Lecture Notes in Computer Science   12945

More information about this subseries at http://www.springer.com/series/7409

Bobbie Fletcher · Minhua Ma · Stefan Göbel ·
Jannicke Baalsrud Hauge · Tim Marsh (Eds.)

Serious Games

Joint International Conference, JCSG 2021
Virtual Event, January 12–13, 2022
Proceedings

 Springer

Editors
Bobbie Fletcher (iD)
Staffordshire University
Stoke-on-Trent, UK

Stefan Göbel (iD)
Technical University of Darmstadt
Darmstadt, Germany

Tim Marsh (iD)
Griffith University
Brisbane, QLD, Australia

Minhua Ma (iD)
Falmouth University
Stoke-on-Trent, UK

Jannicke Baalsrud Hauge (iD)
BIBA, IKAP
University of Bremen
Bremen, Germany

ISSN 0302-9743 ISSN 1611-3349 (electronic)
Lecture Notes in Computer Science
ISBN 978-3-030-88271-6 ISBN 978-3-030-88272-3 (eBook)
https://doi.org/10.1007/978-3-030-88272-3

LNCS Sublibrary: SL3 – Information Systems and Applications, incl. Internet/Web, and HCI

Preface

Serious games operate on the interdisciplinary interactions of art, design, computer science, engineering, entertainment, human computer interaction, psychology, education, and numerous application domains. The Joint Conference on Serious Games (JCSG) has the mission to bring together game designers and developers, researchers and practitioners from diverse backgrounds relating to serious games.

We, as an international Steering Committee, present the conference proceedings of JCSG 2021. The event was the 16th edition of JCSG and its predecessors GameDays and SGDA. The conference merged the GameDays conference and the Conference on Serious Games Development and Applications (SGDA) in 2015. Both conferences were founded in 2010 and have been running for over a decade, taking place in Derby, UK (2010), Lisbon, Portugal (2011), Bremen, Germany (2012), Trondheim, Norway (2013), Berlin, Germany (2014), Huddersfield, UK (2015), Brisbane, Australia (2016), Valencia, Spain (2017), Darmstadt, Germany (2018), Arequipa, Peru (2019), and online (2020).

We initially planned to host JCSG 2021 at Staffordshire University, Stoke-on-Trent, UK as a hybrid conference with delegates joining in person or online. However, due to the ongoing global situation with COVID-19, JCSG 2021 was organised as a virtual event again this year. When this pandemic is all over, we hope to meet you in person and that you will come join us in future JCSG.

After a process of peer review, we selected 20 papers including 6 papers on solving problems through games design and study, 3 games narrative papers from tabletop to narrative frameworks, 4 games in health papers focussing on vulnerable people, 4 papers in the field of competitive gaming and exercise, incorporating papers on esports, exergaming and physical exercise, and finally 3 games in education papers looking at learning soft and hard skills through serious games.

We would like to thank the members of the Program Committee, without whom the conference would not be possible. The JCSG 2021 Program Committee was composed of a wide variety of members of the serious games community representing an ever expanding subject area .

September 2021

Bobbie Fletcher
Minhua Ma
Stefan Göbel
Jannicke Baalsrud Hauge
Tim Marsh
Manuel Fradinho Oliveira

Organization

General Chairs

Minhua Ma   Falmouth University, UK
Bobbie Fletcher   Staffordshire University, UK

Steering Committee

Minhua Ma   Falmouth University, UK
Stefan Göbel   Technical University of Darmstadt, Germany
Jannike Baalsrud Hauge   BIBA-Bremen Institute for Production and
                              Logistics, Germany, and KTH, Sweden
Manuel Fradinho Oliveira   SINTEF, Norway
Tim Marsh   Griffith University, Australia

Program Chairs and LNCS Volume Editors

Bobbie Fletcher   Staffordshire University, UK
Minhua Ma   Falmouth University, UK
Stefan Göbel   Technical University of Darmstadt, Germany
Jannike Baalsrud Hauge   BIBA-Bremen Institute for Production and
                              Logistics, Germany, and KTH, Sweden
Tim Marsh   Griffith University, Australia
Manuel Fradinho Oliveira   SINTEF, Norway

Program Committee

Bobbie Fletcher   Staffordshire University, UK
David White   Staffordshire University, UK
Erik van der Spek   TU Eindhoven, The Netherlands
Esther MacCallum-Stewart   Staffordshire University, UK
Guenter Wallner   Eindhoven University of Technology,
                              The Netherlands
Heinrich Söbke   Bauhaus University Weimar, Germany
Heiko Duin   BIBA-Bremen Institute for Production and
                              Logistics, Germany
Helmut Hlavacs   University of Vienna, Austria
Jannike Baalsrud Hauge   BIBA-Bremen Institute for Production and
                              Logistics, Germany, and KTH, Sweden

Contents

Games Design and Study

Designing Analytic Serious Games: An Expert Affordance View
on Privacy Decision-Making 3
  Patrick Jost and Monica Divitini

Comparison of Serious Games with Established Strategy Games
in the Context of Knowledge Transfer 20
  Ruben Wittrin, Volker Tolkmitt, Max Eibl, Paul Pfleger, Rasmus Wittrin,
  Benny Platte, Christian Roschke, and Marc Ritter

Defining the Mechanisms for Engagement Design Protocol Towards
the Development of Analogue and Hybrid Serious Games: Learning
from FlavourGame 31
  Micael Sousa, Ana Patrícia Oliveira, Pedro Cardoso, Nelson Zagalo,
  and Mário Vairinhos

Designing a Mixed-Reality Sandbox Game on Implementation in Inbound
Logistics 47
  Jannicke Baalsrud Hauge, Anindya Chowdhury, Prabahan Basu,
  Sundus Fatima, and Artem Schurig

Redesign with Accessibility in Mind: A Visual Impairment Study 55
  Jannicke Baalsrud Hauge, Ioana Andreea Stefan,
  Jakob Baalsrud Hauge, Antoniu Stefan, and Ancuţa Florentina Gheorghe

Back to Basics: Explainable AI for Adaptive Serious Games 67
  Florian Berger and Wolfgang Müller

Games Narratives

Participant Centred Framework to Support the Digital Transformation
of Boardgames for Skill Development 85
  H. Almås, M. Hakvåg, M. Oliveira, and H. Torvatn

Designing CBT-Rich Stories for Serious Games 98
  Toka Hassan and Gerard T. McKee

Between Game Mechanics *and* Immersive Storytelling: Design Using
an Extended Activity Theory Framework 113
  Tim Marsh, Ashima Thomas, and Eng Tat Khoo

Games in Health

Creation and Future Development Process of a Serious Game: Raising
Awareness of (Visual) Impairments 131
  Linda Rustemeier, Sarah Voß-Nakkour, Saba Mateen, and Imran Hossain

A Review of Indie Games for Serious Mental Health Game Design 138
  Myfanwy King, Tim Marsh, and Zeynep Akcay

Using Indie Games to Inform Serious Mental Health Games Design 153
  Myfanwy King, Tim Marsh, and Zeynep Akcay

Action-Centered Exposure Therapy Using a Serious Game to Help
Individuals with Alcohol Use Disorder 167
  Flavien Ehret, Yannick Francillette, Benoit Girard,
  and Bob-Antoine J. Menelas

Competitive Gaming and Exercise

Development of a Mobile Exergame to Implement Brief Interventions
to Increase Physical Activity for Adults with Schizophrenia 185
  Yannick Francillette, Bob A. J. Menelas, Bruno Bouchard,
  Kévin Bouchard, Sébastien Gaboury, Célia Kingsbury,
  Samuel St-Amour, Ahmed J. Romain, and Paquito Bernard

Grassroots Esports Players: Improving Esports Cognitive Skills Through
Incentivising Physical Exercise 200
  Bobbie Fletcher and David James

Analyzing Game-Based Training Methods for Selected Esports Titles
in Competitive Gaming 213
  Thomas Tregel, Teodora Sarpe-Tudoran, Philipp Niklas Müller,
  and Stefan Göbel

Physical Exercise Quality Assessment Using Wearable Sensors 229
  Philipp Niklas Müller, Felix Rauterberg, Philipp Achenbach,
  Thomas Tregel, and Stefan Göbel

Games in Education

Development and Validation of Serious Games for Teaching Cybersecurity 247
  Srishti Kulshrestha, Sarthak Agrawal, Devottam Gaurav,
  Manmohan Chaturvedi, Subodh Sharma, and Ranjan Bose

Design and Evaluation of a Serious Game to Supplement Pupils'
Understanding of Molecular Structures in Chemistry 263
   Thomas Bjørner, Louise Gaard Hansen, Miicha Valimaa,
   Julie Ulnits Sørensen, and Mircea Dobre

Using Multiplayer Online Games for Teaching Soft Skills in Higher
Education 276
   Max Pagel, Heinrich Söbke, and Thomas Bröker

Author Index 291

Games Design and Study

Designing Analytic Serious Games: An Expert Affordance View on Privacy Decision-Making

Patrick Jost(✉) [iD] and Monica Divitini

Department of Computer Science, Norwegian University of Science and Technology,
Trondheim, Norway
{patrick.jost,divitini}@ntnu.no

Abstract. With advancing digitalisation and the associated ubiquitous data processing, people face frequent privacy decisions. As personal data is often collected and processed in non-transparent ways, decision-making is tedious and regularly results in unthoughtful choices that resign privacy to comfort. Serious Games (SG) could be instrumentalised to raise awareness about privacy concerns and investigate how better privacy decisions can be encouraged. However, creating a SG that can research and promote better privacy choices while providing exciting gameplay requires carefully balanced game design. In this study, we interviewed 20 international experts in privacy, psychology, education, game studies, and interaction design to elicit design suggestions for analytic Serious Games that can be applied to research and improve privacy decision-making. With a mixed-method approach, we conducted a qualitative affordance analysis and quantified the findings to determine each expert groups' perceptions of how to investigate and educate privacy decision-making with games while keeping an engaging experience for players. The findings suggest that privacy decision-making is best analysed by storytelling that extends to a real-world context and engages the player with curiosity. Decision-making investigation is suggested to either apply unobtrusive in-game monitoring with story-aligned character interrogation, switching to a meta-context or include personal data and devices from daily routines. Conclusively, design implications for analytic SG targeting privacy are synthesised from the experts' suggestions.

Keywords: Serious games · Game design · Analytic game challenges · Privacy · Decision making · Data sharing

1 Introduction

Through ubiquitous computing and the associated data-processing, people are faced with making privacy decisions practically every day. However, while the services we use generally have apparent benefits, the possibilities and threats of private data sharing and processing remain largely hidden to most users. This often results in automatic/instinctive decisions instead of thoughtful privacy decision-making [1]. A group of concern in this regard are teenagers and adolescents who are more susceptible to making less reflected privacy and information sharing decisions [2]. One way to engage this target group and

© The Author(s) 2021
B. Fletcher et al. (Eds.): JCSG 2021, LNCS 12945, pp. 3–19, 2021.
https://doi.org/10.1007/978-3-030-88272-3_1

create awareness is Serious Games [3]. However, creating a Serious Game (SG) concept requires careful balancing of game design. As Dörner et al. [4] define, SGs are games that integrate at least one other goal than pure entertainment (e.g. learning). Additionally, in the case of learning about privacy, a SG may also require including research goals. For example, influences on privacy calculus (weighing risks against benefits) and privacy paradox (acting against better knowledge) such as individual risk propensity or social pressure may be investigated to improve the efficacy of the game [5, 6]. On the other hand, assessing such factors can potentially influence enjoyment by breaking an engaging game flow [7]. Similarly, cognitive factors such as reflection time when deciding about privacy can be affected by extraneous cognitive load from game interaction [8]. While there are SGs about privacy that aim to educate, for example, about social media privacy [9] and cybersecurity [10], potentials for researching privacy decisions and related influences with SGs are so far not explored.

Including the outlined different perspectives in the early stages of game design can help to create such an *analytic SG* – meaning a game that meets educational and research goals while maintaining the players' goal of having an engaging experience. Understanding the different perspectives is important not only for balancing privacy education games but also for SG design toolsets that could incorporate design suggestions for each of the involved roles. In this paper, we explore the multiperspectivity of SG design in the case of privacy to learn about different design proposals and potential design balancing strategies.

1.1 Balancing Analytic Serious Game Design

A recently developed toolset for analytic SG design took the multi-perspective view and synthesised associated affordances from literature and existing Serious Game design toolsets [11]. By taking an action affordance approach, the involved roles – *domain expert*, *player*, *educator*, *researcher*, and *interaction designer* – were used in a goal-driven analysis to identify suggestions on how to design balanced privacy decision game challenges.

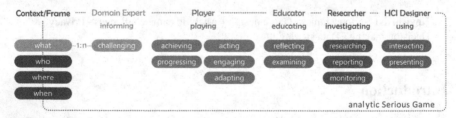

Fig. 1. Multi-perspective affordance framework for balancing analytic SGs as adapted from [11]

The resulting game design toolkit consists of affordance card decks for each goal-driven perspective in an analytic SG (Fig. 1). The cards in each deck are representing design proposals for actualising the affordance generated from the literature analysis. For example, the player affordance (card deck) *engaging* includes suggestions such as competition, curiosity, and gaining awards. The *reflecting* cards of the educator include design proposals such as journal writing or showing decision summaries. The *challenging* cards address privacy domain challenges such as sharing fake data, profiling, and tracking personal location. Additionally, the toolkit entails suggestions for setting the context of the game. These contain design proposals for the domain (*what*), target group (*who*), location (*where*), and time (*when*) the game is planned to be played. In the present study, we apply this proposed action affordance framework to analyse in-depth interviews with international expert groups. Thus, design proposals for balanced game concepts are elicited that are suitable for raising privacy awareness and analysing privacy decision-making while maintaining an engaging game flow. Disclosed design patterns can be utilised for designing analytic SG about privacy choices and adapted for SG design toolkits that consider research aims.

1.2 Research Objectives

The research conducted contributes to the SG knowledge base by eliciting design strategies for balancing engagement, reflection, and assessment in games about privacy decision-making. By taking a multiperspectivity approach, the different viewpoints of international expert groups are explored and synthesised to identify design patterns for balancing analytic SGs. Therefore, the research questions for this study were formulated as:

1. What contextual configurations concerning who, where and when are proposed by the expert groups for analytic SGs about privacy decision-making?
2. What are the preferred SG design suggestions of each expert group regarding the role-oriented affordances of domain expert, player, educator, researcher, and interaction designer?
3. Which design patterns for balancing analytic SGs about privacy emerge from the analysis of the expert interviews?

2 Method

To get a comprehensive insight into how each expert group suggests actualising/designing the affordances, we conducted 20 semi-structured interviews that focused on designing SGs that can analyse and encourage better privacy decisions while maintaining an engaging game flow. International experts regarding privacy, psychology, educational sciences, game studies and human-computer interaction were sampled by e-mail inquiry from six different European universities to conduct a *one-hour interview each*. To be included in the study, experts were required to have at least three years of experience in their respective field while preferably more (Table 1). Moreover, psychologists had to have experience in decision-making, risk-behaviour, or media use, while privacy experts, educators and HCI designers were required to have experience with game-based approaches/projects. We subsequently applied the affordance framework for analytic SGs (Fig. 1) to elicit each expert groups design suggestions from the interviews by deductive-inductive Qualitative Content Analysis (QCA) as proposed by Rädiker and Kuckartz [12, 13] and described in detail in Sect. 2.2.

2.1 Participants

Of the total interviewed experts, 10 were female and 10 were male. The mean age was 40.4 years, while the mean professional experience was 13 years. Table 1 lists the country of origin of each expert and the average years of expertise per group.

Table 1. Demographics and expertise of the interviewed experts

No.	Field of expertise	Age	Gender	Country of origin	Years of expertise	Group expertise (*Mean Years*)
1	Privacy	40	f	Norway	15	13.8
2	Privacy	44	m	Norway	12	
3	Privacy	36	f	Turkey	8	
4	Privacy	45	f	Germany	20	
5	Game studies	42	m	Austria	10	12.3
6	Game studies	32	f	Norway	10	
7	Game studies	45	m	Norway	14	
8	Game studies	36	f	Austria	15	
9	Education	24	f	Norway	3	9.0
10	Education	30	m	India	11	
11	Education	33	f	Greece	6	
12	Education	42	f	Greece	16	
13	Psychology	31	m	Italy	6	22.3
14	Psychology	57	f	Germany	26	
15	Psychology	55	m	Austria	35	
16	HCI Design	46	m	Austria	18	10.6
17	HCI Design	47	m	Switzerland	20	
18	HCI Design	28	m	Austria	6	
19	HCI Design	59	f	Austria	4	
20	HCI Design	36	m	Italy	5	
	Total Average (*Mean Years*)	40.4			13	

2.2 Data Collection and Analysis

Before proceeding to the interview, each expert was informed about the research intent, data processing and research goals. After receiving oral consent on the started recording, a semi-structured interview was conducted. The interview guide was developed from current research on privacy [5, 6], SG design [4, 14] and SG learning/analytics [15] and followed five basic categories: (i) privacy challenges, (ii) engaging game mechanics regarding privacy decision-making, (iii) unobtrusive scientific assessment in games, (iv) reflection and educational practices for analytic games, (v) aspects of games as adequate qualitative/quantitative research instrument. Exemplary open questions included *"What issues come to your mind when thinking about privacy and data sharing?"*, *"What would be enjoyable game goals related to privacy?"* and *"How would you scientifically assess privacy decision-making with a game?"*. The interviews were transcribed and analysed according to a codebook developed from the SG design framework displayed in Fig. 1. After initial coding of the same interview by two researchers, the codebook was refined to reach acceptable intercoder agreement. Thereby, the affordances' overlaps and ambiguities were discussed, and two modifications to the basic framework [11] were made. First, it was established that *challenging* – as representing the domain goal – is, in fact, the main affordance of the domain expert, not the player. While this role is often combined with the educator or researcher, it can also be an additional expert, as in this study, the privacy experts. Second, the researcher affordance *analysing* was adapted to *monitoring* since analysis follows monitoring in research practice. After refining the codebook, adapting coding rules and adding examples for each affordance from the transcripts, an acceptable intercoder agreement of 82% was reached, and each researcher was coding 10 transcripts in a first round. As suggested by QCA methodology [13], the coding followed a two-step process of basic and refined coding. In the first round of coding, researchers applied the context coding of who, where and when design suggestions and then progressed to code each role/perspective iteratively. Thereby they coded with the affordance-oriented questions in mind:

"How does the *(e.g. game expert)* suggest to afford *(e.g. engaging)* gameplay?". In this approach, a design suggestion could be coded with more than one affordance when, for example, the expert suggested having a real-world scenario for *engaging* and *progressing* the player. Subsequently, a second round of inductive fine coding was conducted to group and unfold experts' affordance suggestions. These synthesised suggestions on designing SGs about privacy were quantified and presented in the following findings section.

3 Findings

The following sections present the findings starting with the contextual *who, where* and *when* suggestions and the *challenging* affordance of the domain experts. Subsequently, the results are structured by the role/expert affordances – *playing, educating, researching,* and *using.* The design suggestions of the privacy experts (abbreviated with *P*) are thereby reported first and contrasted with the corresponding role expert proposals and agreements/disagreements from the other groups. The other reporting acronyms for each expert group are: playing – Game studies (*G*), educating – Education (*E*), researching – Psychology (*PS*) and using – Human-Computer-Interaction (*H*).

3.1 Context

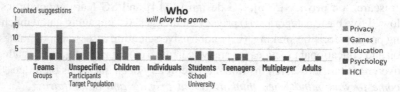

Fig. 2. Counted suggestions on who to target for analytic Serious Games about privacy

Who. When first looking at targeted players for privacy game challenges (Fig. 2), privacy experts were not specifying favoured groups or individuals but would address them broadly: *"...towards everyone, towards the society..." (P-4)*. Game experts and HCI designers, on the other hand, more clearly suggested creating challenges for teams or groups: *"...a collaborative game where you have to collaborate with friends online could be an interesting way. You must decide who needs to know what and be selective about what information is passed to team members." (H-2)*. Psychologists rather referred to *"participants"*, suggesting a research focus while educators did notably not single out students as primary target group.

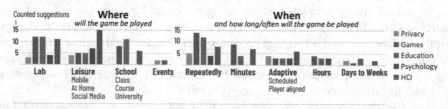

Fig. 3. Suggestions on where and when to apply analytic Serious Games about privacy

Where/When. Privacy experts did make only a few recommendations (Fig. 3) on where and when to play. However, they joined the other experts in suggesting a repeated and adaptive play. Particularly game experts and educators were promoting a recurring experience with a variability of choices/outcomes: *"Where you'd like to go back and play the game again to see if you can use what you have learned to make more informed choices and get another ending." (G-4)*. The same groups also more often suggested the lab as location of play over leisure settings primarily due to the possibility to observe the players reactions/interactions: *"Because I'm a big believer in Serious Games used in a context where it's possible to facilitate discussions and reflections afterwards." (G-4)*. HCI experts, on the other hand, proposed to play in real-world context or combined settings.

3.2 Challenging and Playing

Challenging/Acting. Privacy experts suggested considerably more challenges to address with decision-making games than the other groups (Fig. 4). They strongly suggested addressing the privacy/convenience trade-off and the associated habits/resignation

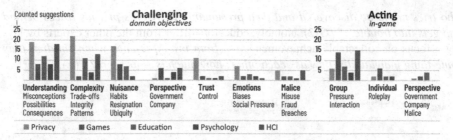

Fig. 4. Suggestions on how to afford *challenging* and *acting* in analytic SG about privacy

from ubiquitous data-processing. Moreover, as expressed by expert 3, privacy experts suggested to convey the experience of consequences: *"Their experience doesn't match the stories they are told. Because they are told a story of potential risk, but they have an experience of actual consequences which is zero very often." (P-3).* Decision complexity and trade-offs were not prominent with game experts, who had few suggestions on this issue. On the other hand, in their domain of playing, they strongly suggested that the in-game acting affords group interaction, as did their peers from HCI and most other experts.

However, while the suggestions were to investigate group decisions and social factors, many also referred to online multiplayer interaction as afforded quality: *"If players in a multiplayer game can chat with each other and collaborate in the game, then you can get exciting data." (G-4).* At the same time, privacy and game experts suggested supporting team and individual perspectives while some also proposed to include switching perspective to government or criminal acting: *"I see that group interaction is very relevant and I think it should be there. But maybe it should be separated." (P-4), "But you know, stepping a little bit into the dark side, that's what you need to create the situations where awareness becomes an issue." (G-1).*

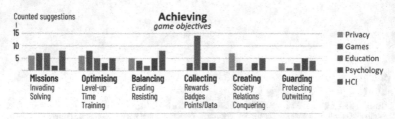

Fig. 5. Suggestions on how to afford *achieving* in analytic Serious Games about privacy

Achieving. Concerning the game objectives, privacy experts held a broad view on suggestions except for collecting rewards, badges, or points/data (Fig. 5). While they regard creating a data-driven society as an intriguing game goal, they are joined by education, HCI and game experts in their opinions that problem-solving missions are generally a good achievement fit. Psychologists suggest evading/protecting action to achieve goals. One game expert describes his evading/resisting plot where the player is: *"...some-one* *who tries not to be discovered and then presumably leaves his privacy traces behind and gets into trouble..." (G-2).* Notably, educators differ from the other experts by laying a focus on collectable achievements: *"...from my experience when children play some-thing individually, they ask each other: how much is your score?" (E-1).*

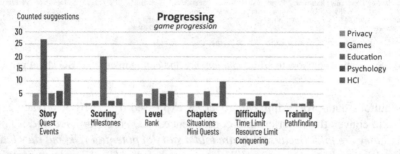

Fig. 6. Suggestions on how to afford *progressing* in analytic Serious Games about privacy

Progressing. While privacy experts commented on game progression in a broad sense with no clear preference (Fig. 6), they did not endorse classical strategies such as scoring, training, or raising difficulty. Contrarily, education experts did strongly suggest affording scoring for progressing the game challenge: *"...you get a new question then you maybe lose points if you don't answer it. So, either you can gain, or you can lose your, yeah, activity level. Because then you have another incentive to make progress." (E-4).* In contrast, game experts, as well as HCI designers and psychologists, did not recommend using a scoring mechanism for progression in a significant number but instead decidedly proposed an event-driven story/quest advancement: *"...maybe it doesn't have a win state. It's just that you read a found smartphone as you would read a novel and every step discloses more personal details about a person you didn't know..." (G-1).*

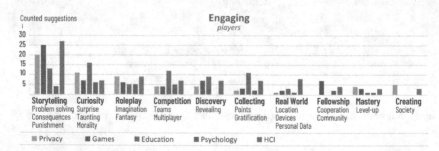

Fig. 7. Suggestions on how to afford *engaging* in analytic Serious Games about privacy

Engaging. When it comes to engaging the player, the experts have made numerous suggestions (Fig. 7). Privacy, game and HCI experts strongly agreed on storytelling with problem-solving activity that entails conveying consequences as most engaging and fitting to privacy decisions: *"So, I would think, that for this kind of game, a solid narrative, relevant choices and branching storylines which will show you different consequences of your actions would be the way to go." (G-4).* Together with the second and third frequent proposals for engagement, curiosity/surprise, and roleplay, it is easily conceivable why several experts from different groups suggested a detective/crime themed narrative that allows for revealing secrets or exposing someone – another suggestion for affording engagement: *"...when it comes to security, often people find it fun to take the role of the bad guy." (P-1), "I could imagine it more in this agent, detective genre, where you naturally take on a concrete role." (G-2).* Different from the other groups, educators also see competition and collecting points as valuable for engagement.

Fig. 8. Suggestions on how to afford *adapting* in analytic Serious Games about privacy

Adapting. Although essential for maintaining an engaging flow experience, experts made few comments about adapting to growing player skills (Fig. 8). Privacy and HCI experts were suggesting changing perspective and extending context for adaption. Thereby, they also often suggested extending to meaningful real-world settings explicitly. *"...if you switch to what if your mother looks at your SMS conversations. Then suddenly it feels more real." (P-3).* Game experts were more suggesting stories that adapt by decision-making: *"...with different branches and choices that you would have to make judgments at relevant points in the game. And then based on the choices the outcome would be very different." (G-4).*

3.3 Educating

Reflecting. The educator affordance of reflecting was commented on quite frequently and in a wide variety by the groups. Suggestions can be classified in in-game and contextual reflection affordances (Fig. 9). Privacy experts were emphasising morality and emotional impact for inducing more reflective choice-making in analytic decision games: *"...you as the player can misuse information that you have available. And then you will think how that feels...let's try for some empathy for the victim." (P-3).* Also, they put forward to clearly visualise judgements for reflection: *"...a visual indicator of how nice you are. And you can see how some people don't care about it and how some people do care." (P-3).* Game and HCI experts, as well as psychologists, however, were recommending more unobtrusive in-game triggering of reflection by plot characters: *"You could have a character that asks questions that make them reflect upon choices that they make." (G-2).*

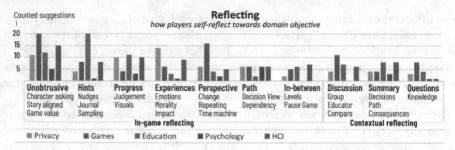

Fig. 9. Suggestions on how to afford *reflecting* in analytic Serious Games about privacy

Game experts also suggested three further strategies. First, combining in-game reflection with contextual interviews in groups or by the educator: *"...you can get some of the data what they think in the moment and then have follow-up interviews later to ask if that influenced their decision-making" (G-4)*. Second, similar to the proposal of privacy experts on adapting by switching or extending to a real-world context, game experts suggested adapting in-game interactions to real-world scenarios: *"...that it's playfully integrated. Where you sit virtually in front of a computer and write an e-mail to someone. You have to type it in and enter something that fits a question accordingly." (G-2)*. Third, they also suggested switching perspective by using time-machine like repetition: *"...after you played it once, you can just rewind the track to decide on different choices and experience different outcomes." (G-4)*. Educators additionally recommend a more interface-oriented reflection by applying subtle decision hints at decision-time: *"...you show them this is important; you should think about it. And then the question should pop up." (E-1)*.

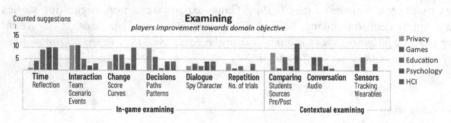

Fig. 10. Suggestions on how to afford *examining* in analytic Serious Games about privacy

Examining. For examining player progress/learning toward the domain goal privacy awareness, privacy and game experts mainly advised to analyse decision paths/patterns and team interaction (Fig. 10): *"...which decision path is he or she following? You could then apply collaborative filtering to find users with similar behaviour." (P-4)*.

Conversely, psychologists, educators and HCI designers are emphasising reflection time as in-game examination of progress: *"... you can always analyse the time they took to think about a decision." (H-2)*. A further recommendation shared by HCI experts and educators is to examine learning progress by the underlying competency model: *"If the score is a good reflection of learning, then you can use the learning curve itself." (E-3)*.

3.4 Investigating

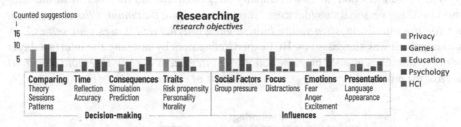

Fig. 11. Suggestions on objectives for *researching* privacy decisions with analytic SG

Researching. Affordance analysis of researching has revealed that suitable research objectives are grouped in researching decision-making and the secondary influences that potentially influence the decision outcome (Fig. 11). Psychologists and privacy experts suggested primarily focusing on comparing decision patterns/situations with dependent secondary variables: *"...could be the time pressure, social factors or discomfort associated with a predicted outcome. And how would I assess for a decision-making game is having different versions of the game in which some of these parameters vary." (PS-1).*

Psychologists and privacy experts also suggested that traits/risk propensity can be a research aim with implemented scales such as cognitive reflection test (CRT) [16] or the balloon analogue risk task [17] in a quest structure: *"For example with the CRT you could make it as you are playing and you meet in the game and you need to sort out a quest." (PS-1).*

Fig. 12. Suggestions on how to afford *reporting* in analytic Serious Games about privacy

Reporting. For assessing subjective measures towards the research objectives while controlling for game activity, most experts agree on having aligned in-game dialogue for questioning players (Fig. 12): *"...someone else will ask the players advice in the game..." (G-1), "...or there is a character that simply asks you why you did that." (P-3).* Besides having dialogue-like asking, experts also had two further suggestions to control for confounding influences from gameplay. First, game experts suggested introducing a meta-level aligned on the narrative to set the interrogation context – or breaking the 4th wall – from the in-game role to the actual real-world person for questioning: *"...in this meta-level, where someone explains, hey, it's cool you have taken part in our experiment so far..." (G-2)*. Second, as G-4 exemplary suggested, extend the context to the real-world by using personal data/devices: *"...on a cell phone that mimics the environment that you are usually on when you're browsing the internet and it uses your selfies.".* A third approach was suggested by HCI experts/educators by utilising the interface layer for micro questions aligned on game action: *"...integrate some low-threshold questions that ask for my mood, my feelings, my assessment of certain topics." (H-1)*.

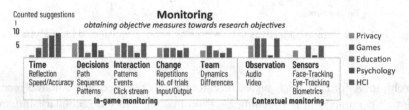

Fig. 13. Suggestions on how to afford *monitoring* in analytic Serious Games about privacy

Monitoring. Unobtrusive in-game monitoring towards the research objectives of privacy decision-making was strongly suggested by HCI experts and psychologists (Fig. 13). The propositions included in-game monitoring of reflection time, decision/interaction paths/patterns and decision outcome changes over time. In contrast to psychologists, the other expert groups were also encouraging in-game and contextual monitoring by observation. The proposed focus was on conversation analysis of intra-team decisions and team differences: *"...record both the screen and the people playing the game, record their social interactions and the dialog." (G-4)*.

3.5 Using

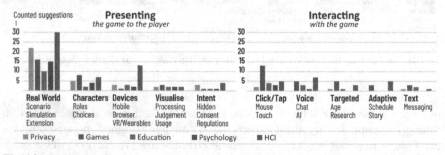

Fig. 14. Suggestions on how to afford *presenting/interacting* with analytic SG about privacy

Presenting/Interacting. Real-world alignment and extension were frequently suggested for presenting analytic SG about privacy (Fig. 14). One HCI expert commented on both design strategies. The first suggestion refers to aligning to a real-world setting by simulating interaction processes in-game: *"...and then I meet persons in the game or find interaction terminals where I can simply indicate my current emotional state via emoticons, or I can give feedback on a certain question via visual analogue scales."* *(H-1).* The second suggestion extends further and connects privacy decision-making to the real world by following the player adaptively: *"Well, ultimately it could be a game that is seamlessly integrated into my everyday life through different channels, different media, different locations." (H-1).* Aside from this adaptive presenting/interacting scenario, experts mostly suggested addressing the mobile platform as the device with the greatest ubiquity and interaction designs with conventional click/touch interaction.

4 Discussion

The analysis of the international experts' suggestions revealed a broad array of design suggestions for the integrated goals of an analytic SG.

When looking at the findings to answer the *first research question* on the *contextual who, where and when* of gameplay, an emphasis on children, teenagers and students as players becomes apparent. While game and HCI experts also emphasise a group focus, the other experts were not showing a clear preference between group and individual play. Both approaches can be seen as equivalent in answering the question of *who* should be targeted, as privacy decisions are often made at an individual level but can also potentially be influenced by peer pressure and thus require group gameplay.

As regards *where* and *when* to apply games about privacy, the suggestions revolved around lab research, school and leisure focus associated with mobile phones and social media. Interestingly, both privacy experts and psychologists were not targeting the school scenario. Eventually, the research objective can act as a detailing factor in determining which context is best to address. The experts strongly agreed on game designs that afford repeated play in any case. This is further mirrored in the suggestions for *examining* and *researching*, where comparing of sessions, reflection time, change over time and repetition as progress/engagement metric were suggested throughout all expert groups.

Regarding the *second and third research questions,* the analysis further revealed expert group preferences for the role-oriented design parts that allow for *several design implications.* Creators of analytic SGs aimed at promoting better privacy decisions can refer to the following insights to maintain an engaging game flow while integrating educational and researching qualities:

First, privacy games are suggested to include challenging goals that transmit tangible, real-world oriented consequences of privacy decisions. Thereby, they should aim to counteract carelessness in trade-offs and resigning to universal data sharing. This becomes apparent when looking at the *challenging* objective where the privacy experts strongly recommended making consequences palpable and revealing the personal downsides of skipping privacy calculus. Biases, misuse, breaches, and fraud, on the other hand, were considered secondary challenges by the experts in terms of privacy decision-making.

Second, engaging gameplay and decision-making analysis may both be supported by team and group playing modes that also allow investigating emotional and social factors. Considering the game experts' proposals on how to design *acting* in the game, a preference for multiplayer/group acting was apparent and supported by the other experts. This design also allows researching peer influences on privacy decision-making as suggested by privacy experts and psychologists and team competition as an *engaging* quality frequently recommended by the educators in this study. However, privacy and game experts have suggested a complementary single-acting perspective, especially in combination with switching to government or criminal acting to demonstrate consequences.

Third, privacy SG designs could integrate storytelling, curiosity, and roleplay in real-world oriented scenarios for game progression through meaningful decision-making. Consequently, allowing more authentic insight into decision influences and motives. In this study, educators favoured scoring/collectable rewarding and competition as designs for engaging the player, progressing the gameplay, and *achieving* game goals. As Chou [14] puts it, this refers to people's inner drive to progress by developing skills to overcome challenges and the widely known strategy of rewarding with points and badges. Privacy experts instead, in accordance with the other groups, preferred design patterns that engage with curiosity and avoidance, which are two other core drivers in Chou's framework [14]. Progression through problem-solving, evasion/resistance and achievements by mission-oriented storytelling, including optimisation or balancing tasks, form the main design pattern for analytical SGs about privacy found in this study.

Competitive games with a scoring mechanism have advantages from an educator viewpoint as they are easily explained in teaching scenarios and quantifiable for comparative evaluation of learning progress. However, scoring as artificial in-game rewarding influences decision-making through game mechanics. Engaging the player through curiosity and progressing through problem-solving to achieve real-world/story-oriented missions characterises a design that, on the other hand, can provide a more authentic insight into decision-making processes and related strategies to encourage reflection. This holds particularly true when also considering the next design implication.

Fourth, the authenticity of in-game decisions can be supported by mapping game interaction to familiar real-world situations, connecting/integrating real, physical devices of daily routine to the gameplay or introducing a metareference. Change of context or alignment to real-world processes were general design patterns that emerged from the experts' suggestions. Game experts proposed to align in-game activities to similar real-world activities, such as writing text messages to peers in the game to encourage reflection. Privacy and HCI experts suggested the same contextual change for adapting to improving player skills while stating it enhances the authenticity of threats. These suggestions to include a reality reference were further emphasised in the design proposals stated for *presenting* the SG. All expert groups strongly suggested including real-world aspects in the game representation with either simulating certain processes or extending the context of play to reality where devices of daily use such as the smartphone get connected to the gameplay. In addition to alignment or extension, a third design proposal to increase the authenticity of decision-making suggested by game experts was to introduce a meta context that breaks the fourth wall when players are asked to state their decision-making motives. Notably, introducing meta-reflection can also contribute to learning gain, as shown by previous research [18]. Thus, the reality and meta references represent balancing design patterns that support the authenticity of players' decision-making while they can also help reflection through context extension/adaption.

Fifth, unobtrusive in-game logging of reflection time, decision paths and team/world interaction allows investigating decision-making improvements while maintaining game flow. Privacy and game experts most frequently suggested *monitoring* decision paths to research decision-making and record interaction between teams/scenarios for *examining* learning progress. Psychologists, educators, and HCI experts proposed more to monitor reflection time to investigate privacy decisions and examine improvements concerning making better choices. The underlying design pattern of recording these parameters unobtrusively in the game can thus be used as a stealth analytics strategy [15] to balance educational and research objectives without interrupting the game's flow.

Finally, in-game questions aligned to the game's story and asked in a dialogue by non-playing characters can help reflection and investigation of privacy decisions. When looking at *reporting* motives behind decisions, psychologists, game and HCI experts suggested most to align questioning to the game story with characters. Similarly, reflecting about decisions was proposed to be integrated with character dialogues as well. While educators showed a preference for questions/hints presented on the game interface, previous studies have shown that dialogic interrogation can be applied for researching decision motives while keeping an engaging game flow [2]. The design pattern can thus help balance a SG to meet the goals of research, teaching, and exciting play.

5 Conclusion

The multi-perspective lens proved valuable for exploring design patterns to balance an analytical SG aimed at privacy decision-making. By qualitative content analysis of the twenty expert interviews, several strategies were uncovered for designing SGs that are engaging while promoting reflection and supporting authentic decision-making research. SG creators can adapt these suggestions to avoid gameplay disruption through assessment or distorted insights into decision reasoning and motives through inappropriate game mechanics. Further research is encouraged to employ the discovered design patterns to create analytic SG about privacy and validate their educational and researching effectiveness as well as their engagement qualities in the field. Ultimately, the elicited design suggestions of each expert group can be integrated into design toolkits that allow non-experts to balance concepts for analytic SGs.

Acknowledgements. This research was funded by the NFR IKTPLUSS project ALerT, #270969. We thank the experts who participated in the study.

References

1. Evans, J.S.B.: In two minds: dual-process accounts of reasoning. Trends Cogn. Sci. **7**(10), 454–459 (2003)
2. Jost, P.: Because it is fun: investigating motives of fake news sharing with exploratory game quests. In: Sampson, D.G., Ifenthaler, D., Isaías, P. (eds.) Proceedings of the 17th International Conference on Cognition and Exploratory Learning in the Digital Age (CELDA 2020), pp. 35–42. IADIS Press, Lisbon (2020)
3. Sorace, S., et al.: Serious games: an attractive approach to improve awareness. In: Leventakis, G., Haberfeld, M.R. (eds.) Community-Oriented Policing and Technological Innovations, pp. 1–9. Springer International Publishing AG, Cham (2018). https://doi.org/10.1007/978-3-319-89294-8_1
4. Dörner, R., Göbel, S., Effelsberg, W., Wiemeyer, J.: Serious Games: Foundations, Concepts and Practice. Springer International Publishing AG, Cham (2016). https://doi.org/10.1007/978-3-319-40612-1
5. Barth, S., de Jong, M.D.: The privacy paradox–Investigating discrepancies between expressed privacy concerns and actual online behavior–A systematic literature review. Telemat. Inform. **34**, 1038–1058 (2017)
6. Trepte, S., Scharkow, M., Dienlin, T.: The privacy calculus contextualised: The influence of affordances. Comput. Hum. Behav. **104**, 106115 (2020). https://doi.org/10.1016/j.chb.2019.08.022
7. Nakamura, J., Csikszentmihalyi, M.: Flow theory and research. In: Snyder, C.R., Lopez, S.J. (eds.) Handbook of positive psychology, pp. 195–206. Oxford University Press, Oxford (2009)
8. Jost, P., Cobb, S., Hämmerle, I.: Reality-based interaction affecting mental workload in virtual reality mental arithmetic training. Behav. Inf. Technol. **39**(10), 1062–1078 (2020). https://doi.org/10.1080/0144929X.2019.1641228
9. Bioglio, L., Capecchi, S., Peiretti, F., Sayed, D., Torasso, A., Pensa, R.G.: A social network simulation game to raise awareness of privacy among school children. IEEE Trans. Learn. Technol. **12**(4), 456–469 (2018)
10. Hart, S., Margheri, A., Paci, F., Sassone, V.: Riskio: a serious game for cyber security awareness and education. Comput. Secur. **95**, 101827 (2020)
11. Jost, P., Divitini, M.: The challenge game frame: affordance oriented co-creation of privacy decision games. In: Fotaris, P. (ed.) Proceedings of the 14th International Conference on Game Based Learning (ECGBL 2020), pp. 277–286. Academic Conferences International Limited, Reading (2020)
12. Kuckartz, U.: Mixed Methods. Springer Fachmedien Wiesbaden, Wiesbaden (2014)
13. Rädiker, S., Kuckartz, U.: Focused Analysis of Qualitative Interviews with MAXQDA. MAXQDA Press, Berlin (2020). https://doi.org/10.36192/978-3-948768072
14. Chou, Y.: Actionable Gamification: Beyond Points, Badges, and Leaderboards. Packt Publishing Ltd, Birmingham (2019)
15. Loh, C.S., Sheng, Y., Ifenthaler, D. (eds.): Serious Games Analytics. AGL, Springer, Cham (2015). https://doi.org/10.1007/978-3-319-05834-4
16. Toplak, M.E., West, R.F., Stanovich, K.E.: The Cognitive Reflection Test as a predictor of performance on heuristics-and-biases tasks. Mem. Cognit. **39**(7), 1275–1289 (2011)
17. Lejuez, C.W., et al.: Evaluation of a behavioral measure of risk taking: the Balloon Analogue Risk Task (BART). J. Exp. Psychol. Appl. **8**(2), 75 (2002)
18. Hagström, L., Scheja, M.: Using meta-reflection to improve learning and throughput: redesigning assessment procedures in a political science course on power. Assess. Eval. High. Educ. **39**(2), 242–252 (2014). https://doi.org/10.1080/02602938.2013.820822

Comparison of Serious Games with Established Strategy Games in the Context of Knowledge Transfer

Ruben Wittrin[1]([✉]), Volker Tolkmitt[1], Max Eibl[2], Paul Pfleger[1], Rasmus Wittrin[3], Benny Platte[1], Christian Roschke[1], and Marc Ritter[1]

[1] Hochschule Mittweida, Technikumpl. 17, 09648 Mittweida, Germany
`wittrin@hs-mittweida.de`
[2] Technische Universität Chemnitz, Str. der Nationen 62, 09111 Chemnitz, Germany
[3] Technische Universität Dresden, 01069 Dresden, Germany

Abstract. Especially in times of distance learning, educational institutions need to diversify their digital teaching methods. Often, they offer only few opportunities for interaction, which is, however, essential for learning motivation. To integrate motivational aspects into digital teaching, this study tests digital games for their compatibility with a learning objectives catalogue of economics. Numerous studies have already shown that serious games have positive effects on learning motivation. In this study, however, not only serious games are considered, but also entertainment games. The main findings include that, on average, there is a 57% thematic overlap with the learning objectives catalogue. 20% of the objectives are explained in a way that makes abstract application possible. The thematic overlap of serious and entertainment games is nearly the same. The results show that there is a lack of games that are compatible with the considered learning catalogue. Remarkably, on average no major differences regarding knowledge transfer were found between the analysed serious and entertainment Games.

Keywords: Serious games · Game-based learning · Economics · Pedagogical use · Higher education

1 Introduction

It is not only since the Covid-19 pandemic and the resulting shift of many teach- ing and learning opportunities to the digital realm that scholars have increasingly concerned themselves with serious games: In a literature review, Zhonggen shows that the number of scientific publications on serious games assisted education rose steadily from 2009 (under 20) to 2017 (over 200) [15]. Other literature reviews show similar conclusions, e.g. [2, 6].

The reason for this is obvious: many studies have shown that serious games can increase both the motivation to learn and the learning success of learners, and thus provide an effective tool for learning, e.g. [3, 7, 10]. Although this is not viewed uniformly in

© Springer Nature Switzerland AG 2021
B. Fletcher et al. (Eds.): JCSG 2021, LNCS 12945, pp. 20–30, 2021.
https://doi.org/10.1007/978-3-030-88272-3_2

academic circles [5] (e.g., Sward et al. could only find a positive influence on motivation, but not on success [12]), this view is now supported by most scholars in the field [13].

A uniform definition of serious Games, on the other hand, has not yet been established. Common definitions describe them as games that, in addition to their entertainment value, also or primarily pursue educational goals [4, 6]. Many definitions go back to C. Abt, "who in 1970 first defined serious games as games that" have an explicit and carefully thought-out educational purpose and are not intended to be played primarily for amusement" [1]. Serious games and related concepts such as simulations have been used successfully for a long time for teaching purposes, especially in the military and medicine sector [6, 8, 11, pp. 29–35]. In classical educational institutions such as schools and universities, however, their use is still in its infancy [8, p. 35], although their potential is considered to be high in this area as well [9].

Among other things, this may be due to the fact that so far, many serious games have been developed for specific skills without taking learning catalogues of university lectures or schools into account. This means that although games can be used to learn individual skills, they cannot (or only partially) accompany or replace large-scale learning formats such as lectures. Also, financial limitations and the particular difficulty of developing serious games for teaching highly complex subjects similar to university courses pose challenges for large-scale use in educational institutions [9].

In a first study, Wittrin et al. already examined the extent to which selected digital games from the entertainment sector can impart knowledge from the field of economics on bachelor/undergraduate level [13]. The aim of this paper is to investigate the extent to which selected digital serious games convey the same learning content and to compare the results from both studies. This leads to the following research question: *To what extent have serious games and selected games from the entertainment sector the potential to impart knowledge in the context of economics reliant on a curriculum-based learning objective catalogue and how do they differ from each other?* Chapter 2 provides an appropriate methodology to answer the posed question.

2 Methodology

This paper is based on the study carried out in [13], where five strategy games from the entertainment sector were examined for their compatibility with a learning catalogue in the field of economics. The results of that paper, which con- tribute data from entertainment games, will be compared to the findings of this study, in which serious games are analysed. The comparison assesses how well serious and entertainment games perform in the context of knowledge transfer in the field of economics.

To ensure comparability, the test followed the same testing methodology established in [13] and applied it to serious games. Hence, the serious games were analysed in three steps: The transmission of the learning objectives catalogue from [13], an identification of suitable games and a test run.

2.1 Learning Objectives Catalogue

The basis of this experiment is a catalogue of learning objectives from the bachelor's degree course in economics at Mittweida University of Applied Sciences. It does not depend on already existing knowledge in the subject area. The under- standing of the learning objectives enables the learners to evaluate basic functionalities of market-based economies. The learning content was divided into 25 learning objectives and categorized into five groups and an assignment of IDs, which is shown in "Table 1". According to [13], the learning objectives were adapted by considering two classes of requirements. Requirement class I investigated a "thematic reference": In the analysed game, a thematic reference to the learning objective must be visible. This means that the game elements must be thematically linked with the content of the learning objective. Content-related learning objective elements are, for example, the existence of an entity, its properties or related terms and chains of effects. The content counterpart in the game can be characters, buildings, explanatory texts, or game mechanisms. The minimum amount of convergence is defined individually for each learning objective.

Table 1. Learning objective catalogue

LO ID	Learning objective
LO.01	The user has knowledge about economic entities and their interests
LO.01.1– LO.01.5	Households; Companies; Banks; Government; Foreign countries
LO.02	The user is aware of the conditions which drive a market economy
LO.02.1–LO.02.3	Competition; Basic freedoms; Monetary stability
LO.03	The user has knowledge about how economic entities interact with each other.
LO.03.1–LO.03.4	Interactions on labour market; Interactions on goods market; Interactions on the capital market
LO.04	The user has knowledge about the objectives of economic policy
LO.04.1–LO.04.6	Full employment; Growth; Foreign trade balance; Ecological balance; Social balance; Price stability
LO.05	The user has knowledge about mechanisms of economic policy intervention and can distinguish perfect markets from realistic market conditions
LO.05.1	The user has knowledge about instruments of economic policies, their characteristics and effects
LO.05.2	The user has knowledge about economic systems, their characteristics and effects
LO.05.3	The user has knowledge on how to achieve goals in general by means of the instruments
LO.05.4	The user has knowledge of market imperfections
LO.05.5	The user is aware of types of market failure
LO.05.6	The user has knowledge on how to tackle market failures in particular through the instruments

Requirement class II "Explanation on abstract levels": This requirement class is based on the first one. But in contrast to that, class II not only requires a thematic reference to the learning objective. Additionally, there has to be a more detailed explanation of the learning content. This explanation is the main condition of requirement class II and includes both an explanation of factual contexts within the learning objective and an explanation on the level of abstraction. Through that, the knowledge gained in the game is raised to a level that allows it to be used in contexts other than the game itself. The acquired knowledge must therefore not only be relevant within the game but must also be applicable outside the game environment and thus be technically correct.

2.2 Selection of Games

In order to pre-qualify serious games fitting the needs of the study, several inclusion criteria were formulated. These are based on the requirements that allow knowledge transfer under academic conditions. Games were only included in the study when meeting all the following criteria.

Enabling a low-threshold implementation of the games in existing learning environments, a *low financial outlay* was deemed necessary. Additionally, considering the potential of serious games in *individual learning*, all games had to be playable alone and without any external guidance. This is especially important in times of distance learning and remote schooling.

To include only games with a high potential to cover the learning objectives catalogue, only games having an *economical background* and *educational content* were analysed. Furthermore, only games which connect game design elements to learning content in multiple ways were included. That led to the exclusion of games based on a single *game mechanic* (such as question and answer-based dialog simulations) because of their lower motivational level they produce [14].

In connection to that, only *digital video games* have been considered because of their independence from physical game materials and suitability for remote schooling scenarios without direct contact between players. This led to the exclusion of bard or card games.

To find suitable serious games, an extensive online research was carried out. In particular, the serious games database from the *Serious Games Information Center* (http://seriousgames-portal.org), which contains over 100 games, was used. Additionally, Google Scholar was searched for publications on serious games with an economic background. The research led to more than 20 potentially suitable serious games.

After the detailed assessment regarding their compatibility with the inclusion criteria however, only four games remained in our selection: *Energetika, Mayor's Table, ars regenti* and *Imagine Earth*. The economical background is given by story elements or integrated quests and game mechanics. However, the main intention of these games is not to impart economic content. Economic issues are thus not the main topic of the games examined but are touched upon. All of them have also a mix of different game mechanics like structure systems, characters, or a story. In this regard, the game mechanics of *Mayor's Table* are compared to the three other games rather simple while *Imagine Earth* has the most complex game mechanics.

2.3   Test Run

Three players tested the serious games in multiple test runs for the learning objectives. As a test protocol, they used a cross matrix which was developed in [13]. It contains the learning objective IDs and the tested serious games. Whether a thematic reference to a specific learning objective was given could be answered in binary form (yes/no). To be able to make a more precise distinction in requirement class II, a third option was added there. Thus, the extent of the explanation on the level of abstraction could be answered in tertiary form (yes/no/proportionate). The thematic reference or explanation on the level of abstraction was assumed as given if the individually defined learning-objective-specific requirements were fully met. Proportional fulfilment is given if at least one element of the defined requirements could be identified. A qualitative assessment of the implementation was not carried out.

3   Results

In addition to the five entertainment games already mentioned in [13], four serious games matching the selection criteria as described in Sect. 2.2 were identified.

3.1   Overview

On average there is a 57% thematic reference and 21% occurrence of explanation on the level of abstraction. The thematic reference of serious games (57%) and entertainment games (56%) are nearly the same. A higher value was expected for serious games. In addition, serious games (23%) only provide on average five percent more explanation at an abstraction level than entertainment games (18%). The intersections of entertainment games and serious games per learning objective category are shown on average in Fig. 1.

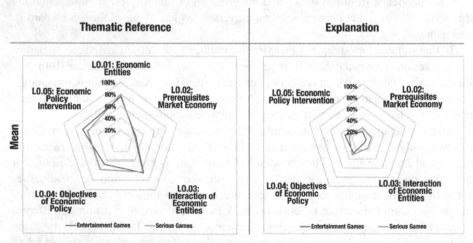

Fig. 1. Intersections of each learning objective category with the two game types "serious games" and "entertainment games"

These values result from the mean value formation of the respective calculated partial achievement values per learning objective, which are shown in Fig. 2 in the lower section of the diagram. These, in turn, are calculated from the binary or tertiary structured data indicated in the cross table. "Available" and "Explained" are each calculated as full compliance, "Partially explained" is considered as half compliance. The mean values obtained from the individual achievement values of the learning objectives are given per learning objective category (below) and per game (right) in decimal notation.

The results show a slight similar distribution of the thematic reference and explanatory values from LO.01 to LO.05 - in all cases, there is only a small explanation rate, and the values of serious and entertainment games differ only slightly from each other. The highest difference of 11% was found for the thematic reference within the learning objective category L.04 (the objectives of economy policy).

The serious game *ars regenti* matches with 88% most of the learning objectives catalogue on the level of thematic reference. Moreover, half of the topics are explained

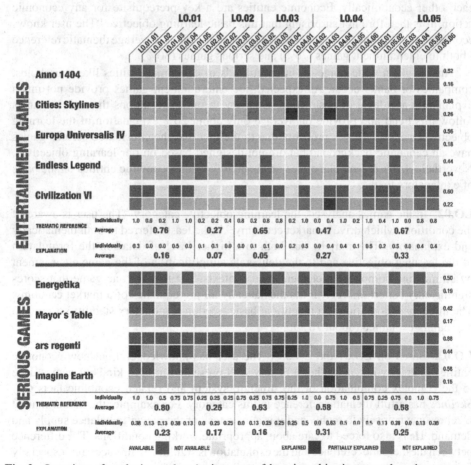

Fig. 2. Overview of analysis results: Assignment of learning objectives to selected computer games within the domains of serious games and entertainment games

on the level of abstraction. Thus, the contents imparted by *ars regenti* show the highest compatibility with the learning objectives catalogue. This shows the potential and the thematic fitness of games as teaching medium in curricular contexts as well. Furthermore, it is remarkable that four of the five entertainment games touch on more than half of the learning objective's catalogue. A reason for this can be found in the placement of the learning objectives at the basic bachelor level. Here, the level of detail in the formulation of learning objectives is still quite wide, in contrast to specialised learning objectives at master levels.

3.2 Intersections of Learning Objective Categories and Games in Detail

Below, the intersections per learning objective category are explained. The results are visualized in "Fig. 3".

LO.01. A game with economic reference needs characters and entities that interact with each other economically. Economic entities are a key prerequisite for any economic action. It is therefore not surprising that this basic learning objective "The user knows economic subjects and their interests" (LO.01) has the highest average thematic reference - both in entertainment games (76%) and serious games (80%).

Amazingly, a wide range of different kinds of economic entities like households, companies or banks occur. As expected, the entertainment games provide not much explanation at a level of abstraction. Contrary to our expectations the serious games follow this trend and provide on average only about 20% explanation of the learning objective category. This is probably due to the fact that the considered serious games have an economic background but are not designed based on our learning objectives. Nevertheless, *ars regenti* elaborates on about 50% of the economic entities on the basis of explanatory texts.

LO.02. In the games analysed, the learning objective category "The user is aware of the conditions which drive a market economy." is the least referred to both thematically and explanatory. This may be due both to a higher level of detail in the formulation of the learning objective and to the deliberate simplification of the game environment by eliminating complicated elements and contexts. But there is one game that scores significantly better: *ars regenti* fits thematically all prerequisites of a market economy. The three main conditions (competition; basic freedoms; monetary stability) occur and are mainly explained (about 70%).

LO.03. Based on LO.01 the LO.03 ("The user has knowledge about how economic entities interact with each other") is very well presented in both kinds of games. Due to the complex combination of the structure system and related economic facts *City Skylines* has a full thematic reference in this category. For example, the labour market is represented closely to reality and it is a main task of the player to balance supply and demand. He is also forced to care about appropriate working conditions. The difference between the thematic reference and the explanation is significant, this accounts especially for the entertainment games.

This can be substantiated, because interactions between economic subjects are elementary for the course of the game and often represent an important indicator of success for the actions and reactions of the player. Interactions are therefore needed for the basic game design. However, since interactions in the real market are sometimes subject to very complex influencing factors and mechanisms, the game environments analysed are mostly greatly simplified. A technically correct representation or explanation on the level of abstraction is therefore not possible in most cases. Here, *ars* regenti is an exception with an explanation rate of 100%.

LO.04. In this learning objective category ("The user has knowledge about the objectives of economic policy"), the difference between the evaluated serious games and entertainment games is the highest. On average, the serious games reach a score of just under 60%, whereas the score of the entertainment games lies at under 50%. Interestingly, three out of the four tested serious games reach the same score of 50%. Only *Energetika* reaches a lower score of just over 30%. In *Mayor's Table*, four avatars representing different interests (for example the "social advisor" representing the needs of the

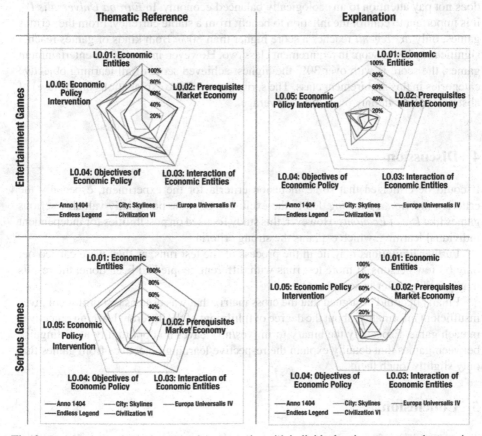

Fig. 3. Intersections of learning objective categories with individual serious games and entertainment games

population or the "environmental advisor" representing the needs of the environment) must be preferably equally satisfied in order to get good results. Through this, the player learns in multiple tasks the necessities of a good and sustainable economic policy.

The difference between the two kinds of games in requirement class II is not as big as it is in requirement class I. The serious games give an explanation on the level of abstraction in around 30% of the cases. The entertainment games reach a slightly lower score.

LO.05. Learning objective category five "The user has knowledge about mechanisms of economic policy intervention and can distinguish perfect markets from realistic market conditions" is met better by the entertainment games (around 50%) than by the serious games (around 40%). This may be since in entertainment games, the challenge for the player often is to cope with crises like wars or natural catastrophes in the most effective way. In serious games, on the other hand, imparting knowledge about how economies work in theory might be seen as more important. *Civilization VI* and *Europa Universalis IV* fit learning objective category five with around 80%. In *Civilization VI* the player needs to cope with natural disasters, global warming, or the rise of the sea level if he does not pay attention to an ecologically balanced economy. In *Europa Universalis IV*, it is important to control the inflation to benefit from a stable currency. From the serious games, only *ars regenti* reaches a score higher than 80%. Both kinds of games reach a significantly lower score in requirement class two. However, in case of the entertainment games, the score is with over 30% the highest achieved score of all learning objective categories in this requirement class. The serious games give explanations on the level of abstraction here in only over 20% on average.

4 Discussion

It could be criticized that some inclusion criteria for the experiment, especially the criterion *individual learning*, led to the exclusion of some potentially valuable serious games like *Isle of Economy*. However, this study focused on possibilities for independent individual learning, which explains the strong criteria.

Further limitations may lie in the process of the test runs, as they were carried out only by few persons. If more test runs with different people had been done, the results may possibly differ in some areas.

Finally, it could be argued that the cross matrix that was used as test proto- col gives insufficient information about the degree of fulfilment of the different learning objectives in each game. Especially the binary form (yes/no) leaves no opportunity to distinguish between games that detailly explain the respective learning objectives from games that only slightly touch them.

5 Conclusion

The comparison of entertainment games and serious games in the context of knowledge transfer might seem predictable, but it led to interesting results: Contrary to what might have been expected, the investigated serious games do not on average convey significantly more learning content than entertainment games. Furthermore, as in entertainment games, only a small part of the learning content conveyed in the selected serious games is explained at an abstraction level. No game with the explicit aim to impart knowledge of learning objects from the economic field based on an established curriculum was found. The content of the games lies in the economic periphery, but the explanation of detailed economic relationships like the construction of supply and demand curve was not the main intention. This leads to a conceivable scenario in which the game with the highest degree of congruence with the learning objectives is selected and played by learners. The deficit of explanation at a level of abstraction can be compensated by additional teaching whereas the thematic congruence in the game is identified by learners and can be reflected within a lecture. The serious games *ars regenti* already has a high thematic compliance (88%) and also a good explanation rate of 44%. Amazingly, *City Skylines* from the entertainment sector has a thematic overlap of nearly 70% and an explanation rate of 26%. This makes us consider the integration of both games in an economic lecture in order to combine the motivational impact of games with the more "serious" character of regular teaching.

Further research potential lies in the integration of motivational aspects related to entertainment and serious games in the field of knowledge transfer. In addition, a serious game prototype based on selected learning objects from the economic field could be developed to compare it on the basis of learning and motivation aspects with the games examined in this study.

References

1. Göbel, S., Ma, M., Baalsrud Hauge, J., Oliveira, M.F., Wiemeyer, J., Wendel, V. (eds.): JCSG 2015. LNCS, vol. 9090. Springer, Cham (2015). https://doi.org/10.1007/978-3-319-19126-3
2. Boyle, E.A., et al.: An update to the systematic literature review of empirical evidence of the impacts and outcomes of computer games and serious games. Comput. Educ. **94**, 178–192 (2016). https://doi.org/10.1016/j.compedu.2015.11.003
3. Chen, Y.C.: Empirical study on the effect of digital game-based instruction on students' learning motivation and achievement. EURASIA J. Math. Sci. Technol. Educ. **13**(7) (2017). https://doi.org/10.12973/eurasia.2017.00711a.   https://www.ejmste.com/download/empiri cal-study-on-the-effect-of-digital-game-based-instruction-on-students-learning-motivation-and-4822.pdf
4. Cody, M.J., Vorderer, P., Ritterfeld, U., (eds.): Serious Games: Mechanisms and Effects. Routledge, New York (2009). http://site.ebrary.com/lib/alltitles/docDetail.action?docID=103 30978
5. Connolly, T.M., Boyle, E.A., MacArthur, E., Hainey, T., Boyle, J.M.: A systematic literature review of empirical evidence on computer games andserious games. Comput. Educ. **59**, 661–686 (2012). https://www.semanticscholar.org/paper/A-systematic-literature-review-of-empirical-on-and-Connolly-Boyle/d935b1ef94761081aa2bcafd0bcb2ed87f72f626
6. Laamarti, F., Eid, M., El Saddik, A.: An overview of serious games. Int. J. Comput. Games Technol. **2014**(3), 1–15 (2014). https://doi.org/10.1155/2014/358152
7. Lamb, R.L., Annetta, L., Firestone, J., Etopio, E.: A meta-analysis with examination of moderators of student cognition, affect, and learning outcomes while using serious educational games, serious games, and simulations. Comput. Hum. Behav. **80**, 158–167 (2018). https://doi.org/10.1016/j.chb.2017.10.040

8. Marr, A.C., Kaiser, R.: Serious Games für die Informations- und Wissensvermit- tlung: Bibliotheken auf neuen Wegen, BIT online Innovativ, vol. 28. Dinges & Frick, Wiesbaden (2010)
9. Mayr, P., Bendl, H., Mörike, F.: Einsatzm"oglichkeiten von serious games in der hochschullehre. In: Baumgart, J., Nagler, G. (eds.) Ausgew"ahlte Aspekte der ange-wandten Betriebswirtschaftslehre und Wirtschaftsinformatik, pp. 253–266. clfme-dia, Walldorf (2015)
10. Pange, J., Lekka, A., Katsigianni, S.: Serious games and motivation. In: Auer, M.E., Tsiatsos, T. (eds.) Interactive Mobile Communication Technologies and Learning, Advances in Intelligent Systems and Computing, vol. 725, pp. 240–246. Springer International Publishing, Cham (2018). https://doi.org/10.1007/978-3-319-75175-725
11. Peery, J.: Questions for serious game development for success. In: 2016 IEEE International Conference on Serious Games and Applications for Health (SeGAH), pp. 1–4 (2016). https://doi.org/10.1109/SeGAH.2016.7586227
12. Sward, K.A., Richardson, S., Kendrick, J., Maloney, C.: Use of a web- based game to teach pediatric content to medical students. Ambul. Pediat.: Off. J. Ambulatory Pediat. Assoc. 8(6), 354–359 (2008). https://doi.org/10.1016/j.ambp.2008.07.007, https://www.sciencedirect.com/science/article/pii/S1530156708001664
13. Wittrin, R., Roschke, C., Tolkmitt, V., Ritter, M.: Exploratory study of established strategy games in the context of knowledge transfer based on selected learning objects from the economic field. In: El Mohajir, M. (ed.) IEEE CiSt'20, pp. 219–224. IEEE, Piscataway, NJ (2020)
14. Wouters, P., van Nimwegen, C., van Oostendorp, H., van der Spek, E.D.: A meta- analysis of the cognitive and motivational effects of serious games. J. Educ. Psychol. 105(2), 249–265 (2013). https://doi.org/10.1037/a0031311. https://www.researchgate.net/profile/CNimwegen/publication/263936571/A-Mea-Analysis-of-the-Cognitive-and-Motivational-Effects-of-Serious-Games/links/5ece14544585152945148fe6/A-Meta-Analysis-of-the-Cognitive-and-Motivational-Effects-of-Serious-Games.pdft
15. Zhonggen, Y.: A meta-analysis of use of serious games in education over a decade. Int. J. Comput. Games Technol. 2019, 1–8 (2019). https://doi.org/10.1155/2019/4797032. https://www.hindawi.com/journals/ijcgt/2019/4797032/

Defining the Mechanisms for Engagement Design Protocol Towards the Development of Analogue and Hybrid Serious Games: Learning from FlavourGame

Micael Sousa[1] , Ana Patrícia Oliveira[2]([✉]) , Pedro Cardoso[2] , Nelson Zagalo[2] , and Mário Vairinhos[2]

[1] Department of Civil Engineering, CITTA, University of Coimbra, Coimbra, Portugal
[2] DigiMedia, Department of Communication and Art, University of Aveiro, Aveiro, Portugal
{apoliveira,pedroccardoso,nzagalo,mariov}@ua.pt

Abstract. There are no perfect recipes to develop a game, even less for creating an effective serious game. Nevertheless, it is crucial to employ methods and protocols to that ensure certain criteria and goals are met during their development. For that intention, we propose the Mechanics for Engagement Design Protocol (MEDP), a procedure that emerges from the need to consider the mechanisms explored through the Design, Play and Experience (DPE) framework's dimensions to meet a serious game's goals, while considering the player profiles according to the Engagement Model. This protocol was implemented and tested during the development of FlavourGame (FG), a serious game that aims to promote discussion and awareness about nutrition for children. The exploration and testing process also allowed to support the MEDP for other serious game projects, as well as to consider the state of the art of current analogue and hybrid games related to food, the theme of FG.

Keywords: Game mechanics · Mechanisms · Engagement design · Serious games · Hybrid games

1 Introduction

Today, hybrid games present themselves as a recent realm in gaming, opening new possibilities, making use of the best of both physical and virtual worlds [1], enhancing players' immersion and interaction in the game as well as its contents, presentation, atmosphere, and control [2]. FlavourGame (FG) is a serious hybrid game for children aged 10–12 years old, which aims to promote discussion and awareness about nutrition, more specifically about everyday choices regarding nourishment and food, integrating emotional and social components of communication.

This paper is organized in three major sections. Section 2 is about how games build meaning, and how mechanisms act as building blocks that bridge theme with player engagement. In Sect. 3, we present a new method to start the design of a Serious Game

B. Fletcher et al. (Eds.): JCSG 2021, LNCS 12945, pp. 31–46, 2021.
https://doi.org/10.1007/978-3-030-88272-3_3

(SG) from existing game mechanisms of analogue and hybrid games: the *Mechanisms to Engagement Design Protocol* (MEDP). Section 4 presents the FG case study where the MEDP protocol was employed, demonstrating how the protocol supported the first steps of development of an analogue and hybrid SG.

2 Towards Engagement

2.1 Objectives and Theme as Starting Points

Serious games reduce the complexity of the reality being addressed to a level of abstraction that allows such subject to be playable [3, 4], but that can jeopardize the balance between playability and serious objectives [5–7]. Therefore, defining game elements, like game mechanisms and their relation to the theme and objectives of the game is essential.

Another important aspect of the implementation of a SG is the support during and after gameplay through facilitation [8]. During a SG it is mandatory to gather information from players' performance and behaviour [5]. The debriefing process must complement the game experience [9], with facilitators that help players analysing and evaluating their decisions and interactions, relating them to the serious objectives of the games [8, 10].

Usually, SG have strong thematic manifestations. It could be something more abstract, like a mathematical learning intention, but even in these cases some theme or story may be included to engage with larger audiences, including the narrative dimension or the possibility to socialize and express creativity through gameplay [11, 12]. So, a SG project should start from the objectives' definition and its thematic integration [5, 6]. Then, project developers will combine knowledge from content experts and game developers, continually testing the game in its playability and ability to achieve the desirable serious goals.

2.2 Mechanisms as Bridging from Building Blocks

Mechanic, Dynamics and Aesthetics (MDA) [13] and its variant Design, Play, Experience (DPE) [7] framework consider *mechanics* as essential elements in game development, but they also identify the purpose of games as artefacts that convey experiences, something Salen and Zimmerman [4] highlighted in their foundational work. The DPE is a variation of MDA for SG applications, introducing new flows between designers and players, considering the learning and narrative dimensions, as well as the role of technology.

Since Board Game Geek (BGG) [14] – the main database for analogue and hybrid games [15, 16] – abandoned the term *mechanics* [17] and adopted the concept of *mechanisms* from Engelstein and Shalev [18], we will follow the same approach. Although mechanics and mechanisms can be described as synonyms, we will consider mechanisms as the building blocks for analogue games [19] and hybrid games, since these kind of games demand that players activate the mechanisms directly to generate the game dynamics.

Mastering a game's mechanisms is a form of learning [20], as well as a way to engage directly with some player profiles that value the mechanical side of the game system [11, 12, 21]. When the mechanisms are integrated with the themes they represent, they can enforce players' behaviours and actions in a meaningful way [4], which can help learning the game and their serious goals [22].

2.3 Engagement as the End Point

When Abt [23] said that games were able to educate, train, and simulate realities where players should overcome challenges to achieve goals, he did not exclude the dimension of fun. Overcoming game challenges, tensions, uncertainties [24] and conflicts [4] can be engaging and fun [25]. The concept of engagement has been discussed over the past decade in different domains from Education [26–28] to Management [29–31] and Marketing [32, 33], particularly with the emergence of social media [34, 35]. In fact, there has been an interest in studying how engagement occurs and what are its effects and patterns on behaviour. In this paper, we follow the perspective of Zagalo [12], who defends that we should "move the research on interactive media design from experience to engagement", because "we need motivational patterns that engage humans, not meanings generated by users while engaged". The author seeks a balance between two opposite sides: a) the subjectivity related to a qualitative mode where the meaning-making and context-dependent factors are present, and b) a quantitative mode related to the digital data that tries to calculate the behavioural change: *engagement*. In this sense, Zagalo looked at the most recent models capable of operating both modes to understand what properties promote engagement and how it can be designed.

Engagement, seriousness, and fun may be difficult to achieve and to balance. Players should never be forced to play a game [36], otherwise, games may fail to be compelling. These games need to be engaging to the player through their design, while maintaining rigorous relation to the theme, narrative and context of simulation, which relate to serious objectives of each SG [37]. To Michael and Chen [38], SG are created to support objectives other than fun, while maintaining it. So, any game can be useful to learn/train something [5], but to create a SG requires a proper design process [6].

One of the main applications of SG is education, and without delivering a compelling experience for players, with the possibility to experiment, explore personal behaviour and get feedback, they would not be such powerful learning tools [9]. Training and simulation are other major applications of SG [39], sometimes used as a global approach, without clear boundaries. Experimentation in these games is essential to their success, relating to the notion of "learning by doing" [40]. The interactivity of gameplay, where players can see the direct consequences of their actions, can be more compelling than a traditional learning or simulation activity, and be a valid way for player to understand new information [41, 42].

Since players bear different backgrounds, preferences and agendas, and act differently during gameplay [11], designers should take player engagement into account when designing a game's mechanics to make such experiences desirable. Zagalo [12] presents three engagement streams: progression, expression and relation. *Progression* is related to the engagement through abstraction and problem solving; *expression* considers the building and creation of the new; and *relation* is understood as a central motivation for the human relationships and their changes. These three streams result from the interaction between players and the game system. According the DPE framework, designers can use game mechanics to deliver the experiences, and the EM explores how these experiences engage different player profiles. Our proposal consists of a protocol that explores existing mechanisms to create a SG that engages different player profiles. That said, certain mechanisms influence the engagement and experiences that a game provides, and this can impact SG's success.

3 The Mechanics for Engagement Design Protocol

3.1 The Overall Process

Mayer [39] refers that SG are related to classifications like "games with purpose", "persuasive games", "social impact games" or simple "learning" or "training" games. The idea to produce a SG usually starts when project developers want to approach a problem, find a solution, change behaviour or help to produce something new. Considering FG's base theme and the objective to promote discussion and awareness around nutrition, we concocted a new planning approach to SG development. Following the previous recommendations [5, 6, 38], we propose an overall solution to guide FG development, also applicable to other SG (see Fig. 1).

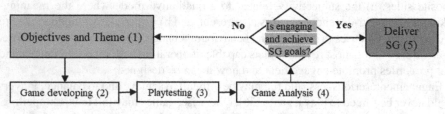

Fig. 1. Overall SG development process. Own source.

Stage 1 starts by defining the objectives and themes at the same time (Yellow). The objectives consist of the achievements to meet by using the game, and the theme sets the context and game environment to be used in the narrative during stage game development (2), always bearing a direct relationship with the objectives of the game. In stage 2, game developers aim to conceive a solution cognizant of the game's objectives and that stimulates and engages players. Stage 2 is where the MEDP protocol is employed. Afterwards, follows a playtesting phase (stage 3) and then evaluation of the quality of the SG (stage 4)[1]. This process suffers many interactions, through which game's design may change which in its turn may also lead to adaptations on theme and to reformulation of the game's objectives. This process continues until the game is ready to be delivered according to the project's requirements.

In hybrid games, the role of digital technology is not limited to the introduction of automatic processes or functional and descriptive mechanisms. In this games, Virtual Reality [43], Augmented Reality [44], and TUI [45] could transform the game's concept, its mechanisms, and even its narrative. Thus, the inclusion of the concept of hybrid games in our model will bring new layers of complexity and possibilities.

---

[1] Between stages 3 and 4, facilitators and debriefing processes play major roles in analysing the quality and efficiency of the game [8, 9, 51]. In analogue games, with no automatization of the game system [52, 53] and limited progressive learning to help new players [54], the facilitator presence is mandatory to teach the players [22]. This is fundamental for FG.

3.2 The Protocol in Detail

The MEDP (see Fig. 2) is a preliminary phase of stage 2 of the overall process (Fig. 1). The MEDP explores the relationship between the DPE and EM frameworks through the engagement dimensions (see Fig. 3).

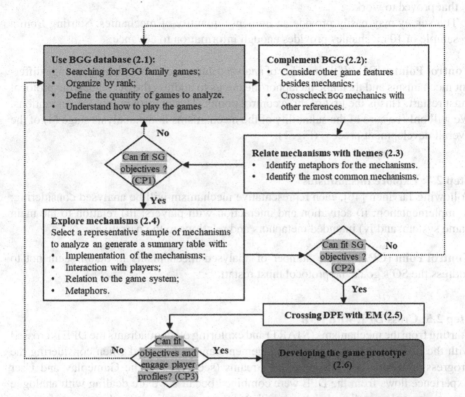

Fig. 2. Diagram of the mechanisms to engagement design protocol. Own source.

The Protocol (see Fig. 2) consists of the following steps and control points:

Step 2.1: Use BGG database:

- Search for the grouped games families and at BGG.
- Organize the games by rank that represents the most enjoyed games.
- Define the quantity of the sample of the most ranked games to analyse.
- Read rulebooks and what tutorial to learn the games in the sample.

Step 2.2: Complement BGG:

- Consider game features like the recommended age to play, player count, duration, complexity and other that can relate to the SG goals.
- The BGG identification of mechanisms can have gaps and inconsistences. [17] There is a need to crosscheck games with other references [18].

Step 2.3: Relate mechanisms with themes

- Identify the metaphor/meaning of each mechanism within each game system, as it is necessary to connect the mechanism to the themes.
- Identify the most common mechanisms in the sample to innovate or to use mechanisms that proved to work.
- The survey may easily provide an immense quantity of mechanics. Starting from a sample of 10 mechanics provides enough information to advance.

Control Point (CP1). If the number of analysed games seem not identify enough different mechanisms and thematic metaphor/meanings to address the SG's goal, the protocol must restart. This is the first of three control points. This control points are perceptions. We will only be sure of the suitability of the mechanisms in the analysis stage (4) of the overall development process (Fig. 1).

Step 2.4: Explore mechanisms
Following Järvinen [46], each representative mechanism will be analysed considering: i) implementation; ii) activation and interaction with players; iii) relation to the main game system; and iv) intended metaphors and relations to the narrative.

Control Point (CP2). If the number of analysed mechanisms in detail seem not to address the SG's goals the protocol must restart.

Step 2.5: Cross DPE with EM.
Starting from the mechanisms (START) and exploring other quadrants the DPE is crossed with the EM to detail how player engagement can be improved when considering the progression, expression and relations streams (see Fig. 3). The Gameplay and User Experience flows from the DPE were combined because we are dealing with analogue games where players directly interact with the game mechanisms for the game to function

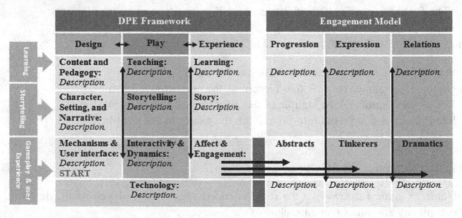

Fig. 3. Relation between the DPE and EM frameworks (STEP 2.5)

[19, 47]. The DPE and the EM are linked by the engagement quadrant. The EM details how the engagement can be explored.

Control Point (CP3): If the number of analysed mechanisms seem not to engage players and address the SG's goals the protocol must restart.

This protocol shows how challenging is to identify and consider all the possible mechanisms and how demanding is to know the games in detail. When the protocol is applied, it offers a set of mechanisms, which developers know that work in specific contexts. Besides that, the protocol's flexibility gives new perspectives for innovation, because developers, if need be, could create new mechanisms for their SG.

4 Use Case: The Mechanisms for Engagement Design Protocol in the Conception of FlavourGame

4.1 Searching for Game Mechanics Related to the Theme

We start by searching for well-established board and tabletop game mechanics to help develop a new SG. The BGG platform has more than 125.000 registered games, but not all are ranked[2]. Searching for the best ranked games associated to a specific BGG theme or family type of game guaranties that the games provided valuable game experiences to players, otherwise they would not be played this much and with players actively evaluating them and recording their play statistics [15, 17, 48, 49]. Nevertheless, even in successful entertainment games, mechanisms may not provide the required metaphors [46], the kind of interaction desirable in a SG, and may ignore players' profiles [12]. Those games can be mechanically engaging but the relationship with the game theme or the metaphor might not be perceived by the players, due "pasted up" themes on mechanisms [50]. So, a deeper research for the mechanics, their implementation and meaning is mandatory.

4.2 Finding the Most Successful Analogue and Hybrid Games About Food

The STEPs (S#) mentioned below are represented in Fig. 2. Considering the FG project's objectives, the family "Theme: Food/Cooking" provided the most games from BGG database (S2.1). The family "Medical: Nutrition/Dieting/Weight Loss" did not have sufficient evaluation in the BGG platform to enter the ranking. BGG considers 956 games associated with the family "Theme: Food/Cooking" but only 207 are ranked. We considered only the 50 topmost ranked games for this family. Taking into account the purposes of the FG, the healthy level of the food promoted in each game was recorded, as the general game features from BGG (2.2): complexity; duration of play; the number of allowed players; and minimum age to play.

Profiting from the availability of the game rules and video explanations at BGG, the research team learned the basic concepts involved in each game. 5 games were

---

[2] Games enter the BGG ranking with at least 30 evaluations from users. The ranking is established through "Bayesian averaging", which prevents games with less evaluation to climb the tops [14]. When a game reaches the top, it was played and appreciated by many users.

collaborative. Only 6 games deliberate promoted healthy food consumption, 28 were neutral and 16 promoted directly candies and fast food. Some games promote ethnic food. Pizzas appear in 7 games and Sushi in 5 games. 5 games introduce phantasy into the "Theme: Food/Cooking". The games were grouped by the main activity represented (Table 1). It is common to have games where the cooking and eating are related, or the production (including harvesting) and delivery are connected.

Table 1. Food and cooking activities in the top BGG games' theme: cooking/food.

Cooking	Eating	Production	Delivering	None
24	13	6	4	3

From the 50 games, 14 should be played over 12 years old, and 43 games can be played in less than an hour. Only 4 games can be played to a maximum of 8 players. The sample shows 15 games that are fitted to a maximum of 4 players and another 15 to a maximum of 5. According to BGG, 34 games have equal or less than 2,00 of complexity (from 1 to 5). 45 games were designed since the 2000s, and 22 in the last 10 years. This means that the industry is producing new games and they are reaching the BGG high ranks quickly, proving their quality and notoriety.

From the 50 games, only "Soviet Kitchen" was a hybrid game. It uses an app to read the cards metaphorically game introduced into a grinder to produce unrealistic recipes to feed the soviet army during war. The app introduces the narrative automatically with multimedia (video and sound). Only one device is needed to play the game which reinforces the cooperation. It is a 2018 game, recommended for players above 12 years old, due to the war theme and suggested absurd and dangerous recipes.

4.3 Testing the Mechanics to Engagement Design Protocol in Practice

The identified mechanisms in each game at BGG proved to be incomplete after learning each game. Based on Engelstein and Shalev [18] new mechanisms were considered and added to the analysis table (S2.2)[3]. The gathered data (S2.1 and S2.2) was completed with the metaphors and relationships to the theme and narrative of each mechanic in each game (S2.3). The following table (Table 2) reflects the most used mechanics (present in # games), the meaning they generated to the theme and the possibilities to support the narrative (S2.3).

Choosing a representative quantity of mechanisms, which are related to the objectives of the game, helped to go deeper on how they are implemented in games addressing the theme and enabling the narrative development. The quantity may vary from process to process, from game to game, and this might only be achieved during an interactive process of finding the proper mechanisms (CP1, CP2 and CP3), that might continue during the prototyping. Choosing 10 mechanics for the first interaction (S2.3) produced the following table (Table 3).

---

[3] Available at http://flavourgame.web.ua.pt/docs/Games_and_Mechanisms_Table.xlsx.

Table 2. Relations from the Mechanisms to the themes, metaphors, and narratives (2.3).

Adopted mechanics	# BGG = TM[1]	Relation themes, metaphors, and narratives
Action points	2■	Limit of actions to do in a turn: quantities of what can be eaten/cooked. A complex job can consume more action points
Action Timer	3■	Simulates the pressure to get food/cook to satisfy needs
Adding and Blocking Buildings	8□	Different stage activities are divided into different activation spaces in a common board. Can represent a market, a kitchen, the cooking stages, or the human body. Adding and blocking action spaces generate interaction and visual planning
Area Majority/Influence	2■	Influence of players in markets, customers, or even areas of the human body where the eaten food can produce impacts
Auction	3□	Auction ingredients/tools in a market, shop or private goods
Card drafting	13■	Choosing ingredients in a market to produce recipes, food in a buffet to form a meal, orders from customers
Card Draw, Limits & Deck Exhaustion	14□	Relation to the limit that a player can eat, pick, use in a recipe, or other activity. Way to control the game duration and to generate randomization, uncertainty in the available resources
Combo abilities	41■	Combining simple actions to unleash new options, scoring opportunities, and powers. Combos can be the recipes or cooking
Contracts	19■	Recipes that generate victory points or provide special abilities. May change the player's powers and unlock new options
Dice rolling	14*	Uncertain and temporary available food in a market, the result of cooking, and the temporary skills of the workers to do a job
Grid coverage	9■	Relationship between tiles/other components representing food and recipes. Linked ingredients make recipes
I Cut, You Choose	3■	It symbolizes the balance between slicing a meal and the distribution of it to the players
Memory	11■	Remembering food attributes, recipes, and cooking sequences

(continued)

Table 2. (*continued*)

Adopted mechanics	# BGG = TM[1]	Relation themes, metaphors, and narratives
Modular board	7*	Change the board, considering the game state, developing character skills for cooking, or a production facility
Physical Action	4☐	Manipulating a game component that can model a real object, like a cooking utensil or the quantities of ingredients
Push your luck	5■	Risking obtaining rare food or doing a complex recipe
Set collection	39■	Combining elements to produce complex/better products. Collecting ingredients to create recipes or gather tools that allow accessing new actions like cooking or travel
Simultaneous Action Selection	10■	Simultaneous play, eating at the same time, cooking in rival restaurants, processing food into their body simultaneously
Tech Tree/Tech Tracks/Track Bonuses	7■	Development of characters and skills. Moving in the tech-tree or individual tracks represent the increasing available actions, resources and allow to produce complex recipes
Tile-placement/Tile-Laying	16■	Placing ingredients, food, and recipes into the game environment. Tiles represent quantities/variety. Their location relates to the stages of the production, cooking, and eating
Trading	4■	Players trade resources, like ingredients, building an economy
Variable Player Powers	6■	Players can have different starting powers or gain special abilities by eating specific foods, cooking, and fulfilling contracts
Worker placement	7☐	Restaurant employees introduce the action choosing aspect, the multiple steps to do a goal, and the notion of timing

■Direct relation ☐Some relation *Not considered by Engelstein and Shalev [18].

Table 3. Relations from the mechanisms to the themes, metaphors, and narratives (STEP 2.3).

Mechanics	Implementation	Interaction with players	Relation to game system	Metaphors
Competitive*	Only one player can achieve objectives	Blocking, be first, remove, steal, and destroy	Exhaustible, racing, and limited resources	Eating/cooking the best/healthiest meal or in a fast way. The most knowledge
Combo abilities	Cards, tiles, dice, and tokens to combine	Picking pieces. Controlling game areas	Combining, Owning/unlock limited resources/ abilities	Knowledge and progression. System simulation (e.g. cooking, metabolism)
Set variation	Cards, tiles, dice, and tokens to combine	Game variation and novelty	Random or predetermined process	Available ingredients, orders from customers, chaotic kitchens, and human metabolism
Contracts	Cards and tokens	Picking unique available contracts to fulfil	Resource and objectives variability	Recipes, customers' desires, market demands and player's preferences
Tile-Laying	Cards and tokens	Adding tiles or cards change game state	Activate/unlock abilities, powers, and scoring	Interactive space where players produce, exhibit food and recipes. System representation
Card Draw, Limits & Deck Exhaustion	Limited quantity of cards	Getting resources first and faster	Definition a process. Control game duration	Available of goods, cooking capacity of a cuisine, time to do cook, deliver food and live
Dice rolling	Type of dice, quantity, rules use the dice	Rolling and using dice in different ways	Generate outcomes, manipulation/choosing	Random results from the production and demand from customers
Card drafting	Drafting from a pool. Adding to personal stack	Picking and reducing player's options	Setting available options and game duration	Picking goods and food, customers to satisfy in a market with some open information

(*continued*)

Table 3. (*continued*)

Mechanics	Implementation	Interaction with players	Relation to game system	Metaphors
Memory	Sequences and quantity of information	Remembering	Introduction and removal of information	Common knowledge. Knowledge from the experience. Complex information
Simultaneous Action Selection	Timer or action synchronization. Simultaneous cards/tiles flip	Playing at the same time. Respecting the available time	Reduce downtime and induces stress	Players are doing the same activity (e.g. cooking competitions or being part of a cooking team)

*Considered a mechanism by Engelstein and Shalev [18] and omitted in BGG

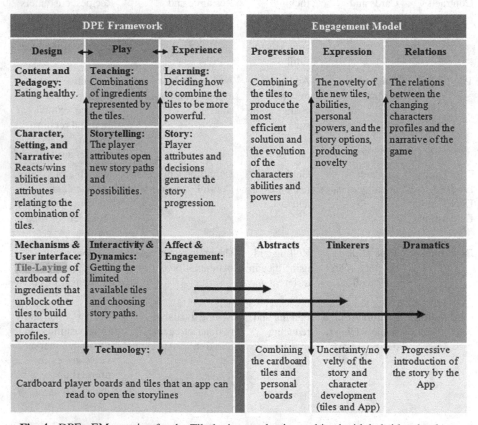

Fig. 4. DPE - EM crossing for the Tile-laying mechanic combined with hybrid technology.

The survey identified many relevant mechanics for the FG development, enough to start relating to the serious objectives of the game and desirable engagement (S2.5). Next step was critical; it consisted on filling the mechanisms' quadrant of the DPE model and linking it to the engagement quadrant of the EM, to establish the relationships with the three streams and related player profile typologies (see Fig. 4).

5 Discussion and Future Work

Following this protocol, in the conception of a SG, we explore the mechanisms in the DPE as a base for its development, and then establish the relations to the EM, planning to engage with the different player profiles through the same game. When the mechanisms do not provide the desirable outcomes, the MEDP can be restarted, at different moments considering its three control points.

The advantage of employing the MEDP in the conception phase before game's development is to save time and have a background of mechanisms to start a SG project. The protocol offers a set of mechanisms, which developers know that work in specific contexts. Game developers can analyse where they can innovate and if they need to create new mechanisms for their SG.

The analysis of the top ranked BGG games guaranties that the mechanisms were already properly tested and enjoyed by many players. Through their mechanisms we can understand the way they were developed towards the theme, the content, the context, and the target audience. Accordingly, the proposed protocol focusses on the relationship that mechanisms have with player engagement, considering different player profiles. We hope this can provide new tools for designers, in order to understand the fascination of interacting with analogue game mechanisms. This fascination determines the boundaries game designers' need to explore in hybrid games: what to digitalize and what to maintain in physical form.

Despite having only explored the Tile-Laying mechanisms, the protocol is viable to explore other mechanisms (Fig. 2). This approach allows predicting what would be the hybrid technology requirements, what to do digitally without losing any of the analogue player engagement and even benefit from some of the possibilities the digital technologies can provide. Exploring the Tile-Laying mechanic through the DPE and EM crossing expressed how a mechanism can engage different player profiles.

Although only one hybrid game appeared in the survey, in the use case of FG, it helped us to understand how a mobile device can do something that analogue design could not. The instantaneous feedback from the combination of ingredients, the media introduction, and the automation that introduces the narrative of the game seem to be powerful features to apply in FG. Besides, eating healthy was not the most popular theme, which may be a problem to FG.

One of the limitations of the MEDP is that the model allows us to predict how the mechanisms may engage players, but that is only verifiable during the playtesting stage with actual players. The fact that mechanisms tend to be abstract and must be combined with other game elements (graphics and components) is a limitation. Future research should focus on these relationships. Another limitation is the BGG databases. Because it is so dominating in the modern board game industry and hobby community there are no other platforms to compare and establish a comparative critical analysis.

The next steps for the development of FG are the prototyping, the narrative development, and the introduction of digital technology. With only one hybrid game in the sample (found during S2.1), and with no reference to any specific mechanisms regarding its hybrid nature, these games are not yet widespread in the analogue game community, making them a clear novelty to explore. While this can be a limitation, as demonstrated by the lack of examples, it is also an opportunity to deepen the potential relationships between analogue and digital games.

Acknowledgments. The authors would like to acknowledge POCI-FEDER and FCT for funding this Project, under the Grant Agreement No. POCI-01–0145-FEDER-031024.

References

1. Oliveira, A.P., Sousa, M., Vairinhos, M., Zagalo, N.: Towards a new hybrid game model: designing tangible experiences. In: 2020 IEEE 8th International Conference on Serious Games and Applications for Health, SeGAH 2020 (2020). https://doi.org/10.1109/SeGAH49190.2020.9201838
2. Wehrum, T.: Evaluating the advantages of physical and digital elements in hybrid tabletop games (2014)
3. de Heer, J., de Groot, T., Hrynkiewicz, R.: Serious gaming is serious business in urban planning. In: Next generation infrastructure systems for eco-cities, pp. 1–6 (2010)
4. Salen, K., Zimmerman, E.: Rules of Play: Game Design Fundamentals. MIT Press (2004)
5. Dörner, R., Göbel, S., Effelsberg, W., Wiemeyer, J. (eds.): Serious Games. Springer, Cham (2016). https://doi.org/10.1007/978-3-319-40612-1
6. Iuppa, N., Borst, T.: eds: End-to-end game development: creating independent serious games and simulations from start to finish. Routledge (2012). https://doi.org/10.4324/9780080952246
7. Winn, B.M.: The design, play, and experience framework. In: Ferdig, R.E. (ed.) Handbook of Research on Effective Electronic Gaming in Education, pp. 1010–1024. IGI Global, Hershey, PA, USA (2009). https://doi.org/10.4018/978-1-59904-808-6.ch058
8. Crookall, D.: Serious games, debriefing, and simulation/gaming as a discipline. Simul. Gaming. **41**, 898–920 (2010). https://doi.org/10.1177/1046878110390784
9. Garris, R., Ahlers, R., Driskell, J.E.: Games, motivation, and learning: a research and practice model. Simul. Gaming. **33**, 441–467 (2002). https://doi.org/10.1177/1046878102238607
10. Mayer, I., et al.: The research and evaluation of serious games: toward a comprehensive methodology. Br. J. Educ. Technol. **45**, 502–527 (2014). https://doi.org/10.1111/bjet.12067
11. Fullerton, T.: Game design workshop: a playcentric approach to creating innovative games. AK Peters/CRC Press (2014). https://doi.org/10.1201/b16671
12. Zagalo, N.: Engagement Design: Designing for Interaction Motivations. Springer Nature (2020). https://doi.org/10.1007/978-3-030-37085-5
13. Hunicke, R., Leblanc, M., Zubek, R.: MDA: a formal approach to game design and game research. AAAI Work. - Tech. Rep. **1**, 1722–1726 (2004)
14. BoardGameGeek | Gaming Unplugged Since 2000. https://boardgamegeek.com/. Accessed on 01 May 2021
15. Rogerson, M.J., Gibbs, M.: Finding time for tabletop: board game play and parenting. Games Cult. **13**, 280–300 (2018). https://doi.org/10.1177/1555412016656324

16. Sousa, M., Bernardo, E.: Back in the game. In: Zagalo, N., Veloso, A.I., Costa, L., Mealha, Ó. (eds.) VJ 2019. CCIS, vol. 1164, pp. 72–85. Springer, Cham (2019). https://doi.org/10.1007/978-3-030-37983-4_6
17. Kritz, J., Mangeli, E., Xexéo, G.: Building an ontology of Boardgame mechanics based on the BoardGameGeek database and the MDA framework. In: XVI Brazilian Symposium on Computer Games and Digital Entertainment, pp. 182–191. Curitiba (2017)
18. Engelstein, G., Shalev, I.: building blocks of tabletop game design: an encyclopedia of mechanisms. CRC Press LLC (2019). https://doi.org/10.1201/9780429430701
19. Sousa, M., Zagalo, N., Oliveira, A.P.: Mechanics or Mechanisms: defining differences in analog games to support game design. In: 2021 IEEE Conference on Games (CoG). In Press (2021)
20. Gee, J.P.: What Video Games Have to Teach Us about Learning and Literacy. Palgrave Macmillan (2003)
21. Cook, D.: What are game mechanics. Lost Garden. https://lostgarden.home.blog/2006/10/24/what-are-game-mechanics/
22. Sousa, M., Dias, J.: From learning mechanics to tabletop mechanisms: modding steam board game to be a serious game. In: 21st annual European GAMEON® Conference, GAMEON®'2020. Eurosis, In press (2020)
23. Abt, C.C.: Serious Games. University Press of America (1987)
24. Costikyan, G.: Uncertainty in Games. MIT Press (2013)
25. Koster, R.: Theory of Fun for Game Design. O'Reilly Media, Inc. (2013)
26. Antonetti, J.V, Garver, J.R.: 17,000 Classroom Visits Can't Be Wrong : Strategies That Engage Students, Promote Active Learning, and Boost Achievement (2015)
27. Butin, D.W., Seider, S., (eds.): The Engaged Campus. Palgrave Macmillan {US} (2012). https://doi.org/10.1057/9781137113283
28. Moore, D.T.: Engaged learning in the academy. Palgrave Macmillan US (2013). https://doi.org/10.1057/9781137025197
29. Rothmann, S.: Employee engagement. In: The Wiley Blackwell Handbook of the Psychology of Positivity and Strengths-Based Approaches at Work, pp. 317–341. John Wiley & Sons, Ltd (2016). https://doi.org/10.1002/9781118977620.ch18
30. Saks, A.M.: Antecedents and consequences of employee engagement revisited. J. Organ. Eff. People Perform. **6**, 19–38 (2019). https://doi.org/10.1108/JOEPP-06-2018-0034
31. Seijts, G.H., Crim, D.: What engages employees the most or, the ten C's of employee engagement. Ivey Bus. J. **70**, 1–5 (2006)
32. Brodie, R.J., Hollebeek, L.D., Jurić, B., Ilić, A.: Customer engagement: conceptual domain, fundamental propositions, and implications for research. J. Serv. Res. **14**, 252–271 (2011). https://doi.org/10.1177/1094670511411703
33. Harmeling, C.M., Moffett, J.W., Arnold, M.J., Carlson, B.D.: Toward a theory of customer engagement marketing. J. Acad. Mark. Sci. **45**(3), 312–335 (2016). https://doi.org/10.1007/s11747-016-0509-2
34. Harrigan, P., Evers, U., Miles, M., Daly, T.: Customer engagement with tourism social media brands. Tour. Manag. **59**, 597–609 (2017). https://doi.org/10.1016/j.tourman.2016.09.015
35. Voorveld, H.A.M., van Noort, G., Muntinga, D.G., Bronner, F.: Engagement with social media and social media advertising: the differentiating role of platform type. J. Advert. **47**, 38–54 (2018). https://doi.org/10.1080/00913367.2017.1405754
36. Lastowka, G., Steinkuehler, C.: Game State? Gamification and governance. In: Walz, S.P. and Deterding, S. (eds.) The Gameful World: Approaches, Issues, Applications, pp. 501–512 (2014)
37. van den Berg, M., Voordijk, H., Adriaanse, A., Hartmann, T.: Experiencing supply chain optimizations: a serious gaming approach. J. Constr. Eng. Manag. **143**, 4017082 (2017). https://doi.org/10.1061/(ASCE)CO.1943-7862.0001388

38. Michael, D.R., Chen, S.: Serious Games: Games that Educate, Train and Inform. Thomson Course Technology (2006)
39. Mayer, I.S.: The gaming of policy and the politics of gaming: a review. Simul. Gaming. **40**, 825–862 (2009). https://doi.org/10.1177/1046878109346456
40. Hussein, B.: A blended learning approach to teaching project management: a model for active participation and involvement: insights from Norway. Educ. Sci. **5**, 104–125 (2015). https://doi.org/10.3390/educsci5020104
41. Torres, M., Macedo, J.: Learning sustainable development with a new simulation game. Simul. Gaming. **31**, 119–126 (2000). https://doi.org/10.1177/104687810003100112
42. Bakhuys Roozeboom, M., Visschedijk, G., Oprins, E.: The effectiveness of three serious games measuring generic learning features. Br. J. Educ. Technol. **48**, 83–100 (2017). https://doi.org/10.1111/bjet.12342
43. Jerald, J.: The VR Book: Human-centered Design for Virtual Reality. Association for Computing Machinery (2016)
44. Schmalstieg, D., Hollerer, T.: Augmented Reality: Principles and Practice. Pearson Education (2016)
45. Xu, D., Read, J.C., Mazzone, E., MacFarlane, S., Brown, M.: Evaluation of Tangible User Interfaces (TUIs) for and with children – methods and challenges. In: Jacko, J.A. (ed.) Human-Computer Interaction. Interaction Platforms and Techniques. pp. 1008–1017. Springer Berlin Heidelberg, Berlin, Heidelberg (2007). https://doi.org/10.1007/978-3-540-73107-8_111
46. Järvinen, A.: Games without frontiers: theories and Methods for Game Studies and Design (2007)
47. Duarte, L.C.S., Battaiola, A.L.: Distinctive features and game design. Entertain. Comput. **21**, 83–93 (2017). https://doi.org/10.1016/j.entcom.2017.03.002
48. Kosa, M., Spronck, P.: Towards a Tabletop Gaming Motivations Inventory (TGMI). In: Zagalo, N., Veloso, A.I., Costa, L., Mealha, Ó. (eds.) VJ 2019. CCIS, vol. 1164, pp. 59–71. Springer, Cham (2019). https://doi.org/10.1007/978-3-030-37983-4_5
49. Woods, S.: Eurogames: The Design, Culture and Play of Modern European Board Games. McFarland, Incorporated, Publishers (2012)
50. Rören, J.: Best of Both Worlds: A Platform for Hybrids of Computer Games and Board Games (2007)
51. Lederman, L.C.: Debriefing: toward a systematic assessment of theory and practice. Simul. Gaming. **23**, 145–160 (1992). https://doi.org/10.1177/1046878192232003
52. Xu, Y., Barba, E., Radu, I., Gandy, M., Macintyre, B.: Chores are fun: understanding social play in board games for digital tabletop game design. In: Proceedings of DiGRA 2011 Conference: Think Design Play (2011)
53. Zagal, J.P., Rick, J., Hsi, I.: Collaborative games: lessons learned from board games. Simul. Gaming. **37**, 24–40 (2006). https://doi.org/10.1177/1046878105282279
54. Sato, A., de Haan, J.: Applying an experiential learning model to the teaching of gateway strategy board games. Int. J. Instr. **9**, 3–16 (2016)

Designing a Mixed-Reality Sandbox Game on Implementation in Inbound Logistics

Jannicke Baalsrud Hauge[1,2,3](✉) (iD), Anindya Chowdhury[1,3] (iD), Prabahan Basu[1,3] (iD), Sundus Fatima[1,3] (iD), and Artem Schurig[1] (iD)

[1] BIBA – Bremer Institut Für Produktion und Logistik GmbH, Bremen, Germany
baa@biba.uni-bremen.de
[2] KTH-Royal Institute of Technology, Södertälje, Sweden
[3] Universität Bremen, Bremen, Germany

Abstract. Practical lab exercises and haptic games are often used to create understanding and awareness of how technologies can support the quality of warehouse operations. However, not all students have access to a suitable physical lab or game environment. A Mixed reality sandbox mode was planned, a game mode of free form that emphasises freedom of movement and offers the player a lot of flexibility and ingenuity in completing tasks and coming up with solutions to the game objectives with a combination of Augmented Reality and physical tools. The purpose of playing this game is to promote the importance of using sensors to increase the efficiency of inbound logistics remotely.

Keywords: Educational serious games · Mixed reality · Logistics operation

1 Introduction

Damages on goods and loss of goods are significant issues within warehouse operations [1]. In addition, there is also a risk that the operators may get exposed to various risks like forklift crashes, pallet rack collapses, and spill occurrence of hazardous materials inside the warehouse, etc. [2]. Even though the likelihood of such an event is low, the impact is high, and thus the avoidance is given a high priority. The implementation of internet of things technology for continuously tracking goods [3] and better visualisation [4] can help in reducing both the likelihood as well as the impact of those risks [5]. To implement, use and rely upon this supportive technology, there is a need for qualification and training of warehouse operators [7] as well as of the management involved in the decision making process of selecting the right technology for implementation, taking infrastructural boundaries into account [5, 8]. For this purpose practical lab exercises, haptic games, field visits etc. play a vital role in the engineering education [9]. However, not all students have access to such facilities [10]. Moreover, the recent pandemic has shown the impact of not being able to be physically in a lab or taking part in a field trip on the learning outcome.

On the other hand side, years of using digital games for educational purposes on decision making related to technology assessment has also shown some limitations related

© Springer Nature Switzerland AG 2021
B. Fletcher et al. (Eds.): JCSG 2021, LNCS 12945, pp. 47–54, 2021.
https://doi.org/10.1007/978-3-030-88272-3_4

to the deep understanding of barriers, boundaries and opportunities in implementing advanced technologies in existing facilities [11]. Based on our experiences with both operating labs and providing fully digital teaching, and in an attempt to overcome the discovered limitations we aim to set up a mixed reality experiment to investigate the boundaries and the opportunities of offering a mixed reality game with remote access. This early work reports on the first mockup experiments of our Mixed Reality Sandbox game can enhance their experience of real-time inbound logistics [9, 12] in terms of sensor selection and related IoT environment. To address the research questions, the rest of the paper is structured as follows, how can a mixed reality sandbox game enhance the learning and prerequisite knowledge of a warehouse employee, and how can they analyse and evaluate the benefits and disadvantages of incorporating modern technologies like sensors in a warehouse environment.

2 Research Methodology and Approach

We used an agile approach to design the game [12]. A similar digital game and experiments using digital twins for logistics warehouse operations were used as starting points for the re-design [5, 6]. For the analysis of the existing game and the design of the new MR-game, we used the theory-based activity model for serious games (ATMSG) [13]. The design of the game is briefly described in [9]. The part of the game flow for which we have carried out the experiments reported in this article is shown in Fig. 1.

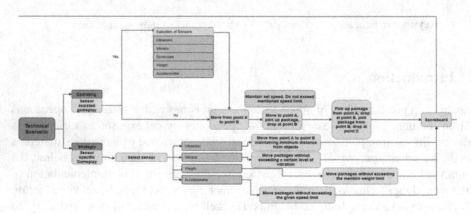

Fig. 1. Game flow diagram

The focus of this paper is related to the part of the sandbox game that concerns the process of sensor selection. The next chapter, therefore, briefly describe our design choices.

3 Design Choices

This section presents the technologies we intend to employ with regards to simplicity, modularity and expandability and in-house competence, we selected Raspberry Pi 4

Model B as server and input device simultaneously. The existing game [6] was realised with Unity Engine, so this engine was also selected for further development. It will be running on an Android tablet. Its camera is used for environment recognition. The software accesses the real-time sensor data wirelessly via the REST interface. This data is presented to the player visually on display as an overlay using augmented technology [5, 14].

In terms of the sensor technologies, these technologies are an integral part of data-driven warehouse logistics and a fundamental component of cyber-physical systems [15]. Sensors are devices that detect, sense, record, indicate, measure physical properties. The intention is to make the player realise and practice simultaneously the advantages of having integrated support of existing technologies while carrying out warehousing operations. The players can also experience the disadvantages or the drawbacks of using sensor technology in the same environment. The acquired knowledge while exploring will be need to be re-visited and applied at later stages in the gameplay. Futhermore, according to the theory of experiential learning, this should also enable the players to investigate what impact such usage may have on the overall experience in the practical world. We have therefore selected sensors which are quite often used in data-driven logistics. The sensors planned to be used in this game are Ultrasonic sensor, Vibration sensor, Touch sensor [16, 17]. The different sensors are used to collect various data during the game to assist the player while playing the game and collect and display real-time data [15]. The sensors will be installed in the forklift that the player will use to play the game. The player need to be able to see live sensor data on the tablet's screen that they will use to control the forklift. During the gameplay, the player can choose to access individual sensor data, helping the player realise the advantages or disadvantages of a sensor assisted environment. The player will also experience how a sensor works and how it can improve performance or safety in a working environment. The interface of this game is the Android tablet that the player use to control the forklift and also see information about the game in general. In the mixed reality scenario, the player can see the forklift through the tablet and on the forklift, the player can see where the sensors are located virtually. By touching the sensors in their tablet, they can read more about the sensor; collect more information about how the sensors work and why the sensors are positioned where they are positioned. This should vastly increase the knowledge and understanding of the users about sensors. Although that is not the primary motivation of this game, the sensors do play an essential role in enhancing the overall learning experience for this game.

4   Mock-Up Learning Scenarios

The game flow is seen in Fig. 1. The potential users of the sandbox game are an inhomogeneous group both in terms of the experience of warehouse management and operation and on technical skills. It is therefore imperative that the game can be adapted to fit the different learning needs. In the first testing, we therefore created a paper mock-up to test if the flexibility was sufficient. The mockup tests were carried out using the paper mockup where we played the various game activities and focused on the flow, the adaptability in the design (for the inhomogeneous groups) as well as on the decision the player would need to make in terms of sensor selection and what feedback it would be required to receive in order to make informed decisions. The initial starting interface is shown in Fig. 2.

Fig. 2. Prototype

The game started with a pre-test, serving as input for changing and adapting the game settings. This was followed by an introduction to the gameplay itself to keep the player engaged throughout the play and explain what the player lacking experience should need to observe (Fig. 3).

Fig. 3. First paper mock-up

The mockup tests showed a need for carrying out some changes- firstly, it needs to be an introduction to the topic that is adapted to the player's knowledge. I.e. if a player has no experience in logistics operation, she will get a different introduction, support, and feedback while playing than one with more experience. The same would be the case in terms of the technologies used-i.e., the current mockup related only to the sensor selection. For a player with little knowledge of sensor technologies, she might only choose between the three types of sensors described in the previous section. In contrast, a more advanced player would get the possibility to select different types of sensors in the same category to emphasise deeper understanding. The mockup testing also revealed the need for better-customised feedback (in our case via the tablets) to keep track of what is relevant and what is not. Based on the experience with the mockup, we also introduced (as an integral part of the game) a tutorial. The tutorial's sole objective is to teach players about the game's basic topology and controls. This will broaden the players' general understanding and understanding of warehouses. We also think that in some cases, it would be suitable to let the player acquire prior knowledge by exploring the sensor technology and the interfaces by free-roaming in the sandbox mode.

5   Results and Impact on Game Design

In addition to the changes in the game flow, the mockup results provide the first insight towards an investigation of using Augmented Reality (AR) with the tablet. AR interaction and controls with tablets seem to engage players significantly in terms of interactivity in the learning process while playing games. Therefore, Augmented Reality technology interfaces combining virtual objects and the integration of data with the highest possible extent of amplifying collaboration and interaction will be developed.

AR Technology provides us an opportunity in making a new design, combining physical interaction of the real world to interactivity and computing capabilities of a digital game. With a focus on the processes revolving around the design of a mixed reality game, it was decided to experiment with low cost augmented reality technologies to investigate functionalities that could improve player experience. Game design pursues an iterative process that follows a path of designing and testing throughout this process. The mockup test resulted in first finding in developing an initial interactive prototype. This on-going iterative process will further improve the concept and design of the game and its implementation. Balancing between virtual and real-world objects is an essential factor to make appropriate use of the medium incorporated in the design. Virtual objects exhibit and allow data visualisation and automation. Hence, this is reasonable to have augmented reality as a medium of display with a substantial property of emergence. Accommodating AR in the design process is a demanding task because of its evolving and growing nature of technology and considering the factors that would produce engaging player experiences with impressive fidelity.

6   Next Steps: Implementation of AR Development and Sensors Development

The presented test results are based on a paper mockup, but we already have parts (see Fig. 2) of the physical environment on the hand side and the existing game on the other hand [6]. However, the analysis has shown that we need to change that extensively, but some digital components can be re-used. Therefore, a primary concern in the new MR setup is the interaction between the digital and physical components. Unity 3D game engine is used as Unity to develop interactive interaction Unity is a multiplatform development tool used to generate 2D and 3D gaming and highly immersive experiences. It is used to make User Interface (UI) follow the game art of simplicity for initial interactive mockup. It will be a simple screen on a tablet with basic controls to navigate the forklift. The complete package of Unity will include scenes with multiple Game Objects controlled by scripts (C#, JavaScript etc.). In addition to using Unity, we need to develop the AR. Here we have selected Vuforia, an Augmented Reality (AR) software development tool kit used to create dynamic user experiences as development environment. Vuforia utilises computer vision technology to see 3D objects in a natural environment and is used to place virtual objects using camera viewfinders and position objects in real surroundings. Vuforia engine package will be added to the Unity project. The Vuforia integration to Unity will optimise performance, synchronise functions, and with Unity flow, it will produce a highly interactive player experience (Fig. 4).

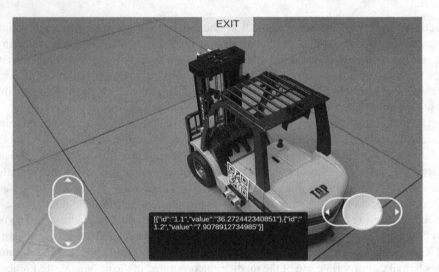

Fig. 4. Concept image of augmented reality

The initial mockup was considered to keep interactions trivial and straightforward to observe player experience first. Since the mockup is in the development phase, the proposed UI contains essential interaction components with tablets: 1) Joystick Controller1 to move forklift backwards and forward. 2) Joystick Controller2 to move forklift right and left. 3) Exit Button to stop the scene. Since it is a prototype, it is to observe players' immersive experience when interacting with these trivial interactions.

7 Discussions and Conclusions

The presented game is based on previous games used for teaching technology assessment in a warehouse environment. The mockup experience ensured us to go for developing a sandbox game, with a narrative evolving as the game is played. It is currently only tested for single player usage, but the underlying design is also for multi-player usage. Initially, the instruction part should educate the players on how to manoeuvre the forklift around and operate the forks using the controls in the gameplay environment. There may also be information spots in the sandbox mode throughout the warehouse that the player may activate to get random information about the warehouse during the scenario. Also, a player can freely roam around and to experience the advantages and disadvantages of different sensors. In the later part of the game, the specific tasks will involve utilising the controls to execute basic tasks in order to increase the player's extrinsic motivation. The conceptual goals and the learning may be tested and helps to improve game efficiency with the progressive growth of the game.

Acknowledgements. This work is funded by the German Federal Ministry of Education and Research (BMBF) through the project DigiLab4U (16DHB2113).

References

1. Sai Subrahmanya Tejesh, B., Neeraja, S.: Warehouse inventory management system using IoT and open-source framework. Alexandria Eng. J. **57**(4), 3817–3823 (2018)
2. V.: Four Common Warehouse Accidents and Steps to Prevent Them (2017). MSDSonline. https://www.msdsonline.com/2016/09/21/four-common-warehouse-accidents-and-steps-to-prevent-them/
3. Zafarzadeh, M., et al.: A systematic review on technologies for data-driven production logistics: their role from a holistic and value creation perspective. Logistics **2021**(5), 24 (2021). https://doi.org/10.3390/logistics5020024
4. Wang, W., et al.: Application of Augmented Reality (AR) technologies in inhouse logistics; E3S Web Conf. **145**, 02018 (2020). https://doi.org/10.1051/e3sconf/202014502018
5. Baalsrud, H., et al.: Employing digital twins within production logistics. In: 2020 IEEE International Engineering, Technology and Innovation (ICE/ITMC) (2020)
6. Oliveri, M., et al.: Designing an IoT-focused, Multiplayer Serious Game for Industry 4.0 Innovation. IEEE ICE/ITMC (2019). https://doi.org/10.1109/ICE.2019.8792680
7. Leal, L.F., et al.: Starting up a Learning Factory focused on Industry 4.0, Procedia Manuf. **45**, 436–441 (2020). ISSN 2351-9789
8. Suárez Fernández-Miranda, S., et al.: The challenge of integrating Industry 4.0 in the degree of mechanical engineering. Procedia Manuf. **13**, 1229–1236 (2017). ISSN 2351-9789.https://doi.org/10.1016/j.promfg.2017.09.039.Managementselection
9. Hauge, J.B., Basu, P., Sundus, F., Chowdhury, A., Schurig, A.: Design of a mixed reality game for exploring how IoT technologies can support the decision making process. In: Auer, M.E., Bhimavaram, K.R., Yue, X.-G. (eds.) Online Engineering and Society 4.0: Proceedings of the 18th International Conference on Remote Engineering and Virtual Instrumentation, pp. 281–288. Springer International Publishing, Cham (2022). https://doi.org/10.1007/978-3-030-82529-4_27

10. Höhner, N., et al.: The next step of digital laboratories: connecting real and virtual world. In: Joaquim, J., (eds.) Virtual-Reality Continuum and its Applications in Industry. VRCAI '19. Brisbane, QLD, Australia, 11/14/2019 - 11/16/2019, pp. 1–2. New York, USA: ACM Press. https://doi.org/10.1145/3359997.3365727
11. Hauge, J.B., Zafarzadeh, M., Jeong, Y., Li, Y., Khilji, W.A., Wiktorsson, M.: Digital and physical testbed for production logistics operations. In: Lalic, B., Majstorovic, V., Marjanovic, U., von Cieminski, G., Romero, D. (eds.) APMS 2020. IAICT, vol. 591, pp. 625–633. Springer, Cham (2020). https://doi.org/10.1007/978-3-030-57993-7_71
12. Hoda, R., et al.: The rise and evolution of agile software development. IEEE Softw. **35**(5), 58–63 (2018)
13. Carvalho, M.B., et al.: An activity theory-based model for serious games analysis and conceptual design. Comput. Educ. **87**, 166–181 (2015)
14. Kumar, R., Rajasekaran, M.P.: An IoT based patient monitoring system using Raspberry Pi. In: 2016 International Conference on Computing Technologies and Intelligent Data Engineering (ICCTIDE'16), pp. 1–4 (2016). https://doi.org/10.1109/ICCTIDE.2016.7725378
15. Zafarzadeh, M., et al.: Data-driven production logistics - an industrial case study on potential and challenges. Smart Sustain. Manuf. Syst. **3**(1), 53–78 (2019)
16. Carotenuto, R.: An indoor ultrasonic system for autonomous 3-D positioning. IEEE Trans. Instrum. Meas. **68**(7), 2507–2518 (2019)
17. Baxter, L.: Capacitive Sensors, p. 138. John Wiley and Sons (1996). ISBN 978-0-7803-5351-0

Redesign with Accessibility in Mind: A Visual Impairment Study

Jannicke Baalsrud Hauge[1,2]([✉]) [ID], Ioana Andreea Stefan[3] [ID],
Jakob Baalsrud Hauge[1,4], Antoniu Stefan[2] [ID], and Ancuța Florentina Gheorghe[2]

[1] BIBA – Bremer Institut für Produktion und Logistik GmbH, Hochschulring 20,
28359 Bremen, Germany
{hau,baa}@biba.uni-bremen.de, jmbh@kth.se
[2] Royal Institute of Technology, Kvarnbergagt.12, 15134 Södertälje, Sweden
{antoniu.stefan,anca.gheorghe}@ats.com.ro
[3] Advanced Technology Systems, Str. Tineretului Nr 1, 130029 Targoviste, Romania
ioana.stefan@ats.com.ro
[4] Hochschule Fuer Technik, Stuttgart, Germany

Abstract. The role of the teacher is to help students improve their knowledge and skills. While it is acknowledged that learning occurs within specific activities and contexts, the adaptation of learning settings to distinct didactical objectives and learner needs remains a challenge. Under these premises, the authors explore the demanding endeavour of creating and tailoring game-based learning activities for specific subjects. The design and personalisation of rich media applications require an extra effort on the teacher side and imply advanced skills. The paper explores the opportunity to reuse gamified lesson plans using an authoring pipeline that reunited authoring tools, game narratives and minigames.

Keywords: Minigame · Metagame · Reuse · Adaption of lessons paths

1 Introduction

For supporting the rapid growth of digital learning, a wealth of learning resources and tools has been developed to enable teachers to create positive and motivating learning environments while trying to spark interest amongst the students and ensure a successful learning process. Within this context, using games for learning has become a great way to make learning motivating and engaging [1], and numerous studies have highlighted the potential of game-based learning [2, 3].

However, the design of Digital Educational Games (DEG) is not an easy undertaking. [4] has highlighted the difficulty to leverage DEG outcomes, stating that their success depends on the context, the content, the topic, and the pedagogical competencies of the teachers. These factors, coupled with the diversity of game genres, the multitude of age groups targeted by serious games [5], and the difficulty of transferring the DEG learning outcomes to the real world [6], make DEG design challenging. Research has also explored the use of learning versions of existing games [7], highlighting a new

B. Fletcher et al. (Eds.): JCSG 2021, LNCS 12945, pp. 55–66, 2021.
https://doi.org/10.1007/978-3-030-88272-3_5

dimension of complexity to the learning design. Research efforts to support a better DEG design have been diverse, stressing the importance of the learning design phase. The iLearnTest Framework [8], for example, has focused on providing game templates that could facilitate game construction. The Activity Theory-based Model of Serious Games (ATMSG) discussed by [9] provided a representation of how the game elements are interconnected and how these elements contribute to achieving the desired pedagogical goals. [10] have presented the evaluation of Collaborative-Competitive SG (CCSG) design and identified a set of guidelines for future educational CCSG.

In this context, the key aim of the Beaconing project was to provide an ecosystem that reunites tools that enable teachers to construct, adapt and easily reuse playful pervasive learning experiences. The Gamified Lesson Path (GLP) is the core concept around experience building. Such GLPs can be created and customised using two main authoring tools: the Authoring Tool for Gamified Lesson Paths and the Authoring Tool for Context-Aware Challenges. These authoring tools enable different levels of the customisation of metagames, which are narratives that drive the gameplay on the student side and minigames used as the primary assessment tools of the learning outcome. With the support of these tools, teachers can personalise the learning units to the specific student's needs [11]. To ensure the reuse of the different learning paths, a set of templates and a taxonomy have been developed [12].

Starting from the critical experiences extracted from the Beaconing large-scale piloting that have involved more than 6000 participants, this paper looks into the accessibility of existing GLPs created in Beaconing, and explores the possibility to adapt them for students with visual impairments starting from existing standard and practices. This study aims to support the development of GLPs that can be played by sudents with visual impairment as part of the INCLUDEME Project (Inclusive Digital Environments to Enable High-Quality Education for Disadvantaged and Disabled Learners). In previous applied research [9–11], significant experience has been gathered in GLP personalization and reuse. For this paper, applied experimnents were executed to determine the specific reuse capability of exiting GLPs for students with disabilities and evaluate the adaptations required to be performed to ensure user-friendliness. The paper advances recommendations that could support the adaptability for accessibility of present and future GLPs.

2 Accessibility Considerations

Accessibility represents an essential requirement of educational environments, and it supports their primordial mission of providing equal and broad access to undergraduate and graduate education. This mission includes prioritising universal access to facilities, information, and technologies, supported by various standards and guidelines.

In recent years it has become mandatory to meet the requirements of the Web Accessibility Policy, and the websites of public institutions, organisations and educational institutions must comply with the Web Content Accessibility Guidelines (WCAG). The top guidelines that are used to make content available are the Web Content Accessibility Guidelines (WCAG), the Authoring Tool Accessibility Guidelines (ATAG), the User Agent Accessibility Guidelines (UAAG), and the Accessible Rich Internet Applications

(WAI-ARIA) [13]. The WCAG 2 developed by the World Wide Web Consortium aims to guide the creation of accessible learning content. WCAG is divided into four principles: perceivable, operable, understandable, and robust. Each principle is divided into testable success criteria. Success criteria are rated A, AA, or AAA depending on how important and demanding achieving the required standard is.

Applying such standards and recommendations in education remains an issue, as awareness of accessibility and its requirements is limited among those creating educational content and those designing and developing educational websites and applications [13]. Efforts to provide accessible learning content are not new [14–16].

However, research has highlighted the critical limitations that still exist today, even at a basic access level, such as providing accessible higher education websites [17, 18]. In this context, many exiting learning resources remain inaccessible, and it has become critical to analyse the adaptability of existing recourses and provide guidelines for accessibility adaptation.

3 Case Studies – Adapting Existing Beaconing GLPs for Accessibility

The Beaconing project intended to provide 'anytime and anywhere' learning by exploiting pervasive, context-aware and gamified techniques and technologies using a problem-based learning approach [19, 20]. The solution's backbone is a platform that offers teachers the possibility to create just one gamified lesson and reuse it in different ways by using an authoring tool. This is to lower the barrier for STEM teachers to introduce and use personalised and pervasive learning as a part of their classes.

A case study has been carried out to analyse the accessibility of the components of two of the GLPs created in Beaconing in the context of the INCLUDEME Project that specifically tartgets the use of gamified lesson paths with students with disabilities. The accessibility tests focused on visual impairment and were carried out for the graphical elements (images) and the minigames included in exiting GLPs, testing mainly the compatibility between backgrounds and text in the minigames. Two images from two GLPs have been tested for accessibility, and compatibility with different types of visual impairments is discussed below.

GLP 1 – The Stolen Files, a Chemistry Adventure

This GLP was designed for middle school students and was used for testing chemistry knowledge.

The first image that we have tested for accessibility offers clues for the answer to the minigame linked to this part of the narratives and includes a representation of three chemical elements: Neon, Chromium and Mercury. The colour scheme for the original image included red-orange for the first element (Chromium), green for the second element (Mercury), two types of blue for the third element (Neon) and background and dark grey for the atomic representation of the elements (Fig. 1).

Each colour of the problematic areas from the image identified using the GIMP application and colors were tested using the colour generator to extract the HEX and RGB codes for further analysis. As it can be seen in Table 1, the codes for the Neon

Fig. 1. Color scheme of an image used in the narration of the GLP

Table 1. Color codes of the tested areas

Area picked	HEX code	RGB code
Chromium	#FF4100	255, 65, 0
Mercury	#35D02F	53, 208, 47
Neon	#50BFB3	80, 191, 179
Background	#8DBFB3	141, 191, 179
Aomic representation	#223A3A	34, 58, 58

element and background have the same values for the green and blue components. Therefore these two areas are identified as problematic from the start.

Figure 2 provides an estimation of how viewers with perception anomalies might perceive an actual image. The Cr element and Hg element are projected for Protanopia and Deuteranopia in similar colours and cannot be distinguished. The Ne element overlaps with the background of the image and cannot be determined. The Hg and Ne are projected for Protanopia and Tritanopia in similar colours and cannot be distinguished.

Fig. 2. Simulated colour perception

Most people who suffer from colourblindness have some form of red-green colourblindness, such as deuteranopia or protanopia. It can be difficult or impossible to distinguish whether a given colour is red or green, and even if there are used different shades of red or green, the contrast between them can be low, and the colours cannot be distinguished.

As shown in Table 2, both for Protanopia and Deuteranopia, the red – orange and green colors for Chromium and Mercury elements are colored in two different shades

Table 2. Color codes of the tested areas

PROTANOPIA			
	Area picked	HEX code	RGB code
	Chromium	#9B8A1D	155, 138, 29
	Mercury	#D0BA1B	208, 186, 27
	Neon	#B1ACA8	177, 172, 168
	Background	#B9B4AD	185, 180, 173
	Aomic representation	#233B3A	34, 59, 58

DEUTERANOPIA			
	Area picked	HEX code	RGB code
	Chromium	#A27A1A	162, 122, 26
	Mercury	#E5AE3C	229, 174, 60
	Neon	#B8A8B8	184, 168, 184
	Background	#B8A8B8	184, 168, 184
	Aomic representation	#223A3A	34, 58, 58

TRITANOPIA			
	Area picked	HEX code	RGB code
	Chromium	#A27A1A	255, 62, 63
	Mercury	#5DC8D7	93, 200, 215
	Neon	#59BBCB	89, 187, 203
	Background	#92BCCB	146, 188, 203
	Aomic representation	#233B3A	35, 59, 58

of yellow, and the background and the Neon element colours are similar for protanopia and same for deuteranopia. For Tritanopia, we have identified three types of blue shades for two of the elements and the background.

We created a new colour scheme adapted for Protanopia and Deuteranopia, using a purple based colour for red tones as they are perceived light blue tone and yellow tone for the green colour. For Tritanopia, the blue tone of the third element was slightly modified to a more aqua tone. (Fig. 3). We did not alter the background, but we changed the contrast of the atomic representation to black (Table 3).

GLP 2 – Elisa Leonida Zamfirescu. Who was she?
The GLP was designed to present the life and legacy of a remarkable Romanian personality – Elisa Leonida Zamfirescu, the first woman with an engineering degree.

The image in Fig. 4 is a snapshot of Elisa Leonida Zamfirescu. The majority of the images used in the GLP were black and white (Fig. 5). A sightly denaturation of the

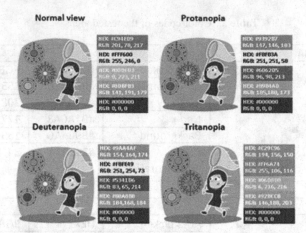

Fig. 3. Proposed colour scheme and simulated colour perception

image's colour can be seen in all images, but overall the image can be perceived by all three types of colourblindness. According to WCAG Accessibility Guidelines, it is recommended, if it is possible, to use black and white graphical representations.

In general, sepia tones, such as those in the picture shown, are perceptible by colour blindness people. Text and backgrounds must have a high level of contrast to allow players to distinguish shapes purely by tones and not colour. The image used for our study is presented in sepia tones and it is classified as an old heritage image. The images were further processed to see how they could be displayed for the selected types of colour blindness and the colour codes were extracted for further analysis, to understand better if they are compatible to be used together with a text. For the analysis, we extracted five critical points of the images. After extracting the colour codes, we identified 3 areas in the image in which text could be integrated. After the analysis, two area could be classified as accessible only for the AA (18pt+) WCAG requirements, but the areas are also limited in terms of space. The text colours used for the test were both white and black and font size at 18pt (Fig. 6).

Our recommendation for using old images, in sepia or grey tones, is to process them by creating dark/or light background areas, depending on the colour used for the text. Therefore, in order to be able to use such images, the authoring tool should have options to alter the images by adding accessible frames, previously tested with different font color/size, in the desired areas of the image. According to WCAG Accessibility Guidelines, many colourblind people find it difficult to distinguish blue from orange, for example, or red from green (and either red or green from grey). It is recommended to avoid the combination of these colours. Regarding the colours, there are two main accessibility concerns regarding the use of colours, contrast and colour dependence:

– Colour contrast is the ratio of the foreground colour (text) and the background colour. The baseline recommendation is at least 3:1 for larger text, but for smaller text (up to 18px), the ratio should be at AA (4.5:1) or AAA (7:1).

Table 3. Proposed colour scheme and simulated colour perception

PROPOSED COLOR SCHEME			
	Area picked	HEX code	RGB code
	Chromium	#C94ED9	201, 78, 217
	Mercury	#FFF600	255, 246, 0
	Neon	#00DFD3	0, 223, 211
	Background	#8DBFB3	141, 191, 179
	Aomic representation	#000000	0, 0, 0

PROTANOPIA			
	Area picked	HEX code	RGB code
	Chromium	#9392B7	147, 146, 183
	Mercury	#FBFB3A	251, 251, 58
	Neon	#6062D5	96, 98, 213
	Background	#B9B4AD	185, 180, 173
	Aomic representation	#000000	0, 0, 0

DEUTERANOPIA			
	Area picked	HEX code	RGB code
	Chromium	#9AA4AF	154, 164, 174
	Mercury	#FBFE49	251, 254, 73
	Neon	#5341D6	83, 65, 214
	Background	#B8A8B8	184, 168, 184
	Aomic representation	#000000	0, 0, 0

TRITANOPIA			
	Area picked	HEX code	RGB code
	Chromium	#C29C96	194, 156, 150
	Mercury	#FF6A74	255, 106, 116
	Neon	#06D8D8	6, 216, 216
	Background	#92BCCB	146, 188, 203
	Aomic representation	#000000	0, 0, 0

Fig. 4. The image used in the narration of the GLP

Fig. 5. Simulated colour perception

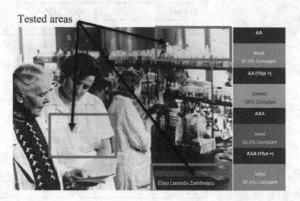

Fig. 6. Tritanopia image addaption with text over

- Colour dependence is the need to see colour to understand the information. In our game case, the users might not distinguish red text for the ending time from the background, and so they will not know that the game is over.

WCAG 2 Success Criterion 1.4.5 (Level AA) requires that images are not used to present text if the authentic text can achieve the same visual presentation (Fig. 7).

- Question area: the contrast between foreground and background has a ratio of 9.35. The colour scheme is accessible.
- Answer area (boxes with letters): the contrast between foreground and background has a ratio of 3.74. The colour scheme is not compatible with small text or images but is compatible with larger text.
- Buttons (See solutions and Undo): the contrast between foreground and background has a ratio of 9.35. The colour scheme is accessible.

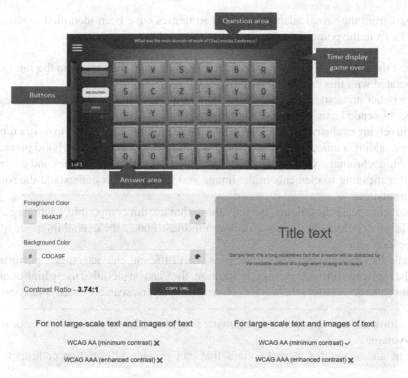

Fig. 7. Testing colour for the Swipe and Seek minigame of Eliza Leonida Zamfirescu GLP

- Time display game ongoing: the contrast between foreground and background has a ratio of 7.6. The colour scheme is accessible.
- Time display game over the contrast between foreground and background has a ratio of 1.73. Moreover, the colour scheme is not compatible both for small and large text or images.

4   Discussion and Conclusions

This research aimed to provide insights that would ease the adaptability of existing GLPs and the design of new ones from an accessibility perspective. Based on the analysis presented in section three, we propose integrating two options in the designing process. The first option is to give the designer, when s/he is creating the narratives of a GLP, the possibility to recolour the images using an image section colour picker and provide accessible colour schemes. The colour picker should have integrated default colour schemes adapted for specific disabilities such as euteranopia, Protanopia and Tritanopia, and a custom scheme that can choose the colour for the critical sections in the images for those who the preset colours do not apply. The second option is to offer the designers the opportunity to use already accessible images previously tested. This option is preferable, as the time spent for redesigning can be much shorter, but it also involves a much greater effort to develop and maintain the application.

Apart from the visual adaption, several strategies have been identified to redesign the GLPs from the point of view of visually impaired players:

- Adjust the colours of the elements as they offer clues to the answer to the minigame associated with this part of the narratives.
- For a better understanding, the text of the elements should be increased, although it is recommended to avoid using text in images.
- Avoid relying exclusively on colours. If the game requires each player to have a unique colour, adding a unique glyph or symbol is a handy option for colourblind players.
- Use Monochromatic Color Schemes in combination with various tones and contrasts to offer meaning to elements in the image and let the player understand the role of different areas
- Do not change all the colours, but only those that are not compatible. Changing all of the different colours to those with colourblindness makes the overall interface of the game look unnatural.
- Visuals like narrative scenes, interactions with different characters, task performing can be replaced with audio scenes. In addition, they can be modified using high contrast colour schemes, colour schemes for colour blind players, scalable fonts, zoom options, etc.
- Transform the text into speech by allowing the integration of a screen reader or using self-voicing.
- Use of audio cues for natural sounds that can provide information or hints to the player.
- Use of sonification to convey information using changes in pitch, amplitude or tempo [21], such as sound effects that indicate different objects or actions.; earcons provide different tones; an alert sound mechanism, like the one used in the pedestrian crossings, provides information on different paths that the player must follow.
- Use haptic stimuli to replace the cues from a non-accessible game that generally come from the visuals.

The relevance of inclusive design of learning resources like serious games that fit a wide variety of specific needs is increasing, but the experience of designing such games leads to compromises in aesthetics and the play experience of other user groups. Research is still needed to balance the different aspects and investigate how the further adaption to specific requirements influences the user and gameplay experiences.

Acknowledgements. The work presented herein is partially funded under the Erasmus+ Program of the European Union, INCLUDEME – Inclusive Digital Environments to Enable High-Quality Education for Disadvantaged and Disabled Learners, Grant Agreement 621547-EPP-1–2020-1-RO-EPPA3-IPI-SOC-IN.

1. References

1. Iten, N., Petko, D.: Learning with serious games: Is fun playing the game a predictor of learning success? Br. J. Edu. Technol. **47**(1), 151–163 (2016)

2. All, A., Nuñez Patricia Castellar, E., Van Looy, J.: Digital game-based learning effectiveness assessment: reflections on study design. Comput. Educ. **167** (2021). ISSN 0360-1315. https://doi.org/10.1016/j.compedu.2021.104160

3. Rajendran, D., Santhanam, P.: Towards digital game-based learning con-tent with multi-objective reinforcement learning. Mater. Today: Proc. **2214–7853** (2021). https://doi.org/10.1016/j.matpr.2021.03.156.

4. Giessen, H.W.: Serious games effects: an overview. Procedia – Soc. Behav. Sci. **174**, 2240–2244 (2015). ISSN 1877-0428, https://doi.org/10.1016/j.sbspro.2015.01.881

5. Mouaheb, H., Fahli, A., Moussetad, M., Eljamali, S.: The serious game: what educational benefits? Procedia – Soc. Behav. Sci. **46**, 5502–5508 (2012). ISSN 1877-0428, https://doi.org/10.1016/j.sbspro.2012.06.465

6. Mayer, I.: Towards a comprehensive methodology for the research and evaluation of serious games. Procedia Comput. Sci. **15**, 233–247 (2012). ISSN 1877-0509, https://doi.org/10.1016/j.procs.2012.10.075

7. Khenissi, M.A., Essalmi, F., Jemni, M.: comparison between serious games and learning version of existing games. Procedia – Soc. Behav. Sci. **191**, 487–494 (2015). ISSN 1877-0428, https://doi.org/10.1016/j.sbspro.2015.04.380

8. Paiva, A.C.R., Flores, N.H., Barbosa, A.G., Ribeiro, T.P.B.: iLearnTest – framework for educational games. Procedia – Soc. Behav. Sci. **228**, 443–448 (2016). ISSN 1877-0428, https://doi.org/10.1016/j.sbspro.2016.07.068

9. Carvalho, M.B., et al.: An activity theory-based model for serious games analysis and conceptual design, Comput. Educ. **87**, 166–181 (2015). ISSN 0360-1315, https://doi.org/10.1016/j.compedu.2015.03.023

10. Buchinger, D., da Silva Hounsell, M.: Guidelines for designing and using collaborative-competitive serious games. Comput. Educ. **118**, 133–149 (2018). ISSN 0360-1315, https://doi.org/10.1016/j.compedu.2017.11.007

11. Munekata, N., Kunita, I., Hoshino, J. (eds.): ICEC 2017. LNCS, vol. 10507. Springer, Cham (2017). https://doi.org/10.1007/978-3-319-66715-7

12. BEACONING project. D3.3 Learning Environment System Specification (2017)

13. Stefan, I.A., Baalsrud, H.J.M., Sallinen, N., Stefan, A., Gheorghe, A.F.: Accessibility and education: are we fulfilling state of the art requirements?. The 17th International Scientific Conference eLearning and Software for Education 2021, eLse, Bucharest (2021)

14. GLP.

15. de Macedo, C.M.S., Ribas, U.V.: Accessibility guidelines for the development of learning objects. Procedia Comput. Sci. **14**, 155–162 (2012). ISSN 1877-0509, https://doi.org/10.1016/j.procs.2012.10.018

16. Gutiérrez y Restrepo, E., Benavidez, C., Gutiérrez, H.: The challenge of teaching to create accessible learning objects to higher education lecturers. Procedia Comput. Sci. **14**, 371–381 (2012). ISSN 1877-0509, https://doi.org/10.1016/j.procs.2012.10.043

17. Ben Salah, N., Bayoudh Saadi, I, Ben Ghezala, H.: A multidimensional framework to study accessible guidance in u-learning systems for disabled learners. Procedia Comput. Sci. **176**, 490–499 (2020). ISSN 1877-0509, https://doi.org/10.1016/j.procs.2020.08.051

18. Ismail, A., Kuppusamy, K.S.: Web accessibility investigation and identification of major issues of higher education websites with statistical measures: a case study of college websites. J. King Saud Univ. – Comput. Inf. Sci. **1319–1578** (2019). https://doi.org/10.1016/j.jksuci.2019.03.011

19. Acosta-Vargas, P., González, M., Luján-Mora, S.: Dataset for evaluating the accessibility of the websites of selected Latin American universities. Data Brief **28** (2020). ISSN 2352-3409, https://doi.org/10.1016/j.dib.2019.105013

20. Baalsrud Hauge, J., Stefan, I.: Improving learning outcome by re-using and modifying gamified lessons paths. In: Ma, M., Fletcher, B., Göbel, S., Baalsrud Hauge, J., Marsh, T. (eds.) JCSG 2020. LNCS, vol. 12434, pp. 150–163. Springer, Cham (2020). https://doi.org/10.1007/978-3-030-61814-8_12
21. Barrass, S., Kramer, G.: Using sonification. Multimed. Syst. **7**(1), 23–31 (1999)
22. Bell, B.: Investigate and decide learning environments: specializing task models for authoring tool design. J. Learn. Sci. **7**(1), 65–105 (1998). https://doi.org/10.1207/s15327809jls0701_3
23. Wiley, D.A.: Connecting learning objects to instructional design theory: a definition, a metaphor, and a taxonomy. Inst. Use Learn. Objects **2830**(435), 1–35 (2000)
24. Martinez, M.: Designing learning objects to personalise learning margaret martinez in Wiley, D.A. Inst. Use Learn. Objects **2830**(435), 151–172 (2000)

Back to Basics: Explainable AI for Adaptive Serious Games

Florian Berger[1]([✉]) and Wolfgang Müller[2][iD]

[1] University of Europe for Applied Sciences, Dessauer Str. 3-5,
10963 Berlin, Germany
florian.berger@posteo.de

[2] Pädagogische Hochschule Weingarten, Kirchplatz 2, 88250 Weingarten, Germany

Abstract. The spread of AI technologies has given rise to concerns regarding the fairness, appropriateness, and neutrality of machine-made decisions. Explainable AI aims at countering this by enforcing simple or transparent solutions. Adaptive serious games themselves have long been a playground for various approaches to achieve machine-regulated adjustments for increased learner success or player satisfaction. Results have been commendable, but can not readily be complemented with explainability. Analysing 18 models of adaptivity in game-based learning and related domains, we propose a simple and explainable adaptivity model for serious games. It is designed as a rule-based, short-term decision making algorithm, proposes game progress as a reliable learning progress indicator, and adapts to both under- and over-performing learners. We present the implementation of the model in two distinct serious games, and the result of an evaluation in a controlled trial ($n = 80$), demonstrating its suitability for adaptive serious games. In conclusion, we underline the importance of designing serious games both as teaching and playing experiences, and of an iterative design process to assure the quality of the final product.

Keywords: Adaptivity · Game-based learning · Explainable AI

1 Introduction

There is an ongoing paradigm shift in the application of technologies of artificial intelligence. For decades, refinement of algorithms up to mimicking nerve structures, in combination with increasing computing power, developed into a situation where the means and gains would justify the methods—however complex, or even incomprehensible to laypersons they became.

This has resulted in impressive achievements especially regarding machine learning. However, as these technologies have started to permeate everyday life, provide counsel for HR management as well as criminal risk assessment, and start to produce spectacular "deep fakes", they are stirring public concern. Aside from perpetuating biases in the training data, contemporary machine learning

© Springer Nature Switzerland AG 2021
B. Fletcher et al. (Eds.): JCSG 2021, LNCS 12945, pp. 67–81, 2021.
https://doi.org/10.1007/978-3-030-88272-3_6

systems by design face difficulties explaining why and how exactly a concrete decision has been achieved.

The scientific community has recognised these concerns as a critical factor for the future acceptance of this technology and related research. Proposals for "Explainable Artificial Intelligence (XAI)" [1] have set new research directions in motion which aim at building accountable, transparent decision-making systems. Serious games, together with computer-based learning and entertainment games, have used and advanced AI techniques since their inception, and consequently are also targets for the demands brought forward by XAI.

2   Background

Up to now, automated adaptivity has not gained widespread use as a core mechanic in both commercial serious and entertainment games, in spite of assumed or even established advantages for both players and producers. Amongst other reasons, Charles et al. have attributed this to the major issues that adaptivity causes for quality assurance—which would have to evaluate all possible adaptations in a game—and even for liability [4]. Conversely, adaptive serious games have long been a fruitful subject of academic research, with a sizeable body of models, prototypes, and evaluations being produced. Their history reflects the evolution of paradigms in adaptivity techniques, ranging from optimised scheduling algorithms [3], plan-based approaches and sophisticated knowledge modeling [9], along with their scalability problems [19], to neural networks [6], although their experimental application was more common in adaptive entertainment games [25].

In their particular use cases and trials, most of them have been successful on a smaller scale. However, for practically all of the historical approaches, implementation details, especially the source code, have not been disclosed; and for solutions based on machine learning, the course of their decision-making remains hidden by the very nature of the technique. As a consequence, this makes them unfitting for XAI, where a system can be held accountable for its decisions even by laypersons. This situation motivates the development of a model that, based on historic successes, combines a general approach with transparency and simplicity.

3   Identification and Analysis of Model Candidates

First step in the development process of a generalised model was the selection and evaluation of seminal historical models. Model candidates were identified by a systematic keyword search in the ACM, IEEE, and Google Scholar databases regarding "adaptive serious games" and "adaptivity in game-based learning". Works were included when they explicitly described a model of adaptivity, and excluded when the model matched or merely augmented a previously described one. The search was extended to references of included works, and to related fields of computer-based learning and entertainment games, following the same method.

The identification process yielded 10 distinct models of adaptivity in game-based learning, 5 from computer-based learning, and 3 from entertainment games.

The models then were analysed and compared using seven criteria, based on comparison criteria of adaptive systems formulated by Albert et al. [2], Martens [16], and Kickmeier-Rust et al. [8]. For brevity, this paper discusses four major criteria: the *basis* of the adaptation, i.e. the source variable that triggers adaptive interventions; whether the model allows for *short-term* interventions, which is crucial for real-time games; the *origin of the reference* that sets the baseline for deviations that require adaptive adjustment; and finally whether or not *over-performing learners* are served by the model.

The structure of the models was also visualised as a flowchart, creating these from the verbose description if no visualisation was provided by the original authors.

The following will highlight four key examples of adaptivity models from the literature.

On the side of computer-based learning, *Martens* presented an adaptivity model for her research on adaptive case-based intelligent tutoring systems (ITS) already in 2006 [15]. She proposed a *Tutoring Process Model* as the central component of a generalised adaptive ITS architecture. Subject of the adaptation are the building blocks and actions of the learning experience, along with help and feedback. The basis is a learner profile building upon a knowledge model. Input for the adaptation process is gathered before a building block is displayed, hence the model is not designed for short-term adaptation. While the origin of the reference baseline remains unclear, the goal of the adaptation is defined as optimal support for the training effects of the application. The model supports both under- and over-performing learners. Since it is a comparatively early, but thoroughly designed model, foreshadowing a lot of the elements used in later adaptivity models for serious games, and has been put to use in practice, it is significant for the construction of a new generalised model.

One year later, Thue et al. presented a very simplistic, but yet effective model of adaptivity for entertainment games, specifically for games with sequential encounters, such as role-playing games [21]. The adaptation manipulates time, place and manners of encounters, the availability of side quests as well as non-player character reactions. The basis of the adaptation if a factorial player model based on five simplified player types, comparable to an earlier approach by Charles et al. [4]. The adaptation time is before each encounter, which allows for short-term adaptivity. The player model is updated based on the player actions taken during the encounter. The origin of the reference is the game designer crafting the parameters of an encounter. Goal of the adaptation is an improved player experience, fun, and replay value. Due to the factorial player model, a notion of over- or under-performing is not applicable to this model. In spite of looking simple, even straightforward, the model of Thue et al. is significant because of being both minimalist and effective at the same time. As such, it has inspired lots of other implementations, while its coincidental similarities to Martens' model, from an entirely different domain—building blocks versus encounters—hint at

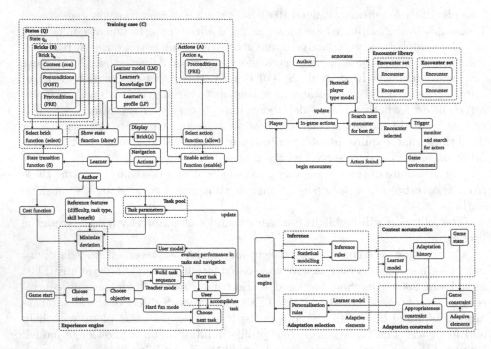

Fig. 1. Flowcharts of the adaptivity models of Martens [15] (top left, from description), Thue et al. [21] (top right, from description), Bellotti et al. [3] (bottom left, extended from [3, p. 265]), and Peirce [17] (bottom right, adapted from [17, p. 109])

an underlying mechanism offering prospects of generalisation. Also, Thue et al. evaluated the model in a controlled trial ($n = 90$) to satisfying results.

Moving to the domain of serious games, Bellotti et al. presented a model that took proven ingredients, as the user model and sequential tasks, and augmented these with a detailed authoring mechanism [3]. Also, the model explicitly targeted "sandbox serious games" that offer a free choice of interactions in an open world. The subject of the adaptation is the character and order of tasks to be completed. The adaptation basis is the learner profile in conjunction with the parameters of the tasks, as designed by an author. The system adapts before a series of tasks ("mission"), which prevents short-term adaptation. The origin of the reference is a cost and difficulty function, as set forth by an author. The adaptation goal is vaguely described as "more efficient learning". In contrast to all other adaptivity models we analysed, Bellotti et al. were the only ones who outright focused on over-performing players, trying to establish fitting challenges for them. In passing, this caters for under-performing players as well. The value of this model for a generalised re-design lies in the explicitly defined role of a game's author. Not only is that person requested to design the tasks; the model also explicitly requires the design of semantic metadata such as difficulty, task type, skill benefits, and a cost function which the system translates into a

Table 1. Adaptivity models in serious games

Authors	Basis	Short-term	Reference origin	Over-performers
Torrente et al. [22]	Learner preconditions, context	No	**Not clear**	**Not explicitly**
Magerko et al. [12]	Player type, motivation	No	Test	*n/a*
Sancho et al. [18]	Learner model	No	**Not explained**	*n/a*
Bellotti et al. [3]	Learner profile, reference features	No	Authored cost function	Yes
Conati and Manske [5]	Learne model	*Conditionally*	Pedagogical presumptions	No
Hodhod [7]	Learner model	*Partly*	Actions tagged "good" by an author	No
Grappiolo et al. [6]	Learner model	No	Hidden function approximated by a neural net	No
Kickmeier-Rust et al. [9]	Learner model and development	Yes	Planned learning path	No
Peirce et al. [17]	Learner behaviour and success	*Conditionally*	Author rules	**Not satisfying**
Koidl et al. [10]	Player-, learner- and pedagogical model	Yes	Authored learning- and story engine setup	No

learning curve. This is a very different approach from the implicit author that all other analysed models silently assume.

No analysis of models for adaptive serious games would be complete without considering the tremendous amount of work that has gone into the adaptive serious games "ELEKTRA" and its successor "80Days". The underlying model is called ALIGN and has been presented by Peirce in 2013, titled "The Non-invasive Personalisation of Educational Video Games" [17]. The model concentrates on the granular details of the decision making, proposing a succession of "Inference – Context Accumulation – Adaptation Constraint – Adaptation Selection". ALIGN exclusively adapts cognitive and meta-cognitive feedback to the players. The basis for adaptation are the player's actions, and a reasoning about their previous successes. The adaptation time is after a player's interaction, making the system short-term reactive in theory, depending on the combinatorial complexity of the computations. The reference origin are the rules applied to the four steps of decision making, as designed by an author. The goal is to understand the sources of player successes and failures, and to motivate, help and challenge players. While an adaptation to over-performers is possible in theory, it remains under-explored in the original work. The value of ALIGN is first its proven successful implementations in two distinct high-value serious games, and second its notion of distinguishing between *possible* versus *appropriate* adaptations by means of adaptation constraints.

Table 2. Adaptivity models in computer-based learning

Authors	Basis	Short-term	Reference origin	Over-performers
Krichen [11]	Pre-test results	**No**	Design of the pre-test	Yes
Martens [15]	Learner model from knowledge profile	**No**	**Not explained**	Yes
Teo and Gay [20]	Learner model of the cognitive structure	**No**	Expert knowledge	**No**
Mao and Li [14]	Facial expression, emotional layer of speech and writing	Yes	Pre-set database	*n/a*
Magnisalis and Demetriadis [13]	Learner model, group model, script model	*In theory*	Author's script, learner demands at runtime, evaluation	Yes

Table 3. Adaptivity models in entertainment game

Authors	Basis	Short-term	Reference origin	Over-performers
Charles et al. [4]	Player performance, factorial player model, player presets	Yes	**Not explained**	Yes
Thue et al. [21]	Factorial model of player types	Yes	Design of encounter details	*n/a*
Van Lankveld et al. [23]	Player skill, difficulty preset	*Turn-based*	Author's rules	Yes

All four models are visualised in Fig. 1, while Tables 1, 2, and 3 summarise the results of the analysis of all selected models.

4   Generalisation of an Explainable Model

The models analysed above share the traits that all their decisions are explainable by a set of human-understandable rules applicable to given parameters and circumstances, and that they feature an—implicit or explicit—strong human authoring component. A simple fallback to one of these models however would not suffice, as they also present some shortcomings in the additional constraints.

The adaptivity models for serious games we analysed demonstrated severe shortcomings in short-term adaptation, which is a requirement for a lot of game genres. Also, none of them save the model of Bellotti et al. address overperforming learners and players, excluding a relevant part of the audience from the benefits of a personalised experience.

The latter requirement was much better addressed by adaptivity models from computer-based learning, but they also, by the nature of the medium, were not appropriate for short-term adaptation.

Conversely, the models for adaptive entertainment games we analysed had no problems neither with short-term adaptation nor adapting to over-performing players. As a consequence, we believe that the strengths of the models from these different domains can be combined, this way also making up for each other's weaknesses.

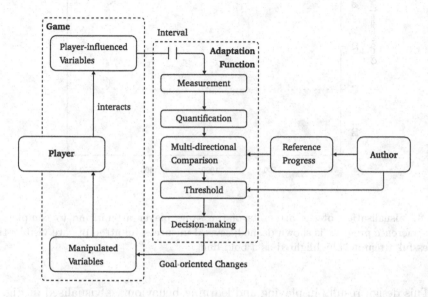

Fig. 2. Flowchart of a generalised explainable adaptivity model for serious games

Our model is visualised in Fig. 2. It builds on an assumption of an adequate *game* being adapted, rather than a mere container for text-based learning; that means support for a high interaction rate, player agency, an actual game logic, and overall playful handling. One core presumption is a *congruence of gameplay and learning actions* by design, which means that game design is carried out by humans qualified for teaching.

The consequence of this design is that, since in-game actions equal learning behaviour, the *in-game progress* constitutes a *direct measurement* of *learning progress*. Hence, basis of adaptation are the properties of the game world that will be influenced by the player at runtime, showing the player's progress.

Whether or not this progress calls for an adaptive intervention depends on a baseline reference of expected progress. The origin of this reference is a human author that is able to judge both the expected progress and the relevance of deviations, and explicitly sets these parameters. That author is preferably an expert in the domain being taught, or is advised by one.

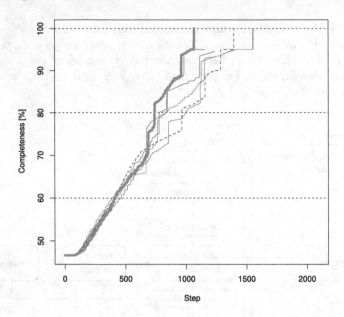

Fig. 3. Visualisation of the attempts of the same player attempting to complete a task: reference progress is shown dashed; several unsuccessful attempts are visible; the successful attempt is highlighted as a bold line.

This design results in playing and learning behaviour as visualised in Fig. 3, which is an actual gameplay recording from the implementation in "Team Leader", detailed below. The authored reference progress over time ("steps", i.e. the number of iterations of player action evaluation and possible adaptation, see Sect. 5 below) is shown as a dashed line. Several player attempts at completion are visible, with the first ones taking too many steps (completing after the dashed reference, and thus failing), the following ones cancelled for not meeting in-game requirements, and the final successful playthrough highlighted as a bold line, finishing well before the reference expected the player to. This succession documents a learning process over the several attempts, until a successful strategy is found and applied.

The adaptation itself is designed as a regulator circuit of player interaction, measurement, comparison to the reference, and possible adaptive intervention. Measurements will be carried out in intervals that allow for an appropriate short-term adaptation. The adaptation mechanism itself is rule-based, a design that is straightforward for humans to comprehend.

Contrary to traditional one-sided models especially from computer-based learning, the generalised explainable model processes a performance below the reference as well as above the reference. In that manner, under- and over-performing players can be catered for using a single mechanism.

Subject of the adaptation are parameters of the game world, or the meta-interaction with the game. While under-performing players will receive established forms of feedback, guidance, and self-reflection, over-performers will experience diegetic interventions that change the in-game situation in a way that makes it more challenging.

The goal of the adaptation always considers the game as a means to an end, and as such lies in the support of the teaching situation that the adaptive serious game is a part of. That situation is bound to have a teaching goal, and it is that—as such, game-external—goal that the interventions are to help achieve. This design is in line with demands of Whitton, who called for the "appropriateness" of serious games as a teaching device, and in this way aligned them to a game-external curriculum, exams, and teaching subjects [24].

The aim of this proposed model is to close the gaps we found in historical models, while at the same time achieving explainability by a simplistic design that can readily be understood by humans. The model makes no assumptions about the subject being taught, only about an alignment of in-game progress and learning success. In line with views formulated by Charles et al. as early as 2005 [4], we believe that abandoning the notion of the successive completion of a player knowledge model is more fitting for the dynamic nature of teaching and learning situations. Instead of an abstraction of knowledge and learning, progress is being embedded in the domain expert's authorship of a desired learning progress, and interventions are only dependant on the current behaviour being displayed by the player.

5 Implementations

The general explainable model we propose has been implemented in two distinct serious games. "Team Leader" is a desktop computer time- and resource management game teaching project management. "akrobatik@home" is an exergame controlled by body posture sensors, putting physical therapy for people affected by thalidomide syndrome in a playful context.

"Team Leader" is meant to be played alongside lessons in project management. It simulates a corporate production environment, where different products need to be produced under time and budget constraints. The player manages a group of workers of different skills, motivation, and productivity. Only by target-oriented workload distribution can the goals of the respective levels be achieved; hence, succeeding in the game is a display of having mastered skills required by the problem domain.

The adaptation is based on the state and tendency of the in-game progress, which is assumed to be linked to player skill. The origin of the reference is an intended learning curve per level, designed by an author. That person also configures adaptation thresholds as a prevention of jittery interventions when performance is close to the intended curve. The adaptation algorithm evaluates the player performance every 2, 1 and 0.5 s in levels 1, 2 and 3 respectively, allowing for short-term interventions and reflecting the increasing challenge.

Negative deviations from the reference learning curve will be met by assistive meta-interventions (see Fig. 4 left); positive deviations will trigger diegetic challenges that require advanced management techniques from the player, such as parallelising task execution (see Fig. 4 right).

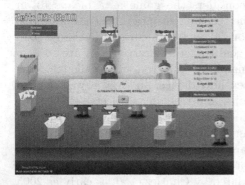 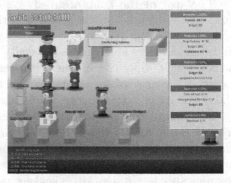

Fig. 4. Context aware feedback as a helping intervention, hinting at what to do next (left), diegetic intervention of slowing down a worker, making the game harder (right)

"akrobatik@home" is a mobile game for tablet computers. The game itself is an endless runner game in third person view, where the player must constantly avoid obstacles by moving horizontally. This movement is controlled by body posture sensors placed on the seat and on the shoulders of the player. By executing an exercise in form of a pendular torso movement, as developed by physiotherapists for persons with thalidomide syndrome, the player avatar is being controlled and moved around the obstacles. The in-game player action and the techniques to be trained align here as well.

Thalidomide syndrome may manifest in very different forms. As a consequence, a fixed difficulty level of a respective exergame is not desirable, or may even be harmful to players. The implementation of our generalised model allowed for a personalisation of the game difficulty, resulting in a fitting training experience. Interventions are again based on the state and tendency of in-game performance. The origin of the reference has been authored together with a physical rehabilitation center. Interventions target the frequency, difficulty, and position of obstacles on the course, and may happen every few seconds. The ability to target over- as well as under-performing players was crucial in this implementation: negative deviations will result in fewer and easier to dodge obstacles, positive deviations will lead to obstacles that require a faster pendular torso movement to avoid them. Figure 5 shows "akrobatik@home" in action.

Fig. 5. The adaptive exergame "akrobatik@home", controlled by body posture sensors

We consider the successful implementation of the generalised explainable model in two complete and published serious games of a very distinct nature an indicator of its broad applicability.

6   Evaluation

6.1   Procedure

The first implementation of the generalised explainable model, "Team Leader", has been evaluated regarding the basic fitness of the adaptivity produced, regarding both the appropriateness and effectiveness of the generated interventions, and the user impression of these. For the former, the software collected data about level iterations; time to completion; number, type, and time of interventions, and their relation to the reference progress. We controlled for confounding variables known to impact performance: gender, age, education, and time per week spent playing digital games. User impressions were evaluated using a questionnaire with three items utilising a 5-point Likert scale.

The game was made available for download from a public website. A stratification algorithm in the download process assigned subjects to one of two subgroups, one playing with adaptation enabled and one with adaptation disabled.

The recorded gameplay took place on the subjects' own computers, and they could freely decide when and how much to play. Upon level completion, the recorded data was uploaded to a server.

The adaptation for level 1 was turned off in both groups to gather a baseline performance from each player.

6.2   Results

The game had been downloaded by 165 persons, 80 of which successfully played all three levels of the game. 44 of the subjects identified as male, 36 as female. Subjects were aged 17 to 38 years, with an age median of 27 and a MAD of 4 years. The stratification resulted in statistically uniform groups: there were no significant deviations in possibly confounding variables (Chi-squared and ANOVA tests).

As assigned by the stratification algorithm, 36 subjects played the game with adaptation enabled, and 44 played it with adaptation disabled. All of the adaptive players received interventions, ranging from 44 to 262 interventions with a median of 92. The vast majority received a mixture of challenging and helping interventions over the course of the game.

To understand the effect of the adaptation, we looked at three dimensions of the recorded data: the total time taken to complete the game[1] ("steps"); the relation of adapting steps, i.e. steps with an intervention, to non-adapting steps; and the relation of help to challenge as the L1-normed relation of challenging steps to the sum of challenging and helping steps, allowing for each to be zero. The result is shown in Fig. 6.

The plot shows that players who took longer received comparatively more help (marked with a circle), and players who played shorter received more challenge (marked with a cross), indicating a correct identification of weaker and stronger players. Also, players with an above-median amount of interventions were predominantly the ones who, in comparison, received either a lot of help, or a lot of challenges; this means that players with a more balanced performance received less interventions, which also underlines the algorithm's correct heuristics.

We could also show that the amount of help received positively correlates with the distance from the reference progress when comparing levels 2 and 3. (linear regression, $p \ll 0.0001$, Pearson Correlation Coefficient 0.7847). We conclude that the algorithm correctly identifies the need for assistance, and acts accordingly.

Results of the comparison with non-adaptive players, however, were less encouraging. Playing with adaptivity disabled resulted in a 15 to 30% faster playthrough (ANOVA, $p < 0.0061$ and $p < 0.0041$ for levels 2 and 3, respectively). Additionally, completion of level 2 took players without adaptation about a third less attempts (ANOVA, $p < 0.0325$).

Asking about the appeal of the game in the questionnaire, subjects who received a lot of interventions rated the gameplay less engaging than all players

---

[1] While, with adaptivity enabled, the total time taken was influenced by adaptive interventions, it was still usable as a performance indicator: assistive meta-interventions by themselves can reasonably be assumed to impose a negligible delay on completion time, and challenging interventions still allowed most of the top-challenged players to complete the game faster than over 50% of all players.

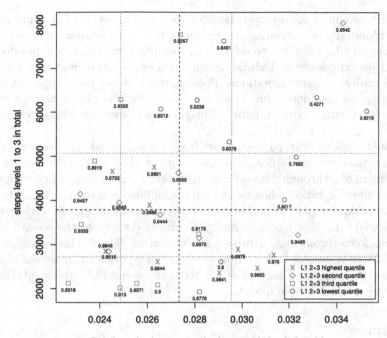

Fig. 6. L1 challenge vs. help plotted against amount of adaptive steps received, and total playing time taken, with quantiles marked as lines

without adaptivity (Kruskal-Wallis test, $p < 0.0499$), and also experienced the rising challenge as less motivating[2] (Kruskal-Wallis test, $p < 0.002$).

The qualitative results clearly contradicted the aims of the algorithm design, and required closer inspection.

7   Conclusions and Future Work

We perceive the results of the evaluation as an encouragement that a simple, explainable, rule-based algorithm is able to produce quality adaptation results in implementations. Aligning gameplay and teaching subject evidently makes players plan, try, and discard solutions until the have mastered a task. The algorithm applied interventions correctly, especially assistive ones.

Investigating the contradictory player feedback, we found that the implementation dealt too much challenge to the players, slowing the players with adaptivity enabled down, and requiring more attempts. The cause was an author reference that in itself was not challenging enough, expecting players to underperform much more than they actually did. While this was justifiable from a perspective of the problem domain, it did create subpar gameplay.

---

[2] Non-adaptive players also experienced a rising challenge as the levels themselves increased in difficulty.

We followed up on some players with a strong contradiction of in-game success versus a reportedly demotivating impression of the game. Somewhat unexpected, the discrepancy had nothing to do with the adaptation: the players pointed out flaws in user experience and visual design, such as an insufficient user interface for some critical in-game situations. These issues had not been apparent in the test sessions we conducted, but these only had a limited player base ($n < 10$). They surfaced with a larger number of players, and especially high-performance players.

In conclusion, we learned that, apart from a good visual and user experience design, an iterative game design process with a thorough evaluation of how actual human playthrough data reflects on the author reference, is key to optimal results for the adaptation when using such a simplified algorithm. Regarding our implementation, we plan to gather more player data from an adjusted version.

Also, while the user feedback and preliminary data from the second implementation looks promising, a proper evaluation of "akrobatik@home" is still ongoing. With a careful look at how the reference performs in actual training situations, we plan to gather and report more usage data of implementations of the generalised explainable model.

References

1. Adadi, A., Berrada, M.: Peeking inside the black-box: a survey on explainable artificial intelligence (XAI). IEEE Access **6**, 52138–52160 (2018)
2. Albert, D., Hockemeyer, C.: State of the art in adaptive learning techniques. D03 Requirements Specification, EASEL Consortium (2000)
3. Bellotti, F., Berta, R., Gloria, A.D., Primavera, L.: Adaptive experience engine for serious games. IEEE Trans. Comput. Intell. AI Games **1**, 264–280 (2009)
4. Charles, D., et al.: Player-centred game design: player modelling and adaptive digital games. In: Digital Games Research Conference 2005, Selected Papers Publication, pp. 285–298 (2005)
5. Conati, C., Manske, M.: Evaluating adaptive feedback in an educational computer game. In: Ruttkay, Z., Kipp, M., Nijholt, A., Vilhjálmsson, H.H. (eds.) IVA 2009. LNCS (LNAI), vol. 5773, pp. 146–158. Springer, Heidelberg (2009). https://doi.org/10.1007/978-3-642-04380-2_18
6. Grappiolo, C., Cheong, Y.G., Togelius, J., Khaled, R., Yannakakis, G.N.: Towards player adaptivity in a serious game for conflict resolution. In: 2011 Third International Conference on Games and Virtual Worlds for Serious Applications (VS-GAMES), pp. 192–198 (2011). https://doi.org/10.1109/VS-GAMES.2011.39
7. Hodhod, R.: Interactive narrative for adaptive educational games: architecture and application to character education. Ph.D. thesis, University of York, February 2010
8. Kickmeier-Rust, M.D., Steiner, C.M., Albert, D.: Non-invasive assessment and adaptive interventions in learning games. In: International Conference on Intelligent Networking and Collaborative Systems, INCOS 2009, pp. 301–305, November 2009. https://doi.org/10.1109/INCOS.2009.30
9. Kickmeier-Rust, M.D., Marte, B., Linek, S., Lalonde, T., Albert, D.: Learning with computer games: micro level feedback and interventions. In: Proceedings of the International Conference on Interactive Computer Aided Learning (ICL), Kassel (2008)

10. Koidl, K., Mehm, F., Hampson, C., Conlan, O., Göbel, S.: Dynamically adjusting digital educational games towards learning objectives. In: Proceedings 4th European Conference on Games Based Learning, pp. 177–184, Copenhagen, Denmark (2010)
11. Krichen, J.P.: Dynamically adjusting to learner's competencies and styles in an online technology course. In: SIGITE 2005: Proceedings of the 6th Conference on Information Technology Education, pp. 149–154. ACM, Newark (2005)
12. Magerko, B., Heeter, C., Fitzgerald, J., Medler, B.: Intelligent adaptation of digital game-based learning. In: Proceedings of the 2008 Conference on Future Play: Research, Play, Share. Future Play 2008, pp. 200–203. ACM, Toronto (2008)
13. Magnisalis, I., Demetriadis, S.: Modeling adaptation patterns in the context of collaborative learning: case studies of IMS-LD based implementation. In: Daradoumis, T., Caballé, S., Juan, A.A., Xhafa, F. (eds.) Technology-Enhanced Systems and Tools for Collaborative Learning Scaffolding. SCI, vol. 350, pp. 279–310. Springer, Heidelberg (2011). https://doi.org/10.1007/978-3-642-19814-4_13
14. Mao, X., Li, Z.: Implementing emotion-based user-aware e-learning. In: CHI EA 2009: Proceedings of the 27th International Conference Extended Abstracts on Human Factors in Computing Systems, pp. 3787–3792. ACM, Boston (2009)
15. Martens, A.: Modeling of adaptive tutoring processes. In: Web-Based Intelligent E-learning Systems: Technologies and Applications, pp. 193–215 (2006)
16. Martens, A.: Adaption formal. Zeitschrift für E-Learning, Themenheft Adaptivität 3, 29–39 (2008)
17. Peirce, N.: The non-invasive personalisation of educational video games. Ph.D. thesis, Trinity College Dublin, Dublin (2013). http://hdl.handle.net/2262/67775
18. Sancho, P., Moreno-Ger, P., Fuentes-Fernández, R., Fernández-Manjón, B.: Adaptive role playing games: an immersive approach for problem based learning. Educ. Technol. Soc. 12(4), 110–124 (2009)
19. Sugandh, N., Ontañón, S., Ram, A.: Real-Time Plan Adaptation for Case-Based Planning in Real-Time Strategy Games. In: Althoff, K.-D., Bergmann, R., Minor, M., Hanft, A. (eds.) ECCBR 2008. LNCS (LNAI), vol. 5239, pp. 533–547. Springer, Heidelberg (2008). https://doi.org/10.1007/978-3-540-85502-6_36
20. Teo, C.B., Gay, R.K.L.: A knowledge-driven model to personalize e-learning. J. Educ. Resour. Comput. 6(1), 3 (2006)
21. Thue, D., Bulitko, V., Spetch, M., Wasylishen, E.: Interactive storytelling: a player modelling approach. In: Schaeffer, J., Mateas, M. (eds.) Proceedings of the Third Artificial Intelligence and Interactive Digital Entertainment Conference. AAAI Press, Menlo Park (2007)
22. Torrente, J., Moreno-Ger, P., Fernandez-Manjon, B.: Learning models for the integration of adaptive educational games in virtual learning environments. In: Pan, Z., Zhang, X., El Rhalibi, A., Woo, W., Li, Y. (eds.) Edutainment 2008. LNCS, vol. 5093, pp. 463–474. Springer, Heidelberg (2008). https://doi.org/10.1007/978-3-540-69736-7_50
23. van Lankveld, G., Spronck, P., van den Herik, H.J., Rauterberg, M.: Incongruity-based adaptive game balancing. In: van den Herik, H.J., Spronck, P. (eds.) ACG 2009. LNCS, vol. 6048, pp. 208–220. Springer, Heidelberg (2010). https://doi.org/10.1007/978-3-642-12993-3_19
24. Whitton, N.J.: An Investigation into the Potential of Collaborative Game-based Learning in Higher Education. PhD Thesis, Edinburgh Napier University (2007)
25. Yannakakis, G.N., Hallam, J.: Real-time game adaptation for optimizing player satisfaction. IEEE Trans. Comput. Intelligence. AI Games 1(2), 121–133 (2009)

Games Narratives

Participant Centred Framework to Support the Digital Transformation of Boardgames for Skill Development

H. Almås[1,2]([✉]) [iD], M. Hakvåg[1], M. Oliveira[3], and H. Torvatn[3]

[1] House of Knowledge, Trondheim, Norway
{havard.almas,magnus.hakvag}@hoknowledge.com
[2] Norwegian University of Science and Technology, Trondheim, Norway
[3] Sintef, Trondheim, Norway
{manuel.oliveira,hans.torvatn}@sintef.no

Abstract. As a pandemic spread throughout the world in 2020, restricting possibilities of physical presence, 'going digital' became acutely necessary for analogue serious game providers. Digitalization of analogue serious games based on player interaction is an arduous task requiring a substantial rethinking of the relationship between players, the facilitator(s), the game, and technology. Empirical research on the matter is inadequate, leaving practitioners without proper guidance in carrying out the digitalization process. This paper presents a novel framework, called the 'Participant Centred Framework', that can aid in moving from the analogue to the digital medium. The framework consists of several categories of relationships we believe instrumental in reimagining games for the digital realm. For each of these categories, several factors or topics to consider are included. The Participant Centred Framework is presented alongside a detailing of what we learned during our own, iterative digitalization process – mapped to the categories and factors of the framework.

Keywords: Digitalization · Board games · Facilitation · Serious games

1 Introduction

The use of serious games can be an important tool in the acquisition of tacit knowledge and competence development on abstract concepts such as negotiation, business strategy development, stakeholder analysis, and so on [1]. However, when developing the simulation driving such serious games, it is necessary to take a closed world assumption – limiting the sophistication of the competence developed. Consequently, it becomes beneficial to provide facilitated experiences usually held in a physical workshop involving multiple participants engaged in a role-playing experience, captured in boardgames. What happens when this acquisition needs to happen digitally?

With the recent upheaval caused by the global pandemic, the learning richness afforded by physical workshops with social interaction has been compromised as people are isolating. Consequently, the new normal is working remotely, by transferring

© Springer Nature Switzerland AG 2021
B. Fletcher et al. (Eds.): JCSG 2021, LNCS 12945, pp. 85–97, 2021.
https://doi.org/10.1007/978-3-030-88272-3_7

the necessary processes into the digital domain. This has created persistent challenges, particularly when considering training that has relied on analogue serious games in physical settings. Although the digital transformation of boardgames has taken place in the past, with literature documenting a few cases of comparative studies between different modalities of boardgames [2], guidelines for handling the transition are lacking. For practitioners of analogue serious games this change has been especially challenging, as no ready-made tools could be picked up, learned, and applied – the move to the new medium required the creation of an entirely new product. This can be an unnecessarily resource-intensive task when a good analogue game exists, and one that can be avoided with the right tools. However, the process is further complicated by the fact that simply making a digital version of an analogue game is insufficient. To maintain the strengths of analogue games, face-to-face interaction, communication, and collaboration, thinking anew regarding the strengths and weaknesses of the digital platform is necessary. As Kriz put it in the August 2020 issue of Simulation & Gaming "Under what conditions … can learning outcomes be reached if the focus of the game … includes the embodied experience and related tacit knowledge of the participants?" [3]. One assumption to make in identifying such conditions is that games cannot be "copy-pasted" to a novel medium, they must be reimagined and redeveloped – preserving the strengths of analogue games and translating them to the digital medium. For instance, it cannot be taken for granted that participants will interact in the same way with digital tokens as physical tokens. More profoundly, however, it cannot be assumed that players meeting digitally via video chat will interact and collaborate in the same manner as they would in a face-to-face setting. Despite these challenges, how can designers avoid "starting from scratch" when moving into the digital realm? In moving from analogue to digital, what can be done to ensure the experience of play is not being hindered by the limitations of the new medium? And how can novel opportunities be exploited?

There is a lack of literature providing documented evidence for this move of boardgames from face-to-face workshops to virtual setups in the digital realm. Even though some comparative studies of boardgames in different mediums do exist [2, 4], it is rare to find the transitioning reported with a set of milestones or guidelines for others to follow. Thus, in place of empirical evidence, we explored the role game design principles/frameworks can have in the transformation process, as we believed that could be fruitful. There are manifold frameworks claiming to facilitate the game design process. Therefore, in the interest of brevity, only some of the most popular approaches [5] will be explored here. First, the Mechanics, Dynamics and Aesthetics (MDA) framework [6] aims to provide a foundation to support the iterative process of game design, building upon the relationship between the game designer and the player. However, the focus is chiefly on the game, neglecting the user experience and the impact of technology. Although the framework can be used for analysis of existing serious games, the focus is on entertainment games, and it fails to address the pedagogical underpinnings foundational to the design of a serious game. Secondly, the Design, Play and Experience (DPE) framework [7] expands on the MDA to address the shortcomings of its application to serious games, including addressing technology and its impact on game design. Yet, it still does not support the digitalization of a physical tabletop game. Lastly, the triadic framework consisting of pedagogy, play and fidelity proposed by Rooney [8] takes a comprehensive approach to linking the targeted three aspects of game design, but the approach is mainly theoretical with limited practical association to design decisions based on impact of technology. None of the frameworks analysed provided practical guidance for supporting the transformation from physical to digital, thus there was little understanding of the necessary trade-offs implicated in the many design decisions to be made along the way. In lieu of a framework guiding the process, we applied a trial-and-error approach with prototyping to work out how we could retain the advantages of the analogue game whilst utilizing the advantages of the digital medium – a "journey" that will be presented and reflected upon in the next sections. When taking this kind of explorative approach, the digital transformation of games is a fuzzy, complex process that can be challenging to manage. One solid 'footing in the bog' we relied on is the psychological and pedagogical principles underpinning how people communicate, act, and interact in situations of learning and knowledge exchange – gleaned in part from the presented frameworks. Therefore, we focused on the four relationships of participant with other participants, facilitator, game, and technology. The transformation lessons to be presented are categorized based on these relationships.

This paper presents in Sect. 2 the boardgame to be transformed, *War Room*, and the theoretical principles on which it is built. The process of digital transformation was iterative, and as such the initial digital mock-up is presented in Sect. 3, which yielded the current digital version, presented in Sect. 4. In Sect. 5 the journey culminates in the presentation of the *Participant Centred Framework* for digital transformation of boardgames, which is the synthesis of the lessons learnt throughout the process. Finally, Sect. 6 contributes to the discussion and conclusions on how to go about the digitalization of analogue boardgames for the purpose of facilitated learning and skill development in workshops.

2 The War Room Learning Experience

War Room, the game to be transformed, is a commercial learning game revolving around complex problem solving and discussion in a team setting, using uncertainty and time constraints to create an engaging experience. The main goal of the game is to provide an understanding of Intellectual Property (IP), Intellectual Property Rights (IPR), and competitiveness. These concepts should not only be memorized, but rather understood for their significant role in business strategy, both as a potential problem and as something that can be beneficial to the organization. This is achieved by creating opportunity for participants to extract and sort relevant information in order to make informed strategic decisions. Before delving into how such learning can be achieved, a short description of the game as an artefact and the progression of play is in order.

The game, in its original, analogue format, consists of a large board/canvas and playing cards providing contextual information and happenings, as can be seen in Fig. 1. These parts are used by players divided into groups of up to five, commonly with several groups simultaneously. Cards are presented in a specific order by a facilitator at set intervals or when deemed necessary. Based on information received from the cards, participants put sticky notes on the board to keep track of extracted information and decisions made throughout the play session. The facilitator(s) is available for aiding

Fig. 1. *War Room* in action

participants when needed during the play phase, both for team dynamic and in process facilitation to provide novel insights, challenge participants, and provide contextual input. In addition to the playing of the game, there is a briefing and a debriefing that is considered part of the process. During the briefing the expert facilitator presents the basic IP/IPR concepts that must be applied to successfully manoeuvre the challenges that arise throughout the play phase. This provides players with the basic vocabulary (explicit knowledge) needed to play. In the debriefing phase, groups of participants come together to recap concepts, discuss solutions, and evaluate applicability outside the game with the facilitator. A full playthrough of the game can take, depending on the needs and skill level of the players, two to seven hours.

How, then, does *War Room* provide a meaningful learning experience to players? To answer this, central game mechanics are presented alongside the overarching theories that make them viable – leveraging certain psychological and pedagogical (or andragogical [9]) principles that promote learning through *action* and *interaction*. First, participants are presented with an actual business case as a starting point which is elaborated and that they expand on, taking on the roles of employees in the company. The information provided in the game must be "digested" throughout, and relevant details extracted to deal with several contextual constraints and fictious happenings presented on the playing cards. Furthermore, the game offers opportunity for participants to obtain new information from the game as well as other players and the facilitator(s), combine this with what they already know [10, 11], apply it in a novel setting, and reflect on how it can be used in real-life situations [12, 13]. This provides players a way of *acting* on information, solving problems, and making decisions – based on new knowledge and existing experience [14, 15]. Second, dealing with these challenges requires participants to discuss possible solutions within their groups, often involving a certain degree of creativity. The problems discussed rarely have a single correct answer, can have built-in "traps", and requires players to collaborate to provide a viable strategy that includes protecting their intangible assets [16–18]. Thus, this represents an opportunity to *interact* with other players in a team setting and learn from the knowledge and experiences of each other – on a topic of shared interest and benefit [19, 20].

3 "Quick and Dirty" Prototype

For the digitalisation of the analogue tabletop game, a user centred design approach was taken, starting with the creation of a quick digital prototype (Fig. 2). The purpose of this first step of the journey was to understand the key differences when transposing from the physical environment to a digital one. Therefore, the tabletop was replicated as closely as possible with minimum design effort beyond making the serious game playable digitally. As such, the following digital artefacts were used:

- a digital whiteboard was used for sharing the canvas that held the joint context of the gameplay. The participants were able to place sticky notes of different colours.
- a video conferencing tool was used for multi-participant communication. The participants were encouraged to share video, but due to screen size the streaming was done via thumbnail sized images that conveyed little in terms of nonverbal communication (NVC) cues.
- mobile phones were used to access the game cards (happenings and information), which required some time to setup appropriately.
- links were used to share additional information via URLs. In this type of game, information is an essential part of the gameplay used for decision making – part of the game mechanics is time constraints and restricted information access to impose uncertainty.

The initial session was conducted with four participants, an observer that was acquainted with the gameplay, and an experienced facilitator of the serious game in physical settings. With the focus on participant centred relationships, the key findings were:

Participant with Participant: The video conferencing tool was inadequate at conveying a sense of social proximity, with inability of leveraging NVC cues. There was no concurrent communication as this would introduce noise into the dialogue between participants and the facilitator. Finally, the group size was deemed borderline as participants struggled to contribute effectively.

Participant with Facilitator: Although the facilitator was very experienced, it was difficult to be fully aware of the interaction across all the participants. Attempts were made at supporting additional simultaneous groups, but barriers to effective monitoring and facilitation restricted the group number to one. The importance of the briefing

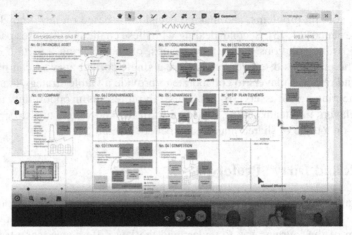

Fig. 2. The prototype

was underestimated when considering the transition, clearly indicating necessity of a framework to convey rules of engagement and understanding of the game.

Participant with Game: Although the game was functional, the intuitiveness of key functions was low, making interaction unnecessarily difficult. Furthermore, as several different digital applications were used concurrently, efficient information management was hindered by screen real estate constraints.

Participant with Technology: The participant population is one with high digital literacy, but still there were difficulties experienced in both the setup and execution of the gameplay. This has a high cognitive cost and potentially dilutes the play experience.

The game was play-tested in two further rounds at this stage, one with an interaction designer subcontractor, and one with a client. Each session had only one team, one facilitator, and observers. In comparison, the analogue game has previously been played with more than 20 groups simultaneously.

4   The Digital Arrival

In moving towards the fully digital version, two overarching goals guided design mitigations from the "quick and dirty"-prototype. First, retaining the key underlying mechanisms, like gameplay, interaction, and the "War Room-experience", when transforming to the final digital medium. Second, understanding how to utilize the benefits of digital media to improve the learning experience offered in the analogue format. The completed digital game was tested by several groups, from which some feedback is included here to support the changes made.

Participant with Participant: To improve communication from the prototype, players are divided into smaller groups and communication via sticky notes was made more

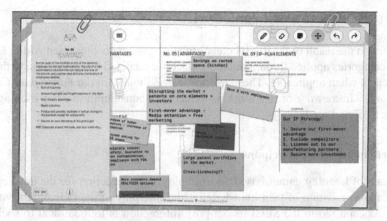

Fig. 3. The digital arrival

intuitive. This mitigates some NVC challenges by reducing the number of video feeds to follow. Play testers experienced interaction in the new version as providing opportunity for realistic discussion and strategizing. What is more, the need for concurrent communication is reduced by having fewer players in each group.

Participant with Facilitator: Measures were implemented to alleviate some of the work that fell on the facilitator in the previous version – in part to ensure consistency. This is necessary because the digital medium allows the facilitator to engage with only one group at a time, with limited possibility of moving between groups to pick up on problems. To achieve this, videos and links were provided for players to use on their own initiative to achieve some of the insight previously provided by the facilitator. This led to less need for the facilitator to provide information, freeing up more time to facilitate interaction.

Participant with Game: To make the interaction between participant and game more seamless than in the prototype, minor animations and sounds that mimic materiality in the analogue game (e.g., flipping cards in a pile) was implemented. Additionally, the onboarding process was simplified by making the login process smoother and by including an informational page prior to the game starting. Lastly, some alterations were done to reduce the issue of real-estate to improve information management (see Fig. 3). Play testers overall experience of the game was reported both as enjoyable and beneficial/ helpful in strategic thinking and decision making.

Participant with Technology: To alleviate issues of cognitive cost and digital literacy, the design of the game interface was improved to better user interaction. For instance, button functionality was made more obvious when using the sticky note functionality, as well as making it easier to navigate through the cards. These alterations led to play testers reporting far less technical difficulties when using the current digital version compared to the prototype.

5 Participant Centred Framework

In this section the result of the digital transformation process is presented within each of the four categories applied throughout the text, contextualized by connection to theoretical concepts when applicable. These lessons learned make up the *Participant Centred Framework*, a framework of relationships to take into consideration when moving from analogue to digital media.

5.1 Participant with Participant

At the heart of learning games based on (role-playing) interaction for the development of skills and acquisition of tacit knowledge is the interplay of the individuals with one another. As captured in the SECI model [18], interaction is foundational to socialization, externalization, combination and internalization in the creation of knowledge. In a physical face-to-face setting, there is a richness of social interaction between individuals, which is significantly compromised and requires rethinking when transitioning to a digital medium. These challenges can be aggregated into four distinct dimensions:

- **Nonverbal Communication.** In the physical world, people have a high bandwidth for communication, including NVC cues, which makes it easier for users to coordinate interventions and reduce the necessity for explicitly conveying their reasoning when taking actions. In the digital domain, NVC richness is reduced due to the constraints in the medium.
- **Social Proximity.** Close physical proximity between participants contributes to higher level of engagement [21], a factor not applicable in the digital domain. This can lead to lower engagement in digital games.
- **Concurrent Communication.** Closely related to both social proximity and NVC, is the ability of supporting concurrent communication. In a physical setting, where there is implicit acceptance of rules of engagement, concurrent communication happens naturally. It is, however, harder to support digitally. Smaller groups can support concurrent communication, but at the cost of hindering flow of communication.
- **Group Size.** In the face-to-face setting, participants understand the actions of one another based on engagement with each other, the board, and the sticky notes. In the digital version, however, there are limitations to the attention and focus of the users, causing larger groups to pose a potential challenge.

5.2 Participant with Facilitator

Although the learning experience of multiple participants relies on their social interaction, the power and influence of the facilitator in ensuring the best outcome for all those involved is unquestionable [20]. Thus, the second relevant relationship to consider is that of participant and facilitator. There are four key processes that are, in our experience, severely impacted by the digital transition:

- **Monitoring.** The facilitator needs to have a good understanding of the full context of the learning situation and the participants. Consequently, they are constantly monitoring and assessing the situation. When transitioning to digital media, several barriers emerge that makes it harder for the facilitator to be fully aware of this context.
- **Consistency.** The unfolding of learning afforded by the analogue boardgame is dependent on the expertise of the facilitator, who draws on their experience to facilitate the learning experience. In the digital version, the facilitation can become more consistent as the facilitator may be supported by automated in-game activities and rule enforcement. However, dynamic adaptation to unpredictable and unforeseen circumstances is lost due to the limitations of the underlying model that support automation.
- **Communication.** In the physical setting, the facilitator can be called to groups or intervene in groups limited only by the number of groups requiring facilitation. In the digital it can be difficult for groups to call out for help, and due to less concurrent monitoring, communication is weakened.
- **Briefing and Debriefing.** The quality of the experience depends significantly on the facilitator and both phases are fundamental in the pedagogical underpinning of learning with tabletop games [22]. In the digital version, de-/briefing necessarily encompasses additional topics, and can therefore be more challenging.

5.3 Participant with Game

A third noteworthy relationship is between participant and game. This covers the issue of interaction with physical game elements vs. digital interaction. We identified four relevant core processes:

- **Materiality.** Tangible physical artefacts anchor the experience of users and support emotional engagement [4]. Nonetheless, the manipulation of physical artefacts may also introduce extraneous strain [23]. In the digital domain, however, all artefacts are intangible.
- **Onboarding.** Engagement with the physical artefacts is intuitive (e.g., write and submit sticky notes, roll die, move game pieces), but there might be barriers to interaction in the digital game due to less intuitiveness. Interaction onboarding should therefore be especially prioritized when using a digital medium.
- **Time Management.** Time management, i.e., adjusting or controlling pace, is an important skill of analogue game facilitators that may be supported by physical artefacts, which impacts participant interaction with the game. In the digital domain strong opportunities to manage the time exist, both for the facilitator and as a function of gameplay, yet time management opportunities can be hindered by reduced visibility of participant engagement and progress.
- **Information Management.** In a physical environment, it is possible to have immediate access to all relevant decision-making information simultaneously, as real estate constraints are virtually non-existent. In the digital version, presentation is limited to relatively small screens.

5.4 Participant with Technology

The final relationship to consider is that of the participant with technology, as the impact of the digital transition is proportionate to the digital literacy of the individual. For this relationship, three main factors are identified.

- **Cost.** Individual, cognitive cost of using the medium significantly impacts the experience of the participant and the overall group experience. In the digital, this cost can be high if not combatted by appropriate measures to increase intuitiveness.
- **Flexibility.** In a physical game, the unfolding of the game state depends very much on the experience and skill of the facilitator – without guarantee of consistency, but with great flexibility and adaptability. Using the digital medium, consistency can be improved (at the expense of flexibility), which has the benefit of reducing the potential strain of participant-technology interaction.
- **Interfaces.** In the real world, the rules of engagement are transparent. In the digital form, however, the potential utility of the boardgame cannot be reached unless the usability is reasonably high.

6 Discussion and Conclusions

The Participant Centred Framework for digital transformation has been created incrementally as a way of capturing the insights and lessons learnt along the journey. When moving from the analogue version to the prototype we identified the ways in which the digital format provides both limitations and possibilities. Consequently, the prototype was instrumental in recognizing how to properly utilize the strengths of this novel format when moving towards the fully digitalized version. Thus, the journey of the digital transformation of *War Room* yielded interesting insights that have been distilled into the Participant Centred Framework, as a means of facilitating the transition from physical to digital in commercial serious games. A final analysis is presented below to show how the relationships in the framework were useful in the process of digitalization:

Participant with Participant: The nonverbal communication richness was greatly hampered by the constraints of online communication. The video portals provided a segmented view of the group that implies an increased cognitive load as more video portals are shown. This necessitated limiting the number of users or redesigning the interface to facilitate the orchestration of large number of users. With regards to backchannel communication, the digital design can highlight, support, and guide participants' attention and focus, assisting in situational awareness.

Participant with Facilitator: The digital facilitator cannot provide adequate hands-on aid to a large number of groups in the same manner that the physical format allows. This is especially relevant in relation to the role the facilitator has in spotting and aiding subpar intragroup communication. Irrespective of the orchestration design features of the digital game, the need to invest in more onboarding time and clear rules of engagement became clear. In the case of large groups of participants where there are constraints with oral communication, it is possible to ameliorate the sharing of information with written communication – at the cost of the significant benefits of the spoken word.

A strong advantage of digitalisation is the possibility of automating tasks that traditionally would be managed by the facilitator, such as time keeping or the release of events affecting the game state progression. The story progression can be dependent on a multi-variable simulation, but the facilitator must retain the option of overriding the system to drive the learning trajectory toward the desired outcomes.

Participant with Game: The physicality element of gameplay is significantly affected when going digital as the game board size is limited by the physical size of the device used by the participant. This means the whole play area is reduced to sometimes as little as 17×25 cm (approx. size of $10''$ tablet), as opposed to the 59×84 cm (A1 paper) *War Room* canvas plus additional table space. It is important to be aware of this limitation and be careful regarding how to provide mechanisms of scope/focus without losing participants in their navigation of the game state, either as an individual or a group.

Participant with Technology: Digital transformation allows for easy access to information, such as how we used QR codes to let participants easily retrieve information for better decision making. However, it is necessary to accommodate the difference in digital literacy amongst the participants and focus on strong support where the most common problems are seen or foreseen. Visual cues and labelling should guide participants during normal use, and especially when issues occur (e.g., network problems).

6.1 Evaluation and Direction

A main strength of this framework is that the factors listed should be applicable as a check list to all digital game transformation endeavours. Being conscious of and accounting for the different interactions should be beneficial, even if each factor might not be relevant in every situation. Another key strength is that the explication of these relationships can encourage thinking anew about the process of digital transformation more broadly, highlighting that it is not necessarily as straightforward as it might seem. Lastly, the framework explores important ways in which the digital medium creates novel opportunities, especially pertaining to support, focus, automation, and information access which should be useable in most digitalisation efforts. However, due to the limits of reporting on a single game, the framework cannot be claimed to be exhaustive. Each digital transformation is likely to bring specific challenges that cannot be foreseen in a general framework. Furthermore, some common challenges and opportunities could have been missed due to the nature of the researched game. It should also be noted that some of the technical challenges met in this research (e.g., size of play area, use of several different applications) might differ substantially from those met when transforming other games.

Future work should focus on using the framework at the onset of the digital transformation of other analogue boardgames to test its usefulness and applicability under different contextual conditions. What is more, the generalizability of the framework should be tested with different populations to establish how factors like, for instance, age, education, and job characteristics could impact use.

Acknowledgements. The authors wish to thank all play testers for providing the necessary feedback to execute the digital transformation.

References

1. van Haaften, M.A., Lefter, I., Lukosch, H., van Kooten, O., Brazier, F.: Do gaming simulations substantiate that we know more than we can tell? Simul. Gaming 1–23 (2020). https://doi.org/10.1177/1046878120927048
2. Wallace, J.R., et al.: Exploring automation in digital tabletop board game. In: Proceedings of the ACM 2012 conference on Computer Supported Cooperative Work Companion, pp. 231–234. ACM, Seattle (2012). https://doi.org/10.1145/2141512.2141585
3. Kriz, W.C.: Gaming in the time of COVID-19. Simul. Gaming. **51**, 403–410 (2020). https://doi.org/10.1177/1046878120931602
4. Rogerson, M.J., Gibbs, M., Smith, W.: "I love all the bits": the materiality of boardgames. In: Proceedings of the 2016 CHI Conference on Human Factors in Computing Systems, pp. 3956–3969. ACM (2016). https://doi.org/10.1145/2858036.2858433
5. Arnab, S., Clarke, S.: Towards a trans-disciplinary methodology for a game-based intervention development process: towards a trans-disciplinary methodology. Br. J. Educ. Technol. **48**, 279–312 (2017). https://doi.org/10.1111/bjet.12377
6. Hunicke, R., LeBlanc, M., Zubek, R.: MDA: a formal approach to game design and game research. In: Proceedings of the AAAI Workshop on Challenges in Game AI, pp. 1–5. AAAI (2004)
7. Winn, B.M.: The design, play, and experience framework. In: Handbook of Research on Effective Electronic Gaming in Education, pp. 1010–1024. IGI Global (2009). https://doi.org/10.4018/978-1-59904-808-6.ch058
8. Rooney, P.: A theoretical framework for serious game design: exploring pedagogy, play and fidelity and their implications for the design process. Int. J. Game-Based Learn. **2**, 41–60 (2012). https://doi.org/10.4018/ijgbl.2012100103
9. Knowles, M.S.: The Adult Learner: The Definitive Classic in Adult Education and Human Resource Development. Routledge, Oxford (2015). https://doi.org/10.4324/9781315816951
10. Kolb, A.Y.: The evolution of a conversational learning space. In: Baker, A.C., Jensen, P.J., Kolb, D.A. (eds.) Conversational Learning: An Experiential Approach to Knowledge Creation, pp. 67–100. Quorum Books, Westport (2002)
11. Kolb, D.A.: Experiential Learning: Experience as the Source of Learning and Development. Pearson Education Inc, Upper Saddle River (2015)
12. Brown, J.S., Collins, A., Duguid, P.: Situated cognition and the culture of learning. Educ. Res. **18**, 32–42 (1989)
13. Rogoff, B.: Cognition as a collaborative process. In: Damon, W., Kuhn, D., Siegler, R.S. (eds.) Handbook of Child Psychology, Cognition, Perception, and Language, vol. 2, pp. 679–744. Wiley, New York (1998)
14. Barrows, H.S., Tamblyn, R.M.: Problem-based Learning: An Approach to Medical Education. Springer , New York (1980)
15. Hmelo-Silver, C.E.: Problem-based learning: what and how do students learn? Educ. Psychol. Rev. **16**, 235–266 (2004). https://doi.org/10.1023/B:EDPR.0000034022.16470.f3
16. Bandura, A.: Social Foundations of Thought and Action: A Social Cognitive Theory. Prentice-Hall, Englewood Cliffs (1986)
17. Lave, J., Wenger, E.: Situated Learning: Legitimate Peripheral Participation. Cambridge University Press, Cambridge (1991). https://doi.org/10.1017/CBO9780511815355

18. Nonaka, I., Takeuchi, H.: The Knowledge-Creating Company: How Japanese Companies Create the Dynamics of Innovation. Oxford University Press, New York (1995)
19. Hackman, J.R.: Collaborative Intelligence: Using Teams to Solve Hard Problems. Berrett-Koehler Publishers, San Francisco (2011)
20. Schwarz, R.M.: The Skilled Facilitator: A Comprehensive Resource for Consultants, Facilitators, Coaches, and Trainers. Jossey-Bass, San Francisco (2017)
21. Walker, C.J.: Experiencing flow: is doing it together better than doing it alone? J. Posit. Psychol. **5**, 3–11 (2010). https://doi.org/10.1080/17439760903271116
22. Schwägele, S., Zürn, B., Lukosch, H.K., Freese, M.: Design of an impulse-debriefing-spiral for simulation game facilitation. Simul. Gaming. (2021). https://doi.org/10.1177/104687812 11006752
23. Sweller, J.: Cognitive load during problem solving: effects on learning. Cogn. Sci. **12**, 257–285 (1988). https://doi.org/10.1207/s15516709cog1202_4

Designing CBT-Rich Stories for Serious Games

Toka Hassan[✉] and Gerard T. McKee

The British University in Egypt, Cairo, Egypt
{Toka.Hassan,Gerard.McKee}@bue.edu.eg

Abstract. Mental illness has a long history of being stigmatised in societies around the world. This stigma denies individuals who have a mental illness the opportunity to lead everyday lives and leaves them reluctant to seek professional help for their illness. A form of therapy called Cognitive Behavioural Therapy (CBT) has proven to be very effective for various mental health issues. Serious game-based storytelling is a form of digital game that aims to create a virtual environment where the player encounters and solves problems in the games world for purposes other than entertainment, for example health and education. The work reported in this paper addresses how CBT can be incorporated in serious games. It focuses on story analysis and offers an illustrative example and a set of guidelines for incorporating a CBT resilience model based on physical, mental, emotional, and social resilience activities into the game's storyline.

Keywords: Storytelling · Cognitive behavioural therapy · Serious games · Mental health

1 Introduction

Mental illness has a long history of being stigmatised in societies around the world. However, only a small percentage of people with mental illness actively seek professional help for their illness [1]. A form of therapy called Cognitive Behavioural Therapy (CBT) is considered the gold standard in the treatment of a wide range of mental health issues [2]. A serious game is a game that does not solely rely on pure entertainment but instead on honing a specific skill set. Serious games encapsulate various genres. They have been applied for different purposes, such as education, military training, and healthcare [3]. By extending the reach of CBT to a serious game-based product, the possibilities become intriguing. Serious games can increase the impact of therapy interventions via three processes [4]. Firstly, it extends the reach of digital therapy to those who might not otherwise use it. Secondly, it improves the player's immersion through both motivational and game-based mechanics. Thirdly, utilising numerous techniques for change, including therapy techniques and game features. It is considered feasible to translate forms of therapy, such as CBT, to games by exploiting features of games for therapeutic change [4]. This paper focuses on the application of serious games in healthcare.

The goal of serious games in healthcare is to create a simulated world in which the regular path is reversed, meaning that when the player tackles challenges in the virtual world, they gain skills and build the right mental fortitude in the real world [5]. These

B. Fletcher et al. (Eds.): JCSG 2021, LNCS 12945, pp. 98–112, 2021.
https://doi.org/10.1007/978-3-030-88272-3_8

games allow the player the freedom to fail in a non-threatening environment where choices relate to clear consequences. However, an issue with these types of games arises since there is a noticeable decline in their use over time, and it is perceived that players lose interest in them within a short period. This issue is due to the lack of an engaging storyline [6]. Thus, an interactive story in a serious game can help add the hook that will pull the player in, achieve immersion, and encourage them to continue playing [7]. Also, confining the user to one fixed story is another issue because it will always be the same story every time. Therefore, the availability of a selection of stories can keep the player engaged and provide continuing support for their mental health and well-being. The work reported in this paper addresses both issues by exploring how CBT can be incorporated in serious games.

The remainder of the paper is organised as follows. Section 2 provides a literature review. Section 3 describes the target platform for the story analysis presented in this paper. Section 4 presents the story analysis based on a case study, The Selfish Giant by Oscar Wilde. Section 5 discusses the implementation of a story app that provides a target platform for stories incorporating CBT resilience activities in the storyline. Finally, Sect. 6 presents a brief discussion and concludes the paper.

2 Literature Review

2.1 Mental Health and Cognitive Behavioural Therapy

Everyone experiences some degree of anxiety; it is a natural response in our human nature. Stress helps the individual to recognise and respond to a threat by activating fight or flight reflexes. A regular amount of anxiety can help enhance people's performance and trigger actions in response to dangerous situations [8]. However, persistent stress can develop anxiety disorders, phobias, panic attacks and obsessive behaviours [8]. An anxiety disorder causes a great deal of worry and stress intensely and frequently. It also hinders the individual's ability to relax and experience a sense of enjoyment and well-being [9].

CBT has proven to relieve symptoms of anxiety and depression much more rapidly than traditional drug therapy or psychotherapy [10, 11]. The premise of CBT is that the individual's thoughts affect how they feel and how they behave. In other words, it is not the situation that determines how one feels but one's perception of the situation. CBT helps individuals identify their thought patterns and challenges their negative cognitive distortions of situations and events to improve mental regulation and reinforce a coping mechanism that targets analysing and solving current problems. CBT provides a way of prevention. However, it is not a cure. Nevertheless, continual use of CBT in the long term builds the individual's resilience and ability to cope with adversity [10].

2.2 Storytelling and Interactivity

Every culture has told stories throughout its human history. Although different cultures have produced their unique way of storytelling, many aspects of storytelling are universal across all cultures [12]. In [13] the authors argue that, according to German scholar

Gustav Freytag, a story plot comprises five essential elements [14]. The first element is the introduction and exposition, where an author would introduce story characters, establish the setting and present a first glimpse of the conflict to come. The second element is the rising action; this usually holds a series of events that build up to the story's central conflict. The third element is the climax, which is the pivotal point of the story where everything converges. Typically, the main character would have to make some life-changing decisions and face the primary opponent of the story. The fourth element is the falling action, which shows the events and complications resolving; the consequences of the main characters' choices during the climax are revealed to the readers. The fifth and final element is the resolution, which is the conclusion of the story and the consequence of the protagonist's decision throughout the story.

Interactive storytelling gives the audience two essential tools that distinguish it from passive storytelling: choice and control. The audience gets to choose how to act within the interactive world, and their choices impact the story's progression [15]. Taking first-person control of story events and directly taking part in the story are vital elements of a story's interactivity. They induce a sense of belonging and competency in the individual when they feel responsible for the story unfolding. Individuals usually gain skills by witnessing cause-effect events and analysing their relationships. Thus, behaviour development can be improved when these stories address behaviour development issues, and the lesson to be gained from the tale encourages health [16].

2.3 Applications of Mental Health and CBT in Serious Games

The representation of mental health in digital games has been the subject of research. [17] and [18] provide a recent review of games that depict mental illness with varying degrees of implicit to explicit representation. Some of these games are: Hellblade: Senua's Sacrifice, Night in the Woods, and Celeste [19, 20]. Moreover, several researchers have explored the incorporation of CBT into serious games [19–22] and [23]. These are described below.

In [21] and [22] the authors discuss a game called Please Knock on My Door, which is entirely based on its own developer's real-life struggles with depression [24]. It articulates how the mental stability of the main character in the game interferes with his daily routine while struggling with severe depression. The role of the player is to help the in-game character overcome their depression. This can include the player tasking the in-game character with mundane activities, such as having food and going to work. The game does not offer a therapeutic intervention. However, it gives insight and awareness to the player of what goes on in the head of a person who is depressed or experiences social anxiety.

In [23], a platform consisting of an app and a website is discussed, called *SuperBetter*, which aims to engage individuals on a journey to pursue goals and address mental health challenges. The platform adopts a resilience model consisting of four resiliencies: mental, physical, social and emotional. Each type of challenge in the app corresponds to a specific type of resilience. Building resilience is one of the cornerstones of CBT. SuperBetter's resilience model is adopted in this paper as the central approach in designing CBT stories for serious games.

3 The Target Platform

In the work reported here an app was proposed and developed as the target platform for playing CBT-based stories. The focus of the app is to play interactive fiction that incorporates CBT within the storyline as a way of providing therapeutic intervention for the players, who might be experiencing symptoms of mental illness. The interactive nature of the story adds a hook that can pull the player into the game, achieve immersion, and encourage the player to continue playing to push the story along [7]. It also provides support for playing multiple stories. This provides the availability of a selection of stories and storylines that can keep the player engaged in activities that support their mental well-being.

The CBT techniques incorporated in the app follow the resilience model described in Sect. 2.3. The resilience model targets the individual's resilience skill, focusing on four types of resilience: emotional, which describes how well a person copes emotionally with stress and affects the individual's ability to be imaginative and creative; mental, which is referred to as mental fortitude, is the ability to withstand or adapt to adversity and helps develop coping strategies; physical, which is the body's ability to maintain stamina and recover quickly; and social, which helps reinforce positive human contact and social connections.

The work reported here also proposed but did not implement a story editor to support the creation of stories that incorporate CBT. A story is either composed from scratch or selected from a set of existing stories. The story is then analysed to look for ways to incorporate CBT resilience activities. The story editor supports the incorporation of the resilience activities into the storyline, encoding the story as an XML document with associated interactive media into a file that can be downloaded into the app where it can be rendered as a game.

Since story analysis is central to developing CBT stories, this paper focuses on story analysis and offers an illustrative example and a set of guidelines for incorporating CBT resiliencies into serious games.

4 Story Analysis

The authors approached the story analysis for interactive storytelling by selecting a short story and analysing it to discover the scope for the player to carry out CBT activities. The analysis comprised five steps: scene breakdown, character identification, emotions and personality traits, states, and activities. The story adapted for this approach was The Selfish Giant by Oscar Wilde [25]. The story turned out to be very appropriate in the context of mental health since it is full of meaningful and moral undertones. The Giant pushes people away and barricades himself inside his castle, wallowing in sadness and loneliness. This can be interpreted in the same way that people with mental illness deal with their mental health issues by shutting people out and putting up barriers around themselves to stop others from helping them. The following describes each of the analysis steps.

Scenes. The first step was to break down the story into scenes. Freytag's Pyramid plot structure was adopted, stating that a story consists of 5 main plot elements. After breaking the story down into those elements, the scenes could be identified easily. A new scene is identified whenever a new location is presented, or the story moves from one plot element to another. For example, consider the following excerpt taken from The Selfish Giant:

> "One day, the Giant came back. He had been to visit his friend the Cornish ogre and had stayed with him for seven years. After the seven years were over, he had said all that he had to say, for his conversation was limited, and he determined to return to his own castle. When he arrived, he saw the children playing in the garden." [25]

By analysing this excerpt, it is clear that this paragraph can be split into two scenes since this section takes place in two different locations.

Characters. The next step was to extract all characters that play an active part in the story. These include the Giant, the children, birds, trees, snow, frost, north wind, hail and the Little Boy. Sometimes it is unclear who the characters in a story are since they can be whomever the author wishes. Consider the following excerpt:

> "The poor Tree was still quite covered with Frost and Snow, and the North Wind was blowing and roaring above it. "Climb up! Little Boy," said the Tree, and it bent its branches down as low as it could, but the Boy was too tiny." [25]

This excerpt shows that characters can be identified by seeing whether they had any dialogue or interactions with other story objects. If yes, then that story object can be considered a character, as seen when the Tree speaks to the Boy.

Emotions and Personality Traits. The next step was to record the emotional state of the characters in each scene. Emotions are critical for storytelling because it makes the product seem less computerised and more natural. Emotional states were the focus since emotions play an essential role in the mental stability of an individual.

A psychologist called Robert Plutchik theorised that there are eight primary emotions: fear, anger, happiness, disgust, surprise, sadness, anticipation, and trust [26]. Plutchik then created the wheel of emotions to demonstrate the various overlap and levels of emotions [26]. It was decided in the current work to focus on the primary eight emotions.

Then it was time to analyse the effect that different personality traits can have on a character's actions. The most widely used model of personality traits is called The Big Five, a set of five broad, bipolar trait dimensions. Each dimension includes characteristics that can either enhance or mar mental health [27]. These traits are [28]: extraversion, openness, agreeableness, conscientiousness, neuroticism. These traits were analysed to identify the reasoning behind the characters' actions in the story. For example, throughout the first part of the story, the Giant is identified as selfish. Selfishness is associated with the lack of consideration of other people. It could also be associated with withholding one's possessions from other people and not sharing them. This can be very clearly seen from the following excerpt:

"When he arrived, he saw the children playing in the garden. 'What are you doing here?' he cried in a very gruff voice, and the children ran away. 'My own garden is my own garden', said the Giant; 'anyone can understand that, and I will allow nobody to play in it but myself.'" [25]

The Giant refuses to share his garden with the children for no other reason than his selfishness. Therefore, it is seen that the Giant's personality falls on the low end of the agreeableness spectrum. Thus, to help the Giant reach a good emotional state, he would have to be more agreeable.

Identifying personality traits also helps when trying to incorporate a more personalised CBT experience to the player. Since CBT identifies thought patterns and behaviours, its efficacy can be drastically enhanced by considering personality traits [29]. Moreover, identifying these traits adds another level of analysis that reflects the complexity of the real world and its complications.

States. The next step was to record the location and emotional state of every character in each scene. Then, analyse how their emotional state changes with each scene and trigger that emotional state transition. In other words, a finite state machine would be created to represent the different states of the story. This approach was chosen because it is a straightforward way of keeping track of current story events and how to move forward from any given point by triggering an appropriate transition.

Firstly, an initialisation state was created to initialise all the characters states, with their attributes set to null (Fig. 1). Null means the character's attribute at this stage is undefined because the character has not come into the scene yet.

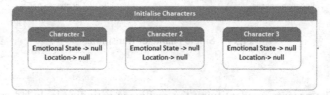

Fig. 1. Initialise states

Then a composite state for each scene was created. Each scene state includes all the currently active character states and their attributes. Then the transition from each scene to the next is either by a CBT activity or a simple scene transition.

Two different ways were created to represent the state machine to enhance the clarity of the transitions and the different emotional states. The first representation shows the complete transitions throughout the story, including scenes and the characters' emotional state and location. This type of representation shows all the states of the characters, even if their state is still undefined or has not changed from one scene to the next. Figure 2 is a sample taken from the complete transition state machine diagram.

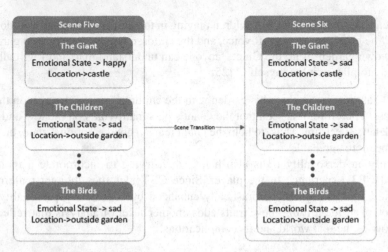

Fig. 2. Partial state transition sample

The second representation shows a single character's transition at a time, choosing to focus on the character's arc at any given scene instead of including every character. Figure 3 is a sample taken from the Giant's transition state machine diagram.

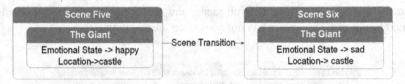

Fig. 3. Single character transitions

Activities. The process of identifying the resilience activities included analysing the story sentence by sentence in search of keywords and specific plot points that indicate where an activity can be integrated to push the story forward. Each type of resilience was mapped to an activity based on the following assumptions:

- The character conversing with other characters through dialogue interactions can suggest a social resilience activity.
- The character experiencing a strong emotion can suggest an emotional resilience activity.
- The character being inquisitive or investigative of their surroundings suggests a mental resilience activity.
- The character engaging in any physical activity, i.e., walking, going up the stairs, can suggest scope for a physical resilience activity.

The following excerpt shows an example of a resilience activity:

"'What are you doing here?' he cried in a very gruff voice, and the children ran away."

This scene gives scope to implement a social resilience activity. The player's role would be to verbally encourage the Giant to interact with the other characters in the most socially appropriate manner. Additionally, that same scene can allude to an emotional resilience activity since the tone of the Giant's speech indicates anger, which is a strong emotion. In the emotional resilience activity the player would reflect on emotionally soothing visionary things, e.g., happy pictures and nature scenes.

The following excerpt shows another example that suggests a resilience activity:

"It is your garden now, little children,' said the Giant, and he took a great axe and knocked down the wall." [25]

This scene holds scope for implementing a physical activity since the Giant knocked down a wall. In this scene, the player's role would be to do a physical resilience activity to encourage the Giant to knock down the wall.

The following excerpt shows scope for implementing the last type of activity, mental resilience:

"I cannot understand why the Spring is so late in coming," said the Selfish Giant, as he sat at the window and looked out at his cold white garden; "I hope there will be a change in the weather."

This scene shows the Giant looking out the window and observing his surroundings. This indicates scope for a mental resilience activity, where the player should be inquisitive and investigative to answer questions relating to the in-game surroundings.

When implementing these activities, it was decided to add additional dialogue cues and CBT activities. However, it was necessary to be respectful towards Wilde's writing and remain as close to the original text as possible. It was then observed that it is possible to integrate the resilience activities within the state transitions created from the previous step in the analysis.

Screenplay. Following the above analysis steps, and to aid the analysis, the story is set out in the form of a screenplay. The traditional screenplay format was adopted, also known as The Master Scene Format. This format typically consists of six main elements: scene headings, the action, character names, parentheticals, character dialogue, and transitions [30].

Fig. 4. Story screenplay

The first element, the scene heading, known as the slug line, is typically written in all caps. It would include INT or EXT for interior or exterior. Then it is followed by the location where the scene takes place and the time of day. The second element is the action. The action describes any action that can be seen or heard. Any sound effects should be written in all caps [30]. The third element is the Character name. The Character name should be written in caps and located in the centre of the page. A character who is speaking in voiceover or is off-screen is designated by V.O or O.S, respectively. The fourth element is Parentheticals. Parentheticals should describe physical or emotional action. It details how the character is speaking the dialogue. The fifth element is character dialogue. Dialogue should be centred on the page; it is what the character says. The sixth and last element is the Transition. The Transition indicates the end of a scene. It is usually written in caps [30]. Going through these steps made it possible to integrate the interactive CBT based storyline with the screenplay format. Figure 4 illustrates, using annotations, how the CBT based activities can be incorporated.

Summary of Analysis. In sum, analysing a story to implement therapy intervention techniques is quite challenging at first. However, it is possible to do so by following a number of straightforward steps after choosing a story.

The first step is to break down that story into sections; these sections represent different scenes in the story. The second step is to try and identify the characters in the story and identify their impact on the story. What are their roles? Are they a hero, villain, or supporting character? In the third step, the author should identify all the characters' emotions and personality traits: to be able to understand how their personality affects their behaviour and to add a level of depth to the reasoning behind their actions. The fourth step is to create states for the characters: to monitor their emotions in each scene, to analyse what triggers their emotions to change, to understand what impacts their emotions, and to find opportunities to induce a change. The fifth step is to identify what CBT activities to incorporate within the story and the most appropriate place for the activities to be incorporated naturally while keeping the flow of the story consistent. After the analysis is done, the next step is to compose the story following the proposed screenplay format.

5   The Story App

The development of the CBT-based serious game consists of three stages. First is composition: the story editor will enable the author to compose a story. The author will be able to choose a visual representation for the characters and scenes in the story and choose to add resilience activities that integrate CBT within the story. The second stage is story mapping, where the screenplay composed by the author is compiled into a jar file. Each resilience activity is mapped to an XML representation in the Editor and a set of java classes in the story app. That jar file includes the screenplay and all media incorporated by the author in the story. The third stage is animation, where the interactive story incorporated in the jar file is played through the story app. The story app can hold an archive of stories composed and uploaded by authors. The player would be able to pick and choose stories to download to the app and play. The story app has been developed and is now a working android application.

5.1   Implementation

The application was developed using Android Studio IDE, which uses the Java programming language and XML. The interface comprises simple graphical elements such as buttons, images, and text fields to avoid overwhelming the interface with different features. A colour scheme was selected for the app based on the psychological properties of colours. In isolation, a single colour on its own has psychological properties, but when combined with other colours, it can produce an emotional response from the user [31]. The right colour combination can act as an unspoken guideline to the user for how to navigate the app [32]. Therefore, it was an important aspect to take into consideration during the implementation. An XML document was created as a representation of The Selfish Giant story and its assets. This document was created using XML Notepad. The parsing of the XML document was implemented through the application's programming interface API: Xml Pull Parser (XPP).

5.2 Walkthrough

The main interface includes guidelines for the player on using different aspects of the app (i.e., resilience activities) and downloading new stories. Furthermore, a scrollable view at the bottom shows the archive of stories (Fig. 5. A). For the present, only The Selfish Giant story is playable. When the player chooses a story, they are taken to that story's interface and prompted to start their adventure (Fig. 5. B). All illustrations used in the story were adopted from the illustrated version of the book [33]. The story's interface is also equipped with a state window that shows the emotions of all in-game characters in any given scene (Fig. 5. C).

Fig. 5. GUI samples

The user can also infer the characters' emotions from the colours used in the interface. For example, when the Giant is happy, the colour of the text view changes to yellow. If he is angry, it changes to red. Moreover, each type of colour representation is accompanied by an animation of the text view that intensifies that feeling, i.e., when the emotion is happy, the whole text view is animated to jump up and down as if it is replicating being happy. If it is angry, then the text view shakes aggressively from side to side.

The player's goal is to maintain the characters' emotional state and the overall state of the game world to achieve harmony. The emotional state is affected by four resilience skills: emotional, mental, social, and physical. Each type of resilience maps to an activity. If the player completes an activity, they will progress through the story. The following figure shows samples of each resilience activity (Fig. 6).

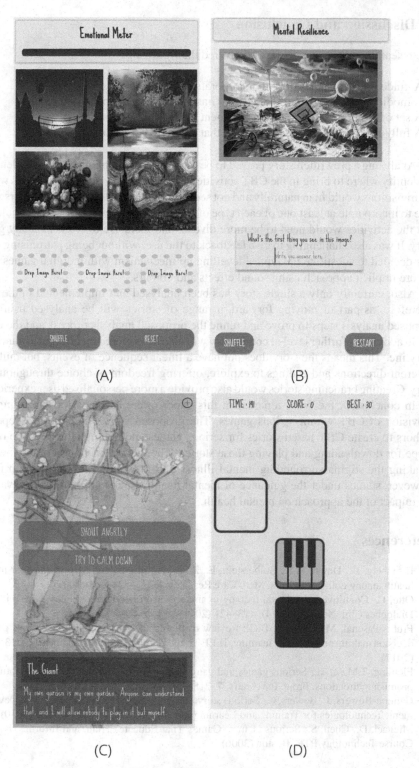

Fig. 6. Resilience activities

6 Discussion and Conclusion

The research reported in this paper delivered the following:

- A guide on analysing a story to incorporate CBT resiliencies.
- A modified story script of The Selfish Giant, following the proposed guide.
- A set of requirements for the development of the story editor.
- A fully functional android application that can play CBT stories.

Analysing a prewritten story proved to be especially challenging. It was challenging to identify where to bring in the CBT activities within the story and finding ways where the transitions would fit in naturally and not seem out of place. However, the authors were able to incorporate at least one of each type of activity within the story. It was concluded that the activities would need to be more diverse and inclusive to work with any given story. It was also challenging to give feedback to the user without being patronising, so it was decided to substitute the typical levelling up mechanism within digital games with a more implicit approach using sound effects and colours.

Also, currently only a single story has been analysed and implemented in the app. Therefore, as part of moving forward, a range of stories will be analysed using the proposed analysis steps to prove and refine the proposed analysis process and the app.

In addition, a further level of complexity will also be explored by offering a branching storyline. This means the story does not have a linear sequence of events, but multiple different directions and endings to explore, offering freedom of choice throughout the story. Creating branching stories would also provide a more personalised user experience.

In conclusion, the work reported in this paper offers a means for expanding the provision of CBT within serious games. The proposed story editor offers scope for authors to create CBT based stories for serious games and the implemented app offers scope for downloading and playing these stories. The work aims to contribute towards breaking the stigma surrounding mental illness and providing help to those in need. However, studies under the guidance of mental health experts are required to evaluate the impact of the approach on mental health.

References

1. Eisenberg, D., Down, M.F., Golberstein, E., Zivin, K.: Stigma and help seeking for mental health among college students. Med. Care Res. Rev. **66**(5), 522–541 (2009)
2. Otte, C.: Cognitive behavioural therapy in anxiety disorders: current state of the evidence. Dialogues Clin. Neurosci. **13**(4), 413–421 (2011)
3. Frutos-Pascual, M., Zapirain, B.G.: Review of the use of AI techniques in serious games: decision making and machine learning. IEEE Trans. Comput. Intell. AI Games **9**(2), 133–152 (2017)
4. Fleming, T.M., et al.: Serious games and gamification for mental health: current status and promising directions. Front. Psychiatry. **7**, 215 (2016)
5. Cannon-Bowers, J., Bowers, C.: Serious storytelling. In: Serious Game Design and Development: Technologies for Training and Learning, pp. 13–30. IGI Global, Hershey (2010)
6. Michael, D., Chen, S.: Serious Games: Games That Educate, Trian, and Inform. Thomson Course Technology PTR, Boston (2006)

7. McDaniel, R., Fiore, S.M., Nicholson, D.: Serious storytelling: narrative considerations for serious game researchers and developers. In: Serious Game Design and Development: Technologies for Training and Learning, pp. 13–30 (2010)
8. Swift, P., Cyhlarova, E., Goldie, I., O'Sullivan, C.: Living with anxiety: understanding the role and impact of anxiety in our lives. Mental Health Foundation, London (2014)
9. Friedlli, D.L.: Mental health, resilience and inequalities. WHO Regional Office for Europe, Copenhagen, Denmark (2009)
10. Burns, D.D.: Feeling Good: The New Mood Therapy. William Morrow and Company, New York (1980)
11. Fenn, K., Byrne, M.: The Key Principles of Cognitive Behavioural Therapy. InnovAiT: Educ. Inspir. Gen. Pract. 6(9), 579–585 (2013)
12. Konigsberg, I.: The Complete Film Dictionary. Penguin Books, New York (1989)
13. Harun, A., Razeef, M., Razeef Abd Razak, M., Nur Firdaus Nasir, M.: Freytag's pyramid: an approach for analysing the dramatic elements and narrative structure in Filem Negara Malaysia's first animated cartoon. In: IEEE Symposium on Humanities, Science and Engineering Research (SHUSER), Penang, Malaysia (2013)
14. Freytag, G.: Freytag's Technique of the Drama: An Exposition of Dramatic Composition and Art. An Authorised Translation from the 6th German Ed. by Elias J. MacEwan. Scott, Foresman & CO, Chicago (1898)
15. Miller, C.H.: Digital Storytelling: A Creator's Guide to Interactive Entertainment, 4th edn. CRC Press/Taylor & Francis Group, NY (2020)
16. Baranowski, T., Buday, R., Thompson, D.I., Baranowski, J.: Playing for real: video games and stories for health-related behaviour change. Am. J. Prev. Med. 34(1), 74–82 (2008)
17. Shapiro, S., Rotter, M.: Graphic depictons: portrayals of mental illness in video games. J. Forensic Sci. 61(6), 1592–1595 (2016)
18. Dunlap, K.: Representation of mental illness in video games. In: Connnected Learning Summit (2018)
19. Berzinka, V.: Computer games supporting cognitive therapy in children. Clin. Child Psychol. Psychiatry 19(1), 100–110 (2012)
20. Jonell, C., Olonde, D.A.: Use of Serious Games in Treatment of Depression (2016)
21. Bostan, B.: Game User Experience and Player-Centered Design. Springer, Istanbul (2020). https://doi.org/10.1007/978-3-030-37643-7
22. Alves, T.: Exploring underrepresented narratives. Social anxiety in games. University of Skovde, Skovde, Sweden (2018)
23. Wang, H., Singhal, A.: Digital games: the secret of alternative health realities. In: Health Communication Strategies for Developing Global Health Programs, pp. 67–82. Peter Lang, New York (2014)
24. Levall, M.: Please knock on my door: a story-driven experience capturing the struggles of depression and social anxiety, 7 September 2017. http://www.michaellevall.com/please-knock-on-my-door/. Accessed June 2020
25. Wilde, O.: The happy prince and other tales. In: The Selfish Giant (1888)
26. Plutchik, R.: The nature of emotions. Am. Sci. 89(4), 334–350 (2001)
27. Costa, P.T., McCrae, R.R.: The NEO inventories. In: Neo PI-R Professional Manual, pp. 223–256. PAR, Inc., Lutz (1992)
28. John, O.P., Robins, R.W., Pervin, L.A.: Handbook of Personality: Theory and Research, 3rd edn. The Guilford Press, New York (2008)
29. Merril, K.M., Strauman, T.J.: The role of personality in cognitive-behavioural therapies. Behav. Ther. 35(1), 131–146 (2004)
30. Field, S.: Screenplay: The Foundations of Screenwriting. Delta, New York (2005)

31. Wright, A.B.: The colour affects system of colour psychology. In: AIC Quadrennial Congress, London (2009)
32. Rider, R.M.: Colour Psychology and Graphic Design Applications (2010)
33. Wilde, O.: The Selfish Giant by Lisbeth Zwerger. Mineedition, Hong Kong (1991)

Between Game Mechanics *and* Immersive Storytelling: Design Using an Extended Activity Theory Framework

Tim Marsh[1(✉)], Ashima Thomas[2], and Eng Tat Khoo[3]

[1] Griffith Film School, Griffith University, Brisbane, Australia
t.marsh@griffith.edu.au
[2] Warrior9 VR, Singapore, Singapore
ash@warrior9.com
[3] Engineering Design and Innovation Centre, National University of Singapore, Singapore,
Singapore
engket@nus.edu.sg

Abstract. This paper outlines the latest work of an on-going long-term sustained research effort to extend and operationalise Leontiev's original hierarchical activity theory framework to model and support the design, development and analysis of games, virtual environments and virtual reality for purpose. While previous work extended Leontiev's activity theory to incorporate both task-based and experiential-based activities and actions performed within a sphere of engagement - corresponding to Huizinga's "play-grounds", "arenas" and "magic circle", and mechanism to analyse and assess the success of purpose, the focus of this earlier work was largely on narrative, scenario and story-based activities, and didn't capture or extend well to gameplay mechanics. The framework described herein describes initial work that builds on and extends earlier work to provide a tool, notation, grammar and building blocks that informs both HCI and practice-based approaches to represent gameplay mechanics *and* narrative, scenario, story-based activities; from game design concepts and ideas, through modelling and analysis, to informing implementation, development and creative practice. The framework is intended to support all delivery platforms and extend to all purposes/sectors (education, health, esports, business, documentary, tourism, social impact, culture, etc.) across the serious games continuum: from games for purpose to experiential environments for purpose. To highlight the versatility of the initial work to extend the activity theory framework, described herein are several examples of serious games, interactive storytelling and immersive VR for purpose developed in research projects, and in the professional immersive storytelling content creation Singapore-based studio Warrior9 VR.

Keywords: Narrative · Story · Mechanics · Games · Serious games · VR · Immersive · Interactive storytelling · Interactive narrative · Framework · Activity theory · Notation · Grammar · Design · HCI · Creativity · Practice-based · Reflective practice

© Springer Nature Switzerland AG 2021
B. Fletcher et al. (Eds.): JCSG 2021, LNCS 12945, pp. 113–128, 2021.
https://doi.org/10.1007/978-3-030-88272-3_9

1 Introduction

The design, development, and creation of games, serious games, VR, AR, immersive worlds, etc. arguably follows one of two approaches – using methodologies from the design and analysis discipline of Human-Computer Interaction (HCI), and practice-based approaches typically embraced by the arts, creative practitioners, and in games and immersive VR studios. While there is some crossover, these two groups largely co-exist independently.

HCI has a long and successful history in iterative design and development, user/player-centered, participatory-design, prototyping, and analysis, evaluation, and assessment of interactive and digital media. While HCI has long looked to the arts to inform methods, and includes creatives, performers and artists in HCI design and development teams, the arts and creativity within HCI typically is incorporated within a traditional engineering and technical design and development iterative cycle.

Practice-based is another successful approach that has a long history in creativity, creative arts, design and making cultures and disciplines. Practice-based approaches are part of a larger family of reflective practice and action-based approaches following Schön's "The Reflective Practitioner" [1] which includes disciplines outside the arts such as, healthcare, medicine, and education, etc. At the heart of action-based approaches is an action-reflection cycle. In the arts, this is iteratively performed in a cycle of making and creating, evaluating/reflecting-in-action, and informing making, and so on. Although creative, making, and practice-based approaches have typically dominated the games industry, and despite the games industry being one of, if not the most profitable interactive digital media industry, over several years there has been several criticisms, and calls for more formal approaches and tools to support and inform game development practitioners in game studios/industry. The advantages being to better support large-scale projects, keeping them on-track, within time and budget, and so help to reduce costs.

As Katherine Neil identifies in her 2016 Gamasutra article [2] "How we design games now and why", that over the years, numerous calls have been made in the games industry to address the making-focused approaches, and make available more games design tools, methods, and formal approaches to support games design and game design thinking in the games industry. For example, going back as early as 1999, game designer Doug Church proposed the need to develop 'formal, abstract design tools' in his well-known article published in the industry's trade magazine *Game Developer* [3]. Later, Raph Koster (2005) drew our attention to "the imprecision of natural language as a tool for designing gameplay", and proposed a graphical notation system in his well-known Games Developers Conference presentation "A Grammar of Gameplay" [4]. While game designer Dan Cook (2007) disparagingly said games design occurred accidentally through habit and guesswork [5].

One thing is clear, that as game and serious games designs and projects became larger, the design documentation also correspondingly became larger. This increases the difficult in managing and keeping track of projects. We've come a long way since these early days with a host of standard texts from writer-practitioners on games design [e.g. Ernest Adams, Tracy Fullerton, Chris Crawford, Katie Salen and Eric Zimmerman, David Perry, etc.] used throughout the world, to introduce, educate, inform and enlighten game practitioners and students (of games design courses and degrees), and researchers, academics and students of HCI and interaction design interested in learning about the craft of game design. In particular, more recently one driver for the HCI communities comes from the strong interest in gamification – applying game elements and characteristics to digital, interactive, online, apps, and services, etc.

Similarly, in the emerging discipline of serious games we witnessed early calls for serious methodologies and design approaches incorporating both research *and* development to address the spate of published work focused on development and practice alone [e.g. 6, 7, 8]. While more recently we've seen an escalation in reports, publications, workshops and conferences focused on serious games design and thinking, and in particular focused on mechanics in serious games these typically adopt HCI focused approaches over art, making, creativity, and practice-based approaches.

Herein, it is argued that both approaches have advantages and could inform and inspire, and feasibly be incorporated with one other. Interestingly, at the heart of both HCI and practice-based approaches is an iterative approach. In HCI, it's the iterative design, development, analysis, evaluation and playtesting cycle; and in practice-based, it's the iterative making/creating, evaluating/reflecting-in-action, and informing making cycle. So for example, it's not difficult to imagine a practice-based creative iterative approach incorporated within an HCI iterative design and development cycle, and vice versa. This paper describes an approach that informs both the HCI design and development cycle and an action-based/practice-based approach for the design and creation of games, serious games, VR and immersive environments. This paper outlines the latest work of an on-going long-term sustained research effort to extend and operationalise Leontiev's (1981) original hierarchical activity theory framework [9]. The framework described herein describes initial work that builds on and extends earlier work to provide a tool, notation, grammar and building blocks to represent gameplay mechanics *and* narrative, scenario, story-based activities; from game design concepts and ideas, through modelling and analysis, to informing implementation.

This paper is organised as follows. In section two, related and previous work to extend and operationalise Leontiev's (1981) original hierarchical activity theory framework is described. Section three describes the notation, grammar and building blocks of the extended framework, and provides examples of serious games, VR and immersive environments gameplay mechanics *and* narrative, scenario, story-based activities represented through the framework. Section four concludes the paper summarising the work and advantages of the framework.

2 Previous and Related Work

Previous work building on the hierarchical activity theory based framework and approach [10–16] has made considerable advances to extend and operationalise Leontiev's (1981) original activity theory to model and support the design, development and analysis of serious games, virtual environments and virtual reality for a variety of purposes along the serious games continuum [17], as shown in Fig. 1.

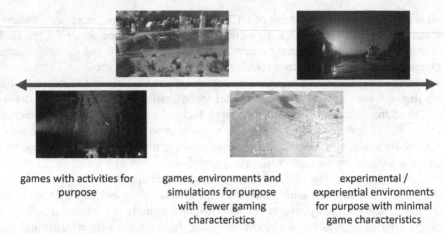

| games with activities for purpose | games, environments and simulations for purpose with fewer gaming characteristics | experimental / experiential environments for purpose with minimal game characteristics |

Fig. 1. Serious games continuum: showing from left to right, games for purpose (with traditional game characteristics) to experimental & experiential environments for purpose (with minimal game characteristics), as follows: Oceans We Make [18] third activity with game characteristics with purpose to collect plastics in the ocean; The Reef Game [19] game-like to slow down or stop harmful human activities to the Great Barrier Reef (second activity); VR Slow Reef Experience [20] swimming through the beauty and wonder of the Great Barrier Reef (first activity); Oceans We Make [18] first activity preparing to go for dive in the ocean

While the previous work [21] developed a framework using activity theory, and interestingly draws on and mixes concepts and frameworks from the two main activity theory systems of Engestrom (1987) [22] and Leontiev (1978) [23], the focus of this work is exclusively on educational serious games. Other earlier activity theory work similarly focusing exclusively on learning games is for example [24]. So while several other published work has explored activity theory and games and serious games, invariably this work focuses on [22] version or hybrid of [22] and Leontiev's later and revised works [23], and focuses on learning or educational games. Interestingly, the English translation of Leontiev's [23] second publication appeared in print before Leontiev's [9] first publication which was translated from Russian to English and published in 1981.

Our activity theory work focused on Leontiev's [9] original activity theory containing the powerful activity concepts of motive and objective that define "activity proper". Our earlier work, referred to as HABS (Hierarchical Activity-Based Scenario approach) focused on interactive narrative, scenario and story-based activities, composed largely of written description or statements of actions/play, similar to a script/scriptwriting, although structured accordingly in a hierarchy of activity, actions, operations, and intention/motive, directed towards objective.

The framework's lens-like ability provided a way to describe and represent any level of abstraction from high-level descriptions of activity to zoom-in to any low-level of actions, sub-actions, sub-sub-actions, and so on, and use of tools and artifacts responding to conditions of action. In [10], we presented the first-steps demonstrating the flexible and powerful ability of the HABS framework applied to the learning game "2020Classroom" (NSF-funded) to zoom-in to any level of detail and complexity, and study results demonstrated the mechanism to analyse, assess and reason about the success of purpose (for undergraduate students to learn about processes of human organs) – through *objective outcome coinciding with motive*. Further refinement to this work was presented in [13].

While this earlier work focused on task-based single-activity and multiple-actions we further extended Leontiev's (1981) activity theory to incorporate experiential-based activities through the *outcome of objective merging with motive*, as well as task-based multiple-activities and actions [14] performed within a Sphere of Engagement [16] corresponding to Huizinga's "play-grounds", "arenas" and "magic circle" [26]. However, the focus of this earlier work on narrative, scenario and story-based activities didn't capture or extend well to gameplay mechanics of loops of interactive play activity/actions that is key to reinforcement of an idea through repeated action [27, 28] and that typically characterise games and games for purpose. Considering the serious games continuum [17] that captures all purposes from all sectors irrespective of platform, it can be seen that our previous work focusing on interactive narrative, scenario and story-based activities, was less effective at capturing or extending to games for purpose with game elements, characteristics and mechanics identified predominately on the left-hand side of the continuum.

Therefore, this called for the next phase in the evolution of the Leontiev's [9] activity theory, to further extend and operationalise our activity theory-based framework and approach to capture core and other game mechanic loops of play activity/actions that typically characterise games and games for purpose, as well as, represent interactive narrative scenario story-based activities.

3   Extended Activity Theory Framework: Notation, Grammar, Building Blocks for Mechanics, Narrative and Story

In this section we present the initial work that builds on and extends earlier work to provide a tool, notation, grammar and building blocks that informs both HCI and practice-based approaches to represent gameplay mechanics *and* narrative, scenario, story-based activities. The framework is intended to facilitate and inform HCI transition from requirements, ideation, design to implementation, and helps practice-based approach transition from ideation, design docs to creation. It's intended to support all delivery platforms and extend to all purposes/sectors (education, health, esports, business, documentary, tourism, social impact, culture, etc.) across the serious games continuum: from games for purpose to experiential environments for purpose.

As demonstrated in our previous work, blending both mechanics and narrative/story provides powerful strategies for design of serious games and immersive environments for purpose. For example, as demonstrated through our exhibited, showcased and published works: The Reef Game [19] and Oceans We Make [18] which incorporate both gameplay mechanics for purpose and experiential environments for purpose, and the VR Slow Reef Experience [20] that incorporates an experiential environment for purpose. As these serious games and immersive VR environments extend across the serious games continuum (Fig. 1), we focus on these examples in this section to demonstrate the extended activity theory framework.

Following Koster (2005), at the heart of our framework is notation and grammar that we have developed. Notation systems are found in the arts, dance and music. As shown in Fig. 2, examples include, the Labanotation which is a visual notation used to record and analyse human movement and the staging of dance and design of choreographed movement sequences, and Musical Notation used to visually represent music played with instruments through the use of symbols and other signs such as for durations, rests, tone dampening and sustaining. In our framework, the notation is derived from extended activity theory concepts and games and serious games design elements and characteristics.

Fig. 2. Notation Systems: (left) Labanotation records human movement sequences for archive and choreography of dance, and (right) Musical notation represents music through symbols and other signs for durations, rests, tone dampening and sustaining.

In the next section we describe the extended activity theory framework, notation and grammar for narrative, story and mechanics, and provide a number of examples including the exhibited, showcased and published works: The Reef Game [19] and Oceans We Make [18] which extend across the serious games continuum (Fig. 1), and the experiential environment VR Slow Reef Experience [20] to demonstrate the versatility of the framework.

3.1 Activity Theory Framework, Notation & Grammar for Narrative, Story & Mechanics	
(circle symbol)	Sphere of Engagement (SoE): corresponds to the environment, "play-grounds" "arena" and "magic circle" (Huizinga's 1955), in which one or more activity is performed – and provides a boundary / demarcation between that which is external / outside of the sphere to that which is internal through either focus of attention / engagement / play or enveloped by technological platform e.g. VR, virtual and game world, gameplay map, and maintain the illusion [25]. Can incorporate either or both task-based and experiential-based activities and actions
M ⟩ O (symbol)	Objective and Motive (O & M) Coincides: task-based activity / actions - towards the fulfilment of goals until objective is fulfilled and / or condition is met. Relationship between O & M provides a means to frame activity and a mechanism to assess / reason about the success of activities / actions through the degree to which outcome of objective *coincides* with motive.
M O (symbol)	Objective and Motive (O & M) Merges: experiential-based activity / actions - relationship between O & M provides a means to frame activity and a mechanism to assess / reason about activities providing an experience as objective outcome *merges* with motive. Merges doesn't necessarily suggest an end point (like task-based) but suggests that as long as actions are contributing to the merging, then motive is being fulfilled or satisfied

(arrow symbols)	Game Start: start of game or experiential encounter; entry to SoE or magic circle (left)	Game End: identifies end of game or experiential encounter (middle)	Transition / Link: linear sequential transition; with direction from one activity / action to (right)

(loop arrow symbol)	Game Mechanic Loop: activity / action(s) performed repeatedly again and again in a loop. Represents the core or other game mechanic loop of *essential play, narrative, environmental storytelling, or experiential activity / actions*
(thick line symbol)	Choice, Decision, Branching, Synchronisation: marks the point at which a choice, decision, branch / branching occurs (can be mandatory or optional) or is synchronisation for players to begin at the same time e.g. start of a race, contest – see examples below.

(rounded rectangle symbol)	(film strip symbol)	Message: title screen, end credits, instructions on gameplay, UI or controls, etc.; introduce or update backstory; can be text, visuals, voiceover.	Cut scene: denotes linear presentation video or animation and duration - to introduce or update story/game, tutorial on gameplay or controls, etc.

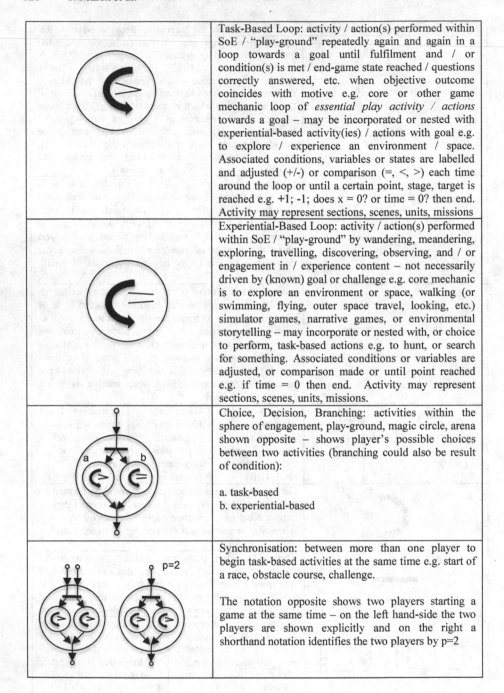

	Task-Based Loop: activity / action(s) performed within SoE / "play-ground" repeatedly again and again in a loop towards a goal until fulfilment and / or condition(s) is met / end-game state reached / questions correctly answered, etc. when objective outcome coincides with motive e.g. core or other game mechanic loop of *essential play activity / actions* towards a goal – may be incorporated or nested with experiential-based activity(ies) / actions with goal e.g. to explore / experience an environment / space. Associated conditions, variables or states are labelled and adjusted (+/-) or comparison (=, <, >) each time around the loop or until a certain point, stage, target is reached e.g. +1; -1; does x = 0? or time = 0? then end. Activity may represent sections, scenes, units, missions
	Experiential-Based Loop: activity / action(s) performed within SoE / "play-ground" by wandering, meandering, exploring, travelling, discovering, observing, and / or engagement in / experience content – not necessarily driven by (known) goal or challenge e.g. core mechanic is to explore an environment or space, walking (or swimming, flying, outer space travel, looking, etc.) simulator games, narrative games, or environmental storytelling – may incorporate or nested with, or choice to perform, task-based actions e.g. to hunt, or search for something. Associated conditions or variables are adjusted, or comparison made or until point reached e.g. if time = 0 then end. Activity may represent sections, scenes, units, missions.
	Choice, Decision, Branching: activities within the sphere of engagement, play-ground, magic circle, arena shown opposite – shows player's possible choices between two activities (branching could also be result of condition): a. task-based b. experiential-based
	Synchronisation: between more than one player to begin task-based activities at the same time e.g. start of a race, obstacle course, challenge. The notation opposite shows two players starting a game at the same time – on the left hand-side the two players are shown explicitly and on the right a shorthand notation identifies the two players by p=2

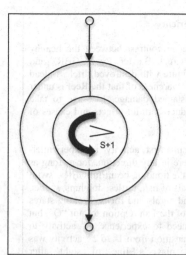

3.2 Basketball Waste Disposal and Recycle Game

Purpose: player learns about the types of trash and the appropriately coloured bin to dispose / recycle it i.e. general waste-green lid; recycle-yellow lid; green waste-lime green lid – learn while playing a fun game!

Activity Statement: task-based, repeatedly sorting waste and recycling trash by shooting baskets into one of three coloured bins, incrementing score s+1 for correctly sorted trash, against the clock-until end game time reached (e.g. 2 minutes). Creates competition between players to get highest number of baskets.

Motive: recycle trash
Objective: sort into correct coloured recycle bin by scoring baskets
[student serious game on BA Games Design, GFS]

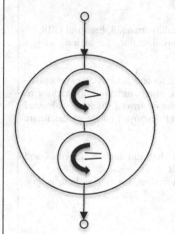

3.2.1 Beach Clear – Pollution-Trash

Purpose: intended to evoke uplifting feeling of accomplishment; beautifying environment creates positive experience. Message: Clean-up & don't litter!

1. Activity Statement: first activity is task-based, repeatedly picking-up trash scattered around the island and loading on a boat until no more trash on island (e.g. with 20 pieces of trash, the core mechanic is repeated 20 times until no trash). As trash is cleared, island progressively becomes more beautiful, sky and sea becomes brighter and bluer, increase in fish swimming and jumping, and birds flying and singing.

Motive: clean-up / clear island of pollution and trash.
Objective: pick-up trash and load on-board boat

When Motive and Objective outcome coincide the activity ends.

2. Activity Statement: second activity is experiential-based, sail away on boat into the sunset

Motive: escape island - enjoy the experience!
Objective: sail boat into / across open sea into sunset

NOTE: the second activity could be incorporated in the first but separating these emphasises the task-based clean-up activity from experiential-based positive and uplifting experience of sailing away into the sunset.

[student serious game on BA Games Design, GFS]

3.2.2 VR Reef Experience

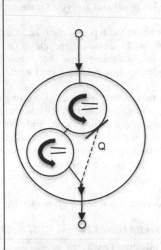

Purpose: To experience contrast between the healthy beautiful, tranquil Great Barrier Reef (GBR) and glimpse a possible future with destroyed, lifeless, dead Great Barrier Reef. Awareness of that the Reef is under threat of further sustained damage. Message to take care of the GBR, reduce harmful effects and causes of climate change.

1. Activity Statement: first activity is experiential-based, swim anywhere in any direction, for as long as you please, through the tranquil, beautiful GBR – swim with clown fish, shoals of fish, turtles, dolphins, sharks, jelly fish, and around corals and rocks. Prolong stares brings-up the name of the fish. Option to quit "Q", but as all participants need to experience 2nd activity to fulfil purpose, the transition from 1st to 2nd activity was positioned in the player's line of sight after predetermined times to encourage transition to 2nd activity.

Motive: experience healthy, tranquil, beautiful GBR
Objective: swim in any direction, for as long as you please

2. Activity Statement: second activity is experiential-based, swim anywhere in any direction, for as long as you please, through the destroyed, lifeless, with dead fish, and bleached and destroyed corals of the future Great Barrier Reef

Motive: awareness of harmful human activities and climate change to GBR
Objective: swim in any direction, for as long as you please

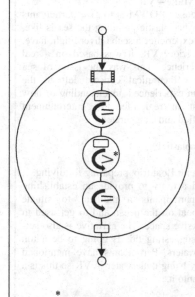

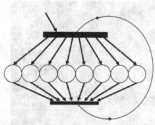

3.2.3 The Reef Game – tablet / smartphone

Purpose: To experience contrast between the healthy beautiful, tranquil Great Barrier Reef and glimpse a possible future with destroyed, unhealthy GBR. Awareness of harmful effects to the Reef from human activities during fun game play. Message to take care of the GBR, reduce harmful effects & climate change. Message: Slow Down / Stop harmful human activities

First, cut scene opening shot moving closer to the game title.

1. Activity Statement: first activity is experiential-based, UI instruction invites the participant to swim and explore anywhere in any direction, through the tranquil, beautiful GBR – swim with clown fish, shoals of fish, turtles, dolphins, sharks, jelly fish, and around corals and rocks – 1 minute.

2. Activity Statement: second activity is task-based, UI instructions to tap on harmful human activities. Game loop is shown opposite; as the harmful events occur in a seemingly random order, the player taps on them to slow down or stop harmful activities. A fun game that gets faster and faster, increasing the challenge, but the ocean inevitably becomes darker, polluted, unhealthy, and game play ends ~1.30mins.

Harmful human activities: farming run off, construction run off, speeding water sports, plastic bags, crown of thorns starfish, over tourism, heavy shipping and smoke / pollution from local industry

3. Activity Statement: third activity is experiential-based, participant to swim and explore anywhere in any direction, for as long as you please, through the destroyed, lifeless, dying reef and bleached corals.

Reef Game ends with thought-provoking message. Further design details can be found in [30, 31].

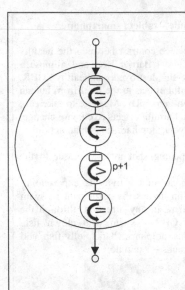

3.2.4 Oceans We Make – VR

Purpose: The purpose of OWM is to give participants an experience of what plastic polluting the sea is like, just like an actual experience a scuba diver might have. Developed by Warrior9 VR, it was based on a real scuba diving experience. This way the issue of sea pollution is not a theoretical concept left to the imagination, but an experienced understanding of how it could manifest in real life. For entertainment purposes it's gamified and exaggerated.

Message: Use less plastic!

1. Activity Statement: Boat trip, preparing for diving.
Experiential-based activity to provide an establishing scene to give participants a moment to situate themselves on a boat on the ocean and to get used to being in an immersive space. The narrative is also set-up by voiceover suggesting this is going to be a fun dive in pristine waters. Participants have mentioned that it can be scary being underwater in VR so this is a way to ease them into it.

2. Activity Statement: Submerged in the sea, and journeying through the beautiful ocean.
Experiential-based activity, participants enter the ocean and get a sense of how beautiful and magical the ocean environment is - particularly those who are afraid of going beneath the surface or who would never get to experience it as they don't Scuba dive. In other words, take people to a place they can't usually get to without a lot of effort. We also purposefully had a shark swim by to make the point that - for the most part - sharks keep to themselves and are not the aggressive villainous creatures portrayed in the media.

3. Activity Statement: Plastics appear, gameplay core loop to capture plastics

Task-based activity; the initial piece of plastic appearing is intended to be a surprise to participants - they're not aware that it is coming. And then slowly the participant sees more pieces of plastic and they are encouraged through UI and audio instruction to enjoy the game-like play loop of trying to collect all the trash using one or both the hands. For each item of plastic successfully collected, a sound is heard and score is incremented. The enjoyment is supposed to take the attention away from the fact that it's actually a bad thing that there's so much trash in this supposedly "pristine" sea. Because that realisation comes later.

As the trash becomes more, the participant struggles to keep-up with the collection, and begins to realise that the game is unwinnable... and is intended to shift their attention back to the fact that actually the sea is horribly polluted, and that's sad/disappointing.

4. Activity Statement: Dive ends, taken out of ocean

Finally, the experience concludes as the participant is pulled out of the sea to see all the trash floating on its surface, as a way of giving participants a bird's eye view of the problem, so they can put it in context, and realize the scale of pollution that overshadows the beautiful ocean - along with an impact statement to show how many pieces of plastic they've collected versus how much is reported to be in the sea. Ultimately the hope of this sentence is to emphasise the fact that using less is the only way that we can reduce the problem, because we can't collect it all.

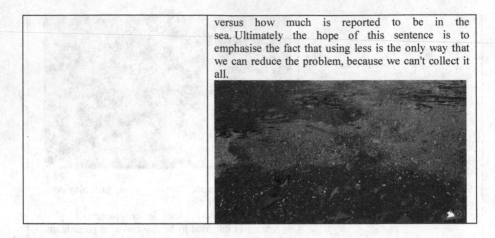

4 Conclusion

This paper presents on-going research to extend and operationalise Leontiev's (1981) original hierarchical activity theory framework. This is the latest work of an on-going long-term sustained research effort. In particular, the main focus of the work presented herein was to extend our activity theory framework to mechanics *and* narrative, scenario and story-based activities performed in sphere of engagement equivalent to Huizinga's "play-grounds" – from high-level to low-level. The framework herein provides a tool, notation, grammar and building blocks that can be incorporated into both HCI and practice-based approaches. The framework is intended to support all delivery platforms and extend to all purposes/sectors (education, learning, health, science, esports, business, tourism, social impact, social justice, cultural heritage, etc.) across the serious games continuum: from games for purpose to experiential environments for purpose. To highlight the versatility of the initial work to extend the activity theory framework, we described several examples of serious game and immersive VR for purpose developed in research projects, and in the professional immersive content creation Singapore-based studios of Warrior9 VR.

References

1. Schön, D.A.: The Reflective Practitioner: How Professionals Think In Action. Basic Books, New York (2008)
2. Neil, K.: How we design games now and why. Gamasutra (2016). https://www.gamasutra.com/blogs/KatharineNeil/20161214/287515/How_we_design_games_now_and_why.php
3. Church, D.: Formal Abstract Design Tools. Gamasutra (1999). https://www.gamasutra.com/view/feature/131764/formal_abstract_design_tools.php
4. Koster, R.: A grammar of gameplay. In: Game Developers Conference (2005)
5. Cook, D.: The Chemistry Of Game Design. Gamasutra (2007). https://www.gamasutra.com/view/feature/129948/the_chemistry_of_game_design.php
6. Zyda, M.: Creating a science of games. Commun. ACM **50**(7), 27–29 (2007)

7. Marsh, T.: Informing design and evaluation methodologies for serious games for learning. In: Proceedings of Learning with Games 2007, Sofia Antipolis, France, pp. 479–485 (2007)
8. Marsh, T., Wright, P., Smith, S.: Evaluation for the design of experience in virtual environments: modelling breakdown of interaction and illusion. J. CyberPsychol. Behav. Spec. Issue Being Presence 4(2), 225–238 (2001)
9. Leontiev, A.N.: Problems of the Development of the Mind. Progress, Moscow (1981)
10. Marsh, T., et al.: User experiences and lessons learned from developing and implementing an immersive game for the science classroom. In: Proceedings of HCI International 2005, Las Vegas, Nevada, USA (2005)
11. Marsh, T., Yang, K., Shahabi, C.: Game development for experience through staying there. In: Sandbox 06 Proceedings of the 2006 ACM SIGGRAPH Symposium on Videogames, vol. 1, pp. 83–89 (2006)
12. Marsh, T.: Staying there: an activity-based approach to narrative design and evaluation as an antidote to virtual corpsing. In: Being There: Concepts, Effects and Measurement of user Presence in Synthetic Environments, pp. 85–96. IOS Press (2003)
13. Marsh, T.: Activity-based scenario design, development and assessment in serious games. In: Gaming and Cognition: Theories and Practice from the Learning Sciences, pp. 213–225. IOS Press (2010)
14. Marsh, T., Nardi, B.: Spheres and lenses: activity based scenario/narrative approach for design and evaluation of entertainment through engagement. In: Pisan, Y., Sgouros, N.M., Marsh, T. (eds.) Entertainment Computing - ICEC 2014, vol. 8770, pp. 42–51. Springer, Cham (2014). https://doi.org/10.1007/978-3-662-45212-7_6
15. Marsh, T., Nardi, B.: Narrative in HCI: interactions, play, games, stories, fictions and envisioning futures using activity theory. In: ACM SIGCHI 2015 - Workshop on Ecological Perspectives in HCI: Promise, Problems, and Potential (2015)
16. Marsh, T., Nardi, B.: Framing activity-based narrative in serious games play-grounds through objective and motive. In: Marsh, T., Ma, M., Oliveira, M., Baalsrud Hauge, J., Göbel, S. (eds.) Serious Games, vol. 9894, pp. 204–213. Springer, Cham (2016). https://doi.org/10.1007/978-3-319-45841-0_19
17. Marsh, T.: Serious games continuum: Between Games for Purpose to Experiential Environments for Purpose. Entertain. Comput. 2(2), 61–68. Elsevier (2011)
18. Thomas, A., et al.: Oceans we Make, Virtual and Augmented Reality. ACM SIGGRAPH Asia, ACM Press, Tokyo (2018)
19. Marsh, T.: The reef game. Available from Google Play. The reef game prototype, showcase. In: Joint Conference on Serious Games-JCSG 2015 (2021)
20. Marsh, T., Jenson, N., Constantine, W., Miller, E.: VR immersive slow reef experience. In: Marsh, T., Ma, M., Oliveira, M., Baalsrud Hauge, J., Göbel, S. (eds.) Serious Games, vol. 9894, pp. 293–296. Springer, Cham (2016). https://doi.org/10.1007/978-3-319-45841-0_34
21. Carvalho, M.B.: An activity theory-based model for serious games analysis and conceptual design. Comput. Educ. 87, 166–181 (2015)
22. Engeström, Y.: Learning by Expanding: An Activity-Theoretical Approach to Developmental Research. Orienta-Konsultit, Helsinki (1987)
23. Leontiev, A.N.: Activity, Consciousness, and Personality. Prentice-Hall, Englewood Cliffs (1978)
24. Oliver, M., Pelletier, C.: Activity theory and learning from digital games: implications for game design. In: Digital Generations: Children, Young People and New Media. Institute of Education, London (2004)
25. Marsh, T., Wright, P.: Maintaining the illusion of interacting within a 3D virtual space. In: 3rd International Workshop on Presence, Delft, The Netherlands (2000)
26. Huizinga, J.: HomoLudens: A Study of the Play-Element in Culture, Beacon Press (1955)

27. Bogost, I.: Videogames and ideological frames. Popular Commun. **4**(3), 165–183 (2006)
28. Barab, S.A., et al.: Pedagogical dramas and transformational play: narratively rich games for learning. Mind Cult. Act. **17**(3), 235–264 (2010)
29. Marsh, T.: Designing for positive and serious experience: devices for creativity, engagement, reflection and learning. In: Göbel, S., Ma, M., Oliveira, M., Wiemeyer, J., Wendel, V. (eds.) Serious Games, vol. 9090, pp. 3–10. Springer, Cham (2015). https://doi.org/10.1007/978-3-319-19126-3_1
30. Marsh, T.: Slow serious games, interactions and play: designing for positive and serious experience and reflection. Entertain. Comput. **14**, 45–53 (2016)

Games in Health

Creation and Future Development Process of a Serious Game: Raising Awareness of (Visual) Impairments

Linda Rustemeier[✉], Sarah Voß-Nakkour, Saba Mateen, and Imran Hossain

Goethe-University Frankfurt, Varrentrappstr. 40-42, 60486 Frankfurt, Germany
{rustemeier,voss,mateen}@studiumdigitale.uni-frankfurt.de,
imran.hossain@web.de

Abstract. Despite the UN Convention on the Rights of Persons with Disabilities and binding laws, digital accessibility is not yet a norm at universities. Therefore (digital) accessibility must be taken into account and be comprehensible to create a university accessible for everyone. Innovative learning methods such as using Serious Games seem suitable for this. A well-designed game narrative can engage and simultaneously lead to proactive thoughts for educators. Moreover, a Serious Game holds the potential to raise awareness among players of the problems students and staff with impairments face at university. The content of our Serious Game "Lola's first semester" showcases initial possibilities for proactive action and raises an identity-creating reference with examples from their own university. For the conception and implementation, the design-based research approach was chosen. This paper presents the results of a first evaluation study of the Serious Game regarding the story, the integrated mini-games and the implementation. Furthermore, it shows how the game is suitable for the described purpose and how it was received. The importance of a well-paced narrative combined with modern visuals and freely available assets are also covered in this paper. Additionally, it is discussed how the next iteration of the development could reach a wider audience. Another goal will be an integration of other impairments, like hearing impairment and mental health issues.

Keywords: Inclusion · Serious game · Accessible educational technologies · Design-based research · Digital accessibility · Gamification · Impairment

B. Fletcher et al. (Eds.): JCSG 2021, LNCS 12945, pp. 131–137, 2021.
https://doi.org/10.1007/978-3-030-88272-3_10

1 A Serious Game for Raising Awareness of Impairments

Fig. 1. Lola's first day at Goethe University Frankfurt

Accessibility is a legal requirement[1] and a necessity, which can be taught in a playful manner. Serious Games can be a medium to simplify complex learning areas. Especially in university contexts, it can be an effective and sustainable self-learning method as well as a suitable, innovative and informative tool of raising awareness. In 2020, we developed a Serious Game named "Lola's first semester"[2] with the aim of raising awareness for the problems of impaired students at universities. The target group are university members who produce digital content. By playing the game, an awareness of the problems should be created and possibilities to reduce digital barriers should be manifested. Digital accessibility needs to be implemented repeatedly to remain in memory and to maintain a learning anchorage. Ideally, the special requirements of impaired persons should be considered from the beginning when, e.g., designing courses, building plans or purchasing systems, so that no barriers do not occur at all. Using a game setting for that process can be the key to learning motivation. In the game, Lola is a first semester student to convey the feeling of being a freshwoman, including all its challenges, but also the support you expect as a student. This brings a narrative advantage. The game design follows the strategies of Dörner et. al ("Serious Games: Foundations, Concepts and Practice") [1]. Within the frame story, there is a clear campus map and five integrated mini-games. Each mini-game looks at a different barrier faced by people with a visual impairment and has a different learning objective: During the "Lecture" game the players need to practice buy-sell decisions signaled by red and green arrows during a stock market simulation. "Online seminar" shows problems in video conferences that the player has to remove by fighting symbolic opponents. "Examinations Office" deals with inaccessible PDFs, which the player has to revise with different tools. "Validator" shows the problem that many machines (e.g., library systems, computer stations or printer) of universities are not barrier-free. The field of view during the game is limited by black borders and pixilation. This mini-game is deliberately difficult to simulate an everyday hurdle of a visually impaired person. "Cafeteria" illustrates the hurdle of time-bound content using the menus in the canteen, involving three different meals displayed, only one is without allergens. Based on the information on the slideshow the correct dishes have to be chosen. In the Serious Game "Lola's first semester", knowledge is conveyed in a

---

[1] Commission Delegated Regulation (EU) 2016/2021 for websites: http://data.europa.eu/eli/reg_del/2016/2021/oj.

[2] Serious Game: https://lolaserstessemester.sd.uni-frankfurt.de/ (In German).

playful way with tasks and further related information. The game concept is designed in a way that can be easily transferred to other types of impairments such as depression, hearing impairments or physical-chronic and psychological-physical impairments. The implementation was carried out with the aim of offering a low-threshold entry so that the players can quickly find their way in and use the game intuitively. The insights gained through the evaluation phase of the Design Thinking process will be incorporated in the revision of the story, the mini-games and the characters. In the first development cycle of the Serious Game, the focus was on the overall game, the acceptance and the experience of visual impairments. The next development cycle will focus even more on User Experience. To make profound and generally valid statements about user behaviour in the further research process, methods from the field of learning analytics can be used. This data can both support the research process and influence the players' gaming behaviour through feedback to users (Fig. 1).

2 Technical Implementation and the Design Thinking Process

The development of the Serious Game "Lola's first semester" followed the process of Design Thinking [2]. The first two phases of empathizing and defining were conducted using data gathered through an online survey in 2019[3]. The survey's aim was to collect data on the current situation of digital accessibility in higher education. Using said data, we were able to pinpoint specific barriers and define challenges. During the phase of ideation, we further generated ideas in weekly team meetups and a Hessian networking meeting. Following, a prototype was implemented and afterwards tested. Using the outcome of the evaluation, we are now in the phase of (re-)defining. We started by scouting for a software, which is easy and free to use. By looking into authoring systems at first, we soon discovered their restrictive nature of pre-implemented features, which would limit the scope of the game [3]. After reviewing the advantages and disadvantages for the technical implementation of various game engines, the decision fell on the open source Godot Engine V.3.2.2 because of its widely supported HTML5 exporting capabilities. The dialogues between Lola and her fellow students were implemented with a combination of the Dialogic[4] add-on, Excel, JSON and Python. The development of the individual characters was done in-house, with the aim of representing a great diversity. Moreover, Audio, which also plays an important role for a better game experience, was taken into account. The whole game is designed to be played only with a mouse accompanied by a narrative conveyed via readable dialogues and distinctive set of characters.

3 Evaluation of the Game and the Integrated Mini-games

After completing the first development cycle, an online survey was conducted. On the one hand, the aim was to evaluate the overall game and the five mini-games in the context of game experience. On the other hand, the goal was to obtain feedback on the

---

[3] http://innobar.studiumdigitale.uni-frankfurt.de/Umfrageergebnisse/Digitale_Barrierefrei heit_an_hessischen_Hochschulen.pdf (in German).

[4] Dialogic: https://github.com/coppolaemilio/dialogic.

concept as well as the current implementation. The feedback results should also provide an answer to the research questions of whether the format of a Serious Game is suitable for creating awareness for the given topic. The Game Experience Questionnaire (GEQ) [4] of the FUGA project (The Fun of Gaming) [5] was used as an instrument and was integrated at the end of the game. The GEQ is characterized by reliability, validity and sensitivity, which are crucial for good measurement. A total of 36 people (13 male, 23 female, 0 diverse) participated in the study with following age groups: 17% under 25, 54% between 25–34, 26% between 35–44, none between 45–54 and 3% above 55. Of the total 36 participants, 25 described themselves as gamers and 11 as non-gamers. There were participants from various lines of work such as educators, tutors, students as well as people working in administration from a network of 11 different universities. Closed questions in the form of a 5-point Likert scale (strongly disagree to strongly agree) were asked in the GEQ. Those statements were assigned to the seven dimensions of Competence, Immersion, Flow, Tension, Challenge, Positive and Negative Effects [3]. The GEQ is followed by an open question at the end of the questionnaire with the possibility to express additional wishes, ideas and criticism. The evaluation followed the Mayring's procedure [6]. The most frequently mentioned statements (n = 7) were that the challenge is well communicated, that the game draws attention to existing challenges and that it is a good game (n = 6). Combined with the result of the best-rated surveyed statements (mean value of over 3 (>=)), the format of the Serious Game appears to be suitable for raising awareness for the topic of accessibility. Participants of various workshops and working groups also confirmed the sensitising effect when playing the game. Negative effects, such as "It put me in a bad mood" and "I felt angry", were hardly mentioned. Both items were rather disagreed with (MW = 1.9). Otherwise, the many pieces of content-related and technical feedback on the game can be incorporated in the next development cycle.

4   Improvements and Further Development

An online survey during the testing phase of the Design Thinking process gave an insight on how the players felt about each aspect of the game. This direct feedback is helpful in improving the game in a phase of (re)defining. Besides overhauling the technical side, another core focus will be to tackle the narrative side. One of the key elements during the development process was to make sure of the technical availability of the game regardless of the available hardware. Although the choice to put the game on the server takes away the steps of downloading a setup file and installation, it still caches (aka downloads) the game first when someone visits the website. Almost every reported technical issue can be traced back to users having slow internet connections and/or hardware with low specifications. The Pixel Streaming technology provided by Unreal Engine (UE4) resolves that problem by making it streamable via server. Playing the game will be like streaming a YouTube video from the user perspective but with the added benefit of controlling the interactive content shown. Moreover, making the game available via a cloud service with an added graphics card can lower the setup cost and time. The results from the GEQ show that the players were distracted and only moderately concentrated. They were not immersed enough to lose track of time or connection to the outside world. Despite having a positive experience, they still felt moderately bored by the game. An introductory onboarding plan could prepare them for the challenging parts. To increase the pressure and challenge, the players need to get in the flow by challenges that are neither too easy nor too hard [7]. By creating metrics, we can easily specify the distracting issues and tackle them. Known distractions are inconsistencies like different designs for the same character. The controls have to be balanced through fine-tuning because of the large impact they have on the game feel [8]. An iterative loop consisting of observation, idea-generation, prototyping and testing can help us embrace the failures [9]. Furthermore, a built-in game analytics functionality could give us insights about player behaviour and help us eliminate more issues. A better User Experience can be achieved by a well-structured head-up display (HUD) and can help players to constantly know which buttons to press when a certain action needs to be done. By using Design Thinking, the capabilities of the audience can be considered and the levels and gameplay can be designed accordingly. Combined with the Gestalt principles in UX [10], the players are faced with an easily comprehensible environment, making the game more accessible. Although the concept was well received, the "Examinations Office" mini-game still faced some criticism regarding gameplay and the presentation of the tutorial. Demanding the players to read a so-perceived overload of instructions before playing the game required more attentional resources. Therefore, more distraction will have a disruptive effect leading to irritation [11]. A good narrative design will bind together the technical and gameplay improvements which will further enhance the User Experience. As the evaluation shows moderately happy players, we want to continue with the structure of our game. A more coherent storyline with an emotional attachment could evoke more empathy. This kind of involvement can create a platform for inducing implicit learning, which, according to some researchers, is more robust than explicit learning mainly because it seems to last longer [12]. Due to its uncomplicated licensing structure, using an industry standard tool like UE4 opens many possibilities. Implementing free to use and highly detailed 3D models and characters can add a modern look to the game in which the players would be embodying and emotionally connecting with the characters. All these processes combined should help to create a lived-in world designed for intrinsic as well extrinsic learning. We started with a focus on visual impairments, but regarding future versions of the game, other impairments are also taken into account. According to the best2 survey[5], studying is made more difficult due to physical or health impairments for 11% of German students. This group includes students with mobility, hearing and speech impairments; mental illnesses; chronic illnesses; dyslexia and other partial performance disorders; autism and AD(H)S. Furthermore, according to the (US) National Center for education statistics, 12% postbaccalaureate students or 19% undergraduate students reported to have a disability.[6] Whether individual impairments, illnesses or other challenges are suitable for a Serious Game like "Lola's first semester" is part of our future research.

---

[5] best2: 21st Social Survey of the German Student Union (DSW), 2016: https://www.studenten werke.de/de/content/studieren-mit-behinderung-%E2%80%93-geh%C3%B6re-ich-dazu.

[6] National Center for education statistics: https://nces.ed.gov/fastfacts/display.asp?id=60 16.05.2021.

5 Conclusion and Future Work

Using Serious Games has helped strengthen the process of inclusion and sensitization. Our lessons learned will be used to construct the next iteration of the game with an expanded target group including the older generation, improved User Experience and a better narrative design whilst upholding the current game structure. A cloud-based deployment could benefit eliminating technical issues and barriers, which will help us elevate our intended goals. A self-evident choice would be to lay the focus on hearing impairments, as the mini-game "Online Seminar" already deals with linked barriers. Another option is to shift the focus on depression, as it is the most common impairment. We have the vision that the concept and implementation of the game could easily be transferred to other contexts at university like orientation events or tutor training. A modular framework and a predefined workflow are required for this, so that elements can be exchanged. A standardized workflow with templates for creating the story and a selection of avatars will help teachers to create a similar Serious Game. The conceptual templates and pre-implemented set of visual elements (e.g., avatars) will be cost and time saving. Furthermore, the described structure will open the game concept of "Lola's first semester" to a wide group of stakeholders. Though this is an ambitious goal, it holds the potential to shift teaching methods at universities into a more gamified learning environment. To underline the need of gamification in teaching and its advantages, future work will deal with the benefit of Serious Games in education.

References

1. Dörner, R., et al.: Serious Games – Foundations, Concepts and Practice. Springer, Cham (2016). https://doi.org/10.1007/978-3-319-40612-1
2. Wolniak, R.: The design thinking method and its stages. Systemy Wspomagania w Inzynierii Produkcji **6**(6), 247–255 (2017)
3. Rustemeier, L., et al.: Spielerische Sensibilisierung durch Erfahrbarkeit von Beeinträchtigungen: Das Serious Game "Lolas erstes Semester". In: Zender, R., Ifenthaler, D., Leonhardt, T., Schumacher, C. (ed.) DELFI 2021 – Die 19, Fachtagung Bildungstechnologien der Gesellschaft für Informatik e.V.. Bonn: Gesellschaft für Informatik e.V. (2021). (in press)
4. IJsselsteijn, W.A., de Kort, Y.A.W., Poels, K.: The Game Experience Questionnaire, pp. 1–47. Technische Universität Eindhoven, Eindhoven (2013)
5. Nacke, L.E.: The fun of gaming. Measuring the human experience of game enjoyment. In: Proceedings of Quo Vadis 2007, Aruba Studios (2007)
6. Mayring, P.: Qualitative inhaltsanalyse. In: Flick, U., et al. (ed.): Handbuch Qualitative Forschung. Grundlagen, Konzepte, Methoden und Anwendungen, pp. 209–213. Beltz - Psychologie Verl. Union, München (1991). ISBN: 3-621-27105-8
7. Chen, J.: Flow in games (and everything else). Commun. ACM **50**, 31–34 (2007). https://doi.org/10.1145/1232743.1232769
8. Swink, S.: Game Feel: A Game Designer's Guide to Virtual Sensation. Morgan Kaufmann, Burlington (2008).ISBN: 978-0-123-74328-2
9. Norman, D.A.: The Design of Everyday Things. Revised and Expanded Edition. Basic Books, New York (2013).ISBN: 978-0-465-05065-9

10. Reed, W.A.: Five UX Principles for Designing Better Products (2014)
11. Lavie, N.: Distracted and confused? Selective attention under load. Trends Cogn. Sci. **9**, 75–82 (2005). https://doi.org/10.1016/j.tics.2004.12.004
12. Reber, A.S.: Implicit learning and tacit knowledge. J. Exp. Psychol. Gen. **118**, 219–235 (1989). https://doi.org/10.1037/0096-3445.118.3.219

A Review of Indie Games for Serious Mental Health Game Design

Myfanwy King[✉], Tim Marsh, and Zeynep Akcay

Griffith Film School, Griffith University, Brisbane, Australia
myfanwy.king@griffithuni.edu.au, {t.marsh,
z.akcay}@griffith.edu.au

Abstract. Mental health disorders present a global challenge being the largest contributor to non-fatal burden of disease. In fact, those who are experiencing symptoms of mental illness often wait ten years before seeking help. This is frequently due to help-seeking barriers such as stigma and cost. One way to combat help-seeking barriers is through increasing the mental health literacy of the public. This has been achieved successfully through digital delivery of mental health information and services, including serious games. Early research suggests that serious games are an effective tool for improving mental health literacy. However, factors such as poor-quality game design and research studies mean that developers face challenges when designing, developing, and analyzing serious games. To address these challenges this paper will provide an analysis of indie games that feature topics of mental health, trauma, and grief. Indie games share similarities to research environments, often being created by small teams on a limited budget. Even with these limitations they can tell impactful and emotional stories, making them a valuable source of inspiration for developers of serious mental health games.

Keywords: Serious games · Mental health · Mental health literacy · Indie games · Independent games

1 Introduction

Mental health disorders are the greatest contributors to non-fatal burden of disease (18.3% as of 2016) and account for eight million deaths per year [1–3]. Mental illness symptoms can affect a person's mental, physical, and social wellbeing and reduce their ability to manage everyday life, for example their ability to attend work or school, go on social outings or care for themselves [3]. Despite the personal cost of these symptoms, it can take up to ten years for a person to seek treatment for a mental illness leading to more severe illness at presentation [4]. This is often due to treatment barriers such as stigma or cost, where stigma is the main reason reported for not seeking help [5–11]. Therefore, reducing stigma and improving the treatment, identification and management of mental health disorders is an imperative global challenge that relies on governments and communities working together.

© Springer Nature Switzerland AG 2021
B. Fletcher et al. (Eds.): JCSG 2021, LNCS 12945, pp. 138–152, 2021.
https://doi.org/10.1007/978-3-030-88272-3_11

One way to increase awareness in communities is through digital interventions that aim to increase mental health literacy (MHL). MHL, first coined by Jorm et al., is a term derived from health literacy and refers to the knowledge of mental health, wellbeing, symptoms, treatment, care, and services [9, 12, 13]. This includes initiatives that reduce stigma and prejudice toward mental health disorders [9, 12, 13]. Digital initiatives such as Beyond Blue aim to do this by providing resources and support to communities [14]. The Beyond Blue initiative has been credited by Jorm, Christensen and Griffiths in helping to increase the publics MHL in Australia [12]. Other interventions aim at augmenting treatment or improving wellbeing. For example, moodgym, an online cognitive behavioral therapy-based course, has been shown to be effective in improving outcomes for those with early symptoms of mental illness when compared to patients on a waitlist [15, 16]. Suggesting that digital interventions are a promising direction for improving MHL. Additionally, there are many mobile application interventions including mood trackers, mindfulness, and meditation applications [17]. Like other digital interventions, serious games present another promising avenue for the delivery of mental health literacy content.

This paper will provide a brief overview of serious games for mental health. Additionally, it will provide an analysis of indie games that explore stories of mental health and mental illness. Through this analysis, suggestions will be provided on ways indie games can inform serious games design. This paper is structured as follows. Section 2 will outline serious game's role in mental health treatment and education. Section 3 explores indie games that provide an insight into the thoughts associated with mental illness and offer a creative look into the design of serious games for mental health. Section 4 will provide a discussion and conclusion to the topics covered in this paper.

2   A Brief Overview of Serious Games for Mental Health

Serious games have been defined by Michael and Chen as games that primarily focus on education, without principally being entertaining [18]. However, they are now further defined to exist on a continuum of gameplay mechanics, narrative, and styles – widening the scope for what is classified as a serious game [19]. Boyle et al. finding articles covering a broad field of topics such as science, health, and business, across several game genres (e.g., simulation and role-playing) in their serious game meta-analysis [20]. Additionally, they found that the benefits of serious game can include but are not limited to behavior change, real world skills development and knowledge acquisition [20]. In fact, both Boyle et al. and Qian and Clark suggest that serious games are ideal for teaching 21st century skills such as communication, problem solving and scientific reasoning [20, 21].

Indeed, MHL should be considered a 21st century skill and is therefore an appropriate field for development of serious games. However, there are challenges in the development of both digital interventions and serious games that utilize mental health literacy. As stated earlier, moodgym is targeted to those who have early signs of mental illness, because it was less effective to those with more severe symptoms of mental illness [15, 16, 22]. Additionally, while there are many mobile applications for mental health, most mobile applications lack research-based examination, may not be backed by current evidence and/or may present damaging information [17]. Moreover, these types of interventions have challenges such as having high attrition and dose dependence; therefore, they are not considered suitable for primary treatment [15, 23–25]. Serious games present a similar challenge to developers in the area of mental health literacy.

Serious games for mental health are a promising, yet emerging field of research. Using them for improving mental health literacy, more specifically for treatment, management, and education, are effective [26, 27]. One example of a serious game for improving mental health literacy in adolescents is SPARX [28]. SPARX is a game and e-health therapy developed for youth that is currently only available in New Zealand [28]. It is divided into several levels, each focused-on learning different skills (e.g., coping with emotions and problems) [29]. SPARX has been shown to significantly improve depression, anxiety, and quality of life with results persisting through to a three-month time point [29]. Results from this study are promising and show the potential of a serious game directed towards youth mental health. However, another study using a variant of SPARX (SPARX-R) that focused on depression, found that there were no significant changes in mental wellbeing or coping [30]. This result was likely affected by high dropout rates and small sample size but touches on a problem with targeting digital interventions to those with mental illness [30].

Targeting young people and teaching them resilience through video games is a natural fit as video games make up a large part of modern culture due to their wide availability over different technologies. However, all the digital initiatives discussed this far fail to address a larger concern and that is offering help and support to those with severe mental illness. In a review on treatment of those experiencing severe mental illness (for example, schizophrenia and psychosis) Fitzgerald and Ratcliffe found that the games were effective and generally accepted by players [26]. However, they also found that factors such as poor design, lack of challenge, lack of contextualization and poor narrative led to users losing motivation and interest in playing the games [26]. In addition, a person experiencing a mental illness, especially a severe one, may have an impaired ability to function or ask for help [26, 31].

Serious games are an emerging field and there are limited examples of research-based games for mental health. In their review, Fitzgerald and Ratcliffe found that research games, existing games and card games were being used in research studies, which is mirrored in an earlier review by Fleming et al. [26, 27]. Interestingly Fitzgerald and Ratcliffe noted that better designed games were more interesting to players, stating that "[h]aving a choice and variety of options, appropriate levels of challenge, easy-to-follow instructions, and familiar, intuitive control devices corresponded to player enjoyment, confidence that they can play the game, and successful delivery of intervention outcomes" [26]. To address the challenge of quality and design in serious games it is important to draw on previous examples. One avenue of investigation for serious games about mental illness are indie games.

3   Indie Games

Video games, by their nature, are a broad and varied field and can be hard to define and indie games are no exception to this [32]. Indie or independent games were originally defined as games that were made on low budgets by small teams who published outside more mainstream channels used by larger companies [32, 33]. As such, for this paper the term indie will refer to games made by one person or small teams that have a limited budget including those that were funded by platforms like Kickstarter. They differ from Triple-A games which are produced by larger companies with larger budgets.

Triple-A games, despite the increase in available platforms for indie games, are an industry standard offering high end aesthetics, grand heroic stories and stunning visuals to players. They are made over many years, have huge budgets, and rely on large teams of people to produce them. However, many of these games utilize formulaic "cookie cutter" gameplay and rely heavily on heroic adventures rather then creating deep and meaningful stories. Indie games on the other hand, tend to be made by one person or smaller teams and are limited by budget. However, they are praised for their innovation, creativity, deep personal stories, authored experiences, and appealing nature. Of course, there are exceptions to these rules, for example *The Last of Us* is a Triple-A game that focuses on story driven gameplay [34]. An indie game example is *Hellblade: Senua's Sacrifice,* which tells a deep story about a character with psychosis using detailed graphics and gameplay that could be found in a Triple-A title [35].

3.1 Indie Games and Mental Illness

Indie games may seem to be more restrictive than larger Triple-A games, but they have a freedom to explore topics that bigger game companies might avoid. These stories can include characters who have a mental illness and/or are LGTBQ+. For example, *Coming Out Simulator* is based on the personal experiences of the developer coming out as gay [36]. This freedom means there are more examples of indie games that explore topics of mental health, mental illness, and trauma. These stories offering a rich narrative world that takes a deeper look at the impact mental illness and trauma can have on those who either experience mental illness or those around them. There are a few exceptions to this, but many popular Triple-A games use trauma as a catalyst for heroic endeavors. For example, *The Last of Us* explores an emotional story of loss and trauma, while games like *Assassins Creed Origin* focus on the hero's journey, where trauma is a catalyst for a heroic adventure rather then the focus of the game [34, 37].

Meaning indie games analyzed in this paper provide insight into the creation of short impactful games that have been created by smaller teams on a limited budget. Drawing on factors such as visual style, storytelling, and gameplay of indie games can help to improve the quality and longevity of serious games. Additionally, these games often provide an example of both positive and negative representation of mental illness that can be used to inform character design. Of course, developers are not limited to video games, additional sources can be found in film, books, and comics. However, the focus of this review is to highlight indie games, which may be overlooked, for use as examples when developing serious mental health games. An overview of these games can be seen in Table 1.

Florence. Florence is a touching and beautifully executed game that explores the beginning and end of a romantic relationship [38]. Regarding mental health, it addresses the feelings of grief and sadness associated with the loss of a relationship and unfulfillment of life goals. Grief itself is not a mental illness as it is a normal response to loss; however, it can affect a person's mental health and wellbeing [14]. Florence is a predominantly visual game that uses minimalistic design and straightforward mechanics coupled with both graphic and visual metaphor to tell the games story. For example, as the relationship grows communication is shown visually through a speech bubble puzzle [38]. The puzzle becoming less complicated over time, as the couple gets to know each other. This is also used when the two have an argument, the puzzle pieces changing color and shape. There are many examples of the use of visual intrigue and clever design dotted throughout Florence. A minimalist design with thoughtful mechanics can help a designer explore how to communicate story visually and mechanically, without the need for a long narrative.

Coming Out Simulator. Coming Out Simulator tells the story of a young man who struggles with coming out as gay to his parents [36]. It also explores the fear, loss and loneliness associated with both hiding and coming out as gay and finally, coming to accept it. A short game, with a minimalist design, it proves that short games and stories can have an emotional impact. Providing both a visual style that is appealing yet minimalist and stories told in short sentences. The players choices are limited, leading to changes in dialogue but not outcome. This can provide inspiration in how to tell small impactful stories that could be used in serious games design, especially in a research setting where time and funds may be limited.

Depression Quest. Depression Quest is surrounded by controversy; however, the focus here will not be on these problems, but on the game itself [39]. Depression Quest is an interactive fiction with minimal design. It explores a twenty something characters life as the symptoms of depression begin to manifest and become worse. Choices can lead to different outcomes, for example getting treatment or taking medication can improve choices, while avoiding treatment and worsening symptoms of depression can cause options to be crossed out. Depression Quest provides insight into the field of narrative design and development for both characters and stories. Additionally, it shows how mechanics can help communicate ideas in story (i.e., crossing out of options when symptoms get worse).

That Dragon Cancer. That Dragon Cancer provides a heart wrenching insight into one family's emotional journey through diagnosis and treatment of their son's cancer and the inescapable death of their son [40]. The game uses metaphors, perspective, and personal discussions to explore the characters feelings during each stage of their child's treatment. They also explore the religious beliefs and how they affect each other's views on what their family is going through. For example, while the mother holds fast that god will save her child, the father is left feeling overwhelmed and alone knowing that their child is going to die. The sense of loneliness and separation of the two characters as they deal with grief and acceptance in their own way is palpable. That Dragon Cancer uses a mixture of metaphor, atmosphere, and personal recollection to tell an emotional story. It highlights the importance of personal stories in the development of character driven serious games.

Keep in Mind: Remastered. Keep in Mind: Remastered is a short game that uses metaphor to explore mental illness and substance use disorder [41]. Players enter an alternate dream world where they need to walk around and speak to monsters, each a metaphorical representation of the symptoms, thoughts and feelings associated with mental illness. For example, one monster represents his past guilt at the loss of a loved one, while another represents his struggle with alcoholism. The use of the monster metaphor is a well-known way a person describes their mental illness, where the experiencer sees the mental illness as a shadow, cloud, or a black dog. In the end Keep in Mind: Remastered is about the acceptance and desire to change and face one's inner demons. It provides designers with examples of how metaphor can be used to communicate not only the symptoms of mental illness, but also the inner fears, thoughts, and feelings of a person's experience.

Actual Sunlight. Actual Sunlight is a somewhat brutal look at mental illness that explores some of the symptoms associated with depression and suicidal ideation [42, 43]. The main character works in a thankless job, has lost pleasure in life and is addicted to video games [42]. You can feel the characters pain, explore his reasoning for suicide and his experience with the symptoms of mental illness. Most confronting is when he decides to act on thoughts of suicide. This is not shown directly but through the metaphorical use of the suns light to express release. This game provides a good example of exploring the thoughts, feelings, and symptoms of someone experiencing a mental illness, including the more challenging thoughts of suicide.

Depression. Depression is a short but clever game developed by Martínez and can be found on the indie game hosting site, itch.io [44]. The developer interviewed participants and asked them to define their experience with depression and then expressed these definitions through game mechanics [44, 45]. The game mechanics are straightforward, get your character (a white square) to a goal using the keyboard. Each of the eleven chapters addresses some aspect of how depression feels. For example, scene two is titled "Sometimes things are a bit more difficult… like you feel … slower" and when the player moves the square it begins to get slower and slower until it crawls to the goal [44, 45]. The act of moving the square provides a mechanical description of the symptom of being slowed down by depression. This game strips away complex visuals, and narrative, in favor of telling a story through mechanics.

3.2 Indie Games, Stigma and Tropes

There are many indie games that explore personal or fictional stories that could be considered serious games. These games innovative designs, visual storytelling, and insightful narratives merit further analysis to learn ways to create impactful and emotional serious games that have longevity. They also provide a portrait of different characters experiences with mental illness to draw from. However, it is essential to be able to recognize inaccurate information and stigma in indie games that serve to misinform the player.

Fran Bow. Fran Bow is a dark tale that explores a child's experience of trauma [46]. The game begins in a mental institution where Fran Bow is being stalked by a shadowy monster and must escape to find her cat Mr. Midnight. Depicting mental institutions is a common and often problematic trope seen in the horror genre that does not reflect modern mental health care practices [46, 47]. Fran Bow also depicts common stereotypes of mental illness where treatment is seen as dangerous, the doctors and staff are viewed as incompetent, and children are being depicted as lobotomized and experimented on [46–48]. While some of the depictions in this game are problematic it must be taken in the context of the game developers lived experiences.

The developer Figueroa using game development as a cathartic experience, stating in an interview "the game itself is a kind of screaming out what I been experienced through my childhood and teenager years. From childhood I have being experiencing traumatic events, from being witness to family violence to unfair personal treatment outside home. And as a teenager being sentenced to be part of a religious sect, being kind of a guinea pig for research with all medicine's doctors gave me to try to cure the mental illness that life was giving me" [49]. In this light, the metaphors of monsters, being trapped in an institution, trying to escape one's past and losing family are brought into context. Fran Bow reminds us firstly that understanding the developers' views can help frame the context of stigmatized depictions. Secondly, having knowledge of these stigmatized depictions allows us to recognize them and know they are not the norm.

The Suicide of Rachel Foster. The Suicide of Rachel Foster is a mystery horror game that follows Nicole as she returns to her parent's hotel years after the suicide of Rachel [50]. The start of the mystery is quite interesting and builds a creepy atmosphere as you walk around the hotel learning about the main characters and the tragedy that unfolded. As Nicole walks around, she discusses the story to an emergency services worker and Rachels brother, Irving. This game deals with several sensitive topics poorly (e.g., Nicole's father having a relationship with Rachel), but the focus here will be on its use of suicide.

Suicide is used as a plot point several times in game, the most confronting of these occurs when the player finds themselves in a car as it fills with exhaust [50]. The player has the choice to stay in the car and die or remain at the hotel forever. Placing the player directly in the role of someone who is acting on thoughts of suicide, with no viable alternative or chance to get help. Several non-research game reviews cover the ending of the game and its use of suicide as a plot point [51–53]. The game does well to build atmosphere; however, its use of suicide as a plot device for shock value detracts from a game that had the potential to tell an emotional story. One that explores the emotional experience of those who have a shared trauma.

Table 1. An overview of indie games that explore mental health topics including their design, core mechanics, advantages, and limitations.

Title	**Florence** [38]
Overview	Tells the story of the beginning and end of a relationship. Showing both the happiness of new love, breaking down of a relationship and the grief that comes at the end of it. Additionally, it shows the personal growth that can come out of grief and loss
Design	A minimalist design with a beautiful art style consisting of muted tones and bright colors highlighted by lines. Backgrounds tend to be sparsely designed when the focus is on the character but detailed when establishing environment
Mechanics	Initially designed for mobile, the game uses straightforward swipe or mouse gestures to browse through the comic panels and complete puzzles
Advantages	• Well-designed gameplay and visuals • Communicates story through gameplay without dialogue • Explores grief, overcoming it and moving on • Good use of emotional gameplay
Limitations	• No text or dialogue used for communication
Title	**Coming Out Simulator** [36]
Overview	Tells the story of a young man's experiences with hiding and coming out as gay and its effect it has on his personal relationships. The ending of the game is more positive, with the character coming to accept who he is and finding a community to help him overcome these challenges
Design	The visual design uses two or three tone colors with line art and faceless characters. Dialogue is shown in colored text boxes that are overlayed above the background and characters. Choices are given at the bottom of the screen in a small grey area that blends will with the other visuals
Mechanics	Players read dialogue through text boxes and make choices by clicking on text below
Advantages	• Straight-forward design • Interesting use of the graphical user interface (GUI) • Tells short but emotional story • Positive and personal representation of LGBTQ+ characters
Limitations	• Characters have no faces, therefore do not show emotions visually
Title	**Depression Quest** [39]
Overview	*Depression Quest* follows the story of a young person as they develop the signs and symptoms of depression. It shows how symptoms of depression can affect everyday life
Design	*Depression Quest* was made using Twine and therefore consist of text, a basic textured grey background, and hyperlinked choices. The side bar contains a title and some information about the game. Above the text is a single image reflecting actions or places in the story. Below the main text and choices is a tracking system consisting of text on top of grey boxes with an animated background

(*continued*)

Table 1. (*continued*)

Mechanics	*Depression Quest* uses interactive fiction mechanics where the player can make choices that affect story and characters, with multiple possible endings reached based on these choices. A tracking system down the bottom of the page shows the level of depression and if the character is receiving treatment. The tracking system is linked to choices, with some being crossed out dependent on the level of symptoms and current treatment
Advantages	• Story told from main characters perspective • Clearly shows how symptoms can affect everyday decisions • Inspired by personal experiences with mental illness • Characters and partners gender are open to players interpretation
Limitations	• Large amount of text to read, players might lose interest • There are mixed reviews despite the fact the game has won awards • Subjectively, not as emotional as other games on this list
Title	**That Dragon Cancer** [40]
Overview	*That Dragon Cancer* follows a family's journey through the diagnosis of cancer, treatment, and death of their young son, Joel. Exploring the thoughts and feelings of Joel's parents and how they each coped with learning that their son was going to die
Design	The design uses a mixture of bright colors and low poly models for most scenes. Dark pulsating tumorous cells are dotted throughout the game and represent Joel's cancer. Additionally, the game uses a variety of colors and metaphors to explore very emotional themes (e.g., drowning under water when feeling alone and overwhelmed). Each chapter of the game plays like a living story book telling different parts of the overall journey
Mechanics	*That Dragon Cancer* is primarily a walking simulator where you explore the world through movement and interaction. There are several points in the game where mechanics are changed to create unique moments within the story. For instance, there is an arcade style game where you need to defeat a dragon
Advantages	• Great example of emotional story telling • Communicates deep emotions and create atmosphere for players • Explores concepts of loss and grief • Might help players who are going through the same experience
Limitations	• Emotional content can be overwhelming • May not be suitable if players have recently experienced loss
Title	**Keep in Mind: Remastered** [41]
Overview	The players follow Jonas into a nightmare world where he encounters representations of his mental illness, fears, and grief. He must visit each one and come to terms with them before he can escape
Design	Colors are a mixture of black, red, and white in the dream world, except for Jonas who is in color. It uses a sparse pixel aesthetic, with real-world scenes being more detailed than those in the dream world
Mechanics	The game is a 2D walking simulator that uses top-down mechanics. The player controls the characters direction and can interact with NPC's

(*continued*)

Table 1. (*continued*)

Advantages	• Metaphorical look at anxiety, grief, and substance use disorder • Uses the monster metaphor to explore symptoms of mental illness • Uses sound to enhance some visual metaphors
Limitations	• Easy to get lost trying to find characters in the game • Subjectively, not as emotionally impactful as some of the other games explored
Title	**Actual Sunlight** [42]
Overview	Actual Sunlight follows Evan Winters, a thirty something year old man, who is experiencing symptoms of depression and game addiction. Players explore his everyday life, struggle with thoughts of suicide and the reasons why he decides to act on those thoughts
Design	*Actual Sunlight* was built in RPG Maker. It has a pixel aesthetic, interspersed with hand drawn images of story moments. It does not use color or metaphor in the same way the other games do, except for the metaphor of sunlight and release to represent suicide
Mechanics	Players discover story elements through interaction with characters and objects. The player moves the character around from a top-down perspective. This game is story driven and is like other interactive fiction/walking simulators
Advantages	• Tells a story about the thoughts and feelings associated with suicide • Tackles a challenging subject well
Limitations	• Best avoided by those who may be experiencing thoughts of suicide or struggling with experiences of mental illness • No attempt made to help the character or find solutions
Title	**Depression** [44, 45]
Overview	Depression is a straightforward game that tells stories of depression through short text statements and mechanics. The creator interviewed people with depression and translated those into game mechanics
Design	The game is set on a dark textured background and consists of small white squares for the main character and as obstacles
Mechanics	The player controls a white square with the keyboard and the aim is to move the square toward a goal. Each level creates different obstacles for the player that represent symptoms or feelings of depression mechanically
Advantages	• Shows how mechanics can be used to explore symptoms of mental illness
Limitations	N/A
Title	**Fran Bow** [46]
Overview	*Fran Bow* is an adventure game that follows a young girl as she escapes a mental institution to search for her cat Mr. Midnight. The game uses horror elements to explore mental illness, grief, and past trauma
Design	The game design is a mix of cute 2D characters with dark horror elements inspired by such stories as Alice in Wonderland. It is a very graphic game depicting for example, dead animals, blood, gore, and murder. Juxtaposing innocent and sweet with death and gore to explore the mind of a child who is experiencing symptoms of psychosis

(*continued*)

Table 1. (*continued*)

Mechanics	Uses adventure game mechanics with the players controlling the character by clicking the mouse on screen. Objects can be interacted with and can be combined in the inventory to solve puzzles. Additionally, the player can interact with different NPCs to have conversations and solve puzzles. The world is divided between reality and a dark dimension that is accessed when Fran takes a pill called Duotine
Advantages	• A metaphorical exploration of trauma and mental illness • Uses tropes and stigma to communicate personal experiences • Explores trauma from the perspective of a child
Limitations	• Traumatic experiences viewed through the eyes of a child • May be challenging to those who have experienced trauma • Contains some use of tropes and stigmatized views of mental illness
Title	**The Suicide of Rachel Foster** [50]
Overview	After the death of her father, the player (Nicole) returns to the family's hotel and uncovers the mystery surrounding the death of Rachel Foster
Design	The design of the game is three dimensional and played from the characters perspective. The hotel environment is well designed, and the game builds a haunting atmosphere through visual, audio and story
Mechanics	The game is a walking simulator, where the player can move around the hotel and interact with objects. The story is told through objects and by talking to Irving (NPC) on the phone, which provides most of the dialogue
Advantages	• Good build-up of atmosphere and mystery at the start of the game
Limitations	• May be challenging to those who have experienced trauma/suicidal ideation • Deals poorly with sensitive topics • Player can participate in suicide • Suicide and past trauma used as plot point and for shock value

4   Conclusion

There are many challenges when developing serious games, including, limited funding, small teams, a need for broad expertise and limited examples for development of both games and studies. These challenges lead to issues of quality in both study and game design. Serious mental health games that target those with mental illness directly face additional challenges. Those with a mental health disorder often have symptoms that can affect their ability to engage with content. This means developing mental health serious games present unique challenges to developers, who must decide how to best address their intended audience.

Currently, researchers are using both commercial games and purpose-built research games to target those experiencing mental illness. Each of these methods have shown promise; however, there are advantages and limitations to both approaches. Research games have the advantage of being backed by a broad range of knowledge and expertise and are often examined to determine their effectiveness. Nevertheless, they are limited by poor quality research studies and low-quality game design. On the other hand, commercial games have the advantage of being more engaging due to their higher quality design and focus on entertainment. However, this focus on entertainment means that the serious objectives identified by researchers may not reach the intended audience.

To address the question of quality in serious games design one source of inspiration are indie games. Indie games that explore both lived experiences with mental illness and emotional stories of grief, trauma and loss provide a unique perspective into the portrayal of complex and relatable characters. Many of these games contain serious content even though they have been created outside of a research context. The examples above are by no means perfect in their portrayals of mental illness; however, their stories can help to inform designers on the creation of characters who are experiencing mental illness that are realistic, informed, humanized, and relatable.

Stigma often demonizes those with mental illness, portraying them as violent, crazy, or insane individuals. To counter these views as developers, creating characters that are well developed, who could be our friends or relatives and who have everyday lives can help to humanize those with mental illness. This extends not only to game development but also to our own analysis of videogames, where a clear understanding of stigma and tropes can help contextualize portrayals. Additionally, an understanding of the symptoms of mental illness and the feelings and thoughts associated with it can aid in accurate and sensitive character portrayals. Although minimizing stigmatized portrayals of mental illness is ideal there are instances where stigma may be appropriate.

When a game explores a creator's personal experiences, what may seem to be a problematic portrayal, could help to give a voice to someone who has experienced mental illness or trauma. These stigmatized views may serve to communicate the experiences of the creator. Additionally, providing players a chance to assess a stigmatized view and challenge their own thoughts could provide an educational moment. Ultimately, developers must consider the role of stigma when designing characters with mental illness for games. Making the characters relatable, honest, and grounded, might help to reduce the impact of stigma in video games.

Indie games provide a rich and diverse example of the use of narrative, mechanics, and aesthetics to tell emotional stories about mental illness, trauma, grief, LGTBQ+ experiences and neurodiversity. One of their greatest strengths lying in the building of honest and relatable characters through narrative design. Indie games are often built on low budgets and with small teams and are ideal examples for researchers who are often in similar situations. In short, although indie games that explore serious mental health topics might fall short of offering an educative outcome, they can provide information on how to create characters, design impactful narratives and create atmosphere. Improving the overall quality of serious games will help to increase their longevity, meaning long term analysis of these games will be much more likely.

References

1. Vos, T., et al.: Global, regional, and national incidence, prevalence, and years lived with disability for 328 diseases and injuries for 195 countries, 1990–2016: a systematic analysis for the Global Burden of Disease Study 2016. The Lancet **390**(10100), 1211–1259 (2017)
2. Walker, E.R., McGee, R.E., Druss, B.G.: Mortality in mental disorders and global disease burden implications: a systematic review and meta-analysis. JAMA Psychiatry **72**(4), 334–341 (2015)
3. Depression and other common mental disorders: global health estimates. World Health Organization, Geneva (2017)
4. Kessler, R., et al.: Lifetime prevalence and age-of-onset distributions of mental disorders in the World Health Organization's World Mental Health Survey Initiative. World Psychiatry **6**(3), 168–176 (2007)
5. Andrade, L.H., et al.: Barriers to mental health treatment: results from the WHO World Mental Health surveys. Psychol. Med. **44**(6), 1303–1317 (2014)
6. Mechanic, D.: Removing barriers to care among persons with psychiatric symptoms. Health Aff. **21**(3), 137–147 (2002)
7. Dockery, L., et al.: Stigma- and non-stigma-related treatment barriers to mental healthcare reported by service users and caregivers. Psychiatry Res. **228**(3), 612–619 (2015)
8. Clement, S., et al.: What is the impact of mental health-related stigma on help-seeking? A systematic review of quantitative and qualitative studies. Psychol. Med. **45**(1), 11–27 (2015)
9. Kutcher, S., Wei, Y., Coniglio, C.: Mental health literacy: past, present, and future. Can. J. Psychiatry **61**(3), 154–158 (2016)
10. Ezell, J.M., Choi, C.-W., Wall, M.M., Link, B.G.: Measuring recurring stigma in the lives of individuals with mental illness. Community Ment. Health J. **54**(1), 27–32 (2018). https://doi.org/10.1007/s10597-017-0156-1
11. Fox, A.B., Smith, B.N., Vogt, D.: How and when does mental illness stigma impact treatment seeking? Longitudinal examination of relationships between anticipated and internalized stigma, symptom severity, and mental health service use. Psychiatry Res. **268**, 15–20 (2018)
12. Jorm, A.F., Korten, A.E., Jacomb, P.A., Christensen, H., Rodgers, B., Pollitt, P.: "Mental health literacy": a survey of the public's ability to recognise mental disorders and their beliefs about the effectiveness of treatment. Med. J. Aust. **166**(4), 182–186 (1997)
13. Jorm, A.F.: Mental health literacy: public knowledge and beliefs about mental disorders. Br. J. Psychiatry **177**(5), 396–401 (2000)
14. Beyond Blue. https://www.beyondblue.org.au. Accessed 31 May 2021
15. Twomey, C., et al.: A randomized controlled trial of the computerized CBT programme, MoodGYM, for public mental health service users waiting for interventions. Br. J. Clin. Psychol. **53**(4), 433–450 (2014)
16. moodgym. https://moodgym.com.au. Accessed 31 May 2021
17. Qu, C.C., Sas, C., Roquet, C.D., Doherty, G.: Functionality of top-rated mobile apps for depression: systematic search and evaluation. JMIR Ment. Health **7**(1), e15321 (2020)
18. Michael, D., Chen, S.: Serious Games: Games That Educate, Train, and Inform, p. 17. Muska & Lipman/Premier-Trade, Boston (2005)
19. Marsh, T.: Serious games continuum: between games for purpose and experiential environments for purpose. Entertain. Comput. **2**(2), 61–68 (2011)
20. Boyle, E.A., et al.: An update to the systematic literature review of empirical evidence of the impacts and outcomes of computer games and serious games. Comput. Educ. **94**, 178–192 (2016)
21. Qian, M., Clark, K.R.: Game-based learning and 21st century skills: a review of recent research. Comput. Hum. Behav. **63**, 50–58 (2016)

22. Twomey, C., O'Reilly, G.: Effectiveness of a freely available computerised cognitive behavioural therapy programme (MoodGYM) for depression: meta-analysis. Aust. N. Z. J. Psychiatry **51**(3), 260–269 (2017)
23. Brijnath, B., Protheroe, J., Mahtani, K., Antoniades, J.: Do web-based mental health literacy interventions improve the mental health literacy of adult consumers? Results from a systematic review. J. Med. Internet Res. **18**(6), e5463 (2016)
24. Schneider, J., Foroushani, P.S., Grime, P., Thornicroft, G.: Acceptability of online self-help to people with depression: users' views of MoodGYM versus informational websites. J. Med. Internet Res. **16**, e90 (2014)
25. Neary, M., Schueller, S.M.: State of the field of mental health apps. Cogn. Behav. Pract. **25**(4), 531–537 (2018)
26. Fitzgerald, M., Ratcliffe, G.: Serious games, gamification, and serious mental illness: a scoping review. Psychiatr. Serv. **71**, 170–183 (2020)
27. Fleming, T., et al.: Serious games and gamification for mental health: current status and promising directions. Front. Psychiatry **7**, 215 (2017)
28. SPARX. https://www.sparx.org.nz/home. Accessed 31 May 2021
29. Merry, S.N., Stasiak, K., Shepherd, M., Frampton, C., Fleming, T., Lucassen, M.F.G.: The effectiveness of SPARX, a computerised self help intervention for adolescents seeking help for depression: randomised controlled non-inferiority trial. BMJ **344**, e2598 (2012)
30. Kuosmanen, T., Fleming, T.M., Newell, J., Barry, M.M.: A pilot evaluation of the SPARX-R gaming intervention for preventing depression and improving wellbeing among adolescents in alternative education. Internet Interv. **8**, 40–47 (2017)
31. Kitchener, B.A., Jorm A.F., Kelly, C.: Mental Health First Aid Manual. Mental Health First Aid, Melbourne (2017)
32. Ruberg, B.: Queering Indie: how LGBTQ experiences challenge dominant narratives of independent games. In: Ruffino, P. (ed.) Independent Videogames : Cultures, Networks, Techniques and Politics. Taylor & Francis Group, Milton (2020)
33. Iuppa, N., Borst, T.: End-To-End Game Development : Creating Independent Serious Games and Simulations from Start to Finish. Focal Press, Waltham (2010)
34. The Last of Us. Sony Computer Entertainment, Naughty Dog, PlayStation (2013)
35. Hellblade: Senua's Sacrifice. Ninja Theory, PlayStation 4 (2017)
36. Case, N.: Coming Out Simulator. Online (2014)
37. Assassin's Creed Origins. Ubisoft, PlayStation 4 (2017)
38. Florence. Mountains, Annapuma Interactive, Steam (2018)
39. Quinn, Z., Lindsey, P., Schankler, I.: Depression Quest. Online (2013)
40. That Dragon, Cancer. Numinous Games, Steam (2016)
41. Melinn, I., Lima, C.: Keep in Mind: Remastered. Little Moth Games, Akupara Games, Steam (2018)
42. O'Neill, W.: Actual Sunlight. WZO Games Inc., Steam (2014)
43. Rock Paper Shotgun. https://www.rockpapershotgun.com/2013/02/11/thoughts-on-actual-sunlight. Accessed 21 June 2019
44. Martínez, M.A.C.: Depression. itch.io
45. https://manuacruz.itch.io/depression. Accessed 27 June 2021
46. Figueroa, N., Martinsson, I.: Fran Bow. Killmonday Games, Steam (2015)
47. Ferrari, M., McIlwaine, S.V., Jordan, G., Shah, J.L., Lal, S., Iyer, S.N.: Gaming with stigma: analysis of messages about mental illnesses in video games. JMIR Ment. Health **6**(5), e12418 (2019)
48. CheckPoint. https://checkpointorg.com/mental-health-representation. Accessed 31 Mar 2020
49. Figueroa, N.: Interview: Killmonday on fran bow, mental health, beauty. In: Walker, J. (ed.). Rock Paper Shotgun Online (2013)

50. The Suicide of Rachel Foster. One-On-One Games, Daedalic Entertainment, Steam (2020)
51. Watts, R.: The Suicide of Rachel Foster. PC Gamer (2020). https://www.pcgamer.com/the-suicide-of-rachel-foster-review
52. Evans-Thirlwell, E.: The Suicide of Rachel Foster review - a Shining-esque riff on Gone Home that doesn't quite dazzle. Eurogamer (2020). https://www.eurogamer.net/articles/2020-02-16-the-suicide-of-rachel-foster-review-shining-esque-hotel-adventure-doesnt-quite-dazzle
53. Gardner, M.: Review: 'The Suicide Of Rachel Foster' Is A Rollercoaster Ride That Plummets At The End. Forbes. https://www.forbes.com/sites/mattgardner1/2020/02/26/review-the-suicide-of-rachel-foster-is-a-rollercoaster-ride-that-plummets-at-the-end

Using Indie Games to Inform Serious Mental Health Games Design

Myfanwy King[✉], Tim Marsh, and Zeynep Akcay

Griffith Film School, Griffith University, Brisbane, Australia
myfanwy.king@griffithuni.edu.au, {t.marsh,
z.akcay}@griffith.edu.au

Abstract. Mental health literacy (MHL) is an important 21st Century skill. Good MHL can help to reduce barriers to help-seeking by equipping the public with the knowledge needed to help themselves or someone experiencing a mental illness. One Australian-based organization that does this through a training course is Mental Health First Aid (MHFA) Australia. There are many digital interventions that aim to achieve this goal and serious games are no exception. Serious games have been identified as ideal for developing 21st Century skills, meaning MHL literacy is a promising candidate for serious games development. In fact, evidence suggest that serious games are effective as a tool for improving MHL. However, they often suffer from poor-quality game design, poor study design, high dropout rates, variability in studies and loss of motivation and engagement of players. This means that there are many challenges to consider when developing serious games. Here we describe our experiences in the development of a serious game prototype that utilizes the principles of MHFA. The aim of this development is to improve the confidence of players in delivering MHFA. Additionally, it aims to address the challenge of serious games quality by taking an artistic approach that combines narrative, aesthetics and mechanics using indie games for inspiration. There are many well-designed indie games that tell emotional and character driven stories of mental illness. They provide inspiration on the development of honest and relatable characters, which offer a positive representation of those experiencing a mental illness.

Keywords: Serious games · Mental health · Mental health literacy · Indie games · Independent games

1 Introduction

Mental health literacy (MHL) is an important 21st Century skill that can help to improve the recognition and treatment of mental health disorders and promote wellbeing. Good MHL means being aware of the different mental disorders and how to access treatment for them [1]. It should also help to decrease stigma and prejudice towards those experiencing mental illness, while simultaneously improving help-seeking through a good understanding of mental health care and available services [1]. This includes the ability to understand what is needed to take care of one's own mental health (i.e., personal

© Springer Nature Switzerland AG 2021
B. Fletcher et al. (Eds.): JCSG 2021, LNCS 12945, pp. 153–166, 2021.
https://doi.org/10.1007/978-3-030-88272-3_12

mental wellbeing) and an understanding of how to help others [1]. Improving MHL is imperative as those who are experiencing mental illness can wait up to 10 years before seeking help, leading to worse symptoms that could have been improved if identified earlier.

There are many digital interventions that are aimed to improve a person's MHL. Beyond Blue is a well-known resource in Australia, providing fact sheets, forums, and help through phone and chat services targeted at those experiencing depression, anxiety, and suicidal ideation [2]. moodgym is an online course that utilizes cognitive behavioral therapy methods to help those with emerging or early symptoms of mental illness [3]. There is also a plethora of mobile applications that offer to help with mental illness [4]. However digital interventions, like moodgym, only target those with milder symptoms of mental illness, since they are not as effective for those with more severe symptoms [3, 5, 6]. One reason for this is that those with mental illness face challenges such as poor motivation, reduced concentration and may not be able to recognize that they are unwell [7, 8]. This means that targeting research towards those around a person with mental illness may be better than targeting those who are experiencing a mental illness directly. One organization that does this is Mental Health First Aid (MHFA) Australia.

MHFA developed the MHFA training course with the aim to increase the publics knowledge of mental health and associated disorders, reduce stigma and provide help in crisis and non-crisis situations [9]. MHFA is "the help provided to a person developing a mental health problem, experiencing the worsening of an existing problem, or in a mental health crisis. This help is provided until professional help is received, or the crisis is resolved"[10]. They provide a range of courses, for example youth and elder MHFA, over different population groups [9, 11]. Their aim is to provide high quality, evidence-based training to the different communities to ensure that those experiencing a mental illness are well supported. Currently in Australia, over nine hundred thousand people have attended a MHFA course, with the support of over two thousand one hundred instructors [11]. The success of MHFA has led to the development of twenty-six accredited MHFA programs around the world that have been adapted for local populations [9]. MHFA itself being a valuable 21st century skill ideal for adaption to a serious game.

Serious games for mental health are an emerging field of study, Boyle et al., and Qian and Clark identifying serious games as a promising avenue for developing 21st Century skills [12, 13]. Therefore, using serious games for developing mental health literacy skills is a promising avenue. However, while there is evidence that serious games are effective for improving mental health literacy there are challenges that must be addressed during design [7, 14]. These challenges include, but are not limited to, the quality of the game design, low-quality studies, mixed efficacy (e.g., SPARX vs SPARX-R), high dropout rates leading to small sample size, and failure of researchers to report effect size [7, 13–16].

This paper will report on the development of a prototype serious game that uses the principles of MHFA, while demonstrating how it sought to address the challenges mentioned above. Specifically, to improve game design the project is taking a creative approach inspired by well-designed indie games that explore topics of mental health. Section 2 will outline the development of the prototype serious game to date. Section 3 will explore the lessons learnt from game development. Finally, Sect. 4 will provide a conclusion and discuss future directions for game development.

2 Development of a Serious Game Using MHFA Principles

MHFA provides an interesting framework for the purpose of serious games development targeted at increasing MHL. In the early phases of development there were several ideas explored that targeted those experiencing mental illness directly. For example, a Plants vs Zombie style game that explores different treatments [17]. These ideas had potential, but the true target for the game was helping a person experiencing a mental illness or expressing thoughts of suicide. As discussed earlier, those experiencing mental illness may struggle to access help and it was thought that targeting a game to those around a person displaying symptoms of a mental illness, would be more effective [7]. This idea led to MHFA Australia, which is designed not only to help those in crisis, but also those experiencing early signs of mental illness. The principles of MHFA (ALGEE) are as follows [8]:

1. Approach the person, assess and assist with any crisis.
2. Listen and communicate non-judgmentally.
3. Give support and Information.
4. Encourage the person to get appropriate professional help.
5. Encourage other supports.

MHFA courses teach strategies for helping someone experiencing mental illness that are guided by the ALGEE principles [8]. The existing MHFA courses are well established and are divided between course work and instructor driven classes [18]. After initial assessment, it was felt that providing serious games as replacement to the traditional and well-established training of MHFA was inappropriate. Instead, the focus was placed on developing a game that would refresh the course for those who had already undertaken training. The advantage of serious games is in their ability to not only motivate and engage players but provide training in 21st century skills, such as communication [12, 13]. Therefore, the focus for this project is on building confidence in providing MHFA to people, rather than purely retraining those who have already undertaken the course. The primary question this research aims to answer is, "can a serious game using MHFA principles improve the confidence of recent MHFA trainees in providing MHFA?" To focus these ideas, five serious objectives were developed as follows:

1. Refresh the principles of MHFA (ALGEE) and steps to use in a crisis.
2. Increase a participant's intention to provide MHFA by building confidence in a safe place.
3. Provide examples of, and moments to practice MHFA principles both in non-crisis and crisis situations.
4. Provide participants with examples and time to develop a self-care plan.
5. Provide participants with positive feedback geared to gently redirect them to the most appropriate answer in role-playing situations.

Another goal of serious game development was to address the design and quality of serious games through taking an artistic approach. An artistic approach utilizes previous examples of creative work to inspire the development of story, visuals, sound, and mechanics. This includes considering how these elements come together to tell emotional and character driven stories, while also integrating serious objectives. Using this approach should improve the overall quality of serious games and hypothetically, increase their longevity. A starting point for this creative exploration were a set of five guidelines developed for a previously unpublished work that inspired the direction of this project [19]. These guidelines are as follows:

1. Provide the game in an accessible way to reach intended audience.
   This principle focused on making the game accessible to an audience. This can include making the interactions easy to use, in a format that targets a more casual gamer. Inversely, the design may need to be more challenging especially for more experienced players.
2. Create an honest character who is empathetic and relatable.
   This guideline is focused on making a realistic character that can help break through the stigma of mental illness. Honest being defined within the context of this project as one that provides a genuine, empathetic, and candid look at mental illness.
3. Provide access to resources in a natural/subtle way as part of the story.
   This guideline was designed to allow players to receive resources as a natural part of the story, while also allowing them to explore resources in their own time.
4. Use the character to explore thoughts and feelings associated with mental illness.
   Allowing players to understand the thoughts and feelings of characters experiencing a mental illness acts to not only humanize them but also provides a way to understand fears, stigma, and other experiences of those with mental illness.
5. Explore the symptoms (both physical and mental) associated with mental illness.
   Similarly, to the previous design principle, characters should display symptoms of mental illness, which when combined with the thoughts and feelings gives a full account of what it is like to have a mental illness.

While this list provides a good starting point to explore stories of mental health, mental illness, and recovery it is by no means complete. Instead, it is designed as a starting structure to frame mental health serious games development, while also supplying guidelines for the analysis of games featuring topics of mental illness. This list can be augmented by the list of exploration points found at CheckPoint (Language, Accuracy, Purpose, Stereotypes, Empathy and Support) and considering the core principles of MHFA [8, 20]. Overall, the aim of these elements is to encourage the development of positive representation of those experiencing mental illness, improve recognition and understanding of mental health disorders, combat stigma and negative stereotypes, and provide resources that empower the public in making more positive changes in their own lives and the lives of others. To address these areas, it was important to explore how narrative, mechanics and aesthetics could be used to communicate serious objectives to players.

2.1 Development to Date

The following section will look at the development of a prototype serious game using MHFA principles. As stated earlier, challenges in quality and design of serious games have been kept in mind during development. With a focus on taking an artistic approach to explore overall game design. This paper will not discuss sound as it is currently undeveloped. However, it is acknowledged that sound design is an important part of creating atmosphere in videogames and is a key part of future development. The indie games explored in this section are reviewed by King, Marsh and Akcay's [21]. The following sections will discuss game development through the lenses of narrative, visual and mechanics.

Fig. 1. An example of the game screen players will see when playing the prototype game. Each element of the GUI is as follows, a) the emotion bar surrounding the background that highlights strong emotions of a NPC, b) the location background for the scene, c) the current NPC talking and their emotion sprite d) the dialogue box that shows the player and NPC dialogue, and scene information, e) the players bar showing dialogue options, players wellbeing and mood, time and day f) a phone GUI that is used in some scenes to send messages.

Narrative is defined in the context of this project as a tool for communicating serious objectives through character development, world building and character identification. Additionally, narrative is an important tool for creating relatable and honest portrayals of characters that are experiencing mental illness. The primary mechanics for the game are those of an interactive fiction that rely on text and visuals to communicate information to the player. Visuals are any part of the viewed world of the player and are one component of aesthetics used to build both the world and atmosphere.

Story and Characters: A Brief Overview. The story follows several characters as they go about their normal lives. MHFA was created with diversity in mind and special attention has been paid to create characters that represent different cultural backgrounds, gender identities and neurodiversity's. The three main characters the player will interact with are Luna (a work colleague and close friend), Greg (the players manager and close friend) and Zeki (the players nephew). There are also several other non-playable characters (NPC) that appear throughout the game. The overall style of the game is pixel based, using voxel models for backgrounds. As this is a prototype visuals, interface, story, and styles are not finalized; therefore, this section will discuss the prototype as it stands currently.

In the main story the player has recently undertaken a MHFA course and will need to use their new skills to help their friends or family members who may be experiencing a mental illness. The game is divided into three chapters as follows, the first chapter gives the player an introduction to the world and characters. The second chapter explores Luna's experiences with mental illness in a non-crisis situation. Finally, the third chapter explores Zeki's experience with mental illness as a LGTBQ+ person in a crisis situation. Each chapter is designed to explore the symptoms, feelings, and experiences of mental illness that the player may encounter in the real world. Figure 1 provides an overview of the main visuals the player will see in game.

Character Identification. Character identification is one tool utilized to help players feel connected to the world and its characters. Character identification is defined by Cohen et al. as "an imaginative experience in which a person surrenders consciousness of his or her own identity and experiences the world through someone else's point of view" [22]. Identification with a story's characters is mediated by factors such as empathy, story perspective, character likeability, reader similarity to character, character morality (e.g., charitableness), reader views or beliefs (e.g., racism and politics) and whether the character is a protagonist or antagonist [23–31]. These factors can facilitate immersion into a narrative, referred to as transportation, and allows an audience or reader to empathize with a character and adopt their beliefs [22, 32]. These articles focus primarily on text and film but can be translated to video games to help improve character identification.

Of these factors, first person perspective, a common trope in interactive fiction, has been shown to increase immersion of players in games [33, 34]. In *Actual Sunlight, Keep in Mind: Remastered, and Coming Out Simulator* the story is told from a third person perspective, which may help to communicate the idea of the player witnessing a personal story [35–37]. Although, the language used is a mix of first person or second person. *That Dragon Cancer* provides an interesting use of perspective, where changes in perspective are used to communicate a variety of experiences to the player [38]. In *Depression Quest* on the other hand, you play from a first-person perspective where the player is being referred to as you (second person) and asked directly by the game "what would you do?" when making choices [39]. While *Depression Quest* is inspired by personal stories its goal is to allow someone to experience what it is like to have a mental illness [39].

In the current prototype, the story is told from a first-person perspective. This perspective was chosen as the focus of the experience is to teach confidence in giving MHFA to a character and it is felt, hypothetically, that the first-person perspective should facilitate this goal. Making the player an active participant in the game world through story and visuals. However, unlike *Depression Quest*, the main story uses a first-person point of view where the player makes choices that direct the dialogue as if talking to the other person (although there are areas where the player will be asked directly about emotions). Visually, the player character is not seen and is placed in front of backgrounds and characters. This design was chosen to facilitate the feeling of being part of the game world.

Mental Illness Representation. Mental health representation is an important consideration when developing stories and visuals in videogames that contain characters who are experiencing a mental illness. Mental illness is highly stigmatized in modern society with many tropes and stigma being seen across media and in video games [40–42]. Stigma is the top concern of those experiencing mental illness and can prevent them from accessing help [1, 43–48]. For many communities it can be hard to find positive representation for those who are considered other. It is only through positive representation that stigma can be broken. It is therefore important to consider how mental health and mental illness are portrayed in media.

In indie games explored in King, Marsh and Akcay's review, there are both positive and negative representations of mental illness [21]. A positive portrayal of a person with mental illness is defined as those that provide honest and relatable characters that explore feelings and/or symptoms of mental illness. While, negative portrayals promote stigmatized views, tropes and utilize mental illness to explain violent behavior and/or as a plot device for shock value. Additionally, negative portrayals may show inaccurate information on the symptoms of mental illness, for example the common belief that those with schizophrenia have multiple personalities.

In development of the prototype game, it felt important to express stigmatized views and allow players to recognize them. For example, an NPC makes a stigmatized comment about Luna's state of mind when she starts showing signs of a mental illness. It is up to the player to recognize and choose whether to correct their colleague. This provides a moment where the player can assess the stigma and react to it or not. Reinforcing concepts from the MHFA course about the use of negative stereotypes and stigmatized language against those experiencing a mental illness. Of course, there is always a possibility that it serves to reinforce the stigmatized view and future development will look at ways to catch these moments to help reinforce the lesson being taught. This is just one example of how stigmatized views can be used to improve knowledge rather than reinforce stereotypes.

Regarding positive representation of mental illness in game, the first chapter was designed to introduce the characters before they begin to display symptoms of mental illness. For example, Luna is introduced to players as a hard worker and caring friend. For example, when the players character is feeling down about Greg leaving the company, she quickly stops probing the player for details when she realizes the player is upset. Instead, she gives the player space and tells them "I am here if you need to talk", showing her supportive and caring nature. These moments are designed to communicate to the player that people with mental illness are human and that mental illness does not define them. They also highlight the contrast in a person's behavior when they begin to show symptoms of mental illness. Meaning, that character development and backstory are essential for stories of mental illness, as they serve to both humanize the character and allow players to assess changes in the characters behavior over time.

Representing Suicide. Suicide is still viewed as a taboo topic throughout the world due to various reasons, including religious and cultural beliefs. However, there is a need to normalize talking about suicide in a non-judgmental way that makes a person feel safe to discuss thoughts openly. In fact, in the MHFA course you are encouraged to ask about suicide directly as it shows you care about the person and allows you to recognize if the person has suicidal thoughts and intentions to act on those thoughts [8]. Like the representation of mental illness in videogames, representations of suicide have challenges and there are important factors to consider before choosing to depict thoughts of suicide or someone acting on those thoughts.

As discussed, Actual Sunlight explores the thoughts, feelings and symptoms that can lead to suicidal ideation [21, 35]. More confronting is the fact that the main character acts on these thoughts of suicide at the end of the game. The act itself is not depicted, however, it is strongly implied, and the author confirms that intent. This is communicated to players through the metaphoric use of sunlight and clearing skies representing the release associated with acting on these thoughts. Another game that explores suicide is The Suicide of Rachel Foster [49]. The game uses suicide as a plot device multiple times and handles other sensitive issues poorly [49]. The most prominent example comes at the end of the game, where the player finds themselves locked in the main characters car as it fills with exhaust [49]. An explicit depiction of attempted suicide that is used for shock value and entertainment, rather than as a genuine exploration of the effects of trauma.

It could be argued that both games used suicide for shock value to some extent, although, they tell their stories differently. Actual Sunlight provides insight into the thoughts, feelings, and symptoms a person might express when contemplating suicide [35]. On the other hand, The Suicide of Rachel Foster presents suicide as an outcome that feels underserved and insensitive [49]. These views are of course subjective and as with mental illness representation, it is important for game developers to assess the appropriateness of depicting suicide in game. Depictions should be thoughtful, provide opportunities to help characters and at minimum, links to resources about suicide and where to get help for suicidal thoughts. In prototype development it was felt that, to build confidence, depicting a character's suicide, even after receiving help, would be too challenging. Instead, players will be able to ask characters about suicide and act appropriately based on the characters response.

Limiting Narrative Choices for Positive Feedback. In all the indie games discussed the player interacts with a virtual world consisting of visuals, character, and dialogue. Keep in Mind: Remastered is a walking simulator where the player wanders around talking to representations of the main characters mental illness [36]. The story is linear, but the player can visit the characters in any order, while still receiving the same story. Depression Quest and Coming Out Simulator have multiple choice elements that give the character a limited number of stories with different outcomes or experiences to explore [37, 39]. For the development of the serious game prototype however, it was necessary to control choices and outcomes. There are three types of choices in the prototype game as follows:

1. Those designed to improve character identification: the first type of choices are designed to help improve character identification. For example, in the first intro-ductory chapter, when Luna asks the players about their current relationship status

the player can choose from several options that best reflect their current real-world relationship. In some ways these choices help to promote player agency into how they would tell their own personal story within the narrative.

2. Those that are in response to symptoms or characters before using MHFA. The second type of choices are in response to the symptoms an NPC character is displaying. These choices allow the player to express how they might feel in each situation in a non-judgmental environment. For example, when Luna turns up late to a presentation that they have been working on for the big boss, there are several responses the player can choose. These choices allow the player to explore potential reactions they might have towards a colleague or friend who may be developing symptoms of a mental illness. This includes times where the player is asked how they feel.

3. Those provided during the mental health first aid portion of the game. The third type of choices are those the player will make while utilizing MHFA. Rather than explicitly telling a player they are wrong; players will be redirected towards the most appropriate answer. This style of learning is utilized during the MHFA course and is also inspired by ReachOut Orbs gameplay [50]. ReachOut Orb was a serious game directed toward young people that unfortunately is no longer available [50]. In ReachOut Orb players where given choices on how to respond to characters, if they responded negatively, they were redirected to a more appropriate response [50].

Limiting choices for current game development is unavoidable, as the story needs to promote specific outcomes. This perhaps is where indie games have a little more freedom than research games. It is common for interactive fiction games, even ones with multiple endings, to use branch cutting [34]. Future developments might see random responses or artificial intelligence used to explore different outcomes, but this is far outside the scope of this project.

Visualizing Emotions. Communicating emotions to players is crucial in a game that is designed to build empathy and connection. The indie games discussed so far use several different techniques to express emotions in game, which could aid developers. In *Keep in Mind: Remastered*, symptoms and feelings are primarily expressed through visual metaphor [36]. While, in *Actual Sunlight* thoughts and feelings are communicated directly through the characters dialogue and through visual thought bubbles [35]. A unique example is *Depression,* it uses short statements coupled with clever mechanics to express the feelings and symptoms of depression [51]. These indie games all have unique ways of revealing the emotions of their characters and like these games, the prototype game needed a tailored way to show the emotion of its characters, including those of the player.

An initial idea was to do something similar to the way perspective changes in *That Dragon Cancer* [20, 38]. This would have been either a trait one could unlock or as part of the story. However, to create a feeling of existing in the real-world, a more natural expression of emotions was needed. The first way to communicate emotion is through facial expression. In the current project each character has a range of facial expression that can be changed throughout the story. A character is displayed when it is their turn to talk and is removed when no one is talking, or the next character is displayed. When expressing strong emotions, a bar around the edge of the character screen flashes a single color that represent the different emotions (e.g., red for anger or blue for sadness). For the player, emotions are shown differently and utilize different mechanics to those used for NPCs.

Enhancing Story Through Mechanics: Player Emotions and Teaching Wellbeing. Player's emotions are shown at the bottom of the screen and change in reaction to story events. Each emotion has a value that can affect the players overall wellbeing either positively or negatively. For example, being happy produces a positive change, while anger produces a negative change. Wellbeing is tracked at the bottom of the screen using a bar that moves left for negative emotions and right for positive emotions. The bar also changes color when the players emotion changes in the story. The goal of this bar was to help the player see how positive and negative emotions can affect their own wellbeing. At one point in the game players are given a chance to choose from a limited range of emotions to express how they are feeling. This leads directly into a section that provides a simple button clicking game that teaches a grounding exercise. The overall aim of this part of the design was to teach players to recognize their emotions and feelings that can lead to them becoming overwhelmed and provide strategies to help to maintain and/or improve their wellbeing (e.g., exercising and meditation). This is considered especially important to help them recover after using MHFA.

3   Lessons Learned from Development

Developing serious games that adhere to a set of serious objectives present a unique challenge for game designers. Crafting a game that looks good, tells an engaging story, and has solid gameplay mechanics, while also successfully communicating serious objectives is a hard goal to achieve, but not impossible. Additionally, assessing the effectiveness of these games following a rigorous methodology is equally challenging due to the wide scope and variety of serious games that often cross several research domains. This scope can make finding examples of well-designed and rigorously validated serious games as a point of reference difficult, and this is true for serious games aimed at increasing mental health literacy. The main reason for this is the emergent nature of serious games and video game research in general.

To address the challenge in design of serious games, this project is focusing on using creative techniques to design a serious game for improving MHL. As part of creative practice, it is important to draw on sources of inspiration. This can cover every aspect of game design; however, the focus of this project has been on narrative, aesthetics, and mechanics. Indie games offer a unique source of inspiration as they share some similarities with research environments, such as small teams and limited funding. Drawing from games that explore issues of mental health and mental illness has provided an insight into the development of positive representation of mental illness. However, while these games are good for drawing inspiration for story, character development, mechanics and design, their primary purpose is largely still entertainment.

Serious games are limited by their serious objectives in ways that entertainment games are not. In the case of current development there are limitations on how to present dialogue and options to players. This is necessary to ensure that players receive positive feedback that can re-direct them to a more appropriate answer. However, doing this limits the replayability of the game. To help with this some choices have been designed to show different responses based on player input, for example, some choices reveal different parts of the story. Serious games are very much curated experiences, where designers choose how players interact with the game to best answer serious objectives rather than create entertaining moments. These elements are not mutually exclusive, nevertheless the approach a designer takes in creating a serious game will be different to how they would develop an entertainment game.

Another area of development that has been difficult is finding the right balance of mechanics, visuals, and storytelling to explore both the player and NPCs emotions. The wellbeing bar seems like a good premise for a game that helps players assess their own emotions and its effect on their wellbeing. However, without the player input, many emotions are best guesses of how a person might feel in each situation. In games that explore emotional topics well, players are not just told directly what their emotions are. Instead, players feel emotions through a combination of story, sound and visuals that create an emotional atmosphere. *That Dragon Cancer* is effective because it uses a variety of techniques to communicate emotions and generate empathy, for example, storytelling, character perspective, visual design, audio, and metaphor [38].

To address this issue of mechanics/superficial representation of emotions for players, the wellbeing bar and stated emotions will need to be removed from the game. Instead, players will be given the opportunity to express their emotions throughout the game and will be given access to wellbeing games from the start. Currently, this area is still in development, but giving players time to reflect on their emotions and possibly their actions will serve to help players identify emotions, learn techniques to improve their wellbeing and assess how this effects their dialogue choices. To improve the communication of NPC emotions drawing on examples such as *That Dragon Cancer* will provide insight into developing emotional games [38]. One example of minimalist game design that expresses complex emotions is *Florence* [52]. *Florence* is an interactive fiction game that uses comic book style panels, life-based mechanics (e.g., brushing Florence's teeth), dialogue-based puzzles and simple animations to communicate not only story but emotions [52]. This minimalistic approach can also be seen in *Coming Out Simulator*, where story is told through dialogue boxes that resemble text messaging on a phone [37]. Drawing from these examples' future development will focus on using short animations to express NPC emotions, as well as improving the overall design of the graphical user interface (GUI).

4   Conclusion and Future Directions

This project explores the development of a serious game designed to build the confidence of players in applying the lessons learnt through Mental Health First Aid. To address the challenges of quality in serious games design this project has taken a creative approach that draws inspiration from a variety of sources, with a particular interest in indie games that explore topics of mental health and mental illness. Indie games that explore personal stories of mental illness can provide insight into the creation of honest and relatable characters through their use of positive representation.

Indie games have provided an in depth look into the development of short emotional stories. They have offered insight into the representation of emotions both visually and narratively. Indie games also demonstrate how to build worlds that are character driven, which allow players to feel part of their characters story. Additionally, they offer an insight into the personal lives of their characters, how they feel, what drives them and how trauma, mental illness and grief can affect them as a person. This is especially prominent in games that are based on real-world experiences. Most importantly indie games provide innovative examples of how mechanics, narrative, and aesthetics can be brought together to tell a story, each individual story uniquely driven by different combinations of these elements.

Conversely, evaluating indie games with poor representation of mental illness can help developers identify common stigmas and tropes. These factors leading to inaccurate portrayals of those experiencing mental illness. However, it is important to consider creator context when assessing stigma in games. Creator context can help identify the difference between a bad representation of mental illness and one that is the result of personal experience. Stigma is a complex subject to manage when developing games that explore stories of mental illness. It is not possible to remove all stigmatized views from media. However, having a good understanding of stigma and treating this topic sensitively will help in building more positive representations of those experiencing mental illness.

Currently a prototype of a serious game has been developed to explore the use of mechanics, story, and visuals to communicate the serious objectives identified for this project. This development process to date has been described in this paper and has highlighted challenges in the design process. Future development will focus on improving how players and NPC emotions are expressed through story and gameplay. This will be accomplished through the addition of animations and improvement of the GUI. Future development will also involve the design of research studies to assess the effectiveness of the game based on the identified serious objectives, with a focus on the confidence of players and their acceptance of the serious game.

References

1. Kutcher, S., Wei, Y., Coniglio, C.: Mental health literacy: past, present, and future. Can. J. Psychiat. **61**(3), 154–158 (2016)
2. Beyond Blue. https://www.beyondblue.org.au. Accessed 31 May 2021
3. moodgym. https://moodgym.com.au. Accessed 31 May 2021
4. Qu, C.C., Sas, C., Roquet, C.D., Doherty, G.: Functionality of top-rated mobile apps for depression: systematic search and evaluation. JMIR Mental Health **7**(1), e15321 (2020)
5. Twomey, C., et al.: A randomized controlled trial of the computerized CBT programme, MoodGYM, for public mental health service users waiting for interventions. Br. J. Clin. Psychol. **53**(4), 433–450 (2014)
6. Twomey, C., O'Reilly, G.: Effectiveness of a freely available computerised cognitive behavioural therapy programme (MoodGYM) for depression: Meta-analysis. Aust. N. Z. J. Psychiatry **51**(3), 260–269 (2017)
7. Fitzgerald, M., Ratcliffe, G.: Serious games, gamification, and serious mental illness: a scoping review. Psychiatr. Serv. **71**, 170–183 (2020)

8. Kitchener, B.A., Jorm A.F., Kelly, C.: Mental Health First Aid Manual. Mental Health First Aid, Melbourne (2017)
9. Mental Health First Aid International. https://mhfainternational.org/the-mhfa-program
10. Jorm, A.F., Kitchener, B.A., Fischer, J.-A., Cvetkovski, S.: Mental health first aid training by e-learning: a randomized controlled trial. Aust. N. Z. J. Psychiatry **44**, 1072–1081 (2010)
11. Mental Health First Aid Australia. https://mhfa.com.au
12. Boyle, E.A., et al.: An update to the systematic literature review of empirical evidence of the impacts and outcomes of computer games and serious games. Comput. Educ. **94**, 178–192 (2016)
13. Qian, M., Clark, K.R.: Game-based Learning and 21st century skills: a review of recent research. Comput. Hum. Behav. **63**, 50–58 (2016)
14. Fleming, T., et al.: Serious games and gamification for mental health: current status and promising directions. Front. Psychiatry **7**(215), 1–7 (2017)
15. Merry, S.N., Stasiak, K., Shepherd, M., Frampton, C., Fleming, T., Lucassen, M.F.G.: The effectiveness of SPARX, a computerised self help intervention for adolescents seeking help for depression: randomised controlled non-inferiority trial. BMJ **344**, e2598 (2012)
16. Kuosmanen, T., Fleming, T.M., Newell, J., Barry, M.M.: A pilot evaluation of the SPARX-R gaming intervention for preventing depression and improving wellbeing among adolescents in alternative education. Internet Interv. **8**, 40–47 (2017)
17. Plants vs. Zombies. Electronic Arts, PopCap Games (2009)
18. Mental Health First Aid Australia. https://mhfa.com.au/courses. Accessed 02 June 2021
19. King, M.: Peggy's Story: A Serious Game for Improving Mental Health Literacy and Reducing Stigma, p. 56. Griffith University (2018, Unpublished)
20. CheckPoint. https://checkpointorg.com/mental-health-representation. Accessed 31 Mar 2020
21. King, M., Marsh, T., Akcay, Z.: A review of Indie games for serious mental health game design. In: Fletcher, B., Ma, M., Gobel, S., Hauge, J.B., Marsh, T., Oliveira, M. (eds.) Joint Conference on Serious Games - JCSG 2021, Stoke-on-Trent, United Kingdom (2021)
22. Cohen, J.: Defining identification: a theoretical look at the identification of audiences with media characters. Mass Commun. Soc. **4**, 245–264 (2001)
23. Batson, C.D., Polycarpou, M.P., Harmon-Jones, E., Imhoff, H.J., Mitchener, E.C.: Empathy and attitudes: can feeling for a member of a stigmatized group improve feelings toward the group? J. Pers. Soc. Psychol. **72**, 105–118 (1997)
24. Hoeken, H., Sinkeldam, J.: The role of identification and perception of just outcome in evoking emotions in narrative persuasion. J. Commun. **64**, 935–955 (2014)
25. Hoeken, H., Fikkers, K.M.: Issue-relevant thinking and identification as mechanisms of narrative persuasion. Poetics **44**, 84–99 (2014)
26. Hoeken, H., Kolthoff, M., Sanders, J.M.: Story perspective and character similarity as drivers of identification and narrative persuasion. Hum. Commun. Res. **42**, 292–311 (2016)
27. Chung, A.H., Slater, M.D.: Reducing stigma and out-group distinctions through perspective-taking in narratives. J. Commun. **63**, 894–911 (2013)
28. Cohen, J., Tal-Or, N., Mazor-Tregerman, M.: The tempering effect of transportation: exploring the effects of transportation and identification during exposure to controversial two-sided narratives. J. Commun. **65**, 237–258 (2015)
29. Igartua, J.-J., Frutos, F.J.: Enhancing Attitudes Toward Stigmatized Groups with Movies: Mediating and Moderating Processes of Narrative Persuasion (2017)
30. Christy, K.R.: I, you, or he: examining the impact of point of view on narrative persuasion. Media Psychol. **21**, 700–718 (2018)
31. Cohen, J., Weimann-Saks, D., Mazor-Tregerman, M.: Does character similarity increase identification and persuasion? Media Psychol. **21**, 506–528 (2018)

32. van Laer, T., de Ruyter, J.C., Visconti, L.M., Wetzels, M.G.M.: The extended transportation-imagery model: a meta-analysis of the antecedents and consequences of consumers' narrative transportation. J. Consum. Res. **40**, 797–817 (2014)

33. Denisova, A., Cairns, P.: First person vs. third person perspective in digital games: do player preferences affect immersion? In: Proceedings of the 33rd Annual ACM Conference on Human Factors in Computing Systems, pp. 145–148. ACM (2015)

34. Ciesla, R.: The (Ancient) art of interactive fiction. In: Ciesla, R. (ed.) Game Development with Ren'Py: Introduction to Visual Novel Games Using Ren'Py, TyranoBuilder, and Twine, 1st edn, pp. 47–77. Apress, Berkeley (2019). https://doi.org/10.1007/978-1-4842-4920-8_2

35. O'Neill, W.: Actual Sunlight. WZO Games Inc., Steam (2014)

36. Melinn, I., Lima, C.: Keep In Mind: Remastered. Little Moth Studios, Akupara Games, Steam (2018)

37. Case, N.: Coming Out Simulator. Online (2014)

38. That Dragon, Cancer. Numinous Games, Steam (2016)

39. Quinn, Z., Lindsey, P., Schankler, I.: Depression Quest. Online (2013)

40. Shapiro, S., Rotter, M.: Graphic depictions: portrayals of mental illness in video games. J. Forensic Sci. **61**, 1592–1595 (2016)

41. Stuart, H.: Media portrayal of mental illness and its treatments. CNS Drugs **20**, 99–106 (2006)

42. Wahl, O.: Depictions of mental illnesses in children's media. J. Ment. Health **12**, 249–258 (2003)

43. Andrade, L.H., et al.: Barriers to mental health treatment: results from the WHO World Mental Health surveys. Psychol. Med. **44**(6), 1303–1317 (2014)

44. Mechanic, D.: Removing barriers to care among persons with psychiatric symptoms. Health Aff. **21**(3), 137–147 (2002)

45. Dockery, L., et al.: Stigma- and non-stigma-related treatment barriers to mental healthcare reported by service users and caregivers. Psychiatry Res. **228**(3), 612–619 (2015)

46. Clement, S., et al.: What is the impact of mental health-related stigma on help-seeking? A systematic review of quantitative and qualitative studies. Psychol. Med. Camb. **45**(1), 11–27 (2015)

47. Ezell, J.M., Choi, C.-W., Wall, M.M., Link, B.G.: Measuring recurring stigma in the lives of individuals with mental illness. Community Ment. Health J. **54**(1), 27–32 (2018). https://doi.org/10.1007/s10597-017-0156-1

48. Fox, A.B., Smith, B.N., Vogt, D.: How and when does mental illness stigma impact treatment seeking? Longitudinal examination of relationships between anticipated and internalized stigma, symptom severity, and mental health service use. Psychiatry Res. **268**, 15–20 (2018)

49. Watts, R.: The Suicide of Rachel Foster. PC Gamer (2020). https://www.pcgamer.com/the-suicide-of-rachel-foster-review

50. ReachOut Orb. ReachOut Australia, ReachOut.com

51. Martínez, M.A.C.: Depression. itch.io

52. Florence. Mountains, Annapuma Interactive, Steam (2018)

Action-Centered Exposure Therapy Using a Serious Game to Help Individuals with Alcohol Use Disorder

Flavien Ehret[1]([✉])[iD], Yannick Francillette[1][iD], Benoit Girard[2], and Bob-Antoine J. Menelas[1][iD]

[1] Université du Québec à Chicoutimi, Chicoutimi, Canada
{flavien.ehret1,yannick_francillette,bamenela}@uqac.ca
[2] Centre de Thérapie La Futaie, Chicoutimi, Canada
http://www.uqac.ca
http://www.centrelatutaie.ca

Abstract. Alcohol use disorder is a worldwide issue causing distress and harm all over societies. The rate of relapse and dropout alcohol addiction treatment shows the necessity to improve those treatments. It is often caused by a lack of motivation or boredom. Cue exposure therapy is an effective treatment that tries to prevent relapses, but it has too many flaws preventing a global inhibition of the addiction. Virtual reality exposure therapy improves cue exposure therapy by using a virtual environment, that way the treatment is less situation-dependent by controlling a virtual world and its context. Serious games are used to address problems that we can find in more classical ways of learning such as motivation and boredom. It also allows the patient to have more active participation. This new approach aims to combine virtual reality exposure therapy, and action-centered exposure therapy, with a serious game to avoid dropout and have better self-commitment from patients. This paper provides key elements to propose a new approach to help tackle AUD. A prototype, to give an example of the implementation, a serious game is also presented.

Keywords: Alcohol use disorder · Action-Centered Exposure Therapy · Virtual Reality Exposure Therapy · Serious game · Interactivity

1 Introduction

Alcohol use disorder (AUD) is also known as alcohol abuse, alcohol dependence, or alcohol addiction. This is a medical condition characterized by the difficulty to control or to stop alcohol consumption[1]. We can note this condition

---

[1] https://www.niaaa.nih.gov/publications/brochures-and-fact-sheets/understanding-alcohol-use-disorder.

Funding: This research was funded by the Natural Sciences and Engineering Research Council of Canada (NSERC); grant number RGPIN-2019-07169.

B. Fletcher et al. (Eds.): JCSG 2021, LNCS 12945, pp. 167–181, 2021.
https://doi.org/10.1007/978-3-030-88272-3_13

is considered a brain and mental disorder by health organizations. It can be diagnosed using the DSM-V [1] and can be specified under three severity categories: mild, moderate, and severe depending on the number of identified symptoms.

AUD leads to excessive alcohol consumption. This can happen in many ways, in binge drinking for example, which consists of consuming several beverages on one single occasion (4 or more for women, and five or more for men). Heavy drinking is another form that consists of consuming several beverages per week (height or more for women and fifteen or more for men)[2]. Besides, Rehm [29] reminds the fact that excessive alcohol drinking is a cause of several disease conditions, such as high blood pressure, heart disease, or cancer for example. Moreover, it can carry short-term risks such as violence, miscarriage, alcohol poisoning. In fact, excessive alcohol drinking can create a vicious cycle that can lead to AUD (see Footnote 2).

It is known that AUD remains a serious public health issue. In 2012, the World Health Organisation revealed that 5.3% of global deaths in the world were caused by alcohol use, alcohol consumption is the first risk factor for premature death and disability among people ages fifteen to 49[3].

We can highlight that, because of the lockdown measures taken by governments in trying to stop the COVID-19 pandemic, alcohol consumption seems to have greatly increased. Moreover, Ramalho presents a survey using the Office for National Statistic of United Kingdom data[4], that shows an increase in the month-on-month volume of alcohol purchased by 31.4% during this period [28] in the United Kingdom.

AUD should not be disregarded by societies, indeed, NIH estimates the cost of alcohol misuses to 249 billion US dollars (see Footnote 3) in 2010 for the United States of America. It also strongly affects the daily life of individuals and their relatives [25]. For example, children of parents with AUD are more likely to be diagnosed by AUD, because of the family environment or genetic factors [25].

AUD is tackle by various well-known organizations. For people having mild to severe AUD, the potential for relapse is high. One of the major challenges is to increase the adherence of patients to treatments. A solution to prevent relapse and to prevent patients from following their impulses is necessary [35]. Another one is the lack of motivation for the treatment that may lead to a dropout [30].

This paper presents two contributions. The first one is recommendations, on key components to focus on, to build tools based on an **action-centered exposure therapy (ACET)** to take care of AUD. ACET use a combination of **cue exposure therapy (CET)** and **virtual reality**, called **virtual reality exposure therapy (VRET)**, and having the patient being active during their

---

[2] https://www.cdc.gov/alcohol/fact-sheets/alcohol-use.htm.

[3] https://www.niaaa.nih.gov/publications/brochures-and-fact-sheets/alcohol-facts-and-statistics.

[4] https://www.ons.gov.uk/businessindustryandtrade/retailindustry/bulletins/retailsales/march2020.

therapy. With those recommendations, we could build a panel of tools to adapt therapies to different profiles of patients.

The second contribution is a prototype to demonstrate how the previous recommendation can be implemented.

This document is structured as follows, Sect. 2 introduces CET to treat AUD. Section 3 presents the related works. Section 4 presents key components for the new approach and an example of a serious game is detailed in Sect. 5. Finally, we present future works, and we conclude this article in Sect. 6.

2   CET to Treat Addiction

Several treatments exist to treat every aspect of AUD, physiological and psychological, respectively with medicines and behavioral therapies[5]. **Exposure therapy** (ET) is a psychological therapy, based on behavior therapy to treat anxiety disorders. It involves exposing the patient to the source of its fear. By repeating it, the extinction of fear happens, feelings of anxiety and distress are reduced. Moreover, Craske et al. provide examples for clinicians about how to apply ET for anxious patients [7]. They aim to explain how to use ET to enhance inhibitory learning and its retrieval. The inhibitory learning model means that the association between a **conditional stimulus** (**CS**; in our case, a bottle of alcohol) and an **unconditional stimulus** (**US**; in our case, the ethanol) learned during conditioning is not erased during the ET. However, a new one aiming to inhibit the first one is created. They recommend using a strategy where the patient will be confronted with a mismatch between his expectancy and the outcome of the ET. As it violates expectancies, it helps inhibitory learning. The patient must also be active, it can be done by asking them what they learned during the session. The therapist and the client must also choose together the goal of the practice in measurable terms. Craske et al. conclude that this model holds promise for improving the efficacy of ET with associative learning mechanisms.

ET has been extended into an approach named **Cue exposure therapy (CET)**, used to treat substance use disorders (drug addiction). It is used to extinguish the association between substances and cues. It consists of exposing patients to cues related to the substance without reinforcement, the consumption of the substance. With repetitive trials, the association between substances and cues is weakened, cravings are then attenuated.

Vollstädt-Klein et al. study the effect of this approach on people suffering from AUD involved in addiction using functional magnetic resonance imaging of the brain (fMRI) [38]. To do so, they compared two groups of patients who underwent a detoxification treatment. One of the groups was a control group the other was assigned to a CET, undergoing fMRI. The patients from the CET group received nine sessions of CET over three weeks. The fMRI has been done before and after the treatments. The study shows less activation of the brain areas relevant for addiction memory for the CET group and enhanced inhibitory

---

[5] https://medlineplus.gov/alcoholusedisorderaudtreatment.html.

control. However, they did not find any differences in craving as scores about self-reported craving did not differ significantly between the two groups. They conclude that CET does have an impact on alcohol-associated brain responses by reducing them, but, this study is not taking into account relapse and drinking behavior, the authors do not take any position about the CET efficacy.

In [21], Loeber et al. investigate the advantages of the CET over the cognitive-behavioral treatment (CBT), a well-established treatment approach. To do so, they made a comparison between two groups of AUD patients, by taking into account two elements: craving and self-efficacy of patients at the end of the treatment. Each group has undergone one of the treatments. The CBT was focused on the development of coping strategies and education about the health consequences of alcohol abuse or relapse. However, the CET was a combination of cue exposure sessions and coping skill training. While doing the cue exposure session, patients were able to put into practice what they learned in the coping skill training. Both had the same time allocated (22.5 h within three weeks). To assess the craving and the self-efficacy of the patients, two questionnaires were used, the Alcohol Craving Questionnaire [27,31] and the Craving Beliefs Questionnaire [2] during the treatment. To assess the development of drinking status, at the end of the treatment, each patient was administered to the TimeLine Follow Back Interview [32] each month for six months over telephone contact. It was also administered in face-to-face interviews three and six months after discharge. Loeber et al., suggest CET has better results as the number of days of abstinence are higher for CET patients than CBT. Ethanol quantities consumed daily are also inferior. They postulate based on this study that a patient with high levels of dependence may profit more from CET.

In [6], Conklin and Tiffany aim to evaluate the efficacy of CET. They have made a meta-analysis of cue exposure addiction treatment outcome studies. They firstly point out some publications that state there is little evidence for the effectiveness of CET [9,11], and [26]. Conklin and Tiffany add a hypothesis that optimal parameters for cue exposure are not yet found. They propose a list of improvements that could be made to the CET. One of them is the usage of cues, they should be used in multiple contexts decreases the context specificity of extinction [16], and allows a general extinction. However, it is complicated to create multiple contexts in a naturalistic setting. Some can even be dangerous such as streets. The extinction learning (decrease of responses when exposed to a conditioned stimulus due to a lack of reinforcement) could be faster when given in a series of short exposures instead of one long session [3]. Coping techniques are also beneficial in case of some situations that could lead to re-addiction. They also suggest using extinction reminders, simple and compact that the person with the addiction can use in anticipation of a high-risk situation as the first CS-US association is not erased.

In their work [24], Monk and Heim presented a systematic review of 80 articles published from 1970 to 2013. They mainly analyzed how the context influences alcohol consumption. They pointed out several publications where contexts (pub, student party, drinking games, after campus, etc.) have been found to be significant predictors of both the frequency and quantity of alcohol consumption.

In [13], Ghiţă et al. investigated alcohol craving levels caused by different elements by testing a group of participants. The kind of elements investigated was the location, the moment of the day or week, the kind of beverage, and the mood. Those participants were diagnosed with AUD according to the DSM-5 [1]. To do so, they asked participants to fill a questionnaire about their cravings. They have identified four triggers that are the most effective. The context associated with the greater craving is a party, a bar, a pub, and a house. The most common craving-related beverages reported by the AUD group are beer, wine, and whisky. The time of the day is also reported to impact alcohol craving as one patient had more urges at night. Likewise, the weekend compared with other weekdays seems to induce a bigger craving. Moreover, they point out that their data indicate a greater craving from a patient with AUD when they have negatives emotions like stress or sadness. In addition, drinking alone or with friends seems to trigger more cravings than drinking with relatives, coworkers, or a partner.

In [22], Manchery et al. study the possibility that intentional bias toward alcohol can be used to predict cue-induced alcohol craving in a population. This bias influence the personal perception that has an individual of their environment. Intentional bias for alcohol-related cues is measured by comparing the reaction time of participants with a task described in the work of Miller and Fillmore [23]. It consists of two pictures side by side with, either alcohol-related content or neutral, that are replaced by a visual probe like a cross. Both pictures disappear and the probe randomly takes the place of one of the pictures. The goal for participants is to indicate as quickly as possible if the probe is on the left side or on the right side. The second task that participants had to perform was to report their craving after completing an alcohol cue-exposure task. For this, participants were exposed to two cues (one alcohol-related and one neutral). They concluded that exposure to alcohol cues elicited significant cravings and heightened attention to alcohol stimuli can significantly impact motivation to consume.

In [34], Stein et al. study the inhibition and the amount of craving for people with AUD. They made a comparison between an AUD group and a control group of inhibition to alcohol-related context and neutral context (pictures with alcohol or neutral cues), as well as assessing the individual amount of craving. Participants had their brain activity recorded while performing a Go-NoGo task involving neutral and alcohol-related stimuli. A Go-NoGo task consists of pressing a button as soon as a picture appears on a screen (Go trials) except when the stimulus is repeated (NoGo trials). Stein et al. conclude that a patient with strong craving will probably have more difficulties inhibiting his drinking urges than patients with weak craving.

3   Related Work

The lack of control of the environment with CET constrains the therapy to take place in a scene with no relation to alcohol consumption. Thus, the context is not available. The search for technology able to improve CET brings us to **virtual reality (VR)**. Ghiţă and Gutiérrez-Maldonado made a systematic review to examine the applications of VR for CET in the case of AUD [12]. They mainly analyzed how VR could improve CET. They found some publications indicating that VR can be used to simulate real-life situations [19] based on relevant stimuli [33], and that it can be kept under control [36]. Those allow individualized assessment and treatment approaches [17]. They also point out some publications [5, 20] supporting that social pressure leads to craving and ask the question about the inclusion of avatars interactive or drinking to create this pressure. Ghiţă and Gutiérrez-Maldonado add that prolonged exposure means less craving with the time passing because of the habituation process and the capacity to build coping strategies. They conclude that CET in VR, also known as **virtual reality exposure therapy (VRET)**, is useful as the results are generally showing positive effects but clinical trials are necessary to find the right parameters and the long-term effect of VRET.

In [4], Bordnick et al. give their own vision of VR usages in the case of CET and treatment against obesity. They state which aspect, VR, can improve. VR allows active participation in a three-dimensional virtual world. It also interacts with most of the sensory channels. When CET is performed or cue-reactivity is studied, it can be done *in vivo*, but it is often too simplified and does not recreate the natural environment of the patient. Even if the proximal cue (an alcohol bottle) is present, the total context is missing (a party). With VR, it is easier to bring a lifelike environment and to reproduce a life experience while being always under control. They also suggest that practicing coping skills while being immersed in a high-risk environment should have better results compared to therapy that relies on talking.

In [14], Giovancarli et al. study three aspects of VRET. Firstly, the effectiveness of CBT coupled with VRET in comparison to CBT alone. Secondly, the impact of VRET with CBT on anxiety, depression, quality of life, self-esteem, and addictive morbidities. Finally, the feasibility and acceptability of VR use. This publication is about a clinical trial of fourteen months, where Giovancarli et al. compares two groups, one CBT coupled with VRET and one with CBT alone in the case of tobacco consumption. The fourteen months are divided into two parts, two months of therapy followed by twelve months of follow-up, consisting of face-to-face interviews aiming to collect data at the end of the therapy followed by three other interviews at three, six, and twelve months after the end of the therapy. The CBT alone therapy followed the keys principle of CBT and was based on international guidelines. For The CBT-VRET, they did a classic CBT session and additionally used a VR headset and a game engine to create the VR exposure. Six different scenarios like drinking in a bar with friends at dusk, having coffee after dinner home, or driving a can on road with traffic. The experimenter could trigger events manually in the virtual environment like an avatar proposing to smoke. In their discussion, they explain that even if CET can be used, it has its limitation, as the presence of only proximal cue (no context), where the VRET might offer an alternative with the context. Giovancarli et al. make the hypothesis that individuals can learn to cope in a VRET just like in the real-life and put into practice what they learned in the CBT session. A VRET can be focused on pleasant scenes to avoid negative impacts such as stress but smokers might be more sensitive when exposed to negative emotions. Finally, as VR is available at low cost and is simple to use, VRET can easily be implemented in the case of clinical practice, and that patients could even practice VR exposure at home.

In [18], **Action-centered exposure therapy (ACET)** is proposed by Kamkuimo Kengne et al. as new approach to treat people with post-traumatic stress disorder (PTSD). They explain that PTSD is dysfunctional beliefs that associate stimuli to dangers or threats, which leads to anxious reactions. ACET consist of proposing patients to take an active role in their treatment by creating an interactive treatment. ACET exploits gamification techniques and interactions between patients and a virtual environment optimized for learning. The authors point out that through an active engagement, several advantages are obtained. The motivation of the patient is enhanced, this may reduce the number of patients giving up their therapy. With the action being observable, it is easier to see progress. They suggest that reaction can become a reflex by creating an association between a stimulus and a reaction through repetition according to behavioral learning theory. By following a succession of stimuli-response processes, one can learn new reflexes with positive outcomes that replace the previous ones with negative outcomes.

Here, we suggest that ACET can be adapted for AUD by including certain elements. The first one is a proximal cue triggering a CS such as an alcohol bottle. The second, is an action to perform towards the cue in response to the CS. An environment related to alcohol is necessary to give a context. A reminder of the inhibition needs to be included, an element that can be reproduced in real life. Finally, an action to associate with the CS is necessary to have a new conditioned response replacing the initial craving for alcohol.

4 Designing Key Components

Action is a key element of ACET. It is the concept of video games as the main actor of the game is the player. Video games also provide a virtual world adaptable to needs. It is then interesting to use this medium to implement ACET.

Moreover, video games are able to use every aspect of VR to improve user engagement, in comparison to a more classical medium such as gamepads, keyboards, mouses, and TV screens. As our game has a medical goal, it fulfills the definition of **serious games**. Serious games aim to change players in a way that persists and by removing feelings of bother [8]. It can be used to learn new knowledge, skill, belief, behavior, etc. In our case, this is the behavior that is targeted even if it is an automatism. We want to change the reaction of the player when confronted in real life to a CS, a bottle of alcohol.

When one wants to use a serious game either to transform players, they must take into account barriers. Barriers are what prevent the player transformation with more classical solutions. Before designing a game, barriers must be found and understood as they can be a hindrance to the impact of the game and its goal. With their knowledge, one can be inspired, this can create game elements meant to overcome those barriers. There is a lot of different barriers that exist, such as motivation, fear, accessibility [8].

Several solutions exist to take care of barriers such as the elimination or workaround. In our case, initial motivation is a barrier to AUD treatment. By using a VR serious game, the player is enticed to try the game. VR technology gained in popularity these past few years, but most people have not been able to try it by themselves. Most of the time, they are surprised by the immersion and have a great time just being in a video game.

As this state does not go on forever, people grow accustomed and lose interest, the game must be fun to retain their will to play. If players like it enough, they could even play it outside of therapy sessions, at home. Moreover, VR headsets are starting to be available at a low cost. Indeed, a fully autonomous device can be available for $300[6].

Based on the analysis of this state of the art, we propose several requirements for a serious game that can help to tackle AUD:

Alcohol-related cue: As proximal alcohol-related cues are the primary elements that trigger craving [22], an element acting as a cue must be present. Usually, a bottle of alcohol can be used. The visual of the cue should be adapted to players given their tastes to have the best performance and to avoid having a beverage that they may not like. Their favorite drink should induce a greater craving.

Interactivity: As this approach is based on ACET, an action to perform toward the cue has to be implemented to have players active during sessions. It helps to keep the player involved in the session. It also allows seeing the reactions of the player when exposed to the stimulus. This reaction is meant to become the reflex replacing the craving by repeating the action when seeing the proximal alcohol-related cue as stated in the behavioral learning theory [18]. That way, the inhibitory learning model is involved [7]. Finally, as the user is not consuming the content of the bottle, the alcohol, there is no reinforcement of the first conditioned response involved.

Reminder: As complicated situations may bring back the first conditioned response [6], a reminder easy to replicate and to carry in real life should be added in the game. It should be in evidence and used during the whole game so it can be associated with the inhibition. That way, players have an item that they can keep on them at all times and use when need to remind themselves of the inhibition.

Environment: As the craving can be triggered just with the environment and its context [24], the right virtual environment that recreates the right context must be used [4]. With prolonged exposure to the context, the player feels less craving and can build copping strategies [12]. The environment should be the most commonly used in VRET, a party, a house, a bar, or a pub [13]. An environment personalized to the player would even be better. It can be

---

[6] https://www.oculus.com/quest-2/.

the one in which the player is used to drink. The ambient sound can also be taken into account. It can be music reminding of parties or chatter, often heard in bars. The use of multiple environments to have multiple contexts is better, as it decreases the context specificity of the game and allows a general inhibition [6].

Avatars: As social pressure leads to craving [12], avatars of people drinking should be added. It would improve the location, add more alcohol contexts, and create social pressure. They could also be interactive with the player by proposing drinks.

Replay value: As a repetitive exposure is necessary [12,18], players have to play the game multiple times. It can lead to a loss of interest until they no longer have the will to play. Some replay value should be implemented to prevent that. To provide some replay value, the goal of the game can be planned with several game rounds insight. More cue positions can be created in advance than the number of cues used in a single round. They are then selected randomly at the initialization of the game. That way, each round is a new challenge.

Game mechanics for player retention: As in most games, games mechanics should be implemented to encourage the player to continue playing. The environment can evolve by accomplishing the main goal. The world could start dark and unwelcoming that become brighter and more pleasant as the player progress toward the end by achieving its objective. It could also be the cleanliness or the tidiness. A feeling of having taken the right decision can arise and push the player to continue further. Achievement associated with rewards can also be implemented to incentive the player to keep playing. For example, after winning the game multiple times, the player can be rewarded with cosmetic elements or badges showing their commitment. These rewards could be lost in case of relapse.

First person perspective: When comparing first and third-person perspectives, a difference between the sense of ownership (self-attribution of the avatar's body) and how it is simple to interact with items can be noted [15]. Indeed, interacting with items precisely is easier and preferred with a first-person perspective. The sense of ownership is also stronger with a first-person perspective. It is easier to project oneself into an avatar with a first-person perspective than third-person perspective [10,37]. Consequently, the first-person perspective is more interesting and should be favored in our context.

5   Usage of This Requirements to Create a Serious Game

The proposed prototype is developed to evaluate the complexity of implementing the previous recommendations in a serious game. As it only focuses on the game elements and less on the interaction part, the elements related to VR are not present (ecological movement, etc.).

The game example has a first-person view to improve the ownership of the game and help the player to interact with the world. The choice of the house with a kitchen, a bathroom, and a living room has been made in accord with the most common places triggering alcohol craving.

The goal for the player is to find all the bottles hidden in the virtual world and to paste a sticker on them (Fig. 1b). The reaction of applying a sticker after finding a bottle is the reaction meant to replace the previous reaction, the craving, and the will to drink the content of the bottle.

This sticker is a reminder of the inhibition actually learned. The bottles of alcohol used are proximal cues meant to trigger craving in players. The texture and shape of the bottle are those of a brand of whisky, in accord with the most common craving-related type of beverages reported by AUD groups [13]. The movement needed to apply the sticker can be associated with a response aiming to replace the previously conditioned response, the need to drink the beverage.

The world is actually divided into different sections by doors to create a new element of gameplay. To open the doors, players must find all bottles available in the areas they have access to (Fig. 2a and b). It helps them to find the bottles and prevent them to be completely lost in a world too big too quickly. By adding new areas one by one to augment the size of the world, players have time to acclimate themselves to the world and learn the topography. It is also a form of reward, by finding all the bottles available, players gain the right to access the next level of the game. It also offers a feeling of progression.

In the current implementation, players start in the kitchen. The first bottle is right in front of them, that way they should not miss the first element on which apply a sticker and understand how it can look like (Fig. 1a). The kitchen is a small area with a door preventing the player to wander off. To open this door, the player must paste the sticker on the first bottle, that way it shows that they have understood the main rule of the game. Once it has been done, they have access to the bigger room of the house, the living room (Fig. 3), and a corridor that lead to closed doors. Behind those doors, there is the bathroom and the restroom.

Only the first bottle is that much in evidence. The others are hidden to increase the difficulty and create a challenge. When players accomplish a feat such as completing a challenge, they have a sense of achievement. It creates enthusiasm for players and gives them the inclination to continue playing.

A scoring system is available to help players keeping track of the number of bottles they have found. The number of mistakes is also tracked and displayed (see Fig. 3 for example). It aims to bring players the will to make the least mistake possible and discourages them to apply a sticker to any elements. That way, players are incited to only paste the sticker on the bottle and to learn correctly the inhibition.

Each bottle can only be marked once. Any attempt to apply a sticker more than once on a bottle is considered a mistake. The game ends once all of the bottles have been found and marked. When it happens, a game over screen appears and shows the score of the player, and the number of mistakes made.

(a) A sticker in the player's hand.

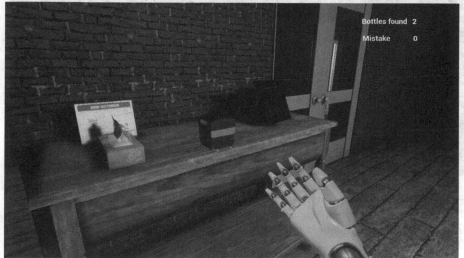

(b) A sticker pasted on a bottle.

Fig. 1. Sticker mechanic, one of the main gameplay elements.

It is possible to personalise the game rules to change the new response that we want to use in the inhibitory learning model. Instead of applying stickers to bottles spread in a virtual world, the goal can be to pour the beverage into a sink to empty the bottle.

As a reward for completing multiple time the game, an achievement with a cosmetic reward for the sticker could be implemented. The sticker can become golden, which can be upgraded to a diamond sticker after even more wins.

(a) Closed door   (b) Opened door

Fig. 2. Unlocking a door allows players to discover new parts of the level.

Fig. 3. Evolution of environment, example of the living room, the luminosity can be dark at the beginning then become lighter. It incites the player to continue playing and transforming the environment into one more pleasant.

6   Conclusion and Future Work

This paper proposed key elements to design a new approach to help tackle AUD. The new approach is based on CET, to which is added interaction to recreate an ACET. It allows the replacement of the craving with a new response through repetition according to the behavioral learning theory. By doing the same exercise repeatedly, the reflex of craving should be replaced by a new reaction. This new approach also possesses all the elements of a VRET with a virtual environment linked to alcohol drinking and its context, proximal alcohol-related cues, and social pressures with avatars. The serious game aspect allows the retention of players by proposing entertainment and challenges.

We plan to analyze the interest of the virtual reality aspect used in VRET and ACET for this approach. Then, we want to integrate it given the results as it may improve the game by reinforcing the presence for players and allow them to reproduce real-life movement. Finally, We plan to run some user tests to assess the effectiveness of this serious game

Acknowledgment. We would like to thank Nathan Sioui and Marly Beaudoin for the 3D Assets of the environment and Pierre Tousignant and Guillaume Côté for the supervision of these 3D artists.

References

1. American Psychiatric Association and American Psychiatric Association and others: DSM 5. American Psychiatric Association 70 (2013)
2. Beck, A.T., Wright, F.D., Newman, C.F., Liese, B.S., Lindenmeyer, J.: Kognitive Therapie der Sucht. Beltz, PsychologieVerlagsUnion (1997)
3. Berman, J.S., Katzev, R.D.: Factors involved in the rapid elimination of avoidance behavior. Behav. Res. Ther. **10**(3), 247–256 (1972)
4. Bordnick, P.S., Carter, B.L., Traylor, A.C.: What virtual reality research in addictions can tell us about the future of obesity assessment and treatment. J. Diabetes Sci. Technol. **5**(2), 265–271 (2011)
5. Cho, S., et al.: Development and verification of an alcohol craving-induction tool using virtual reality: craving characteristics in social pressure situation. CyberPsychol. Behav. **11**(3), 302–309 (2008)
6. Conklin, C.A., Tiffany, S.T.: Applying extinction research and theory to cue-exposure addiction treatments. Addiction **97**(2), 155–167 (2002)
7. Craske, M.G., Treanor, M., Conway, C.C., Zbozinek, T., Vervliet, B.: Maximizing exposure therapy: an inhibitory learning approach. Behav. Res. Ther. **58**, 10–23 (2014)
8. Culyba, S.: The Transformational Framework: A process tool for the development of Transformational games. Carnegie Mellon University (2018)
9. Dawe, S., et al.: Does post-withdrawal cue exposure improve outcome in opiate addiction? A controlled trial. Addiction **88**(9), 1233–1245 (1993)
10. Denisova, A., Cairns, P.: First person vs. third person perspective in digital games: do player preferences affect immersion? In: Proceedings of the 33rd Annual ACM Conference on Human Factors in Computing Systems, pp. 145–148 (2015)
11. Franken, I.H., de Haan, H.A., van der Meer, C.W., Haffmans, P.J., Hendriks, V.M.: Cue reactivity and effects of cue exposure in abstinent posttreatment drug users. J. Subst. Abuse Treat. **16**(1), 81–85 (1999)
12. Ghiţă, A., Gutiérrez-Maldonado, J.: Applications of virtual reality in individuals with alcohol misuse: a systematic review. Addict. Behav. **81**, 1–11 (2018)
13. Ghiţă, A., et al.: Identifying triggers of alcohol craving to develop effective virtual environments for cue exposure therapy. Front. Psychol. **10**, 74 (2019)
14. Giovancarli, C., et al.: Virtual reality cue exposure for the relapse prevention of tobacco consumption: a study protocol for a randomized controlled trial. Trials **17**(1), 1–9 (2016)
15. Gorisse, G., Christmann, O., Amato, E.A., Richir, S.: First-and third-person perspectives in immersive virtual environments: presence and performance analysis of embodied users. Front. Robot. AI **4**, 33 (2017)

16. Gunther, L.M., Denniston, J.C., Miller, R.R.: Conducting exposure treatment in multiple contexts can prevent relapse. Behav. Res. Ther. **36**(1), 75–91 (1998)
17. Hone-Blanchet, A., Wensing, T., Fecteau, S.: The use of virtual reality in craving assessment and cue-exposure therapy in substance use disorders. Front. Hum. Neurosci. **8**, 844 (2014)
18. Kamkuimo Kengne, S.A., Fossaert, M., Girard, B., Menelas, B.A.J.: Action-centered exposure therapy (ACET): a new approach to the use of virtual reality to the care of people with post-traumatic stress disorder. Behav. Sci. **8**(8), 76 (2018)
19. Kwon, H., Choi, J., Roh, S., Yang, B., Lee, J.: Application of virtual reality-cue exposure therapy for reducing alcohol craving. Annu. Rev. Cyberther. Telemed. **4**, 161–166 (2006)
20. Lee, J.S., et al.: Social pressure-induced craving in patients with alcohol dependence: application of virtual reality to coping skill training. Psychiatry Investig. **5**(4), 239 (2008)
21. Loeber, S., Croissant, B., Heinz, A., Mann, K., Flor, H.: Cue exposure in the treatment of alcohol dependence: effects on drinking outcome, craving and self-efficacy. Br. J. Clin. Psychol. **45**(4), 515–529 (2006)
22. Manchery, L., Yarmush, D.E., Luehring-Jones, P., Erblich, J.: Attentional bias to alcohol stimuli predicts elevated cue-induced craving in young adult social drinkers. Addict. Behav. **70**, 14–17 (2017)
23. Miller, M.A., Fillmore, M.T.: The effect of image complexity on attentional bias towards alcohol-related images in adult drinkers. Addiction **105**(5), 883–890 (2010)
24. Monk, R.L., Heim, D.: A critical systematic review of alcohol-related outcome expectancies. Substance Use Misuse **48**(7), 539–557 (2013)
25. Moss, H.B.: The impact of alcohol on society: a brief overview. Soc. Work Public Health **28**(3–4), 175–177 (2013)
26. Powell, J., Gray, J., Bradley, B.: Subjective craving for opiates: evaluation of a cue exposure protocol for use with detoxified opiate addicts. Br. J. Clin. Psychol. **32**(1), 39–53 (1993)
27. Preuss, U., Schütz, C., Koch, J., Soyka, M.: Evaluation of two questionnaires (ACQ and OCDS) for the measurement of subjective craving in inpatient alcoholics. Methodik von Verlaufs-und Therapiestudien in Psychiatrie und Psychotherapie [Methods of process-and outcome-studies in psychiatry and psychotherapy], pp. 200–203 (2000)
28. Ramalho, R.: Alcohol consumption and alcohol-related problems during the COVID-19 pandemic: a narrative review. Australas. Psychiatry **28**(5), 524–526 (2020)
29. Rehm, J.: The risks associated with alcohol use and alcoholism. Alcohol Res. Health **34**(2), 135 (2011)
30. Ryan, R.M., Plant, R.W., O'Malley, S.: Initial motivations for alcohol treatment: relations with patient characteristics, treatment involvement, and dropout. Addict. Behav. **20**(3), 279–297 (1995)
31. Singleton, E., Tiffany, S., Henningfield, J.: Development and validation of a new questionnaire to assess craving for alcohol. NIDA Res. Monogr. **153**, 289 (1995)
32. Sobell, L., Sobell, M.: Alcohol Timeline Followback Users' Manual. Addiction Research Foundation, Toronto (1995)
33. Son, J.H., et al.: Virtual reality therapy for the treatment of alcohol dependence: a preliminary investigation with positron emission tomography/computerized tomography. J. Stud. Alcohol Drugs **76**(4), 620–627 (2015)

34. Stein, M., Fey, W., Koenig, T., Oehy, J., Moggi, F.: Context-specific inhibition is related to craving in alcohol use disorders: a dangerous imbalance. Alcoholism Clin. Exp. Res. **42**(1), 69–80 (2018)
35. Tai, B., Volkow, N.D.: Treatment for substance use disorder: opportunities and challenges under the affordable care act. Soc. Work Public Health **28**(3–4), 165–174 (2013)
36. Valmaggia, L.R., Latif, L., Kempton, M.J., Rus-Calafell, M.: Virtual reality in the psychological treatment for mental health problems: an systematic review of recent evidence. Psychiatry Res. **236**, 189–195 (2016)
37. Vogeley, K., Fink, G.R.: Neural correlates of the first-person-perspective. Trends Cogn. Sci. **7**(1), 38–42 (2003)
38. Vollstädt-Klein, S., et al.: Effects of cue-exposure treatment on neural cue reactivity in alcohol dependence: a randomized trial. Biol. Psychiat. **69**(11), 1060–1066 (2011)

Competitive Gaming and Exercise

Development of a Mobile Exergame to Implement Brief Interventions to Increase Physical Activity for Adults with Schizophrenia

Yannick Francillette[1,2]([✉])[iD], Bob A. J. Menelas[1][iD], Bruno Bouchard[1,2][iD], Kévin Bouchard[1,2][iD], Sébastien Gaboury[1,2][iD], Célia Kingsbury[4,5][iD], Samuel St-Amour[4,5][iD], Ahmed J. Romain[3,5][iD], and Paquito Bernard[4,5][iD]

[1] Université du Québec à Chicoutimi, Chicoutimi, Canada
{yannick_francillette,bamenela,bruno_bouchard,kevin_bouchard,
sebastien_gaboury}@uqac.ca
[2] LIARA, Seminole, USA
[3] Université de Montréal, Montréal, Canada
aj.romain@umontreal.ca
[4] Université du Québec à Montréal, Montréal, Canada
kingsbury.celia@courrier.uqam.ca, bernard.paquito@uqam.ca
[5] Centre de Recherche de l'Institut Universitaire en Santé Mentale de Montréal,
Montréal, Canada
https://liara.uqac.ca/
https://criusmm.ciusss-estmtl.gouv.qc.ca/

Abstract. Schizophrenia and other disorders of the schizophrenia spectrum are the 8th leading cause of disability in the world and affect 1–3% of the general population. These disorders are characterized by the presence of several symptoms, including negative symptoms such as decreased motivation. This type of symptom is particularly troublesome for people suffering from this disorder because it affects their daily life, it makes people have very sedentary behavior. This can have consequences on their health in the long term because a sedentary lifestyle facilitates the development of certain chronic diseases. One solution to this problem is to encourage people to maintain a certain level of physical activity. In this paper, we present a serious game designed to encourage people with this type of disorder to maintain a level of physical activity. This game aims to be integrated into the daily life of the players. We present changes made since our previous work. We present feedback from different people in the target population who have tried the game. The feedback indicates that the lack of aggressive content is nice but that the lack of challenge limits the long-term investment.

Keywords: Exergame · Cognitive impairment · Physical activity · Smartphone · Brief interventions

© Springer Nature Switzerland AG 2021
B. Fletcher et al. (Eds.): JCSG 2021, LNCS 12945, pp. 185–199, 2021.
https://doi.org/10.1007/978-3-030-88272-3_14

1   Introduction

Schizophrenia and schizophrenia spectrum disorders affect 1–3% of the general population, and the World Health Organization ranks this disorder as the 8th leading cause of disability in the world [30]. According to the DSM-V, these disorders are characterized by the presence of several of the following symptoms: delusions, hallucinations, disorganized speech or behavior, catatonic behavior, and negative symptoms (e.g. lack of motivation) [5,28]. This last category of symptoms is particularly challenging because most activities of daily living require motivation to be initiated and maintained, e.g. work, school, groceries, physical activity [10,13]. Because of this motivation deficit, people with schizophrenia spend about 80% of their time in sedentary activities (about 13 hours per day excluding sleep) and are less physically active than the general population [16,29]. 55 to 70% of people suffering from schizophrenia do not meet the recommended level of physical activity and this has an impact on their mental and physical health[27]. Indeed, the lack of physical activity increases the risk of developing chronic diseases such as diabetes, cardiovascular problems, etc. [9].

To address this lack of motivation, several interventions, including physical activity, have been found to foster motivation in individuals with schizophrenia [22,24]. However, studies show that people with schizophrenia have several barriers to physical activity, with lack of motivation being the most common barrier, but also the issue of social support, stress and fatigue [6,23]. We are faced with a circular situation because one of the solutions (doing physical activity) is difficult to apply due to the lack of motivation.

We aim to propose a game that implements the "Brief Script"[1] approach in the field of physical activity for individuals with cognitive disorders. Brief intervention is a method that aims to help a person set goals, identify barriers to achieving those goals, and identify solutions. We base ourselves on the "Volitional Help Sheet" [4], which is a model of brief intervention. This approach has given interesting results in other areas such as alcohol consumption among smokers and emotional eating [2,3]. It seems to show promising results in the field of physical activity [21]. Our approach aims at proposing a serious game that allows to automate and improve this approach after people with cognitive disorders.

In this paper, we propose a mobile exergame that aims to remove the motivation barrier to help individuals with schizophrenia to maintain a level of physical activity. Serious games represent an interesting approach to this problem because they are specifically designed to help remove certain barriers. This game encourages the player to perform physical activity in order to progress faster. We are using some concepts of the "Free to Play" model, especially the idea of being able to spend real money in the game to buy certain elements. In our approach, the player has the possibility to perform physical activity to buy certain items. Moreover, we propose this game on smartphones because on the one hand, it is one of the most important market today with many players. On the other hand,

---

[1] http://www.paha.org.uk/Resource/physical-activity-brief-advice-and-brief-intervention-scripts.

smartphones accompany their users on a daily basis and this allows the game to be played anywhere and anytime.

This paper presents the progress done since our previous publication about this approach [11]. The objective of the paper is to present the changes made as well as the feedback from the target population. The research presented is interested in the usability of this solution with the target population. Thus, we seek to answer the question: is this approach accessible?

This document is organized as follows. Section 2 presents related work. Section 3 presents our approach, introducing game design and game architecture. Section 4 presents our study. Finally, we conclude this paper and present future work in Sect. 5.

2 Related Works

We can categorize propositions in the literature according to the following criteria: The mobility of the platform, static or mobile, i.e. can the player play the game or a game anywhere? the target audience, is the game designed for the general public or for people with cognitive disorders the type of project, is the project an industrial or academic project? And the approach or model of the game. In this paper, we only focus on the works published since 2015 and associated with the key words: exergames, serious games for physical activities, exercise games.

Since the advent of controllers that detect movements or body position, publishers in the video game industry have released several exergames for the general public. Recently, Nintendo's Ring Fit Adventure[2] (Ring Fit) on Nintendo Switch offers players several types of exercises for the lower and upper body using a rigid plastic ring (the Ring-Con) that the player must hold with his hands. The game also uses another accessory (Leg Strap) that allows you to strap one of the Switch's controllers to your leg in order to detect lower body movements. The game combines sequences where the player must run on the spot with combat phases where the player must choose attacks and execute them by performing a series of the attached exercise.

Previously, Nintendo also released the Wii Fit series[3], which uses the Wii Balance, a body scale-like device that calculates the player's center of gravity and inclination using several pressure sensors. The games in this series feature several mini-games, each based on a type of physical exercise that must be performed to win. In their study, authors used these games to observe that they have a positive impact on young adults [8,26]. PDDanceCity is a game that targets people with Parkinson's disease, requiring players to navigate a labirintic level to reach positions given by the game [14]. The game uses the Wii Balance Board or a USB dance mat to calculate the player's movements. The game offers the player the opportunity to work on both thinking and physical skills. They have to find a way to reach the end position and exercise to get there. Other researchers have

---

[2] https://ringfitadventure.nintendo.com/.
[3] https://www.nintendo.com/wiifit/.

proposed games using the Microsoft Kinect device[4], which has several cameras, including one for depth, [7, 20].

Some works use home-made solutions. Running Othello is a version of Othello[5] that follows the same basic rules, but requires the player to complete a physical or cognitive exercise before moving a point [18]. The game loop consists in running towards the token you wish to place, then carrying out the required exercise until the end of the game. The game is played online and the size of the game space is modifiable and each game token is associated with an Radio Frequency IDentification (RFID) tag [1]. This allows the game to be set up in many different places, but the game requires a setup phase at each change of location.

Finally, other works use the smartphone as a game platform. MOBIGAME is a mobile game targeting individuals with type 2 diabetes [15]. The game loop consists in doing physical exercises to gain resources, which allow to manage the maintenance of a virtual garden. The game proposes different types of exercises, to work on different aspects such as, strength, endurance, balance, flexibility. To detect the movement and recognize the exercise, the game is based on the sensors present in the phone. Thus, it does not require any additional electronic device. However, some exercises may require specific equipment such as a chair, a mat, etc. or a particular positioning of the smartphone. The first version of *Ocean Empire* targets individuals suffering from schizophrenia [11]. It proposes to the player to catch fishes to convert them into resources allowing to buy upgrades for a submarine to reach the ocean floor. The player has the possibility to do physical activity in order to gain another type of resources that allow to progress faster. To recognize the physical activity of the players it also uses the sensors of the phone.

3   Material

Ocean Empire is a mobile game for smartphones on Android[6] that uses activity recognition to reward the player for physical activity. It is designed with the Unity 3D engine[7] and is in 2D to run on as many smartphones as possible. It uses several mechanics of Free to Play games to motivate players to do and maintain physical activity. These mechanics are designed to maximize the integration of the game into the player's daily life (Table 1).

Our goal is to promote the achievement of activity through self-regulation and to help users to do this self-regulation. Thus, they have to plan the periods when they want to do activity. The system proposes reminders, and it also proposes interventions to help them fulfill their contract next time if they don't fulfill it. We adopt a strategy based on the "Physical Activity Screening and Brief Advice Script", and the "Volitional Help Sheet" [4, 21].

---

[4] https://developer.microsoft.com/fr-fr/windows/kinect/.

[5] https://www.worldothello.org.

[6] https://www.android.com.

[7] https://unity.com/.

Table 1. Summary of propositions in literature. (^{a}) the study is academic, the game is from industry

Proposition	Platform	Target	Producer	Game approach	Year
Ring Fit	Static	Everyone	Industry	RPG elements attached with exercises	2019
Ocean Empire [11]	Mobile	Schizophrenia	Academic	Clicker with Free to play elements	2018
PDDanceCity [14]	Static	Parkinson's Disease	Academic	Labyrinth	2017
Mobigame [15]	Mobile	Individual with type 2 diabetes	Academic	City-building game	2017
Running Othello [18]	Static	Everyone	Academic	Othello attached with exercises	2015
Cone et al.'s study [8]	Static (Wii Fit)	Young Adult	Academic(^{a})	Wii Fit game	2015

3.1   The Game Loop

The objective is to reach the ocean floor to collect a treasure. However, the submarine is limited in fuel, so the player has to upgrade it gradually in order to progress to the floor. To buy upgrades, he must catch fish that will be exchanged for coins depending on the type of fish. Each fish must be caught with a particular game mechanic, small fish are caught by hitting them, bigger ones must be caught with a harpoon for example.

Unlike many other exergames that make a direct association between physical activity and progress in the game, we propose an asynchronous mode. The player can do physical activity in order to earn a second type of currency (activity tickets) that can be used to buy items to upgrade the submarine. Figure 2 shows game loop of *Ocean Empire*. Figure 1 shows screenshots of the game. The game rewards physical activity that is performed in an unscheduled way, as part of weekly assignments for example. However, to avoid rewarding basic activities such as going to the bathroom, a minimum activity threshold is set. If it is set at 1 min, it means that the person must do 1 min of consecutive walking for this activity to be considered.

Players get more activity tickets when they complete the activities they have planned. The activity must be done within the time period that has been defined. It is a contract that the player defines. For example, if the player plans to walk for 5 min on one day of the week, but does it on another day, they do not get the reward for the planned activity. When the contract expires, a screen asks the player to indicate the reason. This system is part of the brief intervention approach we want to apply. Based on the answer, the system suggests a solution to pass the contract next time. Figure 3 shows screenshots of the different windows related to the planning and completion or not of the planned activities.

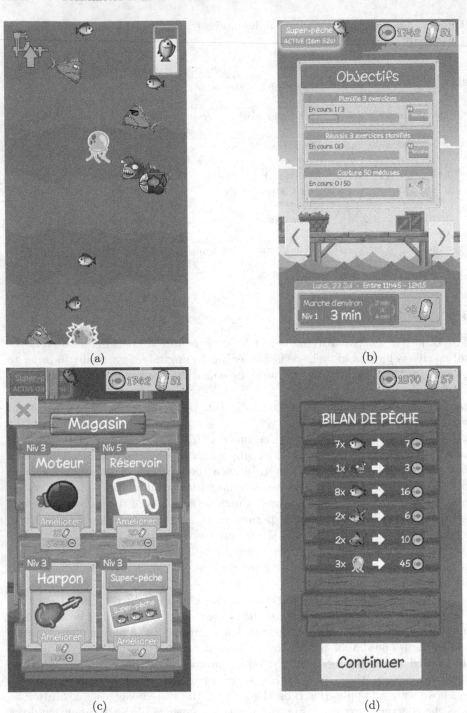

Fig. 1. Screenshots of the game. **(a)** Fishing scene; **(b)** Game mission screen; **(c)** Game shop screen; **(d)** Fishing result screen.

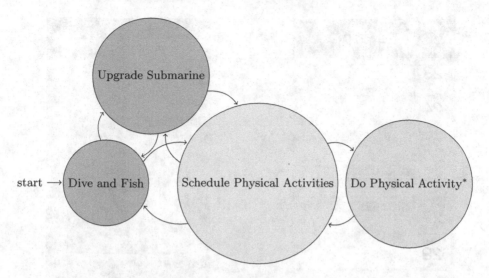

Fig. 2. A scheme of the game loop. (*) Players can do physical activities without planning, but they get higher rewards if they do.

3.2 Activity Recognition

To calculate the physical activity of the player, we use Google's Activity Recognition API[8]. This API is based on the data from the smartphone's sensors (accelerometer and gyroscope) to deduce an activity with a level of confidence. This API can recognize activities such as walking, running, cycling. These are the main activities we are looking to identify for our population.

Our approach is to retrieve at each tick, the activity recognized by the API and save it in a file if the confidence level is above a predefined threshold. Thus, we save a timestamp, the name of the recognized activity, and the confidence level. Figure 5 shows an example file. The activity recognition is performed by a module that is external to the game. This allows the recognition to be performed even when the game is not open. When the game is launched, it reads this file to know the activities that have been performed. It compares the time periods defined in the contracts with the recorded activity periods to validate or not the contracts. The activities are recorded in an encrypted way on the phone. Figure 4 shows a diagram of the application architecture.

4 Study

This game version was evaluated by individuals with schizophrenia, recruited by researchers from the Université du Québec à Montréal (UQAM). The games were played with Alcatel_5044R (IdealXCite) smartphones running on Android

---

[8] https://developers.google.com/location-context/activity-recognition/.

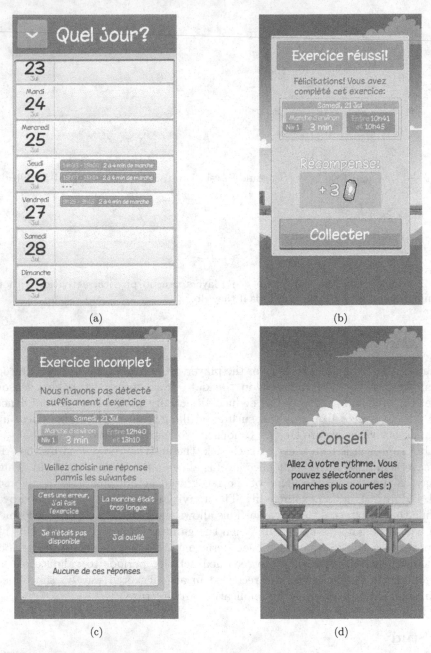

Fig. 3. Screenshot of the planning and execution phase of the exercise. **(a)** the diary where to set the date and time for a physical activity. **(b)** the reward screen when the exercise has been completed. **(c)** the screen when the exercise has not been performed with the questionnaire to help the person identify solutions to the barrier he/she had. **(d)** The screen that displays a suggested solution for the next time (in french: *Go at your own pace. You can select shorter walks.*).

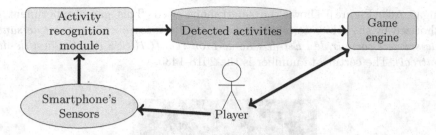

Fig. 4. Scheme of the software architecture and the interactions between the various parts of the system.

Fig. 5. Example of an activity log file. It is displayed in a non-encrypted version from the smartphone. On the left we have the recognized activity separated by a vertical line, the confidence level and then the timestamp of the entry.

Nougat 7.0[9]. Figure 6 shows the smartphone used. This game experiment is authorized by the ethics committee of the *Centre intégré universitaire de santé et de services sociaux de l'Est-de-l'Île-de-Montréal (CIUSS de l'Est-de-l'Île-de-Montréal)*. The certificate number is the 2018-1485.

Fig. 6. Alcatel_5044R (IdealXCite) running *Ocean Empire*.

In the previous study, individuals with no reported mental illness played the game for about 30 min, which was the amount of time provided by the content. In this study, individuals were provided access to the game for 14 days with a presentation of the game on day 1, and two 10-minutes phone interviews on days 7 and 14 to collect feedback regarding the game. Each interview was structured around the following questions:

- What problems have you experienced with the game since the beginning of the study?
- Was it difficult to schedule your physical activity?
- Did the game manage to tell you when you moved?
- If you had a magic wand, what would you like to improve in the game?
- Give me the three negative and positive points of the game?

---

[9] https://www.android.com/versions/nougat-7-0/.

Participants also reported some bugs they encountered during their test. The purpose of this study is to obtain feedback from the target population on the game concept and its use in a real-world context. We regroup the feedback from users around three topics, the game concept, the activity recognition, the difficulty of the game.

Regarding the *game concept*, players reported that they liked the visuals, the simplicity, the accessibility and the "wholesome" aspect (no vulgar or aggressive elements). This tends to confirm what the testers of the previous study reported, that the game does not create stress. The game is perceived as a hobby. One player reported that he played about once a day. However, they complained about the lack of novelty after a certain amount of time, which lowered the level of motivation towards the game. Being able to customise the submarine or other game elements was mentioned as a mechanic that would have been appreciated.

Regarding *activity recognition*, players reported that they liked the fact that they could do physical activity without having the game running and that the game was able to recover it. They also liked the fact that there was a reward for doing physical activity even if it was not planned. One tester reported that he had walked more than he had planned and that he would have liked an extra reward or to be able to add extra minutes to the planned activity. The testers reported several problems with the recognition. The first is that recognition is best done when the phone is in a certain position. For example, one tester reported that some of his activity was not recognised correctly when the phone was in his bag. Another reported that it was possible to cheat and simulate walking by shaking the phone. We can also note that one user reported that he felt that the phone's battery discharged quickly. This point was not considered in the previous study. However, the issue of the application's resource consumption is very important considering the application's planned usage context. Currently, the activity recognition part relies entirely on the Google API. But the fact that we the activity recognition runs continuously in the background has an impact on the battery charge time. By combining the activity recognition with the calculations needed to run the game, the impact on the battery is increased. On the game side, some initial choices such as making the game in 2D, having simple interactions, limiting the need for entities with complex artificial intelligence, were made to reduce the need for computing resources and the impact on the battery. On the activity recognition side, research is needed to reduce the impact on the battery. A simple solution could be to increase the interval of activity detection. However, simply enlarging this interval will have an impact on the detection and with our approach the game may not recognize some periods and cause frustration to the users. Another solution would be to identify if another state-of-the-art approach is more efficient and implement it [25]. Finally, a more advanced solution could be to use a context and battery level adaptive recognition approach. For example, the approach used or the interval could be increased when the user is not in the context of a planned application. When the user is in the context of a planned activity, the interval or approach would be different to improve the detection quality.

Regarding the *game difficulty*, testers indicated that they found the game too simple and that they would have preferred more challenging elements. For example, one tester indicated that he would have preferred the game to limit the number of fishing opportunities per day more to encourage more physical activity. Some mentioned the need for more difficult fishing with more obstacles or constraints.

Ocean Empire has been designed to offer content for 14 days. We wanted to keep the game very simple to avoid creating frustration with elements that would be perceived as too restrictive. However, these feedbacks only point out that having oversimplified the concept seems to have an impact on motivation. Players seem to want difficulty and more restrictive elements. For example, we allow the purchase of several items with both types of game currency, fishing and physical activity, players seem to be willing to not be able to purchase some important items with fishing currency. This would mean that they would be willing to be locked out of some aspect of the game if they did not do physical activity. To offer more variety and diversity, we propose to have levels on different themes. For example, having levels in the dark and requiring the player to spend extra resources each time they want to do that type of level. This level could be generated procedurally with an algorithm that takes into account the level of the equipment of the submarine in order to propose an adapted challenge level [17, 19]. Figure 7 shows a possible example of such a level.

Fig. 7. Screenshot of an example of a potential new level to offer more game situations and challenge. The level is played in the dark in a cave and you have to avoid colliding with the walls.

Finally, personalizing and cosmetic elements seem to be a good way to create the desire to do physical activity. In addition, having special events or items to unlock only in a specific time period could be a motivational element to exploit.

5   Conclusion

In this paper, we have presented the advances we have realized to help people with schizophrenia to maintain a physical activity level with a serious game. This paper presents the advances that have been obtained since the previous work. New features have been added to the game, including a mission system. This game was evaluated by people with schizophrenia who provided feedback after several days of interaction with the game on a daily basis. The feedback suggests that the game concept is enjoyable but requires a higher level of difficulty to keep it interesting in the long run. We are also considering the integration of time-limited events, or events related to the player's context [12], in order to encourage the player to use his resources to complete them and collect the associated rewards. Activity recognition is an important issue to detect the level of physical activity of users on a daily basis. Using google's activity recognition API allowed us to focus on the game design. The recognition is sensitive to the position of the smartphone as well as the walking, running, etc. pattern. Thus, it is important to either present and impose to the player the positions that the smartphone must take, or to propose more flexible methods. A first approach can be to allow a dynamic adjustment of the confidence threshold that we use to validate the recognized activity. Another more elaborate approach would be to use recognition approaches that allow for in-use readjustment of the recognition of user-specific patterns.

In the future, we plan to make changes to the game as players return. We want to move to a new phase of the project which consists in evaluating the acceptability and the feasibility. For this, we plan a 20-day experiment with a questionnaire at the beginning and end of the experiment. We also want to collect physical activity data from the players in order to study the behavior of the players with quantitative data. With these data, we aim to study the impact that gambling has on individuals' daily physical activity.

Acknowledgment. We thank, Éric Boucher, Alexandre Blanchette, Frédéric Bessette for the concept and the implementation of the game. Thanks to Vincent Plourde, Simon Lescieux, Julen Leremboure, Audran Bonnot and Mathieu Bocciarelli for the proposal and implementation of new features.

References

1. Ahson, S.A., Ilyas, M.: RFID Handbook: Applications, Technology, Security, and Privacy. CRC Press, Boca Raton (2017)
2. Armitage, C.J.: Evidence that a volitional help sheet reduces alcohol consumption among smokers: a pilot randomized controlled trial. Behav. Therapy **46**(3), 342–349 (2015)

3. Armitage, C.J.: Randomized test of a brief psychological intervention to reduce and prevent emotional eating in a community sample. J. Public Health **37**(3), 438–444 (2015)
4. Armitage, C.J., Arden, M.A.: A volitional help sheet to increase physical activity in people with low socioeconomic status: a randomised exploratory trial. Psychol. Health **25**(10), 1129–1145 (2010)
5. American Psychiatric Association.: Diagnostic and Statistical Manual of Mental Disorders (DSM 5), p. 70 . American Psychiatric Association, Washington (2013)
6. Bernard, P., Romain, A., Esseul, E., Artigusse, M., Poy, Y., Ninot, G.: Systematic review of barriers to physical activity and motivation for adults with schizophrenia (2013)
7. Campos, C., Mesquita, F., Marques, A., Trigueiro, M.J., Orvalho, V., Rocha, N.B.: Feasibility and acceptability of an exergame intervention for schizophrenia. Psychol. Sport Exerc. **19**(Supplement C), 50–58 (2015)
8. Cone, B.L., Levy, S.S., Goble, D.J.: Wii fit exer-game training improves sensory weighting and dynamic balance in healthy young adults. Gait Post. **41**(2), 711–715 (2015)
9. Correll, C.U., et al.: Prevalence, incidence and mortality from cardiovascular disease in patients with pooled and specific severe mental illness: a large-scale meta-analysis of 3,211,768 patients and 113,383,368 controls. World Psychiatr. **16**(2), 163–180 (2017)
10. Fervaha, G., Foussias, G., Agid, O., Remington, G.: Impact of primary negative symptoms on functional outcomes in schizophrenia. European Psychiatry **29**(7), 449–455 (2014)
11. Francillette, Y., et al.: Development of an exergame on mobile phones to increase physical activity for adults with severe mental illness. In: Proceedings of the 11th Pervasive Technologies Related to Assistive Environments Conference, pp. 241–248 (2018)
12. Francillette, Y., Gouaich, A., Abrouk, L.: Adaptive gameplay for mobile gaming. In: 2017 IEEE Conference on Computational Intelligence and Games (CIG), pp. 80–87. IEEE (2017)
13. Fulford, D., Piskulic, D., Addington, J., Kane, J.M., Schooler, N.R., Mueser, K.T.: Prospective relationships between motivation and functioning in recovery after a first episode of schizophrenia. Schizoph. Bull. **44**(2), 369–377 (2018)
14. Garcia-Agundez, A., Folkerts, A.K., Konrad, R., Caseman, P., Göbel, S., Kalbe, E.: Pddancecity: an exergame for patients with idiopathic Parkinson's disease and cognitive impairment. In: Burghardt, M., Wimmer, R., Wolff, C., Womser-Hacker, C. (eds.) Mensch und Computer 2017 - Tagungsband. Gesellschaft für Informatik e.V, Regensburg (2017)
15. Höchsmann, C., Walz, S.P., Schäfer, J., Holopainen, J., Hanssen, H., Schmidt-Trucksäss, A.: Mobile exergaming for health–effects of a serious game application for smartphones on physical activity and exercise adherence in type 2 diabetes mellitus–study protocol for a randomized controlled trial. Trials **18**(1), 103 (2017)
16. Janney, C.A., Ganguli, R., Tang, G., Cauley, J.A., Holleman, R.G., Richardson, C.R., Kriska, A.M.: Physical activity and sedentary behavior measured objectively and subjectively in overweight and obese adults with schizophrenia or schizoaffective disorders. J. Clin. Psychiatr. **76**(10), e1277-84 (2015)
17. Jennings-Teats, M., Smith, G., Wardrip-Fruin, N.: Polymorph: dynamic difficulty adjustment through level generation. In: Proceedings of the 2010 Workshop on Procedural Content Generation in Games, pp. 1–4 (2010)

18. Laine, T.H., Sedano, C.I.: Distributed pervasive worlds: the case of exergames. J. Educ. Technol. Soc. **18**(1), 50–66 (2015)
19. Lopes, R., Hilf, K., Jayapalan, L., Bidarra, R.: Mobile adaptive procedural content generation. In: Proceedings of the Fourth Workshop on Procedural Content Generation in Games (PCG 2013), Chania, Crete (2013)
20. Pouliot-Laforte, A., Lemay, M., Ballaz, L., Auvinet, E.: Exergame development for dynamic postural control training: Automaticaly detecting the naturally adopted base of support using a kinect camera. In: Virtual Rehabilitation Proceedings (ICVR), 2015 International Conference on. pp. 139–140. IEEE (2015)
21. Romain, A.J., Cadet, R., Baillot, A.: Brief theory-based intervention to improve physical activity in men with psychosis and obesity: a feasibility study. Sci. Nurs. Health Pract/Sci. Infirm. pratiques en santé **3**(2), 1–16 (2020)
22. Romain, A.J., Fankam, C., Karelis, A.D., Letendre, E., Mikolajczak, G., Stip, E., Abdel-Baki, A.: Effects of high intensity interval training among overweight individuals with psychotic disorders: a randomized controlled trial. Schizoph. Res. **210**, 278–286 (2019)
23. Romain, A., Longpré-Poirier, C., Tannous, M., Abdel-Baki, A.: Physical activity for patients with severe mental illness: preferences, barriers and perceptions of counselling. Sci. Sports **35**(5), 289–299 (2020)
24. Sabe, M., Kaiser, S., Sentissi, O.: Physical exercise for negative symptoms of schizophrenia: systematic review of randomized controlled trials and meta-analysis. Gen. Hosp. Psychiatr. **62**, 13–20 (2020)
25. Shoaib, M., Bosch, S., Incel, O.D., Scholten, H., Havinga, P.J.: A survey of online activity recognition using mobile phones. Sensors **15**(1), 2059–2085 (2015)
26. Staiano, A.E., Abraham, A.A., Calvert, S.L.: Adolescent exergame play for weight loss and psychosocial improvement: a controlled physical activity intervention. Obesity **21**(3), 598–601 (2013)
27. Stubbs, B., Williams, J., Gaughran, F., Craig, T.: How sedentary are people with psychosis? a systematic review and meta-analysis. Schizophrenia research **171**(1–3), 103–109 (2016)
28. Tandon, R., et al.: Definition and description of schizophrenia in the DSM-5. Schizoph. Res. **150**(1), 3–10 (2013)
29. Vancampfort, D.: Sedentary behavior and physical activity levels in people with schizophrenia, bipolar disorder and major depressive disorder: a global systematic review and meta-analysis. World Psychiatr. **16**(3), 308–315 (2017)
30. Vos, T., et al.: Global, regional, and national incidence, prevalence, and years lived with disability for 328 diseases and injuries for 195 countries, 1990–2016: a systematic analysis for the global burden of disease study 2016. Lancet **390**(10100), 1211–1259 (2017)

Grassroots Esports Players: Improving Esports Cognitive Skills Through Incentivising Physical Exercise

Bobbie Fletcher[(✉)] and David James[(✉)]

Department of Games and Visual Effects, Staffordshire University, Stoke-on-Trent, UK
{b.d.fletcher,d.james}@staffs.ac.uk

Abstract. Of the three skills needed to play esports, Mechanical Skills, Awareness Skills and Cognitive Skills, this paper focusses on Cognitive Skills. This paper examines how the Cognitive Skills needed by esports player to move from intermediate player to expert player can be improved by exercise. It takes lessons learned from pro players and recognises a need for grassroots player to start good habits around exercise early. It outlines a study done with 109 12–18 year old students to establish once incentivised by the knowledge that exercise improves cognitive skills which improves player skill level, what sort of exercise would encourage them to overcome the barriers they have to taking exercise after every 30 min of play. The paper then goes on to propose how grassroots esports can be supported in the endeavour to encourage exercise breaks as a standard grassroots activity in much the same way as other grassroots sports do in weekend or after school training.

Keywords: Esports · Exercise · Cognitive Skills · Pro players · Grassroots players

1 Introduction

The advent of esports has spawned an entire ecosystem and has given rise to the term e-athletes to describe esports Pro Players. It has also thrown light onto the question is esports a sport? Several countries do consider it a sport, Esports.Net [1]. The most vocal is South Korea, with The Korean Esports Federation spearheading the drive for world recognition of esports as a sport. Early adopters of the idea have been China and South Africa, with USA, Finland, Russia, Italy, Denmark, Nepal and Ukraine joining later.

Discussions have also taken place on allowing esports to be included in the Olympic Games, Grohmann [2] "Competitive esports could be considered as a sporting activity, and the players involved prepare and train with an intensity which may be comparable to athletes in traditional sports", but any future inclusion in the Games would require official recognition of it as an Olympic sport and would also need a governing organization that would guarantee compliance "with the rules and regulations of the Olympic movement." This movement has gathered pace as this summer's Asian Games in Jakarta 2018 held exhibition esports tournaments alongside swimming, soccer, and track and field. At the

© Springer Nature Switzerland AG 2021
B. Fletcher et al. (Eds.): JCSG 2021, LNCS 12945, pp. 200–212, 2021.
https://doi.org/10.1007/978-3-030-88272-3_15

2022 Asian Games in Hangzhou, China, video games will be a medal sport. Organizers of the 2024 Paris Olympics say they are also open to the idea, Nakamura et al. [3].

1.1 The Skills of an Esports Player

It is well documented what skills athletes for traditional sports need, but what skills do esports player need. Dr Anders Frank, Frank [4], in his GDC presentation "Esports Summit" looked at the three aspects of skills development identified in an exploration study by professional DOTA2 players, (Fig. 1) shows how the skill level in each of these skills are demonstrated in players at Novice, Intermediate and Expert levels of play and how these skills change with expertise.

The first are Mechanical Skills. This is the physical clicking of buttons or moving of the joystick to effectively navigate the game. These skills are acquired rapidly by players in the beginning whilst they are learning the mechanics of the game.

The second are Awareness Skills. These are skills that are about the player understanding their place in the game world and their position and actions in relation to players on their own team and that of the opposing team. In the beginning the player learns the consequence of their actions and as time goes on this becomes about finessing their actions in relation to others.

The third are the hardest of all the skills to learn and it is what elevates the player from an intermediate player to an expert. These are the Cognitive Skills. The Cognitive Skills are skills about learning and using that learning to predict the moves and playing tactics of the opposing team. They are also the skills used to switch tactics in the middle of the game when a pre-planned set of moves is not working. It is about reading a situation, learning what that means and adapting.

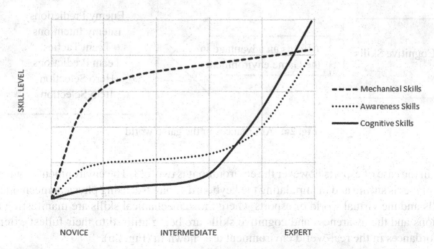

Fig. 1. Pros view on skills development in DOTA 2: adjusting and learning of skills

This directly relates to Gibson's theory of affordance, Gibson [5]. Affordance is mutual relationship between organisms, which in this case are the player, and the environment. Those in tune with the environment has mastered those affordances i.e. all three Mechanical, Awareness and Cognitive skills are all working at an optimal level for the environment. These skills and their associated in game virtual world affordances are described in (Fig. 2a).

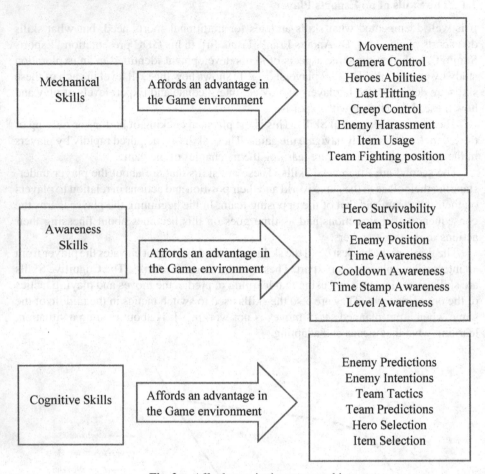

Mechanical Skills — Affords an advantage in the Game environment →

Movement
Camera Control
Heroes Abilities
Last Hitting
Creep Control
Enemy Harassment
Item Usage
Team Fighting position

Awareness Skills — Affords an advantage in the Game environment →

Hero Survivability
Team Position
Enemy Position
Time Awareness
Cooldown Awareness
Time Stamp Awareness
Level Awareness

Cognitive Skills — Affords an advantage in the Game environment →

Enemy Predictions
Enemy Intentions
Team Tactics
Team Predictions
Hero Selection
Item Selection

Fig. 2a. Affordances in the game world

In the case of esports however the environment is twofold. The environment in which the player is sitting and manipulating the keyboard or handset using physical mechanical skills and the virtual world of esports where those mechanical skills are manifesting as actions and the awareness and cognitive skills are being utilised to their fullest extent. Affordances in the real-world environment are shown in (Fig. 2b).

1.2 Cognitive Skills and Exercise

There have been many studies that have suggested that exercise can aid cognitive skills in people of all ages. Erickson et al. [6], says, there is substantial evidence that greater

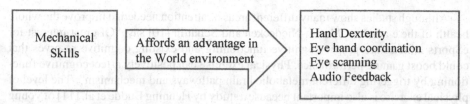

Fig. 2b. Affordances in the real world

physical activity and higher fitness levels are associated with better brain and cognitive health for children and older adults. When specifically looking at the link between cognitive skills in the youth and exercise, Diamond [7] says cognitive skills and motor skills appear to develop through a dynamic interaction.

Research has shown that physical movement can affect the brain's physiology by increasing; cerebral capillary growth, blood flow, oxygenation, production of neurotrophins, growth of nerve cells in the hippocampus, which is the centre of learning and memory, neurotransmitter levels, development of nerve connections, density of neural network, brain tissue volume.

These physiological changes may be associated with the following:

- Improved attention
- Improved information processing, storage, and retrieval
- Enhanced coping
- Enhanced positive affect
- Reduced sensations of cravings and pain

What is of particular interest are the two physiological changes, "Improved attention" and "Improved information processing, storage, and retrieval". These directly relate to the cognitive skills required by esports player to move from intermediate to expert.

1.3 Pro Players, Cognitive Skills, and Exercise

In a study DiFrancisco-Donoghue [8] discovered that at collegiate level in an age range of 18–22 years, esports players practise between 3 and 10 h per day. The most frequently reported complaint was eye fatigue (56%), followed by neck and back pain (42%). eSport athletes reported wrist pain (36%) and hand pain (32%). Forty per cent of participants do not participate in any form of physical exercise. Among the players surveyed, only 2% had sought medical attention.

As the esports industry become more professional the physical training regimes of Pro player becomes more significant. An extensive study of pro player training and physical exercise by Tuomas et al. [9] finds more than half (55.6%) of the professional and high-level esport players believe that integrating physical exercise into their training programs has a positive effect on esport performance. Accordingly, the same study professional and high-level esports players practice around the same number of hours per day as collegiate players but are physically active, those over 18 years old exercising an hour per day.

Although studies show many different areas of attention needed to improve the whole health of the e-athelete, Martin-Niedecken and Schättin [10] say, "Of great interest for eSports athletes are proper cognitive functioning and existing cognitive reserves that could boost gaming performance. Physical exercise can positively affect cognitive functioning by triggering different metabolic brain pathways and mechanism". The level of physical exercise is also important because a study by Henning Budde et al. [11] of young adults with an average age of 23 found that a significant interaction between physical activity participation level and exercise effect on cognitive performance emerged, with only the more physically active participants improving the performance in the cognitive test after the intervention.

1.4   Grassroots Players, Cognitive Skills and Exercise

Grassroots players in esports tend to be young and the World Health Organisation [12] recommends Children and adolescents aged 5–17 years; should do at least an average of 60 min per day of moderate-to-vigorous intensity, mostly aerobic, physical activity, across the week. They should incorporate vigorous-intensity aerobic activities, as well as those that strengthen muscle and bone, at least 3 days a week and should limit the amount of time spent being sedentary, particularly the amount of recreational screen time. It is for this reason school aged grassroots esports players of school age were selected for this study.

The study had two parts, the first a simple discussion about barriers to doing exercise and the second part was a much more in-depth study into what exercise would they select. Both parts of the study had the same 67 school students aged between 12 and 18, from four different schools, who play grassroots esports.

Study Part A
The 109 school and FE College students where asked the question "What barriers do they perceive to having short physical exercise breaks?" The responses that dominated were.

- Technical Limitations (I can't pause the game)
- Flow (I want to finish the game)
- Mood (I don't want to)
- Injury (I can't physically)

Learning from the experiences of the Pro Players there is a need to introduce good habits early and to break down those barriers and incentivise young grassroot esports player to take regular exercise breaks, hence the need for Part B of the study.

Study Part B
With the understanding that cognitive skills are what changes and intermediate player to an expert and the knowledge that cognitive skills are improved by exercise the following research questions where proposed.

"If students knew that a physical exercise break every 30 mins could improve their cognitive skills and help them play esports at a higher level, what exercise would they choose to do?"

2   Methodology of Part B of the Study

Four schools with student ranging from 12 to 18 took part in the study. Participating students were asked to fill in the questionnaire prior to taking part in the focus group. There were various questions asked around how the participants viewed their skills and other about their playing and screen time habits, however for this study only question 6 was used. The way each student answered question determined which focus group they are assigned to (Fig. 3).

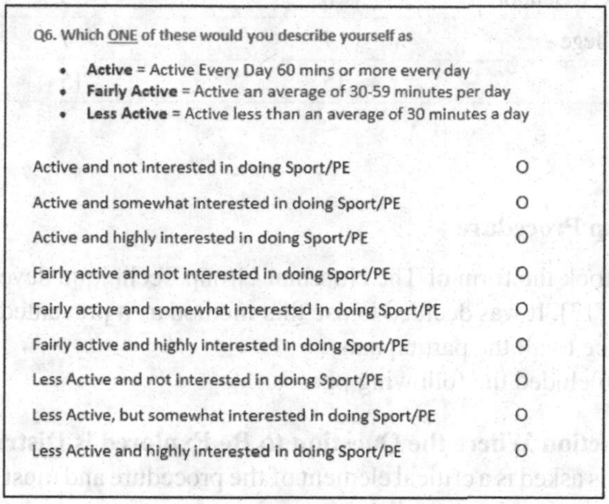

```
Q6. Which ONE of these would you describe yourself as

   •  Active = Active Every Day 60 mins or more every day
   •  Fairly Active = Active an average of 30-59 minutes per day
   •  Less Active = Active less than an average of 30 minutes a day

Active and not interested in doing Sport/PE                         O

Active and somewhat interested in doing Sport/PE                    O

Active and highly interested in doing Sport/PE                      O

Fairly active and not interested in doing Sport/PE                  O

Fairly active and somewhat interested in doing Sport/PE             O

Fairly active and highly interested in doing Sport/PE              O

Less Active and not interested in doing Sport/PE                   O

Less Active, but somewhat interested in doing Sport/PE             O

Less Active and highly interested in doing Sport/PE               O
```

Fig. 3. The question which determined which focus group each student would be in

Table 1. Focus groups by activity and interest

	Less active	Fairly active	Active
Not Interested in sports	Red	Red	Green
Somewhat Interested in sport	Red	Red	Green
Highly Interested in sport	Red	Red	Green

Students were assigned either a Red or Green Group as indicated in the Table 1.

The decision to split up the focus groups in this way was to see whether more physically active students picked different exercises from the less physically active ones. The total number of students in each group relating to each participating school or college and be see in Table 2. In most schools the split was quite even between the Red and Green Groups, but in both CBAT Marling and St. John Fisher schools these were unevenly split.

Table 2. Focus group numbers

School	Red group	Green group
Ballyclare High school	10	8
CBAT Marling	11	4
St. John Fisher	5	16
Prendergast Ladywell School	6	5
Loughborough College	7	7
Barnsley College	15	15

2.1 Focus Group Procedure

The focus group took the form of The Nominal Group Technique developed by Van de Ven and Delbecq [13]. It was decided to use this method as it prevented group think and gave an equal voice to all the participants.

This method included the following phases:

Phase 1: Introduction Where the Question to Be Explored is Distributed
The question that is asked is a critical element of the procedure and must be broad enough to elicit varied responses. for the following participants.

Phase 2: Ideas Generation
The ideas generation phase is necessary to enliven ideas and possibilities but should not lead the participant into making specific choices and progresses in this way.

- Five minutes for silent generation of ideas in writing
- Creation of a numbered list of all ideas on flip chart
- Twenty minutes for a serial discussion of ideas on the flip chart during which items are clarified, defended, elaborated and disputed. Items that emerge from the discussion are added to the list, but items cannot be removed. Some ideas can be grouped as being the same thing
- Five-minute break

Phase 3: Answer Ranking
The ranking phase is where the participant individually weighs up the merits of the activities listed on the flip chart.

- The ranking of priorities where each member chooses the ten most critical elements with ten being the most important and they write their ranking on the flip chart beside the relevant item.
- The numbers are tallied and the solution with the highest score is the most favour and so on to the least

Question Used

The focus group sessions took part at each of the schools and were facilitated by trained staff from the Youth Sport Trust (YST). The focus group sessions they ran all asked the same question to all groups. This is the question that was posed to the students:

It has been proved that physical activity breaks every 30 minutes can help with improving cognitive function. If improved cognitive function could improve your esports ability, what physical activity breaks would you design to make those breaks more appealing?

3 Results

Table 3 is a tabulation of all the raw data from each school or college. The scores were all normalised and that score can be seen in the column next to the rank for each activity.

Table 3. Ranking of physical exercise by school and normalised score

School	Ranked answers red group	Normalised score	Ranked answers green group	Normalised score
Ballyclare High School	1. Exercise Bike	7.7	1. Circuit Training	7.9
	2. Throwing and catching	7.6	2. Kick ups	7.4
	3. Walking (The Dog)	7.4	3. Running	7.1
	4. Trampolining	7.3	4. Cycling	5.8
	5. Jogging	6.0	5. Weightlifting	5.6
	6. Weightlifting	5.7	6. Push ups and Sit ups	5.5
	7. Circuit training	4.7	7. Boxing	4.9
	8. Kick ups	4.5	8. Walking (With Dog)	4.9
	9. Star Jumps	4.0	Golf range	4.5
	10. Pull ups	3.7	10. Throwing and catching	1
CBAT Marling	1. Wii fit (Exergame)	7.8	1. Pull ups	7.5
	2. Trampolining	7.7	2. Basketball	7
	3. Press ups and burpees	7.6	3. Boxing	6.8
	4. Running	6.4	4. Weights	6.5
	5. Basketball	6.1	5. Exercise bike	6
	6. Badminton	6.1	6. Press ups	5.8
	7. Cycling	4.9	7. Sit ups	5
	8. Plank	4.5	8. Treadmill	4.5
	9. Football	4.4	9. Star Jumps	3.3
	10. Walking (the Dog)	3.3	10. Hand Resistance	2.3

(*continued*)

Table 3. (*continued*)

School	Ranked answers red group	Normalised score	Ranked answers green group	Normalised score
St. John Fisher	1. Press ups	7.6	1. Stretching	7.4
	2. Sit ups	7.4	2. Jogging	6.6
	3. Pull ups	7.2	3. Walking	6
	4. Bicep Curls	6.4	4. Cycling	5.7
	5. Stretching	6.2	5. Lift weights	5.6
	6. Running	5.4	6. Sit ups	5.5
	7. Football	4.4	7. Basketball	5
	8. Walking (upstairs)	4	8. Pull ups	4.8
	9. Walking (With Dog)	3.6	9. Push Ups	4.4
	10. Wii sports (Exergame)	2.8	10. Hiking	4
Prendergast Ladywell School	1. Stretching	9.5	1. Cardio	9.8
	2. Jogging	6.5	2. Stretching	8.2
	3. Weightlifting	5.8	3. Walking	6.4
	4. Walking	5.7	4. Press ups	5.8
	5. Cycling	5.7	5. Sit ups	5.6
	6. Sit ups	5.3	6. Gym Workout	5.4
	7.Yoga	4.8	7. Trampolining	5.4
	8. Press Ups	4.7	8. Yoga	4.8
	9. Boxing	4	9. Jogging	4.8
	10. Plank	3.3	10. Swimming	1.2
Loughborough College	1. Stretching	8.4	1. Tennis	7.6
	2. Virtual Reality (Exergame)	6.7	2. Walk (With Dog)	7.1
	3. Push ups and Sit ups	6.6	3. Cycling	6.6
	4. Walking	6.3	4. Stretching	6
	5. Walking (up Stairs)	5.4	5. Skating	5.9
	6. Basketball	5	6. Wii and VR (Exergame)	5.3
	7. Dance Mat (Exergame)	4.9	7. Boxing	5.1
	8. Yoga	4.7	8. Gym Work Out	4.4
	9. Skating	4.6	9. Gardening	3.6
	10. Chopping wood	2.7	10. Juggling	3.3
Barnsley College	1. Jogging	6.5	1. Throw and Catch	7.5
	2. Walking (With Dog)	6.4	2. Stretching	7.2
	3. Calisthenics	6.1	3. Jogging	6.8
	4. Gym	5.6	4. Running	6.3
	5. Cardio	5.2	5. Cycling	5.4
	6. Exercise bike	5.1	6. Table Tennis	5.2
	7. Stretching	5.1	7. Boxing	4.4
	8. Throw and Catch	4.8	8. Walking (With Dog)	4.3
	9. Push ups and Sit ups	4.7	9. Pool	3.5
	10. Yoga	2	10. Trampolining	3.2

3.1 Ranking Evaluation

From the raw data from each school, when the scores were normalised, the following exercises are favoured by each group can be seen in Table 4.

Table 4. Preferred form of Exercise by Group and in Total

Type of Exercise	Red Group	Green Group	Total
Walking (All forms)	42.1	28.7	70.8
Stretching	29.2	28.8	58
Jogging	19	18.2	37.2
Circuit Training-Combinations Press Ups, Pullups, Burpees, Sit ups	23.6	13.4	37
Cycling	10.6	23.5	34.1
Lifting Weights/Weightlifting	11.5	17.7	29.2
Sit Ups	12.7	16.1	28.8
Press/Push Ups	12.3	16	28.3
Exergaming	22.2	5.3	27.5
Running	11.8	13.4	25.2
Boxing	4	21.2	25.2
Trampolining	15	8.6	23.6
Pull Ups	10.9	12.3	23.2
Basketball	11.1	12	23.1
Throwing and Catching	12.4	8.5	20.9
Football/Kick ups	13.3	7.4	20.7
Tennis/Badminton/Table Tennis	6.1	12.8	18.9
Exercise Bike	12.8	6	18.8
Yoga	11.5	4.8	16.3
Gym Workout	5.6	9.8	15.4
Cardio	5.2	9.8	15
Skating	4.6	5.9	10.5
Plank	7.8	0	7.8
Star Jumps	4	3.3	7.3
Bicep Curls	6.4	0	6.4
Calisthenics	6.1	0	6.1
Golf Range	0	4.5	4.5
Treadmill	0	4.5	4.5

(continued)

Table 4. (*continued*)

Type of Exercise	Red Group	Green Group	Total
Hiking	0	4	4
Gardening	0	3.6	3.6
Playing Pool	0	3.5	3.5
Juggling	0	3.3	3.3
Chopping wood	2.7	0	2.7
Hand Resistance	0	2.3	2.3
Swimming	0	1.2	1.2

4 Conclusion

This study has established the type of exercise that school students would like to do. The Red and Green Groups had a lot of similarities in what they chose. Both groups put Walking and Stretching as first and second choices. However, the less active Red Group then placed Circuit Training and Exergaming as there next two choices, whereas the more active Green Groups placed Cycling and Boxing, but as a consensus Jogging came in third place.

Interestingly several groups mentioned Exergaming (Exercise Computer Games) and the Red Group, less active students, ranked this as their 4th favoured physical activity. This has been explored in a study by Martin-Niedecken et al. [10] which states "If designed properly in terms of effectiveness and attractiveness, exergames allow for innovative, motivating and holistic training approaches, which may be extremely suitable and beneficial in eSports athletes to keep and maintain their cognitive, physical and mental processes and thus to increase their eSports-related performance and health." There is one drawback to this approach and that is that it still includes screen time. As has already be said in the paper the World Health Organisation the amount of recreational screen time should be limited, however combining exergaming with esports for less active grassroots players may be a gateway activity to more sport for the less active player (Table 5).

The more active Green Group were more inventive and had a larger range of exercises and in their choices. They also included activities that matched closer to the type of exercises recommended by the World Health Organisation.

So how can the esports industry itself assist in encouraging exercise at grassroots level? In the UK today several dedicated LAN-style esports venues have opened nation-wide. These have been very successful in attracting grassroots players and communities. We are now starting to see this model go one step further and develop venues that include a dedicated space for Yoga and stretching exercises. From this study it is recommended that this idea is taken even further and new venues should consider how they incorporate spaces for exercise including walking, jogging, stretching, circuit training and exergaming.

Table 5. Summary of avenues for the development of esports-specific exergame concepts and the effects of selected physical, cognitive and mental training

Key Influencing Component	Exergame Training & Design Requirements		Potential Positive (Component-Specific) Effects on...
Physical	• Endurance, strength, motor and stretch training • Full-body functional movements • High Intensity Interval Training • Active relaxation training such as yoga and breathing exercises	*Simultaneously vs. sequential* · *Coupled vs. uncoupled* · *Distribution of training components determines training focus*	• Gaming performance (e.g., information processing, executive and attentional functions, perception, and visuo-spatial skills) • Lifestyle (e.g., counteract sedentary behavior) • Musculoskeletal system (e.g., holding musculature of neck and trunk)
Cognitive	• Multisensory stimulation: audio-visual, haptic, proprioceptive level • Game tactics and strategies		• Balanced physical strain • Mental strength (e.g., counteract depression and burn-out) • Self-esteem and bodily security • Gaming behavior (e.g., counteract effects of addictive behavior such as loss of reality and social isolation)
Mental	• Digital/virtual detox: exergaming in the physical space • Simulation of mentally challenging situations • Psychophysiological and psychosomatic training		

Acknowledgements. This study was only possible due to the support of the staff of the Youth Sport Trust, whose staff went into schools and colleges to collect the data.

References

1. Esports.Net: Is Esports a Sport? Countries where Esports is considered a sport (2021). https://www.esports.net/wiki/guides/is-esports-a-sport/
2. Grohmann, K.: E-sports just got closer to being part of the Olympics, Reuters on Insider (2017). https://www.businessinsider.com/e-sports-gets-closer-to-being-part-of-the-olympics-games-2017-10?r=US&IR=T
3. Nakamura, Y., Nobuhiro, E., Taniguchi, T.: Shinzo Abe's party wants Japan ready for video games in Olympics, Mint (2018). https://www.livemint.com/Sports/ATQN0iAS2rVwagVOeGW9MP/Shinzo-Abes-party-wants-Japan-ready-for-video-games-in-Olym.html
4. Frank, A.: "Esports Summit: Skill Progression, Visual Attention, and Efficiently Getting Good at Esports" GDC (2020)
5. Gibson, J.J.: The Theory of Affordances (1977)
6. Erickson, K.I., Hillman, C.H., Kramer, A.F.: Physical activity, brain, and cognition. Curr. Opin. Behav. Sci. **4**, 27–32 (2015)
7. Diamond, A.B.: The cognitive benefits of exercise in youth. Curr. Sports Med. Rep. **14**(4), 320–326 (2015)
8. DiFrancisco-Donoghue, J., Balentine, J., Schmidt, G., Zwibel, H.: Managing the health of the eSport athlete: an integrated health management model. BMJ Open Sport Exerc. Med. **5**, e000467 (2019). https://doi.org/10.1136/bmjsem-2018-000467
9. Kari, T., Siutila, M., Veli-Matti Karhulahti, V.-M.: An extended study on training and physical exercise in eSports. In: Exploring the Cognitive, Social, Cultural, and Psychological Aspects of Gaming and Simulations (2019)

10. Martin-Niedecken, A., Alexandra Schättin, A.: Let the Body'n'Brain Games Begin: Toward Innovative Training Approaches in eSports Athletes (2020)

11. Budde, H., et al.: Intermittent Maximal Exercise Improves Attentional Performance Only in Physically Active Students (2012)

12. World Health Organisation: Physical activity Fact Sheet (2021). https://www.who.int/news-room/fact-sheets/detail/physical-activity

13. Van de Ven and Delbecq: The nominal group as a research instrument for exploratory health studies. Am. J. Public Health (1972)

Analyzing Game-Based Training Methods for Selected Esports Titles in Competitive Gaming

Thomas Tregel(✉) , Teodora Sarpe-Tudoran, Philipp Niklas Müller, and Stefan Göbel

Multimedia Communications Lab - KOM, Technical University of Darmstadt, Darmstadt, Germany
thomas.tregel@kom.tu-darmstadt.de

Abstract. Training approaches in traditional sports are usually extensively documented. In esports and competitive gaming in general, the documentation regarding tactics and methods players can utilize to improve one's skill and thus be a successful player is lacking. To assess and compare the training possibilities in competitive gaming, we systematically select different currently popular gaming genres and analyze them based on their established training methods. Thereby, we analyze game-specific training methods focusing on micro-related skills referring to the players' control over small parts of the game, which highly depends on reflexes, hand-eye coordination, and visual perception. The assessed macro-training methods refer to higher-level game control involving strategy, resource management, and game or map awareness. We conclude this by assessing psychological and physiological aspects on the players' game performance.

Keywords: Training methods · Competitive games · Esports

1 Introduction

Traditional sports have many possibilities to train the skills required for the sport. Soccer player early on exercise their shooting skills on a goal wall, archers practise their aim with targets and for many sports there are specific exercises to stimulate relevant muscles and improve on specific skills to become more successful in the sport [48].

Esports (Electronic Sports) is considered a relatively new sport, and has to deal with a lot of bias. For these competitive games, studies show that the average heart rate of players is similar to that of basketball athletes. Furthermore, players need specific skills, also commonly found in traditional sports, like hand-eye-coordination, reaction time and an increased peripheral vision [49].

Similar to traditional sports, training is esports is highly important. Due to the vast variety of different genres and games, different skill-sets are necessary

© Springer Nature Switzerland AG 2021
B. Fletcher et al. (Eds.): JCSG 2021, LNCS 12945, pp. 213–228, 2021.
https://doi.org/10.1007/978-3-030-88272-3_16

to excel at a certain game [47]. Many games offer in-game training possibilities for the whole game or different game modes. Those consist of different elements, accessible to players, e.g. single- or team-training, bot-games and aim-maps. Additionally, on a game-by-game basis, there are out-of-game training options offered by companies, coaches or the community [10].

Due to key differences in training possibilities and training focuses our goal is to survey popular training options for distinct game genres in their competitive game mode and combining them with the associated learning content or trained skill. Thus, a categorization of training elements is required to describe the trained skill and analyze skill regarding their transferability into other games or game genres [50]. Furthermore, we examine general training approaches used in traditional sports and their use in esports, like the role of psychology and the physiology aspect of esports.

2   Background and Related Work

While there are many electronic games, not every game can be considered an eSport. An eSport has to be a competition between human players using virtual platforms under strict rules. There, players do not win by chance, but by utilizing their experience and skill sets to overcome their opponents. Furthermore, it is important that the players' individual performances are comparable to guarantee a fair rating and evaluation [11,22].

Competitive games and esports game categories develop rapidly with new games coming out each year [24]. Categories differ depending on the main goal of the game, and most popular eSport games are team-games or have direct competitors. For some exceptions like Solo Superplay players compete by comparison of time or high-scores. Due to the vast variety of gaming genres we focus on three categories, selected based on their popularity and their dissimilarity regarding their setup and required skills: Multiplayer Online Battle Arena (MOBA), Team-based Shooters, Real Time Strategy.

In contrast to classical sports, esports games undergo regular (sometimes drastic) rule changes, forcing players to develop new skills and strategies or even switch roles. Even without large game changes popular strategies or characters may change quickly over time, commonly called a changing meta-game.

Micro, which is short for micromanagement refers to the control of the user over small parts of the game. Usually the control over a players character or units. Micro highly depends on reflexes, hand-eye-coordination and the visual skills of the player [29,37]. Macro, which is short for macromanagement refers to higher level control over the game. This usually involves [29,37]:

- *Strategy:* The general strategy used in the game by player and opponents.
- *Resource management:* Refers to an overview over consumption, income, and utilization of available resources within the game.
- *Map awareness:* The user should know what is happening on the map, where other characters, players or units are, and which game timers are currently active.

In most games both micro- and macromanagement are of high importance, with its weighting varying from game to game or based on the platform the game is played on [37].

3   Public Training Methods in Multiplayer Online Battle Arena Games (MOBAs)

In MOBAs, which are immensely popular, two teams compete against each other to destroy the base of the opponent team. They provide a collaborative experience in working together as a team of unique characters in a highly competitive environment against the other team [51]. As characters are selected at the start of a game session, this offers a wide range of strategic options in character selection, team composition and play choices during each game. The amount of variation makes it difficult to predict the opponents future play, increasing the level of challenge and skill required to be successful [51]. Due to its popularity, we assess League of Legends (LoL) [23] regarding its available and utilized training methods. Apart from the different characters for each MOBA and the associated required game experience, most trained skills are transferable to other popular MOBAs like DotA2, Smite, or Heroes of the Storm.

3.1   Game-Based Knowledge Building

In order to make good decisions and stay up to date with current game changes vast game knowledge is necessary, categorized into the following aspects:

- *Champions and Tactics:* It is of high importance to have a good knowledge of the available champions, which not only makes it easier to master a champion, but also helps predict the opponent's move. Certain combinations of champions are strong or weak, depending on their abilities and their resulting synergies. Being aware of these synergies is essential when picking champions for the own team or denying them from the opponent's team [26]. It is commonly recommended for a player to focus few champions and at most two different roles, to be able to master those [25]. Because champions are regularly being updated or new champions are introduced it is essential to stay updated as tactics and synergies can change over time [27,30]. Utilizing a team's champion synergies comes into effect with combinations of skills that work especially well together. Being aware of those for the own team and anticipating combos from opposing champion is detrimental as successful combos often lead to a champion's death. This includes the timing aspects of those combos which need to be trained and communicated.
- *Build and Abilities:* In each game there are several ways to adapt a champion: *Runes, Summoner Spells, Items,* and *Skill Order* [27]. Due to its complexity, general build guides are available for each champion depending on player's focus, covering information about these aspects. Those guides are often created by high-ranked players or by analyzing statistics. As champions are regularly updated it is also important to state that not all guides are recommended

for all seasons [25, 30, 32]. While diverging from a build guide is always possible a deep understanding on the champion, the current state of the game, and both teams is required. Depending on the player preferences and champion's role, there are different *skill orders* to level up a champion's abilities. Especially in the early game this has a high effect, where it decides which abilities a certain champion has available [27].*Runes* (as shown in Fig. 1), *Summoner Spells*, and *Items* all customize the role and the champion and are either chosen prior to the match's start or adapted in the course of the game as a reaction to the opposing champions [27].

- *Professional Games:* To increase knowledge and train reflexes it is not only important to play the game, but also watch and analyze professional league or championship games, which are being broadcasted [46]. League games also have moderators, which explain certain moves or tactics, which can give insight especially to new players. An alternative for using available build guides is watching esports games between teams and paying attention to the attributes the players have chosen for their champions, usually also highlighted and explained by the moderators.

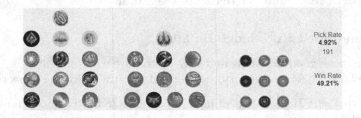

Fig. 1. An example for a rune selection guide for the champion Neeko [34]

3.2   Improving a Player's Gameplay Performance

When playing LoL, both micro and macro play have a high influence on the game's outcome, and both should be equally focused on, when training. Micro in LoL describes the ability to control the chosen champion. Due to the different abilities of the champions, the timings to achieve good results are different. We identified the following main micro abilities players can improve on [28, 29] with a categorization of those aspects in micro training shown in Fig. 2. Here, we do not explicitly list the required perception skills to identify relevant information on the screen, as it is essential for all micro plays.

- Creep score (CS) per minute: CS states how many minions are last-hitted by a champion lead to him receiving more gold and experience points. The champion can time the attacks accordingly to increase the CS.

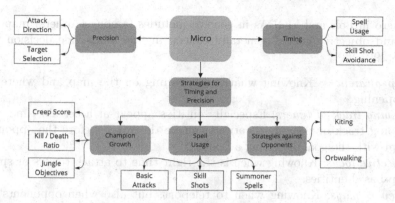

Fig. 2. Developed categorization of skills required in LoL micro.

- Kiting means gaining or keeping distance from an opponent while dealing damage. Distance can be created with movement or abilities. Kiting can be regarded both as an offensive and a defensive mechanism.
- Orbwalking is the performance of attacks and resuming to move again as soon as possible canceling the animation after the attack has already been performed. Thus, timing is required to cancel the animation at the correct moment to gain more time for other actions.
- Skillshots are abilities referring to projectile-based abilities and direction-targeting. Due to the continuous movement of opponents the travel-time of the ability's projectile direction and timing are highly important to get the most out of skillshots.
- Kill/death ratio: More kills against other champions results into more gold and more experience points (XP), which he can spend on items and higher ability levels. As this leads to the champion becoming stronger or more versatile a lead in items and XP over the opponents is advantageous.
- Clearing camps: For players playing the role of a *jungler* it becomes important to clear jungle camps, to not hinder the team in leveling up. There, some objectives can give certain boosts and thus provide a team advantage.

The needed skills focus mainly on the own champion and do not refer to teamwork and thus, a player can improve micro on his own by, e.g., setting a creep score of minions per minute or keeping deaths below a certain number.

Fig. 3. Developed categorization of skills required in LoL macro.

Macro in LoL and MOBAs in general includes (amongst others) map rotations and objective control generally concerning the map-wide decision making [28, 29]:

- *Map awareness:* Knowing what is happening on the map and where it is happening.
- *Keeping track of timers:* Especially entities appear at a certain time, when keeping track of the timer, entities can be destroyed before the opponent's team with the goal of getting a bonus.
- *Objective focus:* Knowing when is the right time to attack towers or specific map-based entities.
- *Teleport plays:* Knowing when to teleport, but also when opponents have teleported, and thus are unable to use the same ability soon.
- *Ganking:* Overpowering the opponent, with the attack of multiple team members.
- *Skill and item information:* Having on overview over which items, health and levels the players have.
- *General Communication and Teamwork*

Macro is harder to improve than Micro, because it usually involves strategies that can mostly be applied in a running game and involves team work. Figure 3 shows a categorization of the possible aspects in macro training [29].

Training and practice tools are useful to improve different individual micro and macro skills. Playing the game in an organized environment and setting goals to oneself to pursue during a match is a valid approach for constant improvement. To aid in this process, external platforms offering personalized training can be utilized [35, 36]. These tools offer dynamic strategies, challenges, collections and rewards as incentives to players wishing to improve their skills. By automatically analyzing the player's game replays those are extracted and provided in a personalized fashion. They provide a detailed breakdown over different game phases, heatmap visualization for positioning, vision, and map exposure coupled with advise on what to improve on.

Individual tools are more focused on training individual required mechanics like improving a player's movement skills in kiting, and dodging [33], or improving individual role skills [31, 32]. As similar tools rose in popularity core aspects are now integrated into the game's built-in practice mode.

4   Public Training Methods in Team-Based Shooters

In shooters the player focuses the actions of an avatar with a weapon against NPCs or other avatars. Usually the weapon is a firearm or other long-range weapon with the focus is on defeating the avatar's enemies or completing map-based objectives. Due to the popularity and long history of the series Counter Strike (CS) and the game Counter-Strike: Global Offensive (CS:GO) was chosen as the Shooter to be analyzed regarding its training possibilities [14]. It is an objective-based, multiplayer first-person shooter. Two opposing teams (Terrorists and Counter-Terrorists) play and commonly compete against each other in a bomb defusal game mode. Unlike MOBAs, team-based shooters utilize a variety of different maps requiring teams to develop individual tactics, practicing them, and analyzing their opponents' tactics [15]. To improve the team's communication map-based callouts need to be remembered (as shown in Fig. 4) and trained to quickly communicate match-events at specific locations.

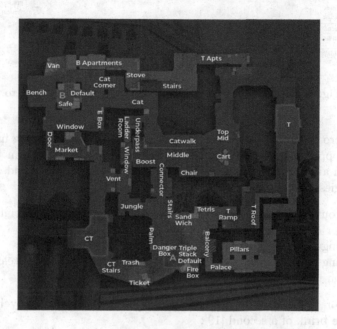

Fig. 4. An example for CS callouts for the map Mirage [45]

Micro in CS:GO is mainly based on the aiming aspect, concerning hitting the opponent's avatar by placing the mouse on it as fast and precise as possible. Thus the training of precision and reflexes is crucial. Figure 5 shows a categorization of the core micro aspects in CS:GO which can be trained and improved on are [10, 12, 16, 19]:

- *Aiming/Cross-hair Placement:* It is recommended to place the cross-hair at head-level as this increased the player's expected damage. Thus, most aiming happens on a horizontal axis, which need to be adapted on non-flat ground or in areas with different plateaus opponents can appear on.
- *Reflexes:* When a player registers a movement, only a limited period of time is available to react to the movement and either hide or fire at the opponent. A good peripheral vision is helpful for these situations.
- *Recoil Pattern:* Each game weapon has a unique recoil pattern. Some weapons start with a bias towards left or right and some climb up and then sway when

the player starts firing. In order to counter this effect during consecutive firing, the player need to memorize the pattern and regularly practice with these weapons.

– *Holding angles:* Players becoming careless and not holding precise angles risk losing their duels when encountering opponents.

Fig. 5. Developed categorization of skills required in CS micro.

For macro in CS, there are two major decision aspects: Gaining information about the opponents team and making decisions for the own team [12,13,19]. Information about the opposing team may lead to the adaption and creation of own strategies. Those factors include [19]:

– Finding out, which of the players in the opposing team is especially good or if a player constitutes a weak link
– Identifying rotating patterns when the opposing team relocates
– Identifying money management of certain players or of the team to gain insight on bought weapons

Decisions for the own team are strategic decisions, which usually have to be made in the brink of a second [19]:

– Knowing the right time to flash for a teammate to blind opponents
– Deciding if a push should be performed instantly or delayed
– Deciding if all corners and hiding places should be checked for opponents
– If an opponent is near, deciding if the bomb should be planted or if a 1vs1 with the opponent would be better

The four important factors in developing macro strategies are pick, trade, flank and economy [20]: *Pick* is the ability to achieve an opening frag. Opening frag refers to opening a site or an area by getting a kill for the team. A prominent strategy for this is to enforce a 5v4 situations and try to take map control *Trade* means getting a trade kill for your team. This means, that a player gets into a situation, where he will presumably die, but possibly leading to a beneficial situation for the team. A weak player goes in first creating space and dies, followed by a stronger player, who can get the multiple follow up kills. This strategy can lead to a 4v3 scenario. *Flank* refers to situations where an opponent is hit from an angle or direction which the opponent did not expect, thus catching the opponent in surprise. The team can try to create multiple projectile angles in such a way, that they cannot be covered from an opponent player at the same time. This can be achieved with strategical positioning in an area. *Economics* limit what individual players can purchase in single rounds. Information about the economics of the opponents team can be used to develop different tactics: If it is known, that the opponent cannot afford certain weapons, e.g., long-range weapons, the team's positioning can adapt based on this information picking strategic spots.

Micro training and practice in CS is mostly based on maps specifically created to improve a skill, like aim-, reflex-, recoil-, prefire-, or grenade-training maps [18]. Similar to replay systems a Demo manager [17] offers after-game analysis and helps to find both team's weak-spots. Especially aim-training is popular with different external tools to practice aim and weapon spray [10,21].

5   Public Training Methods in Real-Time Strategy Games

In a real-time strategy (RTS) game, the players position structures and maneuver units under their control to secure areas of the map and/or destroy their opponents' assets. The typical game in the RTS genre features: resource-gathering, base-building, in-game technological development, unit creation, and indirect control of units. Although some genres share conceptual and gameplay similarities with RTS game, e.g., city-building games, construction and management simulations, and games of the real-time tactics variety they are not considered to be real-time strategy per se. Due to its popularity in research [9] and long history Starcraft II [38] was chosen as the analyzed RTS.

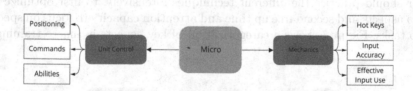

Fig. 6. Developed categorization of skills required in SCII micro.

Micro mechanics are important skills in SC II, with professional players reaching average actions per minute over 300. They comprise of precise and fast use of input elements like mouse or keyboard, but also the strategic setting and use of hotkeys, which reduce the required time to perform actions or combinations [39]. The core commands that are beneficial to master are [39]:

- *Attack-Move:* The units attack any enemy units or buildings in the respective path. When doing an attack move, the units will not fight back if attacked from other positions, but will follow their way to the selected destination.
- *Multiple Unit Groups:* Creating multiple unit groups is better than having one control group, because it allows for better army control.

- *Wire-Frame Selection:* Removing certain units from selections in order to split up a group accurately. This can be used to split up the units to attack different targets.
- *Queuing Commands:* There are certain commands which can be queued, if the player already knows which actions he wants to perform.

Unit positioning is also highly important in extending the life of the player's army and should be performed before every battle. In general, ranged units should be positioned at the back, while melee units and tanks should be positioned at the front [42].

Scouting is the act of gathering information about the opponent and his actions. This can be managed by sending units to the opponent's base, usually a worker unit or a cheap and fast early-game unit. By keeping the unit alive as long as possible using micro skills, players can obtain more information about the opponent and cover larger areas [42].

Harassment is the action of looking for minor holes in the opponent's defenses and using these to gain an advantage by, e.g., interrupting resources gathering, delaying production, or picking of important units, forcing opponents to spend resources on defending or on loss compensation [42].

Unit management during a battle is important as units can be ordered to attack a single enemy unit, which is systematically better than attacking multiple units at the same time. Furthermore, wounded units should be retreated, as it allows them to be healed or repaired, or participate in the fight from range [42]. Individual have special abilities that must be activated and targeted by the player. Knowing when and how to use these abilities is also a part of micro [42].

Macro is considered to be more important than Micro in SCII [39], and the player should practice the different techniques intensively, to first optimize the macro aspects and second free up time and attention capacity to focus on specific micro tasks. Figure 7 shows a categorization of key aspects in macro training.

Fig. 7. Developed categorization of skills required in SCII macro.

Macro in SCII usually involves actions dealing with the match's economy. This includes having an ongoing supply of food to allow the production of new units, without creating supply blocks. With increasing income, it is important to spend the gained resources and construct buildings, train units or get upgrades. This includes planning ahead, as stronger units need require several buildings, which have to be built beforehand. Thus, build orders are important to be memorized and trained [44], as shown in Fig. 8. There are three categories, where resources can be spent [40]:

- *Economy:* Spending on Economy is spending on the supply chain and allowing the harvesting of more resources or increasing the rate at which resources are gathered.
- *Army:* Through the build of units and production buildings, the army size of a player will increase. When the player's resources are growing faster than the players expenses, it is a good tip to produce more production buildings.
- *Tech:* A player can improve the tech by constructing new buildings, which are part of the tech tree. Unlocking new parts of the tech tree allows the built of new, usually more powerful units. Additionally, units can be upgraded with unique techs, making them stronger.

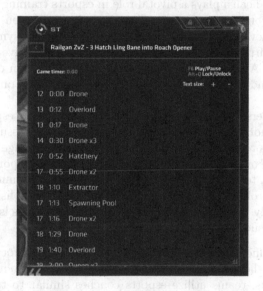

Fig. 8. An example for a SC II buildorder guide for the *Zerg* race [44]

As already mentioned for the micro part, scouting is of high importance in SCII. Gaining information about the opponent can be used in multiple ways but requires game knowledge and experience to utilize the gained information [39]. It can indicate when the opponent is going to attack or when it is weak for an attack. Additionally, knowing the potential opponent strategies allows the player to deduce its current strategy to adapt own strategy accordingly.

Due to the large variety of maps utilized in competitive play, heatmap-based visualization of strategic locations can help players improve their gameplay on each map [41]. These also includes map-based characteristics like the ramp size leading up to the main base location or their closest expansion spot, the distance between the player and opponent location, the presence of ledges and cliffs in strategic locations, the number of base entrances, or the general amount of open space in strategic locations [43].

6   Psychological and Physiological Training

Since esports athletes are constantly required to perform well, selected methods from traditional sport psychology can also be applied in esports. This can be seperated into three main categories [3–5]:

- *Gaming:* The structure and analysis of each training session and tournament matches is of high importance in esports. Especially for teams training together, but also for solo players, a training plan is important to organize training sessions in such a way, that a high level of concentration over an extended period of time can be achieved. Documenting and analyzing this training process is used to measure the personal improved and set new goals.
- *Health:* Mental health plays a pivotal role in esports training, especially when dealing with younger players [7]. This includes addiction prevention happening on all levels of play by looking out for possible symptoms like constant fatigue, irritability, or isolation due to the negative implications on mental health. Another aspect of health is the prevention of injuries occurring through bad posture, extended load, and high strain on individual body parts [4].
- *Personality:* Personality development is important, as especially younger players might not know how to deal with losses, stress, pressure or how to stay motivated. It is recommended to retain a positive self image and have a deep insight into the own strength and weaknesses [7]. Many esports games require players to work together as a team. Schedule planning, communication skills, different team roles and teamwork are important in establishing a successful team. Especially the improvement of communication skills is crucial as it can determine the success of a team.

Since it can be difficult for a player or an aspiring team to focus on all aspects and methods. Furthermore it is challenging for individuals to analyze their own performance. Thus, teams utilize esports coaches similar to traditional sports coaches, which can take over much of the players' much of the cognitive load not directly related with the game. Since the term of an esports coach is not legally defined and everyone who wishes can offer himself as a coach, there are different experiences and qualifications, which can be encountered in people who offer their service as a coach: Sports psychologists, former or currently active players, and people who absolved courses in eSport coaching or sport coaching. The coach's tasks usually can range from nutrition and health aspects to game-related components and mental training to a marketing and sponsoring person in charge. While coaches can help with the success and the progress of a team their role has not been fully defined yet. In 2016, Valve, decided to ban coaches from directly communicating with the players during tournaments. Due to the communication with the coach, the coach started to manage the game and occupied functions usually reserved for the team leader, and thus diminishing the importance of a team leader for the game [1].

Besides psychological training also general physiological training is relevant for esports players due to the required focus and demanded mechanical skills.

In traditional sports the training is customized to fit the requirements of the specific sport. In esports, different games have similar requirements due to similar motoric requirements [6]. These requirements can be categorized into three aspects [5]:

- *Concentration:* In esports, players have to stay highly concentrated for extensive periods of time throughout the entire match. Factors contribution to increased concentration of a players are a regular sufficient sleep schedule as well as a health nutrition.
- *Musculature:* The training of musculature in esports mainly focuses on reducing the risks of injuries to the muscular-skeletal system, which can arise through the process of training or tournaments. Common injuries in esports cover the carpal tunnel syndrome due to repetitive wrist work [2], the tennis elbow, and intense back pain due to bad posture and extensive sitting. Thus, the back musculature is trained, combined with, e.g., running to increase endurance and stretching exercises for muscle flexibility [8].
- *Coordination:* Coordination is the most evident physiological factor in esports consisting of hand-eye coordination, finger coordination, and visual perception. The hand-eye coordination is critical in esports, where hitting a desired spot on the screen using the mouse as fast and precise as possible is important. Finger coordination adds to these challenges as it quickly becomes necessary to input multiple mouse and keyboard actions simultaneously in a coordinated manner. For visual functions many different aspects influence the player's performance like: visual acuity, eye movement, focus, alignment, peripheral vision and awareness, and depth-, colour, and visual perception.

7   Summary, Discussion and Final Remarks

All three monitored games require a vast amount of research in order to be successful in the game. Constant changes in each game due to balancing issues, character, or map changes players need to stay up do date with popular tactics and mechanics. One core similarity for all games is the recommendation to watch professional games, which are being explained either by a moderator or by another player. These usually cover deep insights into the tactical aspect of each game and allow viewers to familiarize themselves with common plays. For the micromanagement aspects each game has their own characteristics players have to focus on to improve their performance. While MOBAs and RTS games have similar input styles, MOBAs are focused on the perfect control of a singular champion, while RTS games are focused on the control of different unit groups. By contrast, micro in team-based shooters mainly concern the optimized control of the player's character in a first-person view. Thus, mouse control regarding firearm management is core here. While especially micro aspects of hand-eye coordination are transferable between games, macro focuses more on the strategic characteristics of gameplay and thus are not directly transferable between games. One problem we identified is the lack of detailed documentation for most training methods and the abundance of sources covering individual aspects instead of a coherent guideline for a specific game. We further identified that game independent factors like physiological and psychological training methods should not be neglected, but rather should be trained in parallel to the game-related aspects, as they have a direct influence not only on the player's game performance, but also on its general health.

References

1. Pereira, R., Wilwert, M.L., Takase, E.: Contributions of sport psychology to the competitive gaming: an experience report with a professional team of league of legends. Int. J. Appl. Psychol. **6**(2), 27–30 (2016)
2. Gelberman, R.H., Hergenroeder, P.T., Hargens, A.R., Lundborg, G.N., Akeson, W.H.: The carpal tunnel syndrome. a study of carpal canal pressures. J. Bone Joint Surg. Am. **63**(3), 380–383 (1981)
3. Railsback, D., Caporusso, N.: Investigating the Human Factors in eSports Performance. In: Ahram, T.Z. (ed.) AHFE 2018. AISC, vol. 795, pp. 325–334. Springer, Cham (2019). https://doi.org/10.1007/978-3-319-94619-1_32
4. DiFrancisco-Donoghue, J., Balentine, J., Schmidt, G., Zwibel, H.: Managing the health of the eSport athlete: an integrated health management model. BMJ Open Sport Exerc. Med. **5**(1), (2019)
5. Pedraza-Ramirez, I., Musculus, L., Raab, M., Laborde, S.: Setting the scientific stage for esports psychology: a systematic review. Int. Rev. Sport Exerc. Psychol. **13**(1), 319–352 (2020)
6. Hoffman, J.: Physiological Aspects of Sport Training and Performance. Human Kinetics, Champaign(2014)
7. Esanu, A.: OG's psychologist Mia Stellberg at TI9: "The OG guys are not affected by the cliches of esports" https://www.vpesports.com/dota2/ogs-psychologist-mia-stellberg-at-ti9-the-og-guys-are-not-affected-by-the-cliches-of-esports. Accessed: 20 Mar 2021
8. Witvrouw, E., Mahieu, N., Danneels, L., McNair, P.: Stretching and injury prevention. Sports Med. **34**(7), 443–449 (2004)
9. Vinyals, O., et al.: Randmaster level in StarCraft II using multi-agent reinforcement learning. Nat. **575**(7782), 350–354 (2019)
10. 3D Aim Trainer. https://www.3daimtrainer.com. Accessed: 20 May 2021
11. Hamari, J., Sjöblom, M.: What is eSports and why do people watch it?. Internet Res (2017)
12. Rambusch, J., Jakobsson, P., Pargman, D.: Exploring E-sports: A case study of game play in Counter-strike. In: 3rd Digital Games Research Association International Conference:" Situated Play", DiGRA 2007, Tokyo, 24 September 2007 through 28 September 2007 (Vol. 4, pp. 157–164). Digital Games Research Association (DiGRA), (2007)
13. Wright, T., Boria, E., Breidenbach, P.: Creative player actions in FPS online video games: playing counter-strike. Game Stud. **2**(2), 103–123 (2002)
14. Valve: Counter-Strike: Global offensive. Platforms: Windows, macOS, Linux, PlayStation 3, Xbox 360, Xbox One, August 2012
15. Lux, M., Riegler, M., Halvorsen, P., Dang-Nguyen, D.-T., Potthast, M.: Challenges for multimedia research in e-sports using *Counter-Strike*. In: Elmenreich, W., Schallegger, R.R., Schniz, F., Gabriel, S., Pölsterl, G., Ruge, W.B. (eds.) Savegame. PGS, pp. 197–206. Springer, Wiesbaden (2019). https://doi.org/10.1007/978-3-658-27395-8_13

16. Johnson, N.: Everything you need to know about crosshair placement in CSGO, June 2020. https://win.gg/news/4669/everything-you-need-to-know-about-crosshair-placement-in-csgo. Accessed: 20 May 2021
17. CSGO Demos Manager. https://csgo-demo-manager.com. Accessed: 20 May 2021
18. Vaz, C.: CS:GO - Best training maps 2020, February 2020. https://www.metabomb.net/csgo/gameplay-guides/csgo-best-training-maps-2018. Accessed: 20 May 2021
19. Mokrusch, H.: Time dimensions of decision-making in CS:GO, February 2017.https://medium.com/@hendrikmokrusch/time-dimensions-of-decision-making-in-cs-go-341fa4cd3727. Accessed: 20 May 2021
20. Chui, S.: Fundamentals concepts to understand team counter-strike, February 2019. https://www.vpesports.com/csgo/fundamentals-concepts-to-understand-team-counter-strike. Accessed: 20 May 2021
21. Spray.Training: http://spray.training, last accessed: 20. May 2021
22. eSport-Bund Deutschland: Was ist eSport? (2018). https://esportbund.de/esport/was-ist-esport. Accessed: 20 May 2021
23. Riot Games: League of Legends. Platforms: Windows, macOS, October 2009
24. Besombes, N.: Esports & competitive games by genre, July 2019. https://medium.com/@nicolas.besombes/esports-competitive-games-by-genre-61fcaf9c6a8f. Accessed: 20 May 2021
25. Mobalytics: Absolute Beginner's Guide to League of Legends, https://mobalytics.gg/blog/absolute-beginners-guide-to-league-of-legends, (Jul 2019) last accessed: 20. May 2021
26. Mobalytics: everything you need to know about team comps and teamfighting in league of legends, https://mobalytics.gg/blog/everything-you-need-to-know-about-team-comps-and-teamfighting-in-league-of-legends, (Feb 2021). Accessed: 20 May 2021
27. Mobalytics: All league of legends champions, builds and stats at your fingertips. https://app.mobalytics.gg/lol/champions. Accessed: 20 May 2021
28. Mobalytics: The path to improvement in league of legends, July 2019. https://mobalytics.gg/blog/path-to-improvement-in-league-legends. Accessed 20 May 2021
29. Team Dignitas: Micro vs. macro: what they are and how to improve on both, January 2018. https://dignitas.gg/articles/blogs/League-of-Legends/11733/micro-vs.-macro-what-they-are-and-how-to-improve-on-both. Accessed: 20 May 2021
30. Champion.gg: LoT champion stats, guides, builds, runes, masteries, counters and matchups!. https://champion.gg. Accessed 20 May 2021
31. Smiterino: League of Legends Smite Trainer, http://smiterino.com, last accessed: 20. Mai 2021
32. LolDataScience: League of legends data visualization and analysis. https://loldatascience.com. Accessed: 20 May 2021
33. LoLDodgeGame: https://loldodgegame.com, last accessed: 20. May 2021
34. Op.gg: League of Legends Neeko Mid Lane Statistics. https://www.op.gg/champion/neeko/statistics/mid. Accessed: 20 May 2021
35. Skillinked: https://training.skillinked.com/en. Accessed: 20 May 2021
36. Zar: LoL in-game coaching overlay. https://zar.gg. Accessed: 20 May 2021
37. Kim, J.: Micro vs. macro gameplay, October 2013. https://gamemakers.com/micro-vs-macro-consolepc-vs-mobile-gaming. Accessed: 20 May 2021
38. Blizzard Entertainment, Activision Blizzard: StarCraft II, Platforms: Windows, macOS, July 2010

39. Liquipedia: How to Improve, April 2019 . https://liquipedia.net/starcraft2/How-to_Improve. Accessed 20 May 2021
40. Liquipedia: Macro in StarCraft II, https://liquipedia.net/starcraft2/Macro, (Apr 2020), last accessed: 20. May 2021
41. Map Analyser for LotV, April 2019. https://tl.net/forum/sc2-maps/414326-map-analyser-tool, Accessed: 20 May 2021
42. Liquipedia: Micro in StarCraft II, January 2020. https://liquipedia.net/starcraft2/Micro, Accessed: 20 May 2021
43. Liquipedia: Maps in StarCraft II, September 2019. https://liquipedia.net/starcraft2/Maps. Accessed: 20 May 2021
44. Spawning Tool Blog, October 2018. http://blog.spawningtool.com, Accessed: 20 May 2021
45. Bozhenko, E.: All CS:GO Map Callouts, April 2020. https://dmarket.com/blog/csgo-map-callouts. Accessed: 20 May 2021
46. Matsui, A., Sapienza, A., Ferrara, E.: Does streaming esports affect players' behavior and performance? Games Cult. 15(1), 9–31, (2020)
47. Kari, T., Siutila, M., Karhulahti, V.M.: An extended study on training and physical exercise in esports. In: Exploring the Cognitive, Social, Cultural, and Psychological Aspects of Gaming and Simulations, pp. 270–292. IGI Global (2019)
48. Palmieri, J.: Sport-specific: Speed training for football. Strength Cond. J. 15(6), 12–17 (1993)
49. Hallmann, K., Giel, T.: eSports-competitive sports or recreational activity?. Sport Manag. Rev. 21(1), 14–20, (2018)
50. Nicholls, S.B., Worsfold, P.R.: The observational analysis of elite coaches within youth soccer: the importance of performance analysis. Int. J. Sports Sci. Coach. 11(6), 825–831 (2016)
51. Tyack, A., Wyeth, P., Johnson, D.: The appeal of moba games: what makes people start, stay, and stop. In: Proceedings of the 2016 Annual Symposium on Computer-Human Interaction in Play, pp. 313–325 (2016)

Physical Exercise Quality Assessment Using Wearable Sensors

Philipp Niklas Müller(✉) , Felix Rauterberg, Philipp Achenbach,
Thomas Tregel, and Stefan Göbel

Multimedia Communications Lab - KOM, Technical University of Darmstadt,
Darmstadt, Germany
philipp.mueller@kom.tu-darmstadt.de

Abstract. To ensure health benefits and prevent injuries, the correct execution of fitness exercises is essential, particularly when vulnerable individuals are involved, such as during rehabilitation. As it is difficult for a person to assess the execution quality for themselves and most people cannot afford a personal trainer at all times, an automated assessment of execution quality is desirable. Whereas human activity recognition with modern sensor technologies has become a fundamental topic in scientific research and industry over the past decade, the execution quality of exercises is rarely addressed. In this paper, we assess the applicability of machine learning-based classification to differentiate not just between different fitness exercises, but also their execution quality. For this purpose, we propose three different system variants to recognize three different fitness exercises and at least three typical execution errors each based on acceleration and gyroscope data from up to four body-worn sensors. In our evaluation, we utilize data we recorded from 16 different participants to determine our systems' recognition performance for different application and implementation scenarios.

Keywords: Activity recognition · Fitness · Machine learning

1 Introduction

Despite regular physical activity having significant health benefits, a large portion of the world's population is insufficiently physically active [2, 4]. With mobile sensor devices becoming increasingly accessible and more widespread in the past decade, fitness and health applications have become an important tool to provide support and motivation for physical activity. In Germany alone, the number of people using such applications is expected to increase from roughly 3.4 million in 2017 to 6.6 million by 2022 [3]. Whereas these applications often offer extensive motivational features such as gamification or social aspects, their tracking capabilities are often limited and do not account for proper technique.

Since proper technique when exercising is essential not just to guarantee a training effect but also to prevent injuries such as strains or sprains [1,16], automatically assessing a person's technique based on wearable sensor data would

© Springer Nature Switzerland AG 2021
B. Fletcher et al. (Eds.): JCSG 2021, LNCS 12945, pp. 229–243, 2021.
https://doi.org/10.1007/978-3-030-88272-3_17

be highly beneficial. Based on this assessment, fitness and health applications could then provide the user with individualized assistance on how to improve their technique. A particularly noteworthy application area is rehabilitation, e.g., after an injury, where it is crucial that exercises are executed correctly, and their physician could utilize an assessment of the patient's execution to track the rehabilitation progress.

In this paper, we want to assess the applicability of body-worn sensors and machine-learning-based classification methods for the purpose of determining the execution quality of physical activities. With appropriate preprocessing and feature selection, these methods have shown to provide high classification performance on a vast number of activity recognition tasks. Compared to other approaches such as handcrafted rule-based systems, machine learning approaches generally require less domain knowledge, less implementation effort, and can more easily be transferred to different tasks, i.e., different activities in this case. They are therefore often preferable if enough training data is available for them to be applicable.

However, determining the execution quality of physical activities is generally a more difficult task than typical activity recognition tasks. First, the classes to distinguish between are more similar to another since they represent the same activity with often only small, yet important, differences in execution. Furthermore, it is comparatively difficult to obtain large amounts of training data for incorrect exercise executions without putting participants at risk. Thus, we want to determine whether and under which circumstances machine learning-based classification methods can be utilized for the assessment of physical activity execution quality and under which circumstances different methods need to be employed.

2   Physical Exercises

To get an accurate representation of the capabilities of machine learning-based classification methods for quality assessment, we chose three well-known fitness-related exercises (see Fig. 1) which fulfill a number of different criteria. To record representative data, it was important that each exercise could be correctly performed multiple times in succession, even by amateurs. At the same time, the exercises had to be complex enough to represent most physical exercises with respect to their recognizability and analyzability. In particular, multiple joints and body parts had to be involved and typical mistakes had to be relatively minor deviations from a correct execution.

For the data recording and later evaluation, it was important to have a well-defined correct execution form and clear definition of typical mistakes (see Fig. 1) for each of the three exercises. These were determined in collaboration with a physiotherapist and based on relevant literature in the field of training theory [5–7].

Table 1. Physical exercises with their respective types of deviations

Exercise	Type of mistake	Abbreviation	Mistake description
Squat	Weight shifted forwards	WS	Weight is kept on the balls of the feet during downward motion, knees extend beyond toes, heels are possibly lifted off the ground
	Inward knees	IK	One or both knees are inclined inwards, following a line along the inside of the feet during downward and upward motion
	Outward knees	OK	One or both knees are inclined outwards, following a line along the outside of the feet during downward and upward motion
	Partial repetitions	PR	Hips and upper body are not lowered deep enough, upper thighs do not become parallel to the ground
Push-up	Flared elbows	FE	Arms are flared out wide, elbows point away from the body up to a 90-degree angle during downward and upward motion
	Lowered mid-section	LM	Body does not maintain a straight line due to lowered hip, groin area remains close to the ground throughout exercise
	Partial repetitions	PR	Body is not lowered deep enough, chest remains far from the ground, upper arms do not become parallel to the ground
Bent-over row	Flared elbows	FE	Arms are flared out wide, elbows point away from the body up to a 90-degree angle during downward and upward motion
	Rounded back	RB	Upper and lower back do not maintain a straight line but falls into a rounded or hunched position
	Torso raise	TR	Upper body is raised and lowered significantly during upward and downward movement

3 Related Work

Despite activity recognition, in general, being a well-researched topic and *healthcare and well-being* being one of its primary application contexts [8,9,15], relatively little work exists on the quality assessment of physical exercises using wearable sensors.

Pernek et al. [11] present a basic approach for quality assessment of body-weight exercises and weight training. In their paper, they propose a system that utilizes the smartphone's accelerometer data to track individual exercise repetitions through real-time segmentation and provide qualitative feedback based on the repetition's duration. Whereas their system performs well on the task of real-time segmentation and provides useful feedback on the execution speed, it does not cover other types of execution errors such as incorrect technique.

More closely related to the topic of this paper is the system presented by O'Reilly et al. [10] which is designed to detect seven distinct types of execution mistakes when performing squats. Relying exclusively on the data provided by a single smartphone's inertial sensor, they recorded 10 correct executions and three incorrect executions for each type of mistake for 22 participants. On this data set, they achieve a multi-class accuracy of 56% in distinguishing between different types of mistakes and correct executions using leave-one-subject-out validation. Alternatively, their model achieves an 80% accuracy in the binary classification task of distinguishing between correct and incorrect exercise execution.

A similar approach utilizing multiple sensors is presented by Velloso et al. [14] in the context of weight-lifting exercises, more specifically, the unilateral dumbbell biceps curl. Instead of relying on the smartphone, four inertial sensors are placed on the wrist, upper arm, lower back, and dumbbell, respectively, providing significantly more information about the person's technique. They recorded data for the correct execution and four different types of mistakes from six participants under the supervision of an experienced weightlifter. On this data set, their system achieves a multi-class accuracy of 78% for the task of distinguishing between different types of mistakes and correct executions using leave-one-subject-out validation.

Another approach utilizing multiple sensors is presented by Taylor et al. [13]. Their system is specifically developed for rehabilitation exercises of knee osteoarthritis patients to differentiate between a correct exercise execution and one of up to four different execution mistakes for three different exercises. Their system uses five inertial sensors attached to the waist and the shin and thigh of each leg, respectively. On a data set consisting of 420 total repetitions from nine participants, their system achieves multi-class accuracies of up to 94% for cross-validation across all subjects and up to 80% for a leave-one-subject-out validation. Their approach is later improved upon [12] to include multi-label classification, allowing for the simultaneous detection of multiple execution mistakes.

4 System Design

Our approach follows a typical machine learning pipeline for classification tasks, consisting of data acquisition, preprocessing, training, and validation steps (see Fig. 1). Validation, in particular, took place during system design to find appropriate default hyperparameter values and during our evaluation to assess our systems' performance in different scenarios.

Fig. 1. Machine learning pipeline for classification tasks

4.1 Data Acquisition

Our data acquisition system, shown in Fig. 2, uses four commercially available sensor boards (Thunderboard Sense 2), each featuring a 3-axis accelerometer and a 3-axis gyroscope. In consultation with a physiotherapist, the sensors were decided to be located above both knees and elbow joints to provide the most meaningful information on potential exercise execution mistakes.

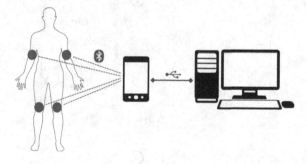

Fig. 2. Data acquisition system consisting of four wearable inertial measurement units and a smartphone for data collection, later connected to a PC for further processing

The measurement ranges of the sensors are set to their maxima of $\pm 16\,$g and $\pm 2000°$/s, respectively, and the sampling rate is set to 95 Hz, allowing our system to record representative data even for quick movements. Whereas it is possible to set higher sampling rates in the sensor boards' firmware, we found 95 Hz to be the highest sampling rate that would still allow all raw sensor data from all four sensor boards to be reliably transferred to the smartphone using Bluetooth Low Energy (BLE), especially when another device was connected to the smartphone via BLE. Furthermore, empirical results showed no significant difference in classification performance for higher sampling rates, suggesting that 95 Hz is sufficient for the selected exercises. The firmware was specifically adjusted for human activity recognition to improve stability and improve power efficiency, disabling unnecessary sensors and features on the sensor board.

Data are recorded on the smartphone using a simple application that lets you connect to multiple BLE devices, control when data are recorded and sent by connected devices, and store the recorded data on the smartphone. Additionally, markers can be set to mark time stamps during which an individual repetition is performed. This is an important feature to accurately label training data for individual repetitions from a recording consisting of continuous repetitions. The stored sensor data and the markers are later transferred to a PC to allow for more time-efficient preprocessing, training, and validation. When an already trained model is used to infer classes during application run-time, this step is skipped, and preprocessing is done directly on the smartphone.

4.2 Preprocessing

For our system, the data acquisition application handles all synchronization between sensor boards and their recorded data, and therefore we can assume all data to have already synchronized timestamps. Thus, our pre-processing consists of the three primary steps depicted in Fig. 3.

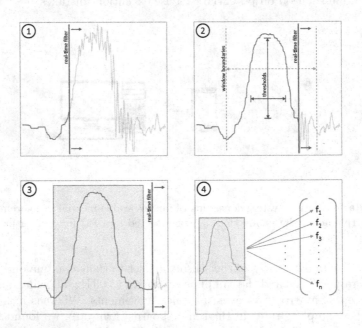

Fig. 3. Preprocessing steps: the sensor data is filtered (1); window boundaries are set when a peak is detected (2); after the filter has passed the right window boundary (3), the enclosed data is used to extract a set of features (4)

First, to remove noise from the data, a median filter is applied to the data of each sensor and each axis, respectively, resulting in smoother data which also improves the reliability of the chosen windowing approach in the second preprocessing step. The median filter replaces the value of each data point by the median of its surrounding values, making it more robust to extreme outliers than, for example, a mean filter. Whereas this approach results in a small delay in the usability of data in a real-time setting, we do not believe this delay of a fraction of a second to be relevant to most activity recognition applications in practice.

A threshold-based peak detection algorithm is employed in the second step to find peaks that surpass a predetermined threshold in the acceleration data. This algorithm is employed on each axis of the accelerometer of each of the four sensor boards. If a peak is found in any of them, time window boundaries are set with a predetermined distance in both directions of the peak. All sensors' data within that time window is then considered to be one potential exercise sample. To label data for later model training, it is then checked whether a marker exists within that time window. If one exists, the sample is given that marker's label. Otherwise, it is considered part of the null class, representing data of no exercise being performed.

Table 2. Features considered for feature subset selection

Feature	Description
Minimum	Smallest acceleration or angular velocity measure in time window
Maximum	Highest acceleration or angular velocity measure in time window
Difference	Difference between minimum and maximum
Mean	Arithmetic mean of acceleration or angular velocity measures in time window
Variance	Average deviation of acceleration or angular velocity measures from the mean
Standard deviation	Square root of variance
Skewness	Asymmetry of signal distribution in time window
Kurtosis	Steepness/tailedness of signal distribution in time window
Body height	Body height of participant in cm

In the last step, each sample is transformed into a set of characterizing properties, i.e., a set of features representing that sample during training and inference. Excluding body height, each feature in Table 2 is calculated for each axis of each sensor individually, resulting in 24 individual feature values for each feature type. Except for body height, all features are statistical measures commonly used for activity recognition in related work. The person's body height was added for test purposes since we expect it to have an impact on the raw sensor data.

To avoid the negative impact of features that are either redundant or do not generalize well, we also performed a feature subset selection by calculating F_1 scores for all subsets of features, all system variants (see Sect. 4.3), and all validation methods (see Sect. 5). Ultimately, this led us to drop the features *Maximum*, *Skewness*, *Kurtosis*, and *Body Height*.

4.3   Machine Learning

We have three different variants for the machine learning part of our system, as shown in Fig. 4. Although the individual classifiers can be any feature-based classifiers, related work suggests that the classifiers best suited for activity recognition tasks are support vector machines (SVM), naive Bayes (NB), random forests (RF), and k-nearest neighbors (k-NN).

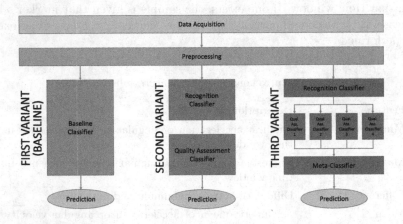

Fig. 4. System overview with three different machine learning variants

The first variant is a simple baseline classifier that contains classes for each combination of exercise type and type of mistake, or lack thereof. Compared to the baseline variant, the other two variants split the prediction of exercise type and type of mistake into two separate tasks. First, a recognition classifier is employed that only distinguishes between exercise types, i.e., whether it was performed correctly or incorrectly. Based on which type of exercise was predicted, a secondary quality assessment classifier is then selected, predicting the type of mistake, or lack thereof, for that specific exercise type. The third variant differs from the second variant in that this quality assessment classifier is replaced by an ensemble of classifiers and a meta classifier. Such an ensemble has the potential advantage of allowing for different types of classifiers to be utilized in the same classification task, making use of their individual strengths in terms of pattern recognition.

5   Results

To assess the applicability of our systems for quality assessment of physical exercises, we conducted an experiment with 16 participants (4 female, 12 male) between 13 and 56 years, with the average age being 30.3 years. All participants were required to engage in regular physical activity, i.e., at least twice a week for at least two years prior to the time of participation, and stated to feel generally healthy with no known impairments that could affect their execution performance.

Each participant was given an information sheet with the training program and short descriptions of each exercise and its variants in advance. For the recording process, the participant was instructed to perform five repetitions for each exercise and each of its deviations. A supervisor was present at all times to provide guidance to the participant, ensure their well-being, and verify that the sensors were properly attached at all times and that all data was properly recorded and labeled. If the recording of an exercise variant was considered erroneous, e.g., because it wasn't performed according to the instructions, it was discarded and, if possible, recorded anew. The resulting data set consists of 923 recordings of exercise repetitions and 96 recordings of null-class activities for a total of 1,019 recorded samples.

5.1   Hyperparameter Values

Before evaluating our systems, it was necessary to select appropriate hyperparameter values, i.e., parameters which aren't adjusted during machine learning, for system-specific and classifier-specific hyperparameters. In both cases, reasonable value ranges for each hyperparameter were determined based on domain knowledge, relevant literature, and empirical results. The final values were then determined using grid search for system-specific and random search for classifierspecific hyperparameters.

System-specific hyperparameters include parameters related to the filtering and windowing steps during preprocessing and directly affect the quality of data samples generated for training and later inference. Table 3 shows the five different parameters and their respective default values determined with grid search on a combination of all systems and validation strategies (see Sect. 5.2).

Classifier-specific hyperparameters were determined individually for each system variant and each validation strategy (see Sect. 5.2) using random search. For the support vector machine, they include the regularization parameter C, the kernel type, and the degree of the polynomial kernel function if a polynomial kernel is used. For the k-nearest neighbors classifier, they include the number of neighbors, the distance metric, and the weight function. For the random forest classifier, they include the number of estimators (trees) in the forest and the number of features to consider when looking for the best split. The individual values selected are omitted in this paper for the sake of clarity. All other hyperparameters are left at the default values set in scikit-learn (v0.24.2).

Table 3. System-specific parameters and their default values

Parameter	Default value	Description
win_size	2.4	Size of each time window (in seconds)
win_shift	10	Amount of window shift to the right from initial position (in percent)
win_overlap	30	Allowed overlap between adjacent windows (in percent)
acc_thresh	3.8	Threshold for accelerometer peak detection (in m/s^2)
kernel_size	48	Size of the median filter kernel (in samples)

5.2   Performance Metrics and Validation Strategies

A number of different performance metrics can be used to measure the performance of a classifier on a classification task. Whereas accuracy, i.e., the portion of all samples classified correctly, is an intuitive and commonly used metric, we believe the macro-averaged F_1-score to be a more appropriate measure in this case. Compared to accuracy, which shows a bias towards classes that occur more often in the data set, the macro-averaged F_1-score is unaffected by an unequal class distribution. For our data set, this can occur in some cases where erroneous recordings had to be removed. In particular, the F_1-score is a specific case of the F-score, which calculates the harmonic mean of precision and recall for each class individually and then averages the calculated values for all classes.

We employ three different strategies for validation, which each represent a different use case of quality assessment models. A separate test set is not employed as it would further reduce the data available for training and validation and because, based on empirical results, our hyperparameter tuning is relatively unaffected by the specific subset of data used.

The first validation strategy, called *within-subjects* (WS), represents the performance of a personalized model, i.e., a model trained exclusively on data of the same person that it is used to predict exercise execution quality for. In this validation strategy, 3-fold cross-validation is performed individually for each participant's data before calculating the average of all cross-validation results.

The second validation strategy, called *leave-one-subject-out* (LOSO), represents the performance of a generalized model, i.e., a model trained with no data of the person that it is used to predict exercise execution quality for. In this validation strategy, 16-fold cross-validation is performed. Instead of the data being randomly split into 16 folds, each fold contains a single person's data. Thus, for each person, a model is trained on all other people's data and then validated only on that person's data.

The third validation strategy is simple *10-fold cross-validation* (10-fold CV) which represents the performance of a hybrid model, i.e., a model trained with data of the person it is used to predict exercise execution quality for in addition to data of other people.

5.3 Performance

To accurately assess the overall performance of each system, the best performing classifiers have to be selected. This is done separately for each classification task in each of the three system variants. Table 4 shows the classifiers which performed best for each of the classification tasks. Overall, k-nearest neighbors, support vector machines, and random forests perform very similarly in most cases. Each of them performs the best at least once, with the best performing ensemble for the third system variant including each of these classifiers. On the other hand, Naive Bayes is never the best performing classifier and regularly performs significantly worse than all other classifiers.

Table 4. Best performing classifiers for each classification task

System/Phase	Cross-validation	Leave-one-subject-out	Within subjects
Recognition	SVM	RF	SVM
System 1 (Qual. Ass.)	k-NN	RF	RF
System 2 (Qual. Ass.)	k-NN	RF	RF
System 3 (Qual. Ass.)	k-NN, RF, SVM	k-NN, RF, SVM	k-NN, RF, SVM
Meta	RF	k-NN	k-NN

Figure 5 exemplarily shows the performance of the baseline system when utilizing different classifiers. As can be seen, even the baseline variant performs relatively well when the training data set contains data for the person whose exercise execution quality is being predicted, reaching an F_1-score of up to 0.9455 for a personalized model (WS) and up to 0.9459 for a hybrid model (10-fold CV). Not shown here, the second and third system variants slightly improve these scores, with the third system variant reaching up to 0.9504 and 0.9628 for the personalized and the hybrid model, respectively. For the generalized model (LOSO), the baseline model performs comparatively poorly, only reaching a maximum F_1-score of 0.5444. The second and third system variants, once again, only perform slightly better, with the third system variant reaching a maximum F_1-score of 0.5723.

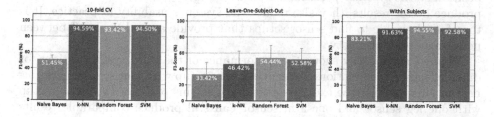

Fig. 5. Performance of the baseline system for different classifiers

It is worth mentioning that the classifier utilized in the recognition phase of the second and third system variants works relatively well, achieving F_1-scores of 0.9549 for the personalized model, 0.9736 for the generalized model, and 0.9934 for the hybrid model, suggesting that both personalized and generalized data is useful to the recognition task. Therefore, the second and third systems only rarely misclassify the exercise type and often misclassify between different deviations of the same exercise. This can also be observed in the systems' respective confusion matrices, exemplarily shown in Fig. 6 for the second system variant. Furthermore, it can be seen that the model performs very differently for different variations of the same exercise, correctly recognizing a raised torso during bent-over rows in 94% of cases but only recognizing the same exercise performed correctly in 55% of cases.

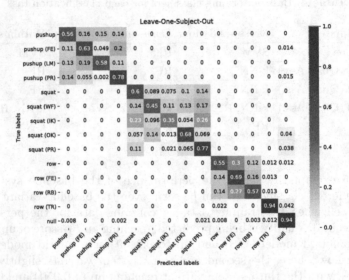

Fig. 6. Confusion matrix for a generalized model (LOSO) of the second system variant

5.4   Number of Sensors

An additional topic of interest is the impact of the number of sensors and their position on the systems' performance. Whereas more sensors can be expected to produce better results, they also reduce the system's usability in practice. It is therefore desirable to find sensor setups that provide a good trade-off between performance and usability.

Figure 7 exemplarily shows the performance of the third system variant for different sensor combinations. As expected, the setup with four sensors performs best in all cases. For the exercises considered in this paper, a two-sensor setup with one leg sensor and one arm sensor can still produce comparable results to a four-sensor setup. However, the difference is significantly larger for the generalized model than for the other two models. Furthermore, sensor setups that exclude the legs perform significantly worse than those which exclude the arms, suggesting that, for the selected exercises, leg movement is more representative than arm movement. Overall, we consider the best trade-offs to be either a full four-sensor setup for maximum performance or a two-sensor setup including one arm and one leg, with one-sensor setups performing insufficiently for practical use.

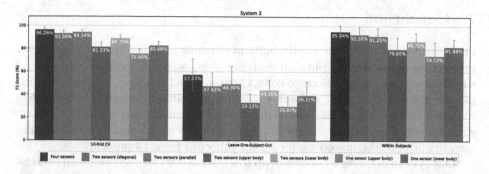

Fig. 7. Performance of the third system variant for different sensor combinations

6 Discussion

Our results seem to confirm that the quality assessment task is significantly more difficult than the activity recognition task for classification algorithms. In particular, a person's sensor data for erroneous executions of exercises does not appear to generalize well to other people, making personalized or hybrid models highly desirable. In practice, however, this means that you would have to record sensor data of erroneous executions for every user of your application and retrain the quality assessment model with that data. In most use cases, this seems highly impractical, especially since erroneous executions can potentially jeopardize the user's health. An exception could be applications that are deployed in collaboration with an expert, e.g., a trainer or a physician. Before deploying the application, the expert could ask the user to perform each exercise and label individual repetitions based on whether they were performed correctly or not. This data could then be used to train a model to assist the user when exercising on their own.

Whereas the limitations of our study cannot allow us to conclusively rule out classification algorithms for quality assessment of physical exercises, our results strongly suggest that classification algorithms are unfit for the task in practice. We believe this to be the case since the primary limitation of our study, i.e., relatively little training data of erroneous exercise executions, would also apply to practical use cases of such a system and cannot be easily circumvented. Furthermore, a more complex and more specialized overall system might produce better results but would also partially defeat the purpose of using machine learning algorithms, to begin with, requiring a large amount of domain knowledge and design effort. For future work, a promising approach to deal with the lack of training data would be the augmentation of data by synthesizing data from existing data or generating entirely new data. For execution mistakes, in particular, data of correct executions could serve as a basis to generate data of execution mistakes.

7   Conclusion

In this paper, we assess the applicability of machine learning-based classifiers for the quality assessment of physical exercises using wearable sensors. We present a system with three variations to collect sensor data from four wearable sensors, process the collected data, and apply machine learning techniques to recognize a recorded exercise's exercise type and potential execution mistakes. The system with its three variations is evaluated for its exercise recognition and quality assessment performance on exercise data collected from 16 participants.

Our system achieves F_1-scores of up to 0.95 and 0.96 for the combined exercise recognition and quality assessment task using a personalized and a hybrid model, respectively, suggesting applicability when data from the user is available for training. Using a generalized model, our system achieves F_1-scores of up to 0.57, suggesting that user data on erroneous exercise executions do not generalize well, and significantly more training data is required when no data from the user is available during training. For practical purposes, the number of sensors utilized can be reduced from four to two, reducing F_1-scores by at most 0.04 for the personalized and hybrid models and at most 0.1 for the generalized model.

Future research will focus on two primary approaches to improve the generalizability of quality assessment models. The first approach is the generation of new sensor data or synthesizing new sensor data from existing data, particularly with respect to sensor data of physical exercise execution errors. The second approach is a different representation of physical exercise execution errors which generalizes better than distinct classes for distinct errors, e.g., by having a clearly defined correct execution technique and measuring how close a recorded execution is to that baseline.

References

1. Sportverletzungen. Verletzungsrisiko & Prävention (2018). https://www.allianzcare.com/content/dam/onemarketing/azcare/allianzcare/de/health-guides/2018/Allianz_Health_Guide_Sports_DE.pdf. Accessed 26 Nov 2020
2. National Health Service - Exercise, October 2019. https://www.nhs.uk/live-well/exercise/. Accessed 08 Aug 2020
3. Nutzerentwicklung bei Wearables und Fitness-Apps in Deutschland in den Jahren 2017 bis 2024, September 2020. https://de.statista.com/statistik/daten/studie/1046996/umfrage/marktentwicklung-von-wearables-und-fitness-apps-in-deutschland/. Accessed 28 Nov 2020

4. World Health Organization - Physical Activity, November 2020. https://www.who.int/news-room/fact-sheets/detail/physical-activity. Accessed 28 Nov 2020
5. Ashwell, K.: The Student's Anatomy of Exercise Manual. New Burlington Books (2016)
6. Boyle, M.: New Functional Training for Sports, 2nd edn. Human Kinetics, Champaign (2016)
7. Earle, R., Baechle, T.: NSCA's Essentials of Personal Training. Human Kinetics, Champaign (2004)
8. López-Nava, I., Muñoz-Meléndez, A.: Wearable inertial sensors for human motion analysis: a review. IEEE Sens. J. **16**(22), 7821–7834 (2016)
9. Olivares Vicente, A., Ramí rez, J., Gorriz, J., Olivares, G., Damas, M.: Detection of (in)activity periods in human body motion using inertial sensors: a comparative study. Sensors **12**, 5791–5814 (2012)
10. O'Reilly, M., et al.: Evaluating squat performance with a single inertial measurement unit. In: IEEE 12th International Conference on Wearable and Implantable Body Sensor Networks (BSN), pp. 1–6 (2015)
11. Pernek, I., Hummel, K., Kokol, P.: Exercise repetition detection for resistance training based on smartphones. Pers. Ubiquit. Comput. **17**, 771–782 (2013). https://doi.org/10.1007/s00779-012-0626-y
12. Taylor, P., Almeida, G.J., Hodgins, J., Kanade, T.: Multi-label classification for the analysis of human motion quality. In: 2012 Annual International Conference of the IEEE Engineering in Medicine and Biology Society, pp. 2214–2218, August 2012
13. Taylor, P., Almeida, G.J., Kanade, T., Hodgins, J.: Classifying human motion quality for knee osteoarthritis using accelerometers. In: 2010 Annual International Conference of the IEEE Engineering in Medicine and Biology Society, pp. 339–343, August 2010
14. Velloso, E., Bulling, A., Gellersen, H., Ugulino, W., Fuks, H.: Qualitative activity recognition of weight lifting exercises. In: ACM International Conference Proceeding Series, March 2013
15. Wang, A., Chen, G., Yang, J., Zhao, S., Chang, C.: A comparative study on human activity recognition using inertial sensors in a smartphone. IEEE Sens. J. **16**(11), 4566–4578 (2016)
16. Wonisch, M., Hofmann, P., Förster, H., Hörtnagl, H., Ledl-Kurkowski, E., Pokan, R.: Kompendium der Sportmedizin: Physiologie, Innere Medizin und Pädiatrie. Springer, Wien (2017). https://doi.org/10.1007/978-3-211-99716-1

Games in Education

Development and Validation of Serious Games for Teaching Cybersecurity

Srishti Kulshrestha[1], Sarthak Agrawal[1], Devottam Gaurav[1(✉)],
Manmohan Chaturvedi[1], Subodh Sharma[1], and Ranjan Bose[2]

[1] Indian Institute of Technology, Delhi, India
svs@iitd.ac.in
[2] Indraprastha Institute of Information Technology, Delhi, India
bose@iiitd.ac.in

Abstract. Serious games have shown great potential as an instructional tool in various fields by providing improved accessibility to simulations, modeling of environments, and visualizations. However, a challenging problem in the design of serious games has been to strike a fine balance between gaming and the pedagogical elements such as content, methodology of instruction, and evaluation. Several models and frameworks have been proposed to support the serious game's design and analysis to address the above-mentioned gap. In this paper, we present a serious game design and validation process in the context of cybersecurity education. We assess the effectiveness of a serious game as an educational tool by using a game designed to teach network firewalls and validate the game's effectiveness to meet the learning objectives by performing a preliminary analysis consisting of objective and subjective parts. The objective analysis is performed by capturing the player's interaction data, while the subjective analysis consists of a survey study to understand the user experience. Furthermore, we also perform an analysis of our game using the Learning Mechanics-Game Mechanics framework to highlight the interrelations between gaming and learning features. Our study demonstrates the significance of objective and subjective analysis, and our preliminary results on using our game to teach security have been found to be encouraging.

Keywords: Serious game · Cybersecurity education · Game-based learning · Quantitative research · Qualitative research

1 Introduction

In the past few years, there has been a major shift in learning from a traditional didactic model to a more learner-centered model [1, 2]. This shift from learning by "listening" to learning by "doing" requires more sophisticated ways of engaging students. In such a context, game-based learning or Serious Games (SGs) is often deployed to bridge the gap between theory and practice. Serious games are computer games designed for purposes

This work is supported by funding received from Government of India, for the IMPRINT project no. 7804.

B. Fletcher et al. (Eds.): JCSG 2021, LNCS 12945, pp. 247–262, 2021.
https://doi.org/10.1007/978-3-030-88272-3_18

other than just entertainment [3]. SGs harness the advantages of gaming technology to create a fun, motivating, and interactive virtual learning environment that promotes user engagement. The use of SGs in the educational sector for teaching and training is gaining importance and will only become more central in the coming years [4].

The digital games are used for learning and education in domains as diverse as health, military, commerce, industry, and vocational education. These can be implicitly customized based on the learning and these also provide instant feedback which allows immediate progress and development for new kinds of understanding. There is also evidence of a high retention power of educational content through playing. Several features that inherently make games engaging and motivating are highlighted by [5].

Hackers are getting smarter every day and count on errors by a human through social engineering attacks to find a way in. As illustrated by the continued success of targeting humans and trained professionals, a gap in cyber security training and awareness can be seen in education and industry. Although there are traditional approaches to training including training manuals, videos, e-learning, and security competitions like DEFCON and Capture the Flag (CTF) [6, 7] which are often found to be effective. These methods require proficiency in the related domain and availability for coaching and tutoring which is expensive. Therefore, there is a felt need to establish innovative, effective, efficient, engaging, and responsive cyber security education and training programs. Thus Serious Games (SGs) make a cost-effective approach for imparting cyber security training. In literature, a few studies have reported positive results indicating that SGs are effective when used for cyber security training and awareness [8–10]. Therefore, our research will motivate individuals and organizations interested in supplementing current methods of training by use of SGs as an innovative and effective means.

However, in designing SGs one has to be careful not to introduce any mismatch between the game and learning mechanics, which we believe is an essential component for a more successful game-based learning solution; case in point is the work in [11], which has demonstrated through case studies that not considering learning mechanics can have adverse outcomes. An effective SG requires a correct balance between pedagogical and game theories for creating an immersive gaming environment [12]. In this regard, one possible approach is to use the *Learning Mechanics-Game Mechanics* (LM-GM) framework [13, 14] (with a pool of pre-defined game feature and pedagogical elements) to design the main pedagogical and gaming features in a game and analyze any/all linkages between them. The LM-GM tool can be used for existing games as a reflection tool, and designers can create a map of dynamics of game mechanics during the flow of a game to show how mechanics change themselves and support each other as discussed in Sect. 4.

Thus, after the design of a SG, assessment is an important aspect. The assessment can target different outcomes such as the gameplay experience, usability, engagement, learning, and motivation. In this work, we are interested in measuring the learning outcome, as it can effectively measure the potential of an SG as an educational tool [15]. The widely used method for the assessment of SGs has been using questionnaires [16]. However, SGs being rich sources of interaction data, can provide in-game interaction data making it a more reliable method for objective assessment [17]. The use of analytic techniques by using in-game data is not new however, only a few studies have reported empirical evidence to inform about the learning process [18]. This paper aims to fill this gap in the literature by providing an objective assessment of our designed game. As opposed to the work done in [19], which classifies the players based on a fixed threshold, we in this paper use more statistics of the in-game data such as mean score across players and clustering to classify players.

In summary, this paper intends to look into two major aspects of assessment that concern SG (i) evaluation of SG learning outcomes, and (ii) evaluation of user experience. Both the assessments are performed within the context of a developed game for teaching the basics of a firewall and its configuration for securing a network.

This paper makes several contributions. The literature shows that the assessments used in prior works for analyzing SGs are either based on general frameworks or on adhoc analyses. We propose in Sect. 2 a methodology that tackles all significant phases of serious game development: from game design, implementation to deployment and learning outcome analysis. Secondly, we use the LM-GM framework for the analysis of the *Firewall* game. The LM-GM framework allows SG mapping that highlights the main learning (LM) and game mechanics (GM) involved in each game situation, and has been presented in Sect. 4. The correct balance between LM and GM is essential for the design of SG and has been used in the process phase in the game design methodology. Thirdly, it evaluates the effectiveness of the game through a preliminary study by inferring the learning outcomes and user experience of the players.

The paper organization is as follows: Sect. 2 discusses the methodology for game design. Section 3 presents the design features and educational objectives of the *Firewall* game. Section 4 discusses the analysis of the *Firewall* game using the LM-GM framework. Section 5 looks at the practicalities of assessment, analytics, and game validation in this context. Section 6 discusses the limitations of this research while Sect. 7 concludes the work and points to a few future directions.

2 Game Design Methodology

The game design methodology comprises three phases: the *input, process,* and *output* based on the works in [20] that describe game-based learning as an input-process-output framework. The input domain consists of defining the learning objectives based on the target audience. The game characteristics and the instructional content are decided based on the identified objectives. The next domain of process describes the game design phase. As shown in Fig. 1, in the design phase the learning goals along with the target population form the basis of game design. The game design process is a cyclic process where a balanced combination of both learning mechanics and game mechanics is required for a good design. To analyze our game for efficient mapping of learning and game mechanics we have used the LM-GM framework which is discussed in Section 2. The result of the input and process domain is the SG which the players will play. The feedback received by the players regarding their progress towards the game task leads to specific learning outcomes that can be seen in the output domain.

Figure 1 shows the development and validation process with the learning outcome analysis. The following methodology helps in the systematic assessment of the effectiveness of the SG as it covers a complete life-cycle of SG from its design to deployment.

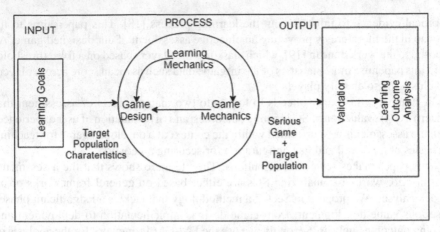

Fig. 1. Methodology of Game Design, Development, and Validation

It also helps in the ease of measurement of the learning outcomes. The game design and development process start with the learning goals being defined for the game considering the target population. The goals are then fed into the design process which itself is an iterative process. The game is then validated with a sample population. This process is repeated till the game is fully validated. The game is then finally deployed.

3 Educational Objectives and Design Considerations

The web-based game is developed using Unity [21], a cross-platform game engine for easy deployment on various platforms. The objective of the game is to teach the players about firewalls. The target audience for the game is entry-level IT users and system administrators. The playable firewall game is accessible at[1].

A firewall is an important topic in the cyber security domain. It filters the incoming or outgoing network packets and only lets through those matching certain predefined conditions based on the organization's policy. Therefore, the use of an effective educational tool helps in the enhancement of the user's practical skills. While there are other simulator tools [22, 23] and games that cover the topic, they teach little on the firewall configuration and without going into the details of the kind of packets being filtered. Based on these limitations, the designed *Firewall* game provides the following educational objectives:

- Adequate functions to implement basic and advanced packet filtering with user-friendly interfaces.
- The ability to verify the consistency and efficiency of the defined filtering rules on the established network sessions.
- Easily modify the order of the filtering rules to adequately reflect the security policy under consideration.

---

[1] http://gost.iitd.ac.in/serious_games/pages/ser.html.

The levels are organized as such that the learning goals are distributed in small clear and structured tasks(cascading info). The game is designed using a first-person approach where the graphics are rendered from the viewpoint of the player. This choice is made as it is appropriate for the sequential level-based layout of the game. It allows the players to experience the action as the protagonist providing greater immersion.

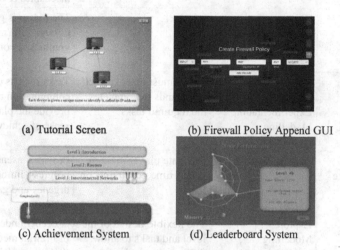

(a) Tutorial Screen   (b) Firewall Policy Append GUI

(c) Achievement System   (d) Leaderboard System

Fig. 2. Screenshots of the Firewall game

In the following Section, we will discuss some of the main design features of the *Firewall* game:

3.1 Tutorial Screen

The tutorial screens are animated graphics that are presented before the start of each level. These are instructional screens that familiarize the players with the terminology, context, and details of the tasks involved in that particular level. Figure 2(a) is an example of a tutorial screen where concepts of computer network, IP address which is essentially the basics of network configuration are explained to the player.

3.2 Firewall Configuration Interface

The Firewall policy configuration interface is shown in Fig. 2(b). This is the main screen where the user can add the rules based on the tasks given in the levels. The interface provides drag and drop buttons for the various elements of the policy like the *INPUT/OUTPUT* chain and the action which can be either *DROP* or *ACCEPT*. The graphical interface helps the player to easily add the rules without remembering the syntax.

Table 1. LM-GM based analysis of *Firewall* Game

Game mechanic	Learning mechanic	Implementation	Usage
Cut scene/Story	Instructional	Animation	Backstory telling the game objectives, mechanics & outcome
Tutorial Cascading Information	Guidance Tutorial	Levels	The Player is guided through informative graphics to complete tasks
Simulate Response Experiment	Observation, Analyze, Experimentation, Modelling Hypothesis	Player must enter correct commands to complete the required tasks	Tasks such as correct configuration rules provide the player with a sense of achievement
Movement Time pressure	Activity/Tasks	Navigate player through levels, time constraints on levels	Provides a sense of progress, immersion, urgency and game mastery
Strategy Planning	Explore Modelling	The flexible design of the level and tasks to allow different strategies to emerge	A deeper understanding of firewall mechanics through modeling
Levels, Feedback, Assessment	Feedback, Motivation, Reflect, Assessment	Advance to the next level. The score shows completion time. Feedback prompts	Reinforces a sense of understanding & progress. Player can reflect on actions taken
Rewards	Motivation, Incentive	Coins and badges	Sense of empowerment and achievement
Behavioral Momentum	Repetition, Reflection	Gameplay repeats through levels	Reinforces behavior change for secure networks

3.3 Achievement System

The achievement system creates a sense of anticipation among players to make the Firewall Game more engaging. The achievement system is provided to the players in the form of rewards like medals. Players are more likely to be rewarded immediately after the successful completion of the level as shown in Fig. 2(c).

3.4 Leaderboard System

The leaderboard system helps the players to see their rank in the Firewall Game in the form of a Radar Chart. The players' rank in the leaderboard system encourages the players to learn more and improve their standing with others as shown in Fig. 2(d).

4 Analysis of Firewall Game Using LM-GM

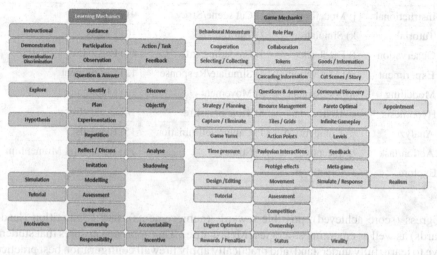

Fig. 3. Learning and game mechanics used as the basis to construct the LM-GM map for a game [14]

The LM-GM framework [13] consists of an exhaustive list of learning and gaming mechanics as shown in Fig. 3. The game designers can refer to these pools while designing to design a game simultaneously with learning activities. Moreover, this tool can be used for existing games as a reflection tool: it helps to identify game and learning mechanics in an existing game and connect them. Furthermore, designers can create a map of the dynamics of mechanics during the flow of a game to show how mechanics change themselves and support each other.

The first step in the application of the framework consists of the identification and description of the actual gaming and learning mechanics. We started with an initial *Firewall* game design with a few gaming and learning mechanics. The game design started with defining the content for the game. To understand the pedagogical intent of the game mechanics, it is essential to understand the content of the *Firewall* game intertwined with the intended learning outcome. We then identified which LM-GM can be applied to each gaming scenario as listed by the LM-GM framework and defined in Table 1.

Firstly, the game context is set through an instructional backstory that defines the player objectives and rationale for subsequent actions. This is achieved using cut scenes. Then the player is introduced to the core mechanics through a short tutorial becoming familiar with the user interface and main controls (cascading information). The core loop of the game is to solve a series of network layout problems in stages, where the player explores each game task (behavioral momentum), tries to understand its structure and how to efficiently solve the problem using a simulate/response approach to observe, experiment and analyze the different commands used to study the behavior of the network under time constraints. The end of each level provides feedback to the player on their

Table 2. LM-GM framework

Learning mechanics		Game mechanics	
a) Instructional	j) Modelling	1) Cut scene/Story	9) Planning
b) Tutorial	k) Simulation	2) Tutorial	10) Levels
c) Observation	l) Feedback	3) Cascading info	11) Feedback
d) Experiment	m) Motivation	4) Simulate/Response	12) Assessment
e) Modelling	n) Assessment	5) Movement	13) Meta-game
f) Hypothesis	o) Reflection	6) Time pressure	14) Competition
g) Analyze	p) Competition	7) Capture/elimination	15) Rewards
h) Action/task	q) Incentive	8) Strategy	16) Behavioral Momentum
i) Explore	r) Repetition		

progress (score achieved), possible rewards (achievements), and competition (leader boards) as well as emerging strategies (Meta-game). This approach ensures that students have to learn, fully understand, and practically apply firewall configuration best practices to complete each stage.

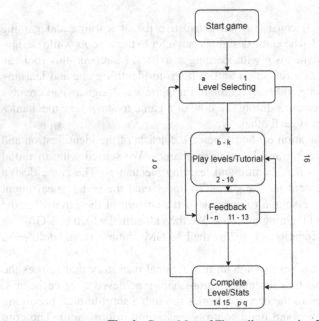

Fig. 4. Game Map of Firewall game using LM-GM

Figure 4 shows a game map constructed through LM-GM based analysis of the Firewall game relating the target learning outcome implemented in the game levels. The map gives a dynamic view of the relationships between the LMs and GMs (defined in Table 2) in the SG flow of actions. It can be observed that the game is designed to cycle through these principles for each learning outcome for different levels. Table 2 list the mechanics used in our game from the exhaustive list of the LM-GM described in [13]. The LM-GM is identified to represent the game-play and the constructivist nature of learning experienced by the player in roughly sequential order from top to bottom.

The Firewall game is divided into three parts covering basic networking, firewall basics, and common network attack scenarios. Each part contains multiple levels. The design principles include a) choosing the level: each level teaches different learning outcomes b) the levels start with an animated tutorial introducing the networking terms that the player should be familiar with before the play c) the gameplay providing the key behavioral determinants. The player tries to solve the level tasks (problem-based solving) and identify the risk involved in case of incorrect steps taken d) the emulated network environment helps the player to observe the consequences of the action. This helps the player to observe and experiment with their choices e) the entire gameplay experience is packaged in an emulated environment with an engaging storyline. The game cycles through the principles for each level effectively reinforcing behavior changes and constructing new knowledge. The learning outcome is the ultimate pedagogical objective of the gameplay which cannot be measured using LM-GM; as a limitation of LM-GM is that it does not expose the connection between concrete mechanics and the high-level educational objectives that the game is supposed to attain [24]. Therefore, we attempt to measure it through the innovative use of Unity analytics that captures the various moves of the player during gameplay. We assess the player both during the teaching phase and the testing phase. The detailed methodology is described in Sect. 5 below.

5 Learning Outcome Assessment

Having evaluated the game mechanics through the LM-GM framework in Sect. 4 above, we measure the learning outcome of a player to test the effectiveness of the *Firewall* game as discussed in [19]. The learning outcome is what makes a serious game effective as unless ultimate pedagogical objectives are achieved the game has failed its intrinsic utility. We follow an analogy of the course assessment process that is (i) a relative grading scheme where performance metrics are relative to the population and (ii) absolute grading with fixed performance metrics. We have used unity analytics to capture the observable within the game. We divide the game into two phases: (i) The Teaching phase and (ii) The Testing phase. Further, the teaching phase and testing phase are divided into five levels respectively. We evaluate the scores obtained in all the levels to categorize the players. Furthermore, to normalize the level of difficulty across the levels, we take the weighted sum of scores obtained in each level. We use the time taken by k^{th} player to complete i^{th} level as t_{ik} as a metric to award the score.

In our game, we have divided both phases into multiple learning goals. The Initial Assessment Score (IA) corresponds to the teaching phase and the Final Assessment Score (FA) corresponds to the testing phase. Therefore for the calculation of IA and FA, a weighted sum of the level scores is required. The score of kth players in the ith level is defined by l_{ik}.

Initial Assessment Score (IA) – It is the score obtained in the teaching phase. The teaching phase is divided into five levels. The time is taken by k^{th} in i^{th} is given by t_{ik}, where $i = 1...5$ and $k = 1...k$.

Final Assessment Score (FA) – It is the score obtained in the testing phase. There are five levels in this phase. For each of these levels, the observable is the time taken to solve the particular level i^{th} level.

The two grading methods to award a score to a player are described below:

Relative Grading (where the maximum and minimum scores are relative to the population) In this grading, we award a score of "1", if a player completes the level in minimum time. A heuristic score which is linear in time is given as,

$$l_{ik} = \max\left\{0, 1 - \max\left\{\frac{t_{ik} - t_{i,min}}{t_{i,max}}, 0\right\}\right\} \qquad (1)$$

where $t_{i,min}$, $t_{i,max}$ is the minimum and maximum time is taken across players to solve the ith level respectively. t_{ik} is the time taken by the kth player to solve the ith level. The level score takes a value of 1 when the player beats the level in minimum time, i.e., $t_{ik} = t_{i,min}$. We can observe that if a player takes more than $t_{i,max} + i^{th}$ level time is awarded "0". Now, IA is calculated as shown in Eq. (2)

$$IA = \sum_{i=1}^{5} w_i l_i \qquad (2)$$

$$w_i = \frac{t_i}{\sum_{i=1}^{10} t_i} \qquad (3)$$

$$FA = \sum_{i=1}^{5} w_i l_i \qquad (4)$$

where w_i is the normalized weight of the ith level, which is calculated as shown in Eq. (3):

The FA is calculated as the weighted sum of all the five Levels given as shown in Eq. (4):-

Absolute Grading (where the maximum and minimum scores are fixed by the instructor) In this grading, we award "1" if a player completes the level in no time, and award "0" if a player completes the level in infinite time. A heuristic score, which is exponential in time is given as,

$$l_{ik} = e^{-t_{ik}/t_i} \qquad (5)$$

where t_{ik} is the time taken by the kth player to solve the ith level. t_i is the average time taken by all the players to solve the ith level. Now, IA and FA are given in Eq. (6–8).

$$IA = \sum_{i=5}^{10} w_i l_i \qquad (6)$$

$$w_i = \frac{e^{t_i}}{\sum_{i=1}^{10} e^{t_i/t}} \tag{7}$$

$$FA = \sum_{i=5}^{10} w_i l_i \tag{8}$$

We have used exponential function assuming that players' learning experience decreases exponentially with time. The difference in the FA and IA forms the basis for measuring the effectiveness of the SG. The change in the results of IA and FA with respect to Initial Threshold (IT) and Final Threshold (FT) determines the phase completion. The thresholds here are taken as the mean values of the time taken across the player to solve the level. We also classify each player in a different learning category based on the change in values of IA with respect to IT and FA with respect to FT as following.

- if FA ≥ FT the players have completed the mastery phase and possess the intended learning knowledge. Based on their IA value, we categorize players as:

  - Active Learners if IA < IT, the player did not have any pre-knowledge but completed the mastery phase.
  - Masters if IA ≥ IT, the players already had some pre-knowledge before playing the game.

- if FA < FT the players failed in the mastery phase and did not possess the intended learning outcome. Based on their IA value we categorize players as:

  - Slow-learners, if IA < IT, the players faced difficulty in the practice phase and progressed slowly.
  - Outliers, if IA ≥ IT, the players completed the practice phase but could not complete the mastery phase.

Results. To study the effectiveness of the developed Firewall game, we have surveyed fifteen Masters's students from Computer Science. The players were provided with the web link and the results were stored on a Firebase database [25].

Figure 5 shows the categorization of players for relative and absolute grading. The player's categorization is done when the threshold taken is the mean of the IA and FA scores. The number of "Active + Slow + Masters" learners is higher than the number of "Outliers". This means that the game is effective in inducing the knowledge.

Another way of categorizing the data is using k-means clustering [26] to dynamically decide the threshold. In Fig. 6, the clustering of the IA and FA scores is shown for relative grading data. The results are divided into the same four categories. In both cases, the number of learners is greater than the "Outliers".

Discussion. To gain insight into our assessment approach, we tried to answer the following questions related to the "Firewall game":

- Did the players have any knowledge gain after playing the Firewall game?

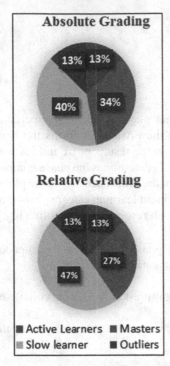

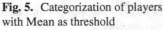

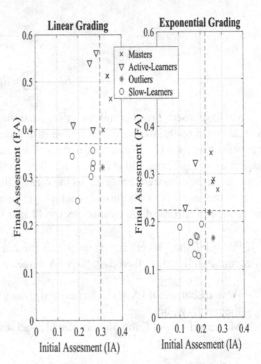

Fig. 5. Categorization of players with Mean as threshold

Fig. 6. Clustering of players for relative grading

- Is the "Firewall game" game effective at teaching the intended knowledge to the players?

To answer the first question, we calculated the level scores for all the phases, to calculate, FA and IA. To determine the knowledge gain we have calculated the difference between FA and IA score, in the case of linear grading the difference was positive in the case of all fifteen players but in the case of absolute grading, only seven players out of fifteen got a positive difference. Therefore, we conclude that the knowledge gain of the player is 100% when their relative performance is being judged but is 46.66% in the case of absolute grading. Hence, we can say that our game is linearly inducing knowledge than exponential [27].

According to the results, most of the players are categorized as "Masters", meaning that that the players already possess some knowledge about the topic. Although, this does not mean that the game is not effective as the learner (Active + Slow + Masters) are more in each case than the "Outliers". When segmenting groups by k-means clustering for (i) linear grading results - the "Firewall" game is effective as the number of "Active" learners is greater than the "Masters", (ii) absolute grading results - the results categorize most players as "Slow learners", meaning that the players had some difficulty while completing the phases.

Table 3. Subjective feedback mean ratings

Dimension	Attribute	Survey item	Mean score
Gaming Experience	Challenge	The experience was challenging. I found the game stimulating	3.45
	Flow		3.40
	Immersion	I was able to achieve the goals set in the game	3.20
	Affect	I remained focused on the game throughout	3.85
		The overall experience was positive	
Learning Experience	Learning Goal	The learning goals of the game were clear	3.65
	Content	The game scenario had relevance to the subject	3.65
	Appropriateness	The game required me to use skills being taught	3.55
	Integration	The game provided opportunities to receive feedback	3.40
	Feedback		
Usability	Interface	The user interface was easy to use	3.15
	Interaction	It was easy to get started with the game	3.4
		I learnt how to play the game quickly	2.95
		The help function was useful to play the game	3.1
Fidelity	Visual Appeal	The playing environment was visually appealing	3.5
	Identification	I can identify with the components used in the game	3.4
	Verisimilitude	I can identify with the story/scenario in the game. The experience felt real	3.6

We also employ subjective analysis to assess the user experience (UX) in SG. The players after finishing the game reflect on the game in a brief anonymous questionnaire embedded within the game. The questionnaire has been devised based on multidimensional aspects of UX and collects information about different attributes based on the study in [28]. The players rated the game on the five-step Likert scales where (1 = 'Strongly Disagree' and 5 = 'Strongly Agree'). The results of subjective feedback are provided in Table 3.

It can be observed that players have provided the highest score for the "affect" attribute. The high score on the "affect" attribute shows a positive experience for the players. This subjective feedback is very well correlated with the objective assessment of the game, discussed earlier, where positive learning was demonstrated. The dimensions of gaming experience, learning experience, usability, and fidelity capture important attributes of UX for SG, providing useful information for developers. Table 3 also shows a lower score on the usability aspect(interaction) namely the statement 'I learned how to play the game quickly'. It was observed while interacting with the players that some users faced difficulty in understanding the mechanics of the game. It is planned to make instructions more explicit to address this issue. Thus, a combination of quantitative results with qualitative feedback and observation is required for effective enhancements to be implemented.

6 Limitations

To test the perceived effectiveness of our designed game, we conducted both objective and subjective analyses. Both the objective analysis and subjective feedback showed promising results in terms of players' knowledge gain on the topic of a firewall. However, there are some limitations to the study. Firstly as a preliminary study, the sample size of fifteen participants is small. Secondly, among the various metrics that can be used to assess the learning outcome, we have limited the assessment based on one metric (time taken). The players are ranked easily on the Leaderboard with the amount of time taken by the players. Hence, the limitation to one observable, i.e., time taken.

7 Conclusions and Future Research

For SGs to be used as a viable educational tool, they must be properly designed and provide some means of testing within the context of the education or training they are attempting to impart. In this paper, we present a methodology for structuring the design and assessment of SG systematically.

In our study for validation of the *Firewall* game, we used a hybrid approach where in addition to objective measures using learning analytic, we also supplemented it by subjective feedback from players. This is an alternative to the commonly used approach of using questionnaires for SG assessment. We used two grading approaches (relative and absolute) for the analysis of the game's effectiveness. While the *Firewall* game proved to be an effective educational tool, but it is unable to capture the initial knowledge level of the players as the IA results were higher. Thus, an accurate assessment of the initial knowledge is required for proper analysis. We also concluded that for our game relative grading is better as the knowledge is being induced linearly.

The methodology presented in this paper can also be used for the design and development of SG in other domains. The assessment is done based on the interaction data captured via a tracker embedded in the game. This is a more objective assessment approach rather than the use of traditional methods like questionnaires. The assessment score method can be easily adapted for other games as well depending on the observable being collected. We have limited the assessment based on one observable (time taken) but in the future, we plan to extend the assessment method by including more observables on a larger data set. The larger data in terms of a number of players will provide us with more insights into the player's progression and knowledge level.

References

1. Harris, M., Cullen, R.: Learner-centered leadership: an agenda for action. Innov. Higher Educ. **33**, 21–28 (2008)
2. Yilmaz, G., Bulut, S.: From a Teaching-Centred to a Learning-Centred Approach to Curriculum Design: Transforming Teacher Candidates, pp. 69–94. Libri Publishing, Oxfordshire (2017)
3. Ulicsak, M.: Games in Education: Serious Games. a FutureLab Literature Review, p. 139 (2010). http://www.futurelab.org.uk/projects/games-in-education

4. Connolly, T.M., Boyle, E.A., MacArthur, E., Hainey, T., Boyle, J.M.: A systematic literature review of empirical evidence on computer games and serious games. Comput. Educ. **59**(2), 661–686 (2012). http://www.sciencedirect.com/science/article/pii/S0360131512000619

5. Prensky, M.: Digital game-based learning . Comput. Entertain. **1**(1), 21 (2003). https://doi.org/10.1145/950566.950596

6. L., M., E., T., B., H.: Capture the flag as cyber security introduction. In: 2016 49th Hawaii International Conference on System Sciences (HICSS), pp. 5479–5486, January 2016

7. Bishop, M.: Teaching computer security. In: SEC, pp. 65–74. Citeseer (1993)

8. Hendrix, M., Al-Sherbaz, A., Bloom, V.: Game based cyber security training: are serious games suitable for cyber security training? Int. J. Serious Games **3**(1) (2016). http://journal.seriousgamessociety.org/index.php?journal=IJSG&page=article&op=view&path[]=107

9. Jones, J., Yuan, X., Carr, E., Yu, H.: A comparative study of CyberCIEGE game and department of defense information assurance awareness video. In: Conference Proceedings - IEEE SOUTHEASTCON, pp. 176–180 (2010)

10. Sheng, S., Magnien, B.: Anti-phishing phil: the design and evaluation of a game that teaches people not to fall for phish. In: Proceedings of SOUPS 2007, pp. 88–99 (2007). http://dl.acm.org/citation.cfm?id=1280692

11. Blunt, R.: Does game-based learning work? results from three recent studies. In: Proceedings of the Interservice/Industry Training, Simulation, & Education Conference, pp. 945–955. National Defense Industrial Association Orlando eFL FL (2007)

12. Rooney, P.: A theoretical framework for serious game design: exploring pedagogy, play and fidelity and their implications for the design process. IJGBL **2**, 41–60 (2012)

13. Arnab, S., et al.: Pedagogy-driven design of serious games: an overall view on learning and game mechanics mapping, and cognition-based models (2015)

14. Lim, T., et al.: The lm-gm framework for serious games analysis (2013)

15. All, A., Castellar, E.P.N., Looy, J.V.: Towards a conceptual framework for assessing the effectiveness ofâ digital game-based learning. Comput. Educ. **88**, 29–37 (2015). http://www.sciencedirect.com/science/article/pii/S036013151500113X

16. Calderón, A., Ruiz, M.: A systematic literature review on serious games evaluation: an application to software project management. Comput. Educ. **87**, 396–422 (2015). http://www.sciencedirect.com/science/article/pii/S0360131515300166

17. Min, L., Jina, K., Sa, L., Wenting, Z., Jeff, H.: Learning analytics as an assessment tool in serious games: a review of literature. Serious Games Edutainment Appl. **2**, 537–563 (2017). https://doi.org/10.1007/978-3-319-51645-5_24

18. Chaudy, Y., Connolly, T., Hainey, T.: Learning analytics in serious games: a review of the literature. In: European Conference in the Applications of Enabling Technologies 2014 (2014)

19. Serrano-Laguna, Á., Manero, B., Freire, M., Fernández-Manjón, B.: A methodology for assessing the effectiveness of serious games and for inferring player learning outcomes. Multimedia Tools Applicat. **77**(2), 2849–2871 (2017). https://doi.org/10.1007/s11042-017-4467-6

20. Garris, R., Ahlers, R., Driskell, J.E.: Games, motivation, and learning: a research and practice model. Simul. Gaming **33**(4), 441–467 (2002). https://doi.org/10.1177/1046878102238607

21. Technologies, U.: Unity game engine. https://unity3d.com/

22. Garrido, J.M., Bandyopadhyay, T.: Simulation model development in information security education. In: 2009 Information Security Curriculum Development Conference. pp. 21–26. InfoSecCD 2009, ACM, New York (2009). https://doi.org/10.1145/1940976.1940983

23. Wang, X., Hembroff, G.C., Yedica, R.: Using vmware vcenter lab manager in undergraduate education for system administration and network security. In: Proceedings of the 2010 ACM Conference on Information Technology Education, pp. 43–52. SIGITE 2010, ACM, New York (2010). https://doi.org/10.1145/1867651.1867665

24. Carvalho, M., et al.: An activity theory-based model for serious games analysis and conceptual design. Comput. Educ. **87**, 166 (2015)
25. Google firebase. https://firebase.google.com/. Accessed 20 Jul 2019
26. Garbade, D.M.J.: k-means-clustering (2018). https://towardsdatascience.com/understanding-k-means-clustering-in-machine-learning-6a6e67336aa1
27. Johnston, K., Aldridge, B.: Examining a mathematical model of mastery learning in a classroom setting. J. Res. Sci. Teach. **22**, 543–554 (1985)
28. Moizer, J., et al.: An approach to evaluating the user experience of serious games. Comput. Educ. **136** (2019)

Design and Evaluation of a Serious Game to Supplement Pupils' Understanding of Molecular Structures in Chemistry

Thomas Bjørner(✉) (iD), Louise Gaard Hansen, Miicha Valimaa, Julie Ulnits Sørensen, and Mircea Dobre

Department of Architecture, Design and Media Technology, Aalborg University, A.C. Meyersvænge 15, 2450 Copenhagen, SV, Denmark
tbj@create.aau.dk

Abstract. This study is initial experiences in the design and evaluation of a serious game to supplement pupils' understanding of molecular structures in chemistry. 27 pupils were included in the study, aged 13–14, with 16 boys and 11 girls. All participants were recruited from two chemistry classes at a Danish elementary school in Copenhagen. A formative evaluation consisted of both a questionnaire, observations, and interviews. The questionnaire was inspired by the User Engagement Scale (UES) short-form. Designing a serious game for pupils with the aim to increase the understanding of molecular structures, is not an easy task. This serious game was to some extend able to engage the pupils within the subject of chemistry. The game itself was reported to be very engaging, but the specific learning outcomes remains uncertain. We can conclude that the serious game was visually appealing, the pupils were absorbed in the game, and wanted to continue playing. However, the designed serious game was also a bit confusing and made too difficult, resulting in frustrations for the pupils. Further, there are still some important challenges in how to increase the validity and reliability when evaluating serious games with children and adolescent as the users.

Keywords: Serious game · Chemistry · Engagement · Evaluation · Pupils

1 Introduction

Many elementary school pupils (ages 12–15) struggle to learn chemistry concepts [1–3], including atomic models and molecule systems, as part of the mandatory curriculum. These difficulties might underpin their entire experience with chemistry [1–3], or even science, technology, engineering, and mathematics (STEM) related disciplines in general [4, 5]. Numerous previous studies have addressed some of the reasons why chemistry is a difficult subject for many pupils [1–6]. Scholars have especially emphasized the gap between abstract, difficult chemistry concepts and the world in which they live; this also includes language and syntax difficulties related to misunderstandings of the connections between models, symbols, and the microscopic and macroscopic levels [6, 7]. Given these difficulties and the imagination required to connect concepts

© Springer Nature Switzerland AG 2021
B. Fletcher et al. (Eds.): JCSG 2021, LNCS 12945, pp. 263–275, 2021.
https://doi.org/10.1007/978-3-030-88272-3_19

to real-life situations [3], various attempts to use gamification and serious gaming to increase learning motivation in chemistry and to fill the gap between the abstract level and the real world have been presented [2, 3, 6, 8–11]. However, there is still a need to direct the serious gaming to address specific learning objectives in chemistry [3]. There also remains the challenge of finding the right match and balancing the interactions among various target groups (e.g., age, gender, motivation), contexts (e.g., cultural, schools, content/curriculum), and serious gaming to create actual learning using an engaging gaming approach. The background of using serious games in education (and, in this study, within chemistry), is based on the idea that games, because of their ability to engage end excite [2, 3, 6, 9–11, 32–35]; can provide a level of learning engagement among pupils. However, it is extremely challenging to outline evidence for improved learning using serious games. There are several reasons for this, such as the low number of participants, different contexts, short evaluation periods, a lack of longitudinal studies, a lack of baseline and control groups, and poorly defined evaluation criteria. This study does not solve all these challenges, but it provides another attempt to improve pupil's difficulties in chemistry using a serious game. This study is based on the following research question: How can one design an engaging serious game that strengthens the understanding of the atomic model and molecular structure, as taught in chemistry in the Danish elementary schools to pupils ages 13–14?

2   Previous Research

The use of serious games for learning purposes is relatively small compared to that of games intended for fun and entertainment [12]. However, serious gaming for learning represent an important part of serious games [2, 3, 8–12, 19, 32–34], and is expected to increase. The worldwide five-year compound annual growth rate (CAGR) for serious games and services is estimated at 33.2%, and revenues will more than quadruple to exceed $24 billion by 2024. The expected growth is especially favorable within learning purposes and correlates to the generation of digital natives [13]; greater adaptability to technological change [14]; and ongoing innovations integrated into next-generation serious games including advances in psychometrics, neuroscience, augmented reality (AR), and artificial intelligence (AI) [12]. Exact predictions such as these are always difficult, as there is no consensus on the definition of serious games, and they are used in divergent ways, focusing on various perspectives depending on their purpose, players' goals, and intended content [15, 16]. Previous definitions have emphasized that serious games are applications that are not designed exclusively for fun [17] or that are intended to be more than entertainment [15, 16]. However, there are still some unsolved categorical problems regarding what constitutes a game and what "more than entertainment" or "not exclusively for fun" actually means. Furthermore, there are often categorical problems within the terminology associated with serious games and gamification [18]. In spite of the diversity of definitions, there seems to be some general agreement on the growth of serious games, and a requirement for successful serious games for learning purposes is including complex reciprocities of engagement and motivation [3, 10, 15, 16, 19].

Engagement has been defined as a quality of user experience [20] and as an indicator of whether a player wants to continue playing [21]. The challenge is that engagement, particularly in the context of serious games, is a complex subject, as it encompasses various related concepts related to the user experience, including immersion, presence, flow, transportation, and absorption. Because of the interrelated nature of these various concepts, engagement is often used without a clear definition, leading to possible confusion in measuring how engaged a user is with, for instance, a serious game. Most often, engagement in serious gaming is a means for providing some kind of learning [17, 22]. Learning is also a multidimensional construct consisting of behavioral, affective, and cognitive engagement [23]. Furthermore, to design an engaging serious game for learning purposes, scholars have emphasized aspects of motivation (especially intrinsic motivation), such as curiosity, a desire for challenge, rewards, feedback, and involvement [13–15, 22–24]. However, the success of a serious game for learning purposes depends on both the teachers and pupils' motivation to begin playing the game and to spend their time, effort, and energy on it. The experiences of flow [25] and enjoyment [26] are crucial to this process. When players have mastered specific challenges, they develop a greater level of skills that can be used and improved with more complex challenges in other levels or games [25]. This can have a positive influence on learning and intrinsic motivation in serious games [22].

Previous studies have presented some empirical short-term evidence that serious games can have a positive effect on student learning achievement and learning attitudes in chemistry [2, 3, 27]. However, as mentioned by other scholars [3], there is still a need for serious chemistry games that act as an interface for presenting specific chemistry concepts.

Previous studies have mainly used pre/post-test, surveys and questionnaires, observations, and interviews [2, 3, 6, 9–11, 32–35] when evaluating serious game with learning purposes targeting pupils and students. A part of the novelty in this study is to learn from this past work, and improve the methodology by including a substantial work in both the teacher involvement, pilot-testing, and evaluation. When evaluating a serious game for pupils it is important not to neglect the challenges finding the right match of both the participants' cognitive abilities and a solid methodological approach.

3 Methods

3.1 Participatory Design and Pilot Testing

An important focus of this study was to involve the teachers who taught the pupils about atomic models and molecules. This was done by following a participatory design approach [31] in which the end-users included both teachers and pupils. The teachers served as gatekeepers who facilitated and controlled the process in areas such as the curriculum's aims, focus, knowledge, skills, and analysis. Therefore, the teachers were involved as co-designers very early in the process. They were asked for input and feedback, but they also worked as partners in the design process regarding changes to aspects of the game's development. Prior to the final game, efforts were made into various pilot testing. The pilot testing were performed in two stages. The first stage included a low fidelity paper prototype, and included 3 participants. The paper prototype was tested in order to make sure that the overall concept of the game could be understood. The second stage of pilot testing consisted of a usability test, and included 7 participants. Both stages of the prototype testing was set up in the school library at the same elementary school for the later evaluation, and it was made sure that the participants for the pilot testing were not included as later participants.

3.2 Participants

27 pupils were included in a formative evaluation. The participants were aged 13–14 with 16 boys and 11 girls. All participants were recruited from two chemistry classes from a Danish Elementary school in Copenhagen. All participants have had chemistry for one year.

All participants and parents gave informed consent and were informed that they could withdraw from the study at any time. We provided all participants with anonymized ID numbers, and all the data were labeled with these IDs. Furthermore, we applied special ethical considerations when recruiting children. Access, permission, and ethical approval were included from the State School. All participants were inform that they were respected on each individual's speed and level, and there was no hurry or judgement based on speed or level.

3.3 Procedure and Analysis

The participants were sampled by the convenience sampling method, also due ethical reasons to make it voluntary to participate. The participants were asked to complete the same mission; to build hydrogen and oxygen and use these elements to construct H_2O and O_2. The participants were encouraged to play the game on their own, but could ask the researchers if they did not know how to proceed.

The data collection consisted of both a questionnaire, observations, and interviews.

The questionnaire was inspired by the User Engagement Scale (UES) short-form [27], and consisted of 12 items on a 3-point Likert scale. The scale was included with smiley faces for ease of conceptual understanding for the pupils.

The observations consisted of observation notes by two of the researchers. The observations included registrations of the participants chosen cards in an included card sorting. The participants were asked to pick up to five cards (out of 12) to describe their experience of the game. The cards had an equal distribution of positive and negative connotations. The wording on the cards were as follows: Pretty, fun, easy, cosy, pleasant, want to play more, confusing, boring, fast, irritation, difficult, and ugly. After picking the cards, the pupils were encouraged to share their reasons for picking these cards.

The questionnaires were analyzed by cumulative frequency. The expert interview were analyzed by traditional coding [29] following four steps: organizing, recognizing, coding, and interpretation.

4   Design and Implementation

The game was designed in Unity. It consisted of first-person perspectives in a 3D environment with the functionality of the atom and molecule builder presented as 2D assets.

Before starting the game, the player was briefed on how to navigate and run the gameplay. The player could look around by using the mouse; walk using the W, A, S, and D keys; and jump by using the space bar, as is often the case in other games. When the player moved the mouse to look around, the vector of the camera view direction changed, so the camera followed the mouse, and the rotation of the player object changed in the game world coordinates. In this way, the movement directions were related to the player object. For example, forward was always the direction in which the camera pointed.

After the briefing, the player entered a 3D spaceship with three floors. In the spaceship, the player could move around and make their way to the two 2D laboratories: the atom builder lab and the molecule builder lab. Each lab was equipped with a desk. Once the player approached either of these desks, the game loaded a corresponding scene. The different scenes and switching between them was handled using Unity's scene manager. The transitions contained a loading screen animation for effect (a black screen that persisted for 2.5 s, with the word "Loading" in the middle). The player had to complete three levels/learning objectives in the game (Fig. 1): 1) find out which element to create, 2) make the atoms for the element in the atom builder lab, and 3) create the molecule for the element in the molecule builder lab. Once finished, they could press the "Back" button to return to the spaceship.

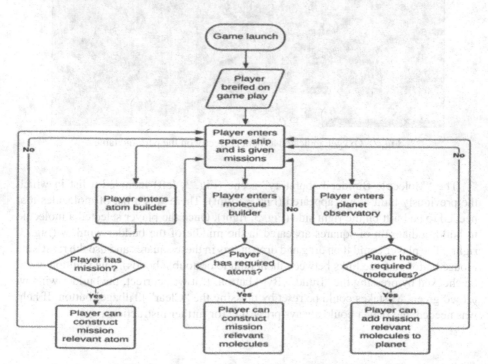

Fig. 1. A flowchart over the game's functionality

268   T. Bjørner et al.

The "Atom Builder Laboratory" scene contained buttons that generated protons, neutrons, and electrons. These could be placed on the concentric circles representing the atomic model, as well as in the atom's nucleus. The player could push another button to display the periodic table and select the element for which they wanted to build an atom. This displayed the information necessary to build the atom (the numbers of protons, neutrons, and electrons). Once the player placed everything on the model, they could press the "Build" [Byg] button to check whether the solution was correct. If the atom was built correctly, it turned green on the periodic table and was available for use in the molecule builder laboratory. Mistakes could be reset by pressing the "Clear" [Tilbage] button. As a set learning objective, pupils were required to build a minimum hydrogen and oxygen in the atom builder lab to continue.

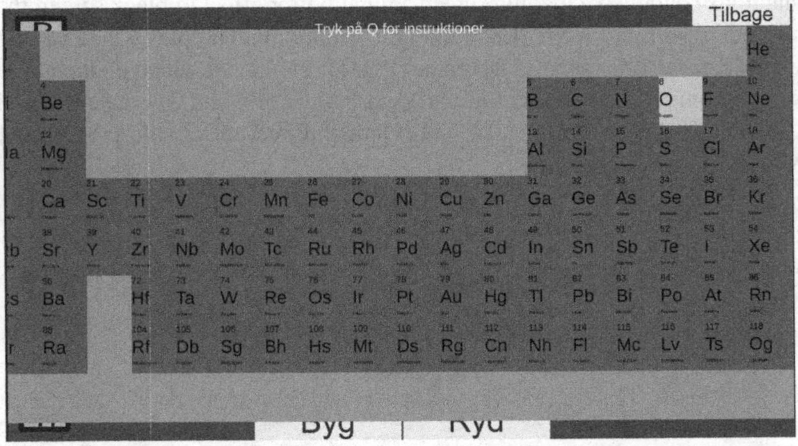

Fig. 2. Oxygen indicated as built correctly on the periodic table

The "Molecule Builder Laboratory" scene (Fig. 3, left) included a list in which the previously built atoms appeared (Fig. 3, right). There was a list of molecules that needed to be built on the right side (Fig. 3, right). Once the player selected a molecule to build, a diagram of squares appeared in the middle of the builder window (Fig. 3, right). The player could then drag and drop atoms in these squares and use the right-side mouse button to trace links between them (single or double bonds). The solution could be checked by pressing the "Build" [Byg] button. If it was correct, the builder window turned green. Mistakes could be reset by pressing the "Clear" [Tilbage] button. If help was needed, the player could always press "Q" for further instructions.

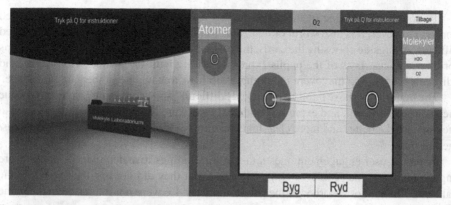

Fig. 3. The Molecule Builder Laboratory (left). Diatomic oxygen built correctly in the molecule builder laboratory (right).

5 Findings

5.1 Positive with Some Confusing and Difficult Elements

The pupils completed the requested mission (to build hydrogen and oxygen and use these elements to construct H_2O and O_2) in the serious game between 9 and 19 min, with an average time of 12.4 min. Most of the pupils (15), spent less than 13 min in the game, with only 4 pupils spending more than 17 min.

The card sorting revealed a clear pattern towards selections of positive cards, based on their immediate response after the gameplay (Fig. 4). 22 pupils picked pretty, 16 picked cozy, 15 picked fun, 13 picked want to play more, and 11 picked fast.

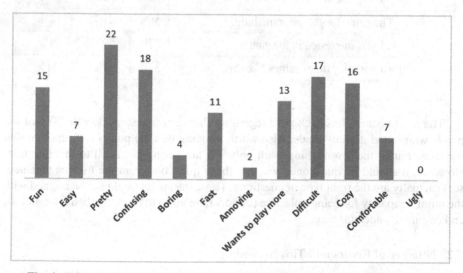

Fig. 4. Selected cards from the card sorting, each pupil could select 5 cards. n = 27.

To contrast this, none of the pupils picked ugly, 2 picked annoying, and 4 picked boring. However, it is also worth of note, that 18 pupils picked confusing and 17 picked difficult. Alongside choosing the cards, the participants were encouraged to give reasons for their choices. Lots of the pupils expressed a long with the picked "confusing" and "difficult" cards, that they were unfamiliar with how to navigate in the game interface.

The majority of those pupils who picked "difficult" and "confusing" were mainly due the chemistry content, and expressed both that they were not good at chemistry, but also they would like better and more clear hints on how to fulfill the chemistry requirements/ the mission.

From the user engagement questionnaire the findings revealed that the pupils were engaged in the game (Table 1). Only 4% stated that they did not lost themselves in the game, 15% were not absorbed in the game, and only 4% were not interested in the game (Table 1).

Table 1. Questionnaire findings. n = 27.

Statement	Very	Normal	Not at all
I lost myself in the game.	37%	59%	4%
I lost my sense of time while I was playing the game.	37%	48%	15%
I was absorbed in the game.	48%	37%	15%
I felt irritated by the game.	4%	33%	63%
I felt irritated while I played the game.	4%	30%	67%
The game was good.	48%	48%	4%
The game was prettily made.	70%	30%	0%
The game taught me something.	56%	41%	4%
I was interested in the game.	37%	59%	4%
I want to play other games like this.	52%	37%	11%

The most positive feedback were regarding the game's aesthetics, with 70% of the pupils who found it pretty made. Also worth noticing that the pupils self-reported that the game taught them something, with only 4% answering not at all to this question. However, it should be questioned whether these questions from the user engagement scale actually are the right type of questions. These questions might not be aligned with the pupil's capacity for being reflective (or not) in relation to his or her behavior, habits, and cognitive understanding.

5.2 Number of Errors and Tips Needed

During the gameplay, the observer noted the number of errors that the pupils made within three different categories: Input errors; chemistry errors, and the number of tips needed.

For the input errors, the findings revealed an evenly distributed amount of errors across pupils. The boxplot (Fig. 5) reveals that the participants had between 0 and 5 input errors, with a median of 2.4 and an interquartile range of 2 to 3. This indicates that the general usability for the game was good. Further, the findings revealed that those pupils being already familiar playing games (playing games several times per week or daily) had fewer input errors, compared to those pupils playing less than several times per week.

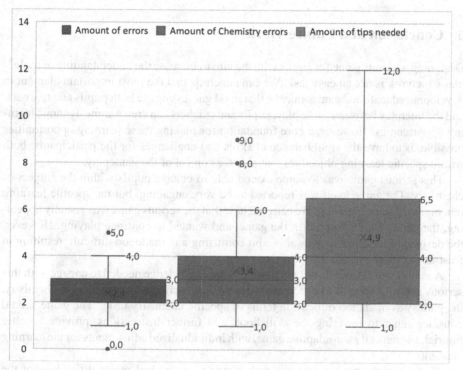

Fig. 5. Boxplot revealing the distributions of participant errors. n = 27.

The number of chemistry errors were a bit surprising, as we anticipated that the majority of the pupils would be able to use previously learned knowledge from their chemistry classes. The findings for chemistry errors revealed a median of 3.4, and an interquartile range of 2 to 4, making it negatively skewed based on the outliers 8 and 9. This findings suggest that the pupils were able to recall certain aspects of the atomic and the molecular structures, but not all. It should also be noted that the number of errors in chemistry had a strong correlation to the number of tips needed. Several pupils did not attempt to perform the tasks without guidance. Only few pupils kept attempting to complete the task/mission without any guidance.

The findings also revealed that the number of tips needed varied wildly between 1 and 12, with a median of 4.9 and an interquartile range of 2 to 6.5 with a negatively skewed tendency. The number of tips could be interpreted as problematically high.

However, it should be emphasized that the tips covered both input and chemistry errors, with most tips provided for chemistry errors. Further, the labelling "errors" is not the perfect terminology, or should at least be understood in a much more holistic learning context. The approach of asking, were a very familiar approach for the pupils, and by that this serious games also reflects the normal instructor approaches and practices within the class room setting. On the other hand, the structure of this serious game could be improved to give the pupils much further opportunities explore the game world on their own and create their own path of knowledge [30].

6 Conclusion and Future Work

Designing a serious game for pupils with the aim to increase the understanding of molecular structures, is not an easy task. We can conclude that the most important element in developing educational games may be that good games engage both pupils and teachers, and the interplay between game play, pupils and teachers can create some dynamic learning opportunities. However, a core foundation for making these learning opportunities possible, is to have the right balance of skills and challenges for the participants; both within specific learning objectives, but also for control of the gameplay.

This serious game was to some extend able to engage pupils within the subject of chemistry. The game itself was reported to be very engaging, but the specific learning outcomes remains uncertain. We can conclude that the serious game was visually appealing, the pupils were absorbed in the game, and wanted to continue playing. However, the designed serious game was also a bit confusing and made too difficult, resulting in frustrations for the pupils.

A majority of the pupils did not have the basic knowledge needed to engage with this serious game. In spite of a participatory design approach with the teachers in chemistry, the game was made too difficult in terms of specific chemistry tasks. The game should consider either to lowering the skill floor, add further instructions, provide a better tutorial, and make it as an adaptive game, with individualized adjustments for the learning elements.

Those participants not familiar with playing games, had major difficulties of the controls and the gameplay. A better introduction, gradually to the mechanics of the game, as well as the principles by which atoms and molecules are built, could possibly have helped mitigate the difficulties. Likewise, the confusion might also have risen from the serious game's lack of story. The pupils simply start on a spaceship, and are given the objective of constructing hydrogen and oxygen, water and atmospheric oxygen without any clear context; neither from the game itself, nor from the teachers. However, this is a mistake by the game designers/researchers, not having the teachers been involved throughout all design stages, and possible also guided the teachers for how to introduce the game.

In research, there also remains much more attention towards how to evaluate serious game targeting children and adolescent. There are still some important challenges in how to increase the validity and reliability when evaluating serious games when children and adolescent are the users. Participants, including the teachers, should be motivated and want to participate – also in the evaluation part. Further, which method should be used, and how to ask the right type of questions, aligned with the child's capacity for being reflective (or not) in relation to his or her behavior and habits. Future work is needed to generate significant evidence and insights regarding pupils' learning of chemistry via serious gaming. First, a much higher number of participants is needed, and baseline and control groups should be included in the research design. Second, further details on the identification of the participants are needed (e.g., their confidence in serious gaming and game genre preferences, current knowledge, motivation, expectations, and technology acceptance). It is important to emphasize that there is no established taxonomy of serious gaming, and serious games are still diverse in their outcomes and certainly understudied as a means to provide knowledge about chemistry. It would also be interesting to create different options in the game design for target groups other than pupils aged 13–14, as well as to make the game more personalized with the inclusion of the participants' own knowledge, motivation, and life stories.

1. References

1. Brecher, J.: Name=struct: a practical approach to the sorry state of real-life chemical nomenclature. J. Chem. Inf. Comput. Sci. **39**(6), 943–950 (1999). https://doi.org/10.1021/ci990062c
2. Wood, J., Donnelly-Hermosillo, D.F.: Learning chemistry nomenclature: comparing the use of an electronic game versus a study guide approach. Comput. Educ. **141**, 103615 (2019). https://doi.org/10.1016/j.compedu.2019.103615
3. Srisawasdi, N., Panjaburee, P.: Implementation of game-transformed inquiry-based learning to promote the understanding of and motivation to learn chemistry. J. Sci. Educ. Technol. **28**(2), 152–164 (2018). https://doi.org/10.1007/s10956-018-9754-0
4. Lamb, R., Akmal, T., Petrie, K.: Development of a cognition priming model describing learning in a STEM classroom. J. Res. Sci. Teach. **52**(3), 410–437 (2015)
5. Noh, T., Scharmann, L.: Instructional influence of a molecularlevel pictorial presentation of matter on students' conceptions and problem-solving ability. J. Res. Sci. Teach. **34**(2), 199–217 (1997)
6. Suits, J. P., Srisawasdi, N.: Use of an interactive computer-simulated experiment to enhance students' mental models of hydrogen bonding phenomena. ACS Symposium Series, pp. 241–271 (2013). https://doi.org/10.1021/bk-2013-1142.ch010
7. Taskin, V., Bernholt, S.: Students' understanding of chemical formulae: a review of empirical research. Int. J. Sci. Educ. **36**(1), 157–185 (2014). https://doi.org/10.1080/09500693.2012.744492
8. Ferrer, V., Perdomo, A., Rashed-Ali, H., Fies, C., Quarles, J.: How does usability impact motivation in augmented reality serious games for education? In: 2013 5th International Conference on Games and Virtual Worlds for Serious Applications (VS-GAMES), pp. 1–8 (2013). https://doi.org/10.1109/vs-games.2013.6624233
9. Garneli, V., Patiniotis, K., Chorianopoulos, K.: Designing multiplayer serious games with science content. Multimodal Technol. Interact. **5**(3), 1–17 (2021). https://doi.org/10.3390/mti5030008

10. Baalsrud Hauge, J., Stefan, I.: Improving learning outcome by re-using and modifying gamified lessons paths. In: Ma, M., Fletcher, B., Göbel, S., Baalsrud Hauge, J., Marsh, T. (eds.) JCSG 2020. LNCS, vol. 12434, pp. 150–163. Springer, Cham (2020). https://doi.org/10.1007/978-3-030-61814-8_12

11. Rastegarpour, H., Marashi, P.: The effect of card games and computer games on learning of chemistry concepts. Proc. Soc. Behav. Sci. 31, 597–601 (2012). https://doi.org/10.1016/j.sbspro.2011.12.111

12. Adkins, S.S.: The 2019–2024 global game-based learning market: serious games industry in boom phase. Metaari's 2019–2024 Global Game-based Learning Market Report (2019)

13. Prensky, M.: H. sapiens digital: from digital immigrants and digital natives to digital wisdom. Innov. J. Online Educ. 5(3), article 1 (2009). https://nsuworks.nova.edu/cgi/viewcontent.cgi?article=1020&context=innovate

14. Burner, T.: Why is educational change so difficult and how can we make it more effective? Forskning og forandring 1(1), 122–134 (2018). https://doi.org/10.23865/fof.v1.1081

15. Ritterfeld, U., Cody, M., Vorderer, P. (eds.): Serious Games: Mechanics and Effects. Routledge, New York (2009)

16. Hookham, G., Nesbitt, K.: A systematic review of the definition and measurement of engagement in serious games. In: Proceedings of the Australasian Computer Science Week Multiconference, pp. 1–10 (2019). https://doi.org/10.1145/3290688.3290747

17. Ciman, M., Gaggi, O., Sgaramella, T.M., Nota, L., Bortoluzzi, M., Pinello, L.: Serious games to support cognitive development in children with cerebral visual impairment. Mobile Netw. Appl. 23(6), 1703–1714 (2018). https://doi.org/10.1007/s11036-018-1066-3

18. Mulcahy, R.F., Zainuddin, N., Russell-Bennett, R.: Transformative value and the role of involvement in gamification and serious games for well-being. J. Serv. Manag. 32(2), 218–245 (2020). https://doi.org/10.1108/josm-05-2019-0137

19. Khan, A., Ahmad, F.H., Malik, M.M.: Use of digital game based learning and gamification in secondary school science: the effect on student engagement, learning and gender difference. Educ. Inf. Technol. 22(6), 2767–2804 (2017). https://doi.org/10.1007/s10639-017-9622-1

20. O'Brien, H.L., Toms, E.G.: What is user engagement? A conceptual framework for defining user engagement with technology. J. Am. Soc. Inf. Sci. Technol. 59(6), 938–955 (2008). https://doi.org/10.1002/asi.20801

21. Schønau-Fog, H., Bjørner, T.: "Sure, I would like to continue" a method for mapping the experience of engagement in video games. Bull. Sci. Technol. Soc. 32(5), 405–412 (2012). https://doi.org/10.1177/0270467612469068

22. Wouters, P., van Nimwegen, C., van Oostendorp, H., van der Spek, E.D.: A meta-analysis of the cognitive and motivational effects of serious games. J. Educ. Psychol. 105(2), 249–265 (2013). https://doi.org/10.1037/a0031311

23. Hookham, G., Nesbitt, K., Kay-Lambkin, F.: Comparing usability and engagement between a serious game and a traditional online program. In: Proceedings of the Australasian ComputerScience week multiconference (ACSW 2016). ACM, New York, pp. 1–10 (2016). https://doi.org/10.1145/2843043.2843365

24. Staiano, A.E., Adams, M.A., Norman, G.J.: Motivation for exergame play inventory: construct validity and relationship to game play. Cyberpsychol. J. Psychosoc. Res. Cyberspace 13(3), article 7 (2019). https://doi.org/10.5817/cp2019-3-7

25. Csikszentmihalyi, M.: Flow: The Psychology of Optimal Experience. Harper Perennial, New York (1990)

26. Sweetser, P., Wyeth, P.: GameFlow: a model for evaluating player enjoyment in games. Comput. Entertainment (CIE) 3(3), 14–27 (2005)

27. Pilli, O., Aksu, M.: The effects of computer-assisted instruction on the achievement, attitudes and retention of fourth grade mathematics students in North Cyprus. Comput. Educ. 62, 62–71 (2013). https://doi.org/10.1016/j.compedu.2012.10.010

28. O'Brien, H.L., Cairns, P., Hall. M.: A practical approach to measuring user engagement with the refined user engagement scale (UES) and new UES short form. Int. J. Hum. Comput. Stud. **112**, 28–39 (2018). https://doi.org/10.1016/j.ijhcs.2018.01.004

29. Bjørner, T.: DataAnalysis and findings. In: Bjørner, T. (ed.) Ualitative Methods for Consumer Research: The Value of the Qualitative Approach in Theory and Practice. Hans Reitzels, Copenhagen (2015)

30. Bjørner, T., Hansen, C.B.S.: Designing an educational game: design principles from a holistic perspective. Int. J. Learn. **17**(10), 279–290 (2010). https://doi.org/10.18848/1447-9494/cgp/v17i10/47275

31. Halskov, K., Hansen, N.B.: The diversity of participatory design research practice at PDC 2002–2012. Int. J. Hum. Comput. Stud. **74**, 81–92 (2015). https://doi.org/10.1016/j.ijhcs.2014.09.003

32. Ibarra, M.J., Ibañez, V., Silveira, I.F., Collazos, C.A., Wallner, G., Rauterberg, M.: Serious games for learning: a quantitative review of literature. In: Ma, M., Fletcher, B., Göbel, S., Baalsrud Hauge, J., Marsh, T. (eds.) JCSG 2020. LNCS, vol. 12434, pp. 164–174. Springer, Cham (2020). https://doi.org/10.1007/978-3-030-61814-8_13

33. Vandercruysse, S., Vandewaetere, M., Clarebout, G.: Game-based learning: a review on the effectiveness of educational games. In: Handbook of research on serious games as educational, business and research tools, pp. 628–647. IGI Global (2012)

34. Rojas-Salazar, A., Haahr, M.: Theoretical foundations and evaluations of serious games for learning data structures and recursion: a review. In: Ma, M., Fletcher, B., Göbel, S., Baalsrud Hauge, J., Marsh, T. (eds.) JCSG 2020. LNCS, vol. 12434, pp. 135–149. Springer, Cham (2020). https://doi.org/10.1007/978-3-030-61814-8_11

35. Iten, N., Petko, D.: Learning with serious games: is fun playing the game a predictor of learning success? Br. J. Edu. Technol. **47**(1), 151–163 (2016). https://doi.org/10.1111/bjet.12226

Using Multiplayer Online Games for Teaching Soft Skills in Higher Education

Max Pagel[1], Heinrich Söbke[1(✉)] [iD], and Thomas Bröker[2] [iD]

[1] Bauhaus-Universität Weimar, Goetheplatz 7/8, 99423 Weimar, Germany
{max.pagel,heinrich.soebke}@uni-weimar.de
[2] Nuremberg Institute of Technology, Keßlerplatz 12, 90489 Nürnberg, Germany
thomas.broeker@th-nuernberg.de

Abstract. In addition to subject-specific (or technical) skills, so-called soft skills or 21st Century Skills, should be essential learning outcomes in almost any higher education curriculum. However, only a limited number of learning activities aiming at the development of soft skills are carried out in current higher education curricula. Multiplayer online games are considered as learning tools fostering soft skills. In this study, an elective course designed for teaching soft skills in engineering disciplines using the commercial multiplayer online game EVE Online is evaluated. Presented are the design of the online course, and evaluation results. Evaluation instruments include a questionnaire on social presence, intrinsic motivation, and expectations of students as well as semi-structured interviews. Overall, the evaluation renders multiplayer online games to be promising soft skills learning tools aiming at digital game-savvy students. Further, the evaluation provides guidance for enhancing the course design and thereby contributes to establishing multiplayer online games as learning tools for soft skills.

Keywords: EVE Online · Meta skills · Instructional design · Serious games · Game-based learning · 21st century skills

1 Introduction

Although there is agreement in literature that skills are divided into the two disjunctive subsets of hard skills and soft skills, there is no unified definition of soft skills. For example, Laker & Powell [1] define hard skills as "technical skills that involve working with equipment, data, software", while they introduce soft skills as "intrapersonal skills such as one's ability to manage oneself as well as interpersonal skills such as how one handles one's interactions with others". Matteson et al. [2] guide through various definitions of soft skills, which, for instance, include innovation, initiative, service orientation, leveraging diversity, communication, leadership, collaboration and cooperation, and team capabilities [3]. Further, the 4C model summarizes collaboration, communication, critical thinking, and creativity as soft skills [4].

Despite the obvious lack of a complete definition of soft skills, their importance for professional success is repeatedly emphasized [5, 6]. This relevance has resulted in

B. Fletcher et al. (Eds.): JCSG 2021, LNCS 12945, pp. 276–290, 2021.
https://doi.org/10.1007/978-3-030-88272-3_20

the term *21st Century Skills*, a set of skills that is defined similar - but not identical - to soft skills. For example, in addition to soft skills, 21st Century Skills also include more technically induced skills, such as media literacy, i.e. being able to deal with new media, or information literacy, i.e. being able to filter out relevant information from a flood of information [7]. While Dede [7] provides various frameworks for categorizing 21st Century Skills, Binkley et al. [8] divide 21st Century Skills into the four categories of *Ways of Thinking, Ways of Working, Tools for Working*, and *Living in the World*. The categories indicate that 21st Century Skills go beyond soft skills in the definition of Laker & Powell. Further, organizations such as Partnership for 21st Century Learning [9]—remarkably also creator of the 4C model—may be seen as a testimony to the enormous relevance attributed to imparting these skills. In summary, and without limiting further definitions, it seems appropriate to use the term soft skills for the remainder of this article, defined as generic skills that can be used in a wide variety of professional contexts to promote positive results.

However, despite all theoretical and organizational efforts to impart soft skills, it is repeatedly criticized that soft skills are not adequately taught in formal learning contexts. This often results in students not being sufficiently prepared for their professional life [10–12]. Thus, the study addresses this challenge by investigating a course promoting soft skills based on a digital game.

Digital games are generally regarded as learning machines [13]. Often digital games are recognized as sources of situational learning [14]. Furthermore, various reviews and numerous single studies suggest strongly that digital games also serve as tools for developing soft skills [15–18]. The massively multiplayer online game (MMOG) EVE Online [19] is one of these soft skill-imparting digital games, owing in part to the nurturing of a large community around the game, sandbox-like developable custom tasks, or programming interfaces for 3rd party software. Since players succeed if they plan carefully, if they specialize, if they collaborate with other players, or if they consult with other players, the development of soft skills is fostered [20].

Based on the objective of proposing a learning activity promoting soft skills for undergraduate engineering students, a course utilizing the MMOG EVE Online has been designed, implemented, and evaluated. The remainder of this paper is organized as follows: Sect. 2 describes the course designed and the research methods used. Subsequently, Sect. 3 reports the quantitative and qualitative study results. Section 4 discusses the results and limitations of the study, while Sect. 5 summarizes the conclusions.

2 Methods

2.1 Course Design

The course's design is based on a set of underlying assumptions: a comprehensive goal, such as making in-game money should prompt the students to engage in activities and specialize in a certain field. The fun of playing EVE Online should lead to a high level of student engagement in these activities. The activities themselves should lead to an implicit training of soft skills and thus to the achievement of the learning goals. The attainment of the learning outcomes would be supported by the requirement for each student to keep an activity diary and to deliver group-wise reports in the weekly plenary sessions to increase reflection. The course took place once in a week for 90 min over 15 weeks in a virtual classroom using the communication software Discord [21] (plenary session). The teaching style was seminar-like, that is, the goals in the game and the actions necessary to achieve them were all discussed. Beyond this weekly teaching session, the students were instructed to deal with achieving the goals in EVE Online on self-organized sessions. The weekly activities were based on the following pre-established phase plan:

Phase 1 - Familiarization. Objectives: Students are enabled to use EVE Online and become familiar with the game. In particular, students learn how to gather information required to perform activities purposefully in EVE Online (Duration: 2 weeks).

Phase 2 - Group Formation and Goal Finding. Objectives: Students form groups. Each group develops an action plan ("business plan") on goals and the strategies to pursue the goals in the game (Duration: 2 weeks).

Phase 3 - Work Phase. Objectives: The groups work on achieving their goals, such as mining ore ("Miners"), producing goods ("Industrialists"), trading ("Traders", or training for fights ("Fighters"). Every week the groups briefly present their results in the plenary session and point out successes and challenges of their actions in the game. Further, the weekly presentations may lead to an exchange of experiences or collaborations, such as "Fighters" protecting "Miners" during mining in non-secure space regions and thereby increasing mining yields. The status is represented by key performance indicators. If necessary, further actions are triggered via intermediate goals. This phase is supervised in an agile manner with the aim of encouraging the students to act and reflect (Duration: 10 weeks).

Phase 4 - Evaluation. Objectives: Assessment of what has been achieved and recommendations for further redesign of the digital learning activity (Duration: 1 week).

Successful completion of the course required regular participation in plenary sessions, keeping activity diaries, and submitting an essay reflecting on soft skills in EVE Online at the end of the course.

2.2 Software and Hardware

For the course, the client software of the MMOG EVE Online was required, which is available in a free version that seems to be sufficient for the purpose of the course. The software runs on any standard notebook, so that neither hardware nor software costs are incurred. Since communication is an essential part of the course and, secondly, playing MMOGs is usually supported by communication channels outside the game, the communication software Discord (2015) was used. A separate server was created specifically for the course. In addition, a corresponding course in the institutional learning management system (Moodle (Moodle.org 2018)) was used for all personal administrative information of the students, such as the submission of the essay at the end of the course and the implementation of the quantitative survey.

2.3 Organizational Integration

In the summer term of 2020 three students successfully completed the course. In the following winter term 11 students did so. In each case twice as many students were initially interested in the course. The course was supervised by a lecturer and a teaching assistant having an affinity for games.

2.4 Measurements

Students were asked to complete a questionnaire prior to the last plenary session. The questionnaire consisted of standardized instruments, as well as self-compiled items. In addition, a semi-structured interview was conducted by the study leader with all students who successfully completed the course. The set-up of the two instruments as well as the results are described in the following section.

3 Results

Demographic data were collected as part of the questionnaire. All students who answered the questionnaire, volunteered also as interviewees.

3.1 Demographics

A total of 14 students, 12 male (86%) and 2 female (14%), participated in the study. Their age ranged from 20 to 30 years (M = 23, SD = 3.2). Among the majors were construction management (8; 57%), civil engineering (4; 29%), and computer science (2; 14%). The high percentage of construction management students is attributable to the low number of elective courses offered in this program.

3.2 Questionnaire

Expectancy Value. The expectancy value items according to Wigfield and Eccles [22] were used to determine the general motivation of the students to participate in this course, e.g. whether the students are more interested in the technical learning objectives of the course or whether the achievable ECTS are the focus. The values of all subscales (Table 1) can be described as high. The highest value is achieved by the subscale Interest (6.0), which may reflect the voluntary, interest-driven choice of the course. Also, for the subscales Importance and Usefulness, comparatively high values are observed. The comparative values originate from an engineering course [23] and are likewise considered being very high already. A possible explanation for the high values might be the high importance and usefulness of the learning objectives of the course as actually agreed upon by the students. Furthermore, it has to be taken into account in both cases that the surveys took place rather at the end of the course and that the approval of the values decreases as the course duration progresses [24].

Table 1. Value subscales ([22], 7-point Likert scale, N = 14)

Value	M (SD)	Reference adopted
Importance	5.5 (1.13)	4.8 (1.37)
Usefulness	5.6 (0.86)	5.8 (1.41)
Interest	6.0 (0.93)	5.7 (1.56)

Table 2 shows the levels of agreement with statements describing expectations on the course. Again, students do not attend the course because of the ECTS to be earned (#8). However, the ECTS are not completely negligible, students are interested in a formal outcome of the course (#11 in Table 3). In terms of content, students expect an overview of soft skills (#1) and learning skills that they can usefully apply in their later professional life (#2, #3). The concrete expectations for learning collaboration (#5) and communication (#7) are present, but rather subordinate. Furthermore, the game-based environment is relevant (#4).

Table 2. Expectancies ([22], 7-point Likert scale, ordered by mean value, N = 14)

#	Expectancy	M (SD)
1	I get a good overview of the subject area of soft skills	6.3 (0.8)
2	I acquire knowledge and skills that I can later use profitably for myself	5.9 (1.0)
3	I acquire knowledge that I can later use beneficially for society	5.4 (1.1)
4	I spend an enjoyable time in an exciting and fun environment	5.4 (1.0)
5	I learn to work well with others	5.3 (1.2)
6	I learn project management methods in general	5.1 (1.2)
7	I learn to communicate well	4.9 (1.6)
8	I can acquire ECTS for my degree with limited effort	3.7 (1.7)
9	I receive concrete instructions for my daily work	3.6 (1.4)

Attitudes. Furthermore, students were asked to express their level of agreement on a number of statements to learn more about their perspectives (Table 3). One concern when designing the course was that another online course in the COVID pandemic caused online semester would be too much. This assumption has not been confirmed (#6, #7). There was also a fear that the abstract, non-subject related in-game goals would be detrimental to motivation. This assumption was neither confirmed (#10), as well as the assumption that the students rather wanted to gain practical experience (#12). The first three statements were intended to identify the extent to which soft skills are subjectively already mastered by the students. The statements #5 and #13 served for estimating how the students assume the effectiveness of a training environment when labelled as a game or a virtual environment. The result shows the expected deviation: games appear less as serious training environments than virtual environments.

Table 3. Attitudes (7-point Likert scale, N = 14)

#	Statement	M (SD)
1	I would describe myself as rather creative	4.3 (1.39)
2	I like to communicate with others	5.4 (1.29)
3	Teamwork suits me	5.1 (1.12)
4	I think it is important to train soft skills in my education	6.4 (0.90)
5	I believe that it is possible to train soft skills in a collaborative virtual environment	6.2 (0.77)
6	I think it is difficult to take such an elective course because the schedule in the study is already very tight	3.5 (1.50)
7	In an online semester, the extra screen hours for a virtual environment are hard to bear	2.8 (1.82)
8	The objective of the course is clear to me	5.9 (0.88)
9	It is unclear to me how a virtual environment can be used to train soft skills	2.4 (1.34)
10	I miss the concrete subject-specific tasks in such a course	3.2 (1.15)
11	For me it is important that credit points can be achieved with the course	5.6 (1.63)
12	Virtual environments do not appeal to me; practical relevance is more important to me	3.1 (1.67)
13	I believe that it is possible to train soft skills in an online game	5.9 (1.06)

Learning Outcomes. With the help of 8 items, the subjectively perceived learning outcomes were queried using communication, collaboration and creativity as an example of soft skills. Communication (M = 5.8, SD = 1.3) was rated best, followed by collaboration (M = 5.3, SD = 1.1) and creativity (4.3). All skills received good scores or scores above the middle of the scale. Based on these skills as examples, the course has been rated as helpful by the students. The order of the values indicates the necessity of the skills in the game: Communication is the basis of most game actions and also of collaboration. Creativity, on the other hand, is most likely to be compensated. Interestingly, the order of learning outcomes is also the order in which students rate their own abilities (#1–#3 in Table 3). Here, a possible relation is still to be analyzed.

Social Presence. Social presence is considered a crucial factor for well-functioning online learning environments [25]. Since this course was designed as an online course, an investigation of social presence was also to be conducted using Lin's measurement [26]. Table 4 shows the uniformly relatively high scores of all three subscales. Subscale #1 indicates the extent to which the group is perceived as helpful for learning success. Subscale #2 measures whether the group members felt comfortable in the group. And subscale #3 indicates the influence of the group on the individual's activities. Overall, the values indicate a sufficiently high social presence.

Table 4. Social Presence subscales [26] (7-point Likert scale, N = 14)

#	Subscale	M (SD)
1	Perception of the Assistance of Group Activity to Learning	5.8 (1.00)
2	Social Comfort of Expressing and Sensing Affect	5.9 (1.08)
3	Social Navigation	5.6 (1.20)

Situational Motivation Scale. The primary learning tool of the course is a game. Since the use of games is strongly intrinsically motivated, the question arises to what extent a high intrinsic motivation is also present in scenarios that are not solely motivated by the game itself. Therefore, the Situational Motivational Scale (SIMS) measurement [27] was used to measure intrinsic and extrinsic motivational components. Concretely, the subscales Intrinsic Motivation, Identified Regulation, External Regulation, and Amotivation—described by Ryan & Deci [28] are assessed. In order of enumeration, intrinsic motivation decreases while extrinsic motivation increases in each subscale. The results received (Fig. 1) are again to be rated as good. Intrinsic motivation and Identified Regulation are very high, while External Regulation and Amotivation are both significantly lower than in an example where SimCity was used in a classroom setting [29].

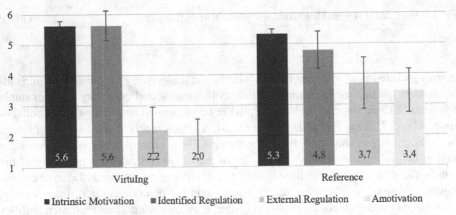

Fig. 1. Situational Motivational Scale [27] (N = 14, Reference: [29])

Concluding Statements. Finally, at the end of the questionnaire, students were asked to indicate their agreement with concluding statements. The responses can be considered very encouraging (Table 5): The highest level of agreement (6.4 out of 7) was given to the statement that students would participate in the course again (#1), followed by recommending the course to their fellow students (#2). However, digital game affinity is a prerequisite (#3). Once again, it is confirmed that the course is a useful learning activity (#4). Rather rejected is the statement that the course is fun but not very educational (#5).

Table 5. Concluding statements (7-point Likert scale, N = 14)

	Statement	M (SD)
1	I would participate in such a course again	6.4 (0.82)
2	I would recommend this course to my fellow students	6.0 (0.93)
3	For participating in the course, one should like digital games	5.8 (1.08)
4	I consider the course to be a useful learning activity	5.7 (0.80)
5	The course is fun, but I do not learn as much	3.4 (1.34)

3.3 Semi-structured Interviews

Semi-structured interviews of about 20 min each were conducted with all participants by the study leader after the end of the course (N = 14). For the interviews, the following topics were determined in an informed brainstorming session by two experts:

1. **Learning.** The aim of every course in higher education is that the students learn in some way. Therefore, it is important to know whether learning has taken place from the students' point of view.
2. **Didactic Design.** The use of media for learning purposes should be optimized according to the rules of instructional design. Thus, a didactic scenario was also designed for this course, of which the success should also be assessed by this study. Therefore, the students were also asked about their assessment of the scenario.
3. **Fun.** The particularity of a course using a game is an increase in motivation through the expected fun of the game. Whether the fun has actually occurred is to be evaluated here.
4. **Social Presence.** The course is conducted completely online. A common problem of online courses is a lack of social presence. However, social presence is conducive to learning outcomes. Therefore, the question of social presence is crucial. Here, a distinction was made between social presence within the cohort of the course as well as within the game.

The statements made during the interviews were documented in written form. Table 6 gives an impression showing a selection of particularly noteworthy statements.

After completion of the interviews, a content analysis according to Schmidt [30] was carried out by the study leader to cluster the data, which was checked by another expert and corrected in discussions.

Table 6. Selected statements in the interviews

#	Statement
S1	You are thrown in at the deep end
S2	All are out to make money and sometimes set traps. You learn people skills
S3	You can take away a lot, especially for the management sector
S4	The general approach of training soft skills using an MMOG is very sound
S5	The course was not wasted time, but something different than usual that set new stimuli
S6	In the game, you can't get far on your own…
S7	You drown if you don't get involved

After clustering the data, the following topics were identified: *learning* (divided into further categories), *didactic design*, *suggested changes*, *fun* and *social presence*.

Learning. The comments on the topic *learning* were so diverse that the clusters were assigned to different categories (Table 7). The first category includes statements about the soft skills taught. Here, *self-organization* (#1) was mentioned most frequently, including references to self-discipline, adapting to circumstances, finding a role in the team, delegating work or time management. This was followed by *organizational skills* (#2). These included planning, leadership, organizing group work, dealing with initially unknown people, or coordinating and dividing tasks. *Social skills* in general were also frequently mentioned (#3). This cluster is supplemented by mentions of people skills, which are particularly necessary to be able to assess previously unknown players in the game. *Communication* (#4) was also mentioned as a skill block taught by the game. In the *media literacy* cluster (#5), the programming interfaces of EVE Online, the operation of Discord, and MS Excel skills were mentioned. *Information literacy* (#6) included, in particular, researching information about EVE Online. In the category *Technical Learning Outcomes* especially the realistic *market models* (#8) were mentioned, while in the *Affective Learning Outcomes* category the *importance of teamwork* (#9) was recognized. Interestingly, there were also mentions of learning outcomes that were not met. Among these was *Creativity* (#10). In the category *General Assessments* there were two clusters, one was the statement that *less could be learned than expected* (#11), the other was that the learning objectives of soft skills do not seem to be perceivable in the same way as technical skills (#12). Both comments may indicate the need for better announcing the course.

Didactical Design. Table 8 shows *problems* (#13) as the most important cluster on the topic of didactical design. However, the high number of mentions results in large part (n = 9) from the difficulty of getting into the game. Most of the students had no EVE Online

Table 7. Interviews: clustered statements regarding topic *learning* (n: occurrences)

Category	#	Cluster	n
Soft skills	1	Self-organization	9
	2	Organizational skills	8
	3	Social skills	5
	4	Communication	5
	5	Media literacy	4
	6	Information literacy	3
	7	Teamwork skills	2
Technical learning outcomes	8	Market models	3
Affective learning outcomes	9	Importance of teamwork	1
No learning	10	Creativity	2
General Assessment	11	Less learned than expected	1
	12	Learning outcomes not directly visible	1

experience and so learning the basics of the game was a major challenge for the students - although a separate phase of the course is dedicated to this. Other problems cited were the varying levels of engagement and the sole goal of making money. Fortunately, *positive characteristics* (#14) followed as the second largest block with a number of favorable qualities: the regular appointments, the unique selling point that the course is completely virtual, the versatility of the game with many different tasks, the Discord channel, which is very helpful for communication and data collection, the pressure to work together as a group, which was perceived as positive, and the ability of the course to balance different skill levels. In the *pre-requisites* cluster (#15), the need for students to have an affinity for digital games was mentioned in particular. *Technology* (#16) pointed out requirements for hardware as well as for internet connections. Although the requirements for EVE Online are comparatively low compared to other games, they should not be neglected.

Table 8. Interviews: clustered statements regarding topic *didactical design*

#	Cluster	n
13	Problems	14
14	Positive characteristics	11
15	Pre-requisites	4
16	Technology	3

Proposed Modifications. From the answers on the topic *didactical design*, the topic *proposed modifications* have been derived (Table 9). The largest cluster could be summarized as *more leadership* (#17). Among the actual demands were more precise goal setting, supervision of results, and higher standards for work results. In general, these statements can be interpreted as a negation of the assumption that the didactic scenario around the game should be built up in a similarly playful way. Instead, a strict didactic scenario is to be preferred, as it is known in other courses in higher education. The cluster *adapt theory part* (#18) refers to the weekly plenary session in which essentially the activities done so far were reflected and the activities were planned. The time spent was perceived as too long in relation to the rather small number of participants, and the proportion of theoretical lectures, such as the connection of this course to the real world, was reported as too low. Furthermore, there were comments that the working time required for the course was too high. However, these concerns could be resolved by jointly recalculating the actual effort with the interviewees. Mentioned only once, but probably relevant in connection with the cluster problems (#13), is the need to *increase the engagement* of some students (#20).

Table 9. Interviews: clustered statements regarding topic *proposed modifications*

#	Cluster	n
17	More leadership	10
18	Adopt theoretical part	6
19	Reduce working time	2
20	Increase engagement	1

Fun. In the topic *fun*, clusters could be formed for the various factors that contribute to experiencing fun. The *social context* (#21) was frequently named as a factor contributing to fun. This was justified with a sense of achievement in teaching others, with the group experience as well as with the general joy of socializing. Also strongly represented was the cluster *game* (#22). Among the reasons given were the statements that it was a game, that learning was very relaxed, that the game helped overcome motivational gaps, and that the course was very diverse. The option of *self-directed play* (#23) was mentioned as particularly motivating. However, a *change in fun over time* was also noted (#24): after familiarization, the fun became greater, although there were still moments of frustration. The characteristic of digital games of *immediate feedback* (#25) also contributed to the fun, as did the increased *knowledge of the game* (#26). Although EVE Online has been on the market for several decades, the *graphics* were still described as motivating (#28). It was also mentioned, however, that there were definitely *individual differences*, as in the case of engagement (#27).

Social Presence. Table 11 shows the clustering of the topic *social presence*. In the cluster *social structure* (#21) answers were summarized, which on the one hand indicated that the students already knew each other in part, but on the other hand showed that a

Table 10. Interviews: clustered statements regarding topic *fun*

#	Cluster	n
21	Social context	6
22	Game	6
23	Self-directed play	4
24	Change over time	4
25	Immediate feedback	2
26	Knowledge of the game	2
27	Individual differences	2
28	Graphics	1

social structure is very important for playing EVE Online itself. The cluster *medium* (#22) collected statements to what extent the communication, mostly conducted via audio chat, is sufficient. In part, audio chat was considered sufficient, but some of the responses also missed a video. Under *game organization* (#23), the importance of sub-corporations for establishing well-functioning corporations was especially emphasized. Through cluster #24, the importance of the topic *social presence* for the course was underlined. It supported a balanced division of roles for efficient collaboration.

Table 11. Interviews: clustered statements regarding topic *social presence*

#	Cluster	n
21	Social structure	7
22	Medium	4
23	Game organization	3
24	Impacts of social presence	2

Final Comments. Final comments on the overall evaluation of the course were almost uniformly positive. There was no participant who would not recommend the course to others. The course was viewed as positive because soft skills have rarely been taught in other courses, the basic structure was described as appropriate, and information management was suggested as an additional learning objective. The visibility of the course in the context of study planning by students needs to be improved.

4 Discussion

The small number of participants in this study implies not being considered representative. However, improvements to the course design can be derived and are currently being tested in a further study.

The soft skills to be trained were not measured directly, for example via a questionnaire, but only indirectly via the interviews. One reason for this was that the learning objectives of the course were not described in detail, but in abstract terms as soft skills. This also, meant that no activity focuses were formed that promoted specific soft skills, which could then have been specifically measured. The design of an MMOG-based course that specifically promotes particular soft skills, such as communication, is therefore a future task.

Several critical issues were identified for the further development of the course. For example, the introduction of the students to the game is mission critical. Although it is a digital game and should allow for easy familiarization, getting students into the game should not be underestimated. Furthermore, the didact scenario needs to be designed more carefully so that it provides guidance and stimuli if students do not develop sufficient initiative. It should not be assumed that the motivating effect of the game will always ensure sufficient engagement. Furthermore, measures need to be developed to account for the possible heterogeneous engagement of learners. In the study presented, the announcement of the elective course was not optimal, so many potential participants were not reached. Nevertheless, the course should probably continue to be placed as an elective, since digital game affinity is considered a prerequisite for participation.

The results are limited by the possibility that both the survey and the interview do not exclude socially opportune answers, e.g., aspects of learning and fun may have been overemphasized in the interview.

5 Conclusions

The study presented investigates the appropriateness of an online course in engineering undergraduate programs using the massively multiplayer online game EVE Online for the development of soft skills. The structure of the course is described, the results of a questionnaire completed by the participants as well as semi-structured interviews with the participants show the appropriateness of such a course to be a generically applicable option for the development of soft skills. It should be noted, however, that the participants of such a course should be digital game-savvy. Future work, besides the development of specific tasks aiming at individual skills, is the actual objective evidence of skill improvement. With the changes suggested for design and implementation of the course derived from the results, the study is contributing to establishing MMOG-based courses aiming at soft skill development in higher education.

1. References

1. Laker, D.R., Powell, J.L.: The differences between hardand soft skills and their relativeimpact on training transfer. Hum. Resour. Dev. Q. **22**, 111–122 (2011). https://doi.org/10.1002/hrdq
2. Matteson, M.L., Anderson, L., Boyden, C.: "Soft skills": a phrase in search of meaning. Portal. **16**, 71–88 (2016). https://doi.org/10.1353/pla.2016.0009
3. Promís, P.: Are employers asking for the right competencies? A case for emotional intelligence. Libr. Adm. Manag. **22**, 24–30 (2008)
4. Sipayung, H.D., Sani, R.A., Bunawan, W.: Collaborative Inquiry For 4C Skills. **200**, 440–445 (2018). https://doi.org/10.2991/aisteel-18.2018.95

5. Kyllonen, P.C.: Soft skills for the workplace. Chang. Mag. High. Learn. **45**, 16–23 (2013). https://doi.org/10.1080/00091383.2013.841516
6. Balcar, J.: Is it better to invest in hard or soft skills? Econ. Labour Relations Rev. **27**, 453–470 (2016). https://doi.org/10.1177/1035304616674613
7. Dede, C.: Comparing frameworks for " 21 st century skills." 1–16 (2009)
8. Binkley, M., Erstad, O., Herman, J., Raizen, S., Ripley, M., Miller-ricci, M., Rumble, M.: Defining twenty-first century skills. In: Griffin, P., McGaw, B., Care, E. (eds.) Assessment and Teaching of 21st Century Skills, pp. 17–66. Springer, Netherlands (2012). https://doi.org/10.1007/978-94-007-2324-5
9. P21: Partnership for 21st Century Learning. https://www.battelleforkids.org/networks/p21/
10. Wilkie, D.: Employers say students aren't learning soft skills in college. https://www.shrm.org/resourcesandtools/hr-topics/employee-relations/pages/employers-say-students-arent-learning-soft-skills-in-college.aspx
11. Stevens, M., Norman, R.: Industry expectations of soft skills in IT graduates a regional survey. ACM Int. Conf. Proceeding Ser. 01–05-Febr (2016). https://doi.org/10.1145/2843043.2843068
12. Pereira, O.P.: Soft skills: from university to the work environment. analysis of a survey of graduates in Portugal. Reg. Sect. Econ. Stud. **13**, 105–118 (2013).
13. Gee, J.P.: What Video Games Have to Teach Us About Learning and Literacy. Palgrave Macmillan, New York (2008)
14. Steinkuehler, C.A.: Games as a highly visible medium for the study of distributed, situated cognition. In: Barab, S.A., Hay, K.E., Songer, N.B., and Hickey, D.T. (eds.) Proceedings of the International Conference of the Learning Sciences. pp. 1048–1049. Erlbuam, Mahwah (2006)
15. Qian, M., Clark, K.R.: Game-based learning and 21st century skills: a review of recent research. Comput. Hum. Behav. **63**, 50–58 (2016). https://doi.org/10.1016/j.chb.2016.05.023
16. Sourmelis, T., Ioannou, A., Zaphiris, P.: Massively multiplayer online role playing games (MMORPGs) and the 21st century skills: a comprehensive research review from 2010 to 2016. Comput. Human Behav. **67**, 41–48 (2017). https://doi.org/10.1016/j.chb.2016.10.020
17. King, E.M.: Guys and games: practicing 21st century workplace skills in the great indoors (2011). ISBN: 9781267065728
18. Gee, J.P.: Affinity spaces : online and out of school. Phi Betta Kappan. 8–13 (2018)
19. CCP: EVE Online. http://www.eveonline.com/
20. Bröker, T.: Wie kommt das Problem ins Spiel? Designprinzipien und Nutzermodell als Entwicklungsgrundlagen für ein Multiplayer Online Game in der Bauphysik. epubli GmbH, Weimar (2016)
21. Discord. https://discord.com/
22. Wigfield, A., Eccles, J.S.: Expectancy – value theory of achievement motivation. Contemp. Educ. Psychol. **25**, 68–81 (2000). https://doi.org/10.1006/ceps.1999.1015
23. Söbke, H.: A case study of deep gamification in higher engineering education. In: Gentile, M., Allegra, M., Söbke, H. (eds.) GALA 2018. LNCS, vol. 11385, pp. 375–386. Springer, Cham (2019). https://doi.org/10.1007/978-3-030-11548-7_35
24. Seifried, E., Kriegbaum, K., Spinath, B.: Veränderung der veranstaltungsbezogenen Motivation über ein Semester und die Rolle von veranstaltungsbezogenen Erwartungen. In: Seifried, E. and Spinath, B. (eds.) paepsy 2017 -Gemeinsame Tagung der Fachgruppen Entwicklungspsychologie und Pädagogische Psychologie 11. - 14. 9. in Münster - Arbeitsgruppe Motivation im Hochschulkontext: Entwicklung und beeinflussende Faktoren (2017)
25. Oztok, M., Brett, C.: Social presence and online learning : a review of research. J. Dist. Educ. **25**, 1–10 (2011)
26. Lin, G.-Y.: Social presence questionnaire of online collaborative learning: Development and validity. 2004 Annu. Proc. – Chicago, vol. 1, PP. 588–591 (2004)

27. Guay, F., Vallerand, R.J., Blanchard, C.: On the assessment of situational intrinsic and extrinsic motivation: the Situational Motivation Scale (SIMS). Motiv. Emot. **24**, 175–213 (2000). https://doi.org/10.1023/A:1005614228250

28. Ryan, R.M., Deci, E.L.: Self-determination theory: Basic psychological needs in motivation, development, and wellness. Guilford Publications (2017)

29. Söbke, H., Arnold, U., Montag, M.: Intrinsic motivation in serious gaming a case study. In: Marfisi-Schottman, I., Bellotti, F., Hamon, L., Klemke, R. (eds.) GALA 2020. LNCS, vol. 12517, pp. 362–371. Springer, Cham (2020). https://doi.org/10.1007/978-3-030-63464-3_34

30. Schmidt, C.: The analysis of semi-structured interviews. In: Flick, U., von Kardorff, E., Steinke, I. (eds.) A Companion to Qualitative Research, pp. 253–258. SAGE Publications, London, UK (2004)

Author Index

Achenbach, Philipp   229
Agrawal, Sarthak   247
Akcay, Zeynep   138, 153
Almås, H.   85

Basu, Prabahan   47
Berger, Florian   67
Bernard, Paquito   185
Bjørner, Thomas   263
Bose, Ranjan   247
Bouchard, Bruno   185
Bouchard, Kévin   185
Bröker, Thomas   276

Cardoso, Pedro   31
Chaturvedi, Manmohan   247
Chowdhury, Anindya   47

Divitini, Monica   3
Dobre, Mircea   263

Ehret, Flavien   167
Eibl, Max   20

Fatima, Sundus   47
Fletcher, Bobbie   200
Francillette, Yannick   167, 185

Gaboury, Sébastien   185
Gaurav, Devottam   247
Gheorghe, Ancuţa Florentina   55
Girard, Benoit   167
Göbel, Stefan   213, 229

Hakvåg, M.   85
Hansen, Louise Gaard   263
Hassan, Toka   98
Hauge, Jakob Baalsrud   55
Hauge, Jannicke Baalsrud   47, 55
Hossain, Imran   131

James, David   200
Jost, Patrick   3

Khoo, Eng Tat   113
King, Myfanwy   138, 153

Kingsbury, Célia   185
Kulshrestha, Srishti   247

Marsh, Tim   113, 138, 153
Mateen, Saba   131
McKee, Gerard T.   98
Menelas, Bob A. J.   185
Menelas, Bob-Antoine J.   167
Müller, Philipp Niklas   213, 229
Müller, Wolfgang   67

Oliveira, Ana Patrícia   31
Oliveira, M.   85

Pagel, Max   276
Pfleger, Paul   20
Platte, Benny   20

Rauterberg, Felix   229
Ritter, Marc   20
Romain, Ahmed J.   185
Roschke, Christian   20
Rustemeier, Linda   131

Sarpe-Tudoran, Teodora   213
Schurig, Artem   47
Sharma, Subodh   247
Söbke, Heinrich   276
Sørensen, Julie Ulnits   263
Sousa, Micael   31
St-Amour, Samuel   185
Stefan, Antoniu   55
Stefan, Ioana Andreea   55

Thomas, Ashima   113
Tolkmitt, Volker   20
Torvatn, H.   85
Tregel, Thomas   213, 229

Vairinhos, Mário   31
Valimaa, Miicha   263
Voß-Nakkour, Sarah   131

Wittrin, Rasmus   20
Wittrin, Ruben   20

Zagalo, Nelson   31

Printed in the United States
by Baker & Taylor Publisher Services